THE BODY IN SOUND, MUSIC AND PERFORMANCE

The Body in Sound, Music and Performance brings together cutting-edge contributions from women working on, and researching, contemporary sound practice.

This highly interdisciplinary book features a host of international contributors and places emphasis on developments beyond the Western world, including movements growing across Latin America. Within the book, the body is situated as both the site and centre for knowledge making and creative production. Chapters explore how, with insightful theoretical analysis, new methods and innovative practices – sometimes within the socio-cultural conditions of racism, sexism, and classism – the body can rise above, reshape, and deconstruct understood ideas about performance practices, composition, and listening/sensing.

This book will be of interest to both practitioners and researchers in the fields of sonic arts, sound design, music, acoustics, and performance.

Linda O Keeffe is a sound artist and Senior Lecturer of Sound Art and Sound Studies at the University of Edinburgh, UK, founder of Women in Sound Women on Sound, and editor-in-chief of *Interference Journal: A Journal of Auditory Cultures*.

Isabel Nogueira is a professor in the Music Department of the Federal University of Rio Grande do Sul, Brazil. She co-ordinates the Sonic Research Group in Gender, Body and Music.

THE BODY IN SOUND, MUSIC AND PERFORMANCE

Studies in Audio and Sonic Arts

Edited by Linda O Keeffe and Isabel Nogueira

LONDON AND NEW YORK

Cover image: Shadows of Light by Lina Espada

First published 2023
by Routledge
4 Park Square, Milton Park, Abingdon, Oxon OX14 4RN

and by Routledge
605 Third Avenue, New York, NY 10158

Routledge is an imprint of the Taylor & Francis Group, an informa business

© 2023 selection and editorial matter, Linda O Keeffe and Isabel Nogueira; individual chapters, the contributors

The right of Linda O Keeffe and Isabel Nogueira to be identified as the authors of the editorial material, and of the authors for their individual chapters, has been asserted in accordance with sections 77 and 78 of the Copyright, Designs and Patents Act 1988.

All rights reserved. No part of this book may be reprinted or reproduced or utilised in any form or by any electronic, mechanical, or other means, now known or hereafter invented, including photocopying and recording, or in any information storage or retrieval system, without permission in writing from the publishers.

Trademark notice: Product or corporate names may be trademarks or registered trademarks, and are used only for identification and explanation without intent to infringe.

British Library Cataloguing in Publication Data
A catalogue record for this book is available from the British Library

Library of Congress Cataloging-in-Publication Data
Names: O'Keeffe, Linda (Sound artist) editor. | Nogueira, Isabel, editor.
Title: The body in sound, music and performance : studies in audio and sonic arts / edited by Linda O'Keeffe and Isabel Nogueira.
Description: Abingdon, Oxon ; New York : Routledge, 2022. |
Includes bibliographical references and index. |
Identifiers: LCCN 2022004352 (print) | LCCN 2022004353 (ebook) |
ISBN 9780367441951 (hardback) | ISBN 9780367441944 (paperback) |
ISBN 9781003008217 (ebook)
Subjects: LCSH: Music–Philosophy and aesthetics. |
Music–Performance–Psychological aspects. | Sound (Philosophy) | Listening.
Classification: LCC ML3800.B714 2022 (print) | LCC ML3800 (ebook) |
DDC 781.1/7–dc23/eng/20220418
LC record available at https://lccn.loc.gov/2022004352
LC ebook record available at https://lccn.loc.gov/2022004353

ISBN: 978-0-367-44195-1 (hbk)
ISBN: 978-0-367-44194-4 (pbk)
ISBN: 978-1-003-00821-7 (ebk)

DOI: 10.4324/9781003008217

Typeset in Bembo
by Newgen Publishing UK

CONTENTS

List of Contributors   *viii*
List of Illustrations   *xiii*

    Introduction   1
    Linda O Keeffe and Isabel Nogueira

PART I
New Epistemologies of Sound   9

1 Forces at Play   11
   Heather Frasch

2 Why Should We Care about the Body?: On What
   Enactive-Ecological Musical Approaches Have to Offer   23
   Lauren Hayes

3 Under *Mar Paradoxo* (Paradox Sea) and *Coastal Silences*   35
   Raquel Stolf

PART II
Gendered Sounds, Spaces, and Places   49

4 Deep Situated Listening among Hearing Heads and
   Affective Bodies   51
   Sanne Krogh Groth

5 The Field is Mined and Full of "Minas": Women's Music in
  Paraíba – Kalyne Lima and Sinta A Liga Crew 65
  Tânia Mello Neiva

6 Working with *Womens Work*: Towards the Embodied Curator 78
  Irene Revell

7 Tejucupapo Women: Sound Mangrove Bodies and Performance
  Creation 92
  Luciana Lyra

PART III
New Methodologies in Sound Art and Performance Practice   111

8 Looking for Silence in the Body 113
  Ida Mara Freire

9 Our Body in #sonicwilderness & #soundasgrowing 128
  Antye Greie-Ripatti (AGF/poemproducer)

10 What Makes the Wolves Howl under the Moon? Sound
   Poetics of Territory-Spirit-Bodies for Well-Living 138
   Laila Rosa and Adriana Gabriela Santos Teixeira

11 Dispatches: Cartographing and Sharing Listenings 153
   Lílian Campesato and Valéria Bonafé

12 Applying Feminist Methodologies in the Sonic Arts:
   Listening to Brazilian Women Talk about Sound 166
   Linda O Keeffe and Isabel Nogueira

PART IV
The Body Technology   179

13 The Sensuality of Low Frequency Sound 181
   Cat Hope

14 Cynosuric Bodies 196
   Susie Green and Margaret Schedel

15 The Violining Body in *Anthèmes II* by Pierre Boulez 214
   Irine Røsnes

16 "Try to Walk with the Sound of My Footsteps So That We
   Can Stay Together": Sonic Presence and Virtual Embodiment
   in Janet Cardiff and Georges Bures Miller's Audio and Video
   Walks 228
   Sophie Knezic

17 Breathing (as Listening): An Emotional Bridge for
   Telepresence 243
   Ximena Alarcón-Díaz

18 Foley Performance and Sonic Implicit Interactions: How
   Foley Artists Might Hold the Secret for the Design of
   Sonic Implicit Interactions 265
   Sandra Pauletto

Index 279

CONTRIBUTORS

Ximena Alarcón-Díaz is a sound artist researcher interested in listening to sonic migrations. She is a Deep Listening® tutor, with a PhD in Music Technology and Innovation. Throughout her career, she has created telematic sonic improvisations and interfaces for relational listening, to understand sensorially her and others' migratory experience in search of a collective interface that holds such sonic in-betweenness. http://ximenaalarcon.net; http://intimal.net

Valéria Bonafé is a composer and researcher. She has worked mainly in the areas of musical composition, musical analysis, sound studies, and feminism. She is a member of NuSom – Research Centre on Sonology, and one of the founders of Sonora: Musics and Feminisms. She is currently developing a postdoctoral research project at the University of São Paulo. www.valeriabonafe.com; www.microfonias.net

Lílian Campesato is a Brazilian artist, scholar, and curator. She is a Research Affiliate at NuSom – Research Centre on Sonology, and a co-founder of Sonora: Musics and Feminisms. Her publications mainly address the investigation of the politics of listening, noise, and aurality. She is currently developing a postdoctoral research project on listening and subjectivity in testimonies of recorded voices of women at the Federal University of the State of Rio de Janeiro. www.liliancampesato.net; www.microfonias.net

Heather Frasch is a composer, performer, and creator of interactive sound installations and digital instruments whose work explores notions of fragility and stillness. Influenced by the dis-embodiment of acousmatic practices, she investigates the re-embodiment of sound and the intimacy between humans and their technological objects. She is Associate Professor of Music Technology at the Norwegian University of Science and Technology, Trondheim, Norway. www.heatherfrasch.net

Ida Mara Freire is a writer and dancer. She is an emeritus professor at the Federal University of Santa Catarina, Brazil, having earned her Doctor in Psychology at the University of São Paulo. She has been a specialist in Scenic Dance at Santa Catarina State University, a post-doctorate researcher in Inclusive Arts at the University of Nottingham, a visiting researcher in 2011 at the University of Cape Town, South Africa, working on Dance and Forgiveness, and is a member of the international editorial board of the journal *Research in Dance Education*.

Susie Green, based in Miami, Florida, blends music, art, and science as a neurodivergent Cuban American composer, vocalist, and sound-designer. Following an engineering internship at Crescent Moon Studios, she signed as a songwriter and published several works. She then undertook postgraduate research at the University of Huddersfield, UK while creating for immersive theatre, short films, and labels and teaching undergraduate composition as a visiting lecturer. She expanded on Rudolph Laban's Movement Theory, incorporating concepts from quantum mechanics, human dynamics, and cosmology, shaping sound though bespoke systems by harnessing the body's movement. Currently, Susie continues her research, publications, and works while supporting STEAM efforts with various organisations and collaborators in her community and worldwide.

Antye Greie-Ripatti, performing as AGF, is a German poetess, vocalist, and media artist who uses language and electronics, and explores speech and spoken word within the depths of electronic music, sculpting glowing post-internet tapestries as @poemproducer. http://poemproducer.com/info.php; http://antyegreie.com; https://twitter.com/poemproducer

Lauren Hayes is a Scottish musician, improviser, and sound artist. Her research explores embodied music cognition, enactive approaches to digital instrument design, and haptic technologies. She is an Assistant Professor in the School of Arts, Media and Engineering at Arizona State University, Director-At-Large of the International Computer Music Association, and a member of the New BBC Radiophonic Workshop. www.pariesa.com; www.laurensarahhayes.com

Cat Hope is an artist scholar whose research interests include animated notation, Australian music, low frequency sound, digital archiving, gender, and music. She is a co-author of *Digital Arts: An Introduction to New Media* (2014) and an active composer and performer. She is currently Professor of Music at Monash University, Melbourne, Australia. www.cathope.com

Sophie Knezic is a writer and visual artist with research specialisms in the metaphysics of transparency, spectrality, temporality, memory, experimental film and video, sound art, and humour in contemporary art. Her PhD on *Transparency, Translucence and the Crystallisation of Time* was completed in 2015. Her writing has been published in *Broadsheet Journal*, *Memo Review*, *Art +* Australia and *Art Monthly Australasia*, and she is a regular contributor to *Frieze* and *Australian Book Review*. She currently lectures in Critical and Theoretical Studies at Victorian College of the Arts, University of Melbourne, and in Art History, Theory + Cultures in the School of Art at the Royal Melbourne Institute of Technology.

Sanne Krogh Groth is Associate Professor of Musicology and Office Director of the Sound Environment Centre, Lund University, Sweden, and Editor-in-Chief of the online journal *Seismograf Peer*. She is the author of the book *Politics and Aesthetics in Electronic Music* (2014), co-editor of *The Bloomsbury Handbook of Sound Art* (2020), and is currently conducting field research on experimental music and decolonial aesthetics in Indonesia.

Luciana Lyra is an actress, director, playwright, and author who co-ordinates and teaches the Graduate Program in Art at the Department of Art Education and Popular Culture at Rio de Janeiro State University, Brazil, and is a collaborator in two graduate programmes at Santa Catarina State University and the Federal University of Rio Grande do Norte. She is a Postdoctoral Fellow in Anthropology at the University of São Paulo, holds a Doctor and Master of Performing Arts from the State University of Campinas, and is coordinator of Mito, Rito e Cartografias feministas nas Artes under the auspices of the Brazilian National Council for Scientific and Technological Development. www.unaluna.art.br; www.lucianalyra.com.br; https://amotinadas.wixsite.com/motim

Tânia Mello Neiva is a musician, performer, educator, and researcher. In 2018, she gained her PhD in Feminist Musicology from the Federal University of Paraíba, Brazil, where she carried out post-doctoral research in 2021. Her interests include women in music, technology, and social studies. Since 2003, she has been developing interdisciplinary works, acting both as performer and composer.

Isabel Nogueira is a professor in the Music Department of the Federal University of Rio Grande do Sul, Brazil. She co- ordinates the Sonic Research Group in Gender, Body and Music.

Linda O Keeffe is a sound artist and Senior Lecturer of Sound Art and Sound Studies at the University of Edinburgh, UK, founder of Women in Sound Women on Sound, and editor-in-chief of *Interference Journal: A Journal of Auditory Cultures*.

Sandra Pauletto is an Associate Professor in Media Production and a Docent in Sound and Music Computing in the Department of Media Technology and

Interaction Design at the KTH Royal Institute of Technology, Stockholm, Sweden. Prior to 2019, she was a Senior Lecturer in Sound Design at the University of York, UK. She has worked on a variety of UK research projects funded by the Engineering and Physical Sciences Research Council, the Arts and Humanities Research Council, British Academy, Wellcome Trust, European Union, and Swenson Stiftelsen, and has published widely both in scientific and humanities venues. She is currently the principal investigator for three projects: "Sound for Energy", exploring sonic interaction design to support energy efficiency behaviour in the household, funded by the Swedish Energy Agency, "The Radio Sound Studio", developing novel digital sound design tools through the modelling of historical sound effects, funded by NAVET, at the KTH Royal Institute of Technology, and "SonicFunc: Sound Design Methods for the Digital Society". www.kth.se/profile/pauletto

Irene Revell is a curator and writer working across sound, text, performance, and moving image. She is Co-Director of Electra, is closely involved in collections including Electra's Her Noise Archive and Cinenova: Feminist Film and Video, and is currently completing a doctorate on Creative Research into Sound Arts Practice at the University of the Arts London, where she teaches on the MA Sound Arts course.

Laila Rosa is a singer-songwriter, composer, violinist, and *rabeca* player, and gained her PhD in Ethnomusicology from the Federal University of Bahia in Brazil and New York University. Since 2011, she has been a professor at the Music School of the Federal University of Bahia, where she teaches on the graduate programmes in Music, and Gender, Women and Feminism, and is a member of Feminária Musical, a research and sound experiment group; the Center for Interdisciplinary Studies on Women; Gender, Art and Culture; and is also a member of the research group Sonic: Gender, Body and Music.

Irine Røsnes is a violinist, academic, improviser, and specialist in performance of repertoire for violin and electronics. Currently pursuing a PhD at the University of Huddersfield, UK, she has presented numerous premieres across Europe and North America and appeared at festivals such as *Huddersfield Contemporary*, *Borealis*, *Gaudeamus*, *Chicago New Music* and *Wonderfeel*. Educated in Bergen, Düsseldorf, Utrecht and Chicago, her concert repertoire extends from the music of the early Baroque era to works of the 21st century. She is a visiting lecturer at the University of Wolverhampton campus in Leicester, UK, where she teaches modules of academic research and violin performance.

Adriana Gabriela Santos Teixeira is an actress, poet, composer, illustrator, and performer, and is a PhD student on the Graduate Program in Performing Arts at the State University of Campinas, São Paulo, Brazil. She has a Fellowship in the Doctorate Sandwich Abroad Institutional Program for Internationalization, an exchange programme between the State University of Campinas and Middlesex University London. She also holds a Master in Performing Arts from the Federal University of Bahia, Brazil.

Margaret Schedel, whose interdisciplinary career blends classical training in cello and composition, sound/audio data research, and innovative computational arts education, transcends the boundaries of disparate fields to produce integrated work at the nexus of computation and the arts. Her diverse creative output spans interactive multimedia operas, virtual reality experiences, sound art, video game scores, and compositions for a wide variety of classical instruments or custom controllers with interactive audio and video processing. A Professor in the Department of Music at Stony Brook University, New York, she currently serves as Chair of the Art Department and teaches computer music at Peabody Conservatory.

Raquel Stolf lives in Florianópolis, Santa Catarina, Brazil. She is an artist and professor in the Department of Visual Arts and the Visual Arts Graduate Program at Santa Catarina State University. She holds a doctorate (2011) and a Master (2002) in Visual Arts from the Federal University of Rio Grande do Sul. Her projects investigate writing processes, experiences of silences, and listening situations. Her current work includes the research groups Contemporary Artistic Propositions and Their Experimental Processes (Santa Catarina State University/Brazilian National Council for Scientific and Technological Development) and Art Vehicles (Federal University of Rio Grande do Sul/Brazilian National Council for Scientific and Technological Development). www.raquelstolf.com/; https://soundcloud.com/raquelstolf; https://soundcloud.com/marparadoxo; https://anecoica.org

ILLUSTRATIONS

Figures

1.1	Objects in Frasch's studio in Berlin, Germany, 2017	12
1.2	Image from Frasch's performance at *Post-Paradise Series*, Birmingham, UK, 2019	14
1.3	Frasch's self-made instrument, Digital Boxes, in Berlin, Germany, 2017	14
1.4	Image from Frasch's performance at *Post-Paradise Series*, Birmingham, UK, 2019	16
1.5	Ryoko Akama in performance	19
2.1	Fluid and dynamic movement is used with a haptically augmented hybrid piano, rather than discrete, choreographed gestures; images from livestreamed performance for Iklectik Art Lab, London, 2020	30
2.2	Setting up in a day centre for adults with learning disabilities with augmented fan, acoustic piano, coloured furniture, haptic listening devices, Skoog musical controller, and participants (obscured)	31
3.1	*mar paradoxo*, 2013–2016, general view of the publication (printed material and audio CDs)	36
3.2	*mar paradoxo*, 2013–2016, documentation of the process	37
3.3	*mar paradoxo*, 2013–2016, detail of note-drawings from and for listening – collapsing silence, by Raquel Stolf	38
3.4	*mar paradoxo*, 1996, detail of *FORA [DO AR]* (OUT [OF AIR]), by Raquel Stolf	40
3.5	*mar paradoxo*, 2013–2016, detail of notes-drawings (seabed typologies), by Raquel Stolf	41
5.1	Luana Flores	67
5.2	Kalyne Lima	68

5.3	Sinta A Liga Crew	69
5.4	Image from the videoclip of Sinta A Liga Crew – "Campo Minado"	71
6.1	(a) *Womens Work*, first issue (1975) cover; (b) *Womens Work*, first issue (1975) colophon; (c) Annea Lockwood's *Piano Transplants*, first issue; (d) *Womens Work*, second issue (1978)	81
6.2	ORGASMIC STREAMING ORGANIC GARDENING ELECTROCULTURE, Chelsea Space (2018), installation view: Annea Lockwood, *Piano Transplant no 1* (1966) and Carolee Schneemann, *Parts of a Body House* (1957–68), re-set by Matthew Appleton	84
6.3	(a) preparing photocopied scores from *Womens Work* for *These are scores*, Sounding Bodies, Copenhagen (2018); (b) 'reading', *These are scores, Art Research Work* conference, Zurich University of the Arts (2017); (c) 'performing', *These are scores*, Chelsea Space, London (2018)	86
7.1	Tejucupapo mangrove forest, 2007	93
7.2	Dona Biu de Vinuca, an oyster gatherer from Tejucupapo, working, 2008	94
7.3	Tejucupapo mangrove forest and oyster gatherers, 2008	96
7.4	Women of Tejucupapo backstage during *A Batalha das Heroínas* (2008)	98
7.5	*Ciranda* music and dance in Tejucupapo, 2008	98
7.6	*Coco* in Tejucupapo, 2008	99
7.7	*A Batalha das Heroínas* (2007)	101
7.8	*Guerreiras* (2010), written and directed by Luciana Lyra, showing actresses Viviane Madu, Simone Evaristo, Cris Rocha, Katia Daher, and Luciana Lyra on stage	103
7.9	*Guerreiras* (2010), written and directed by Luciana Lyra, showing actresses Katia Daher and Viviane Madu on stage	104
7.10	Actress Simone Evaristo in *Guerreiras* (2010)	105
7.11	Scene from the play *Pour Louise ou a desejada virtude da resistência* (2016), direction and dramaturgy by Luciana Lyra	106
7.12	Scene from the play *Homens e Caranguejos* (2012), direction and dramaturgy by Luciana Lyra	107
7.13	Scene from the play *Salema – sussurros dos afogados* (2012), direction by Luciana Lyra	107
8.1	One step	114
8.2	The sound of silence	115
8.3	Touching the invisible	119
8.4	Stillness	123
8.5	Inner silence	125
9.1	Hanoi Leninpark, 2018	129
9.2	*Blueberry techno* score, 2015	129
9.3	Carsten Stabenow, Berlin, 2017	130

9.4	A line of women in the rice fields	132
9.5	*Blueberry techno* score, part 2, 2015	132
9.6	Samiland, 2015	133
9.7	Sonic wild	134
9.8	Hanoi	135
9.9	Skibotn session, Caspar Ström, 2015	136
10.1	*Lunar painting 10.1: Uterus in flower, I snaked*, by Laila Rosa	145
10.2	*Lunar painting 10.2: Lunar Shakti, Siren's chant*, by Laila Rosa	145
11.1	Three frames of *sky-only, a vertigo*	159
11.2	Frames of *or-life* (left), *impulse 1* (centre) and *impulse 2* (right)	162
12.1	Listening during a soundwalk in Porto Alegre, Brazil, August 2018	170
12.2	Biba Meira conducting the group in August 2018	174
12.3	Chatting with Batuca performers over food, August 2018	175
13.1	Video still from Vanessa Godden's video for Thembi Soddell's track 'Erasure', from the *Love Songs* album	186
13.2	A photograph of the performance space in Rosenfeld's *Cannons* installation, Midland Railway Workshop, Western Australia, 2010	189
13.3	Screenshot of the animated notation score for Cat Hope's *Tone Being* (2016)	191
14.1	QR code for www.susiegreen-music.com/handography	197
14.2	*Perception*	198
14.3	*Multi-Dimensional Isolation*	200
14.4	*Multisequence, thumb in*	200
14.5	*Kinesphere of the Hand*	200
14.6	*Shadows of Light*	206
14.7	*((re) frame/bound)*	207
14.8	*Entangled Pulse*	208
14.9	*Entangled Voice*	209
15.1	Pierre Boulez, *Anthèmes II*, "Très lent"	220
15.2	Pierre Boulez, *Anthèmes II*, "III Lent"	221
15.3	Pierre Boulez, *Anthèmes II*, "Nerveux, irregulier"	222
15.4	Pierre Boulez, *Anthèmes II*, "VI Allant"	224
16.1	*The City of Forking Paths*	233
16.2	*Alter Bahnhof Video Walk*	237
16.3	*Night Walk for Edinburgh*	239
17.1	*Listening in Dreams*, via Google Hangouts	245
17.2	*Listening to the Land*, Grån, Norway	246
17.3	Score for *A Migratory Journey* by Ximena Alarcón	247
17.4	The four spheres of migratory memory	248
17.5	The experiments' suits and markers, screenshot from a video capture of Qualisys software	249
17.6	*Experiment 1 Migratory Journeys*, video screenshot	249
17.7	Breathing data from improvisers while performing *Migratory Journeys*, screenshot from plot	251

17.8	INTIMAL System for Relational Listening	252
17.9	Improvisers using INTIMAL in locations in the three cities: Iklektic (London), Melahuset (Oslo), and Phonos Foundation, University Pompeu Fabra (Barcelona)	252
17.10	Use of the mobile phone as a sensor in MEMENTO	253
17.11	Signal flow of RESPIRO: collecting, transmitting, sonifying, and amplifying breathing data	253
17.12	Listening setting: loudspeakers used to listen to the sonification of breathing data via RESPIRO	254
17.13	Signal flow in TRANSMISSION	255
17.14	Time score of *INTIMAL: A Long-Distance Improvisation*	255
17.15	Analysis of INTIMAL and breathing as an emotional bridge using Jensenius' Taxonomy of Body Motion	256

Table

5.1	Lyrics and form of *Campo Minado* – Portuguese and English	72

INTRODUCTION

Linda O Keeffe and Isabel Nogueira

This book sets out to examine the place the body has in shaping sonic art practices from performance through music, dance, theory, and methodology. We chose authors who have examined the body as a site for dissonance and resonance, of politicised, gendered, and racialised spaces, of body politics, and of listening and performative bodies. A number of our authors have asked what constitutes a known or socially constructed body, and where do black, non-binary, radicalised, brutalised, migratory, or virtual bodies exist in sonic art or performance spaces?

In some ways, our approach to editing this book and selecting the writers rests on what Rebecca Schneider (1997) might call an exposition of unfolding the body, making explicit the "signification that surrounds bodies" (ibid., 5) where the explicit, the very obvious aspect of some bodies, being different from other bodies, are weighted with much historical meaning, folded within cultures of colonialism, sexism, racism, ableism, and classism. But equally, our approach to bringing the body to the centre of subjectivity, to the core of theoretical and methodological significance, is shaped by how central the body has become in many women's practices. The starting point for this might begin with Clara Rockmore and Alexandra Stepanoff, who exemplified the embodied performance potential of new musical instruments, or focus on the very explicit bodily engagement of artists such as Yoko Ono or Marina Abramovich, where the potential for physical violence simmers underneath the performance, all the way through to Christine Sun Kim, a deaf artist working with sound, for whom sound is not just something heard or audible, but a force that can be contextualised through body language and performance.

The body as a site of creative practice is situated at the cusp of socially contextualised and political meaning (Ezcurra 2019; Butler 1988); the body also exists within varying forms of social control, contested ideologies, and as Pagnes affirms, "At the empirical level, the body – as an entity to be protected, regulated, punished, included, excluded, etc. – is itself the object of politics" (2017, 4). With the rise of feminism in the 1970s, we see transformations within the arts, where the female body as an object to be viewed is countered by, in some parts, a quantifiable contestation of what is absent, thinking here primarily of the Guerrilla Girls poster campaign of the 1970s which highlighted the absence of women artists in museums and galleries, but the overwhelming presence of their naked forms in works by male artists, "which brought to public discussion the fact that politics are not only a matter of sovereign control but are also intrinsic to the domain of the sexed body" (Ezcurra 2019, 5). There has, however, been an absence of placing the body at the centre of discourse in music technology, music performance, and the sonic arts. That is not to say that there aren't theorists in music and sound that explore these areas. Thompson (2017) has very much argued for the inclusion of black and female bodies in epistemologies of knowledge, while Born and Divine (2015) have critiqued the absence of women in the academic structures of said spaces. Xambo and Jawad (2020) argue that we need to explore a more "diverse and fluid" definition of music technology. But while these may be arguments for the inclusion of certain groups within these spaces, it does not focus on the body as an agent of change, or the body facilitating transformations in practice.

There is a canon of works in the field of music and sound that is founded on the idea that sound and music are neutral spaces where our lived experiences are seen as something less important than our process of learning a body of techniques, or discourses that already exist. If we consider that the canon in art fields is occupied mostly by white men from the Global North, we need also to consider that gender, race, and global localisation are key points of that canon and that there is no neutrality at all. In discussion with our contributors, we asked that they place their experiences, research, and relationship to their practice at the core of their chapters. For us, this approach in itself is an epistemological turn in the sonic arts.

But to wholly focus on the body as a political feminist space, imbued with all the social constructs for which it battles, might lead to ignoring the many other ways in which the body unfolds in practice. In this book, we see and hear the body as one which changes the shape of technological engagement in new performance technology.

Working with Women on Sound

We, Linda and Isabel, first met in 2017 at the Women in Sound Women on Sound (WISWOS)[1] symposium *Educating Women in Sound*, which was organised by Linda, in Lancaster, England. This was the second of two symposiums that Linda had created for WISWOS. The first, in 2016, focused solely on creating a networking space for women working in all areas of sound. However, the purpose of the second WISWOS event was to explore when and how women begin to engage with sound as a medium or concept within their practice and research, and the way in which current pedagogy informs or inhibits their relationship to sound. For this event, Isabel came on board as a WISWOS network member, supporting the development of our call and methods. We found through workshops, focus groups, keynotes, and performance discussions that women were often self-taught, came late to working with technology (in comparison to their male peers), and that for many, the starting point or subject matter was their bodies. This last event led to the creation of an education support tool, co-created with Rebecca Collins, that would be developed for schools and online access, Research in a Box: Educating Women in Sound.[2]

Linda: In 2017, I began to work with human–computer interaction as a method of sound making in both performance settings and within sound design for theatre. Using Wii controllers with the SuperCollider software platform radically altered how I thought of my body as a site of sound making. Every gesture had the potential to change the sound, which led to developing increased sensitivity to every gesture I could make. The body has the potential to alter a number of interactions when it enters a space, and each space affects how we move through and interact with that space. My body has always played a part in my performance work, but usually through the manipulation of pre-recorded sounds or adding my voice in a live vocal performance. This direct link between a body's movement and the sound it produced enhanced my engagement with and experience of shaping sound in a way I hadn't experienced before.

Isabel: I began working with sound from a classical music perspective, then moved towards examining musicology through a feminist lens, focusing on women's experience as performers when using technology. My work with sound and music comes from the perspective of women's experiences, focusing on the body and the dialogue construction in collective works. Women's voice, my own voice, video making, storytelling, and the different approaches the body can have while playing different surfaces have been important in my artistic practice. More recently, I began to work with modular synthesis and sensor technology within my practice, and it has been a turning point for me. I became very aware of the possibilities the body has in the co-creation of sound.

In 2018, we began a collaborative, research-led, and practice-based project in Brazil, where we began to examine, through a series of methods, how women's practices in sound are formed. We created different opportunities to bring women together to discuss their points of view and the difficulties and challenges of being a woman working in sound and music, to offer spaces for networking and emotional support, and to offer peer-to-peer support in finding opportunities for funding and training (see Chapter 12). We also began to explore, within our own practice, the place of the body as a source of information, a site of political and social activities, of oppression and expansion, and this work emerged as a number of performance projects which toured across the north and south of Brazil.

The Idea of the Book

Following this period of research and practice, we began to think about putting a book together, one which would be wholly authored by women from diverse practices and backgrounds. In our time together in Brazil, we had found that some of the key ideas emerging from our collaboration and work with women included a keen sense of a lack of recognition of their contributions to various fields. For many, a key factor was their gender: being identified as woman, as female, placed them automatically on the outside. They were rarely asked to contribute to sites of knowledge sharing, networking, or production, whether as keynotes at conferences, as contributors to books, or as speakers in colleges or universities. They felt a deep exclusion from the fields of sound, music and performance pedagogy, epistemology, and practice. While they acknowledged these walls, they also highlighted the tool kits they had developed to break down barriers, from forming new communities and establishing support networks to developing innovative artistic practices.

What also emerged from our various discussions and collaborations with women was the place of the body as a site of knowledge, where bodily experiences enhance or reshape our engagement with spaces of performance or art making. Their approach to working with sound and technology was fundamentally an embodied and bodily experience, in part because many were self-taught[3] and utilised movement and the voice to engage with new technologies. For others, everyday experiences as women, whether difficult or not, shaped their conceptual approach to making and thinking about their practices.

Our body actions and sensibilities inform daily interactions and shape perception. We are already aware that embodiment "expressed through various forms of nonpropositional knowledge, constitutes the realm of all performers: actors, dancers, mimes, and musicians, to name a few" (Duby and Barker 2017, 2). It is enacted daily by many working in sound, seen by many as essential to how they engage with technology, concepts, and spaces, yet very little is written from that experiential place within the field of sonic art practice and sound studies, particularly in the areas of music technology, composition, and music performance studies. We argue that this is in part due to the fact that *body* works – those that explore the subjective experiences, the lived experiences felt and sensed – are often those produced by women. In this way, it became essential to us to place the body at the heart of this discourse.

Our Authors

By mid-2019, we were ready to think about contributors to this book and began to look at artists, researchers, and theorists who we felt engaged with ideas about the body, bodily practices, or embodiment. We had connections to many networks and access to hundreds of women who could contribute to the book, but we felt that representation of authors from a wide variety of subject areas, theoretical concepts, and methodological approaches would allow our readers see the breadth of work being undertaken by women in the sonic arts. We decided on key themes we wished to explore, themes which had emerged within our research as well as areas we felt were current in sound, music, and performance practice. The chapters are divided into four parts to allow for the collation of certain thematic thoughts. Some of our authors may span more than one of these themes, but the locus of their work, we feel, belongs in the space where we have situated them.

In Part I, "New Epistemologies of Sound", our authors are asking us to think differently about the place of the body both historically and contemporarily in music and performance. For Heather Frasch in Chapter 1, a new theoretical lens is required to understand how instrument building, touch, and memory shape the experience of both the performer and the audience, and multiple perspectives are required to understand the human relationship with the non-human object – the instrument. In Chapter 2, Lauren Hayes argues that there is a need to rethink techniques of human-controlled interactions in order to explore the body as a more integral, centred position within performance. She argues that music's move towards embodied cognition has yet to enfold the theories of social and science and technology studies of the 1980s which recognised the importance of social experiences as embodied processes, and that a larger understanding of how certain technologies can be exclusionary would allow for a more considered discussion around what we build and whom we build for. Raquel Stolf in Chapter 3 brings us an experiential analysis of a body of work created during 2013–2016. She asks how we might document moments of silence, but also questions what theoretically has come to constitute silence. For Stolf, silence is both within and without the body, and in collecting silence, the body also acts as a site of collecting, transforming, and being transformed by different kinds of silence.

In Part II, "Gendered Sounds, Spaces and Places", our authors are observing the ways in which social, political, and epistemological[4] structures have shaped a participation with, or the creation of, bodies of work, from theatrical to musical performances. In Chapter 4 by Sanne Krogh Groth, we hear about two very different listening experiences, set apart by a number of years, two performance events at which she was an attendee. In her analysis of these concerts, she uses feminist theory to understand her embodied reaction and engagement with each of those events. The effect each experience had on her is shaped by a form of "situated knowledge", whereby her own reactions, perturbations, enjoyment, and anxiety are understood within the context of the histories of electroacoustic music (EAM) concerts as particularly masculine spaces. She offers, through an example of one particular event, new approaches to placing EAM events within a more inclusive and open space for both the performers and listeners. Chapter 5 by Tânia Mello Neiva, on the other hand, brings us into the world of rap music in northeast Brazil, and the repositioning of women's bodies and lyrics into a very male-dominated musical world. She examines the work of a female rapper and one rap group through the lenses of racism, sexism, and colonialism, exploring how these female rap lyricists take back ownership of their bodies through the clothes they wear, the lyrics they write, and the videos and concerts they create and perform in. In Chapter 6, Irene Revell examines the role of the curator as an embodied experience when creating potential performance interactions between composer, scores, and the audience. She focuses in particular on the potentially rich experience of the workshopping of women's works, scores that have been ignored or marginalised, and when exhibited, placed behind barriers. In Chapter 7, Luciana Lyra brings us to the forests of Pernambuco, Brazil, to the annual event *A Batalha das Heroínas*

(The Battle of the Heroines), a theatrical work devised, planned, and performed by women as a celebration of the first battle, fought and won by women, against the Dutch in the 17th century. Her artethnographic investigation of this annual performance has had an impact on the development of her theatrical career, where the body as a site of historical forces such as colonial experiences and everyday lived experiences becomes part of the making of theatre works.

In Part III, "New Methodologies in Sound Art and Performance Practice", our authors talk about their processes of making, techniques developed as a response to very particular experiences and places, some resonant with memories of violence and exclusion, such as Ida Mara Freire in Chapter 8, where she explores, through conversations between a poet and a choreographer, the power of the body to remember and move above and beyond colonial violence upon black bodies. In Chapter 9, Antye Greie-Ripatti offers us insights through poetics and performative language, an opportunity to experience different sites where listening occurred and was shared. Through a reading of her text, we can engage with her, ensuring the work doesn't stop at each site. Laila Rosa and Adriana Gabriela Santos Teixeira have created a unique approach to co-creation where the body, spirit, mind, and memory, in combination with a rereading and reacquiring of Brazilian African indigenous poetics of reterritorialising the sacred feminine, are applied to their collaborative performance practice. In Chapter 11 by Lílian Campesato and Valéria Bonafé, we are invited into a shared listening practice that spans space and time as well as the distance created between bodies as a result of a pandemic. In their practice, they have closed this distance through the sharing and remaking of their sonic worlds. They offer an approach to listening, a score which the reader can perform. This score can become an act of feminist political listening and acting. In Chapter 12, we write about a methodology developed in 2018 to work with women artists in Brazil. We developed a process of engagement whereby a number of workshops were designed to nurture the development of performance practices. All activities were constructed in a dialogic process, which subsequently transformed our performative and artistic approaches to collaboration.

Part IV, "The Body Technology", explores how the body shapes the use or design of technology, or how bodies can be shaped by their relationship to technological artefacts or spaces. In Chapter 13, Cat Hope argues for a rethinking of the potential of low frequency sound (LFS) in enabling a more sensorial approach to listening. Emerging technologies have allowed for the amplification of sounds in these ranges, meaning more composers have the ability to manipulate and push the boundaries of LFS through both acoustic and electronic compositions. With LFS, the body becomes a resonating space where corporeality is amplified as our bodies connect with these sounds. In Chapter 14, Susie Green and Margaret Schedel's practice-based research examines the potentiality of the body to interface with technology through a series of exercises where movement, translated to data, becomes sound. However, this translation is far more complex when signifiers of movement, what constitutes forms of communication through gesture, move us beyond simple data sonification. For them, the choreography of these gestures is shaped by far more complex issues related to inclusion in the design of technological interfaces, where different bodies need to be considered in the design of interfaces so that all body types can perform and connect with technology. In Chapter 15, Irine Røsnes argues for a non-hierarchical approach to electroacoustic performances, recognising the importance of the body at the centre of the relationship between technology and the acoustic instrument – in this instance, the violin. For Røsnes, the body of a musician is shaped not just by the many years of training, but the many histories of many musicians training which the body *embodies*. In moving towards an electronic performance, what place does the body have in this new form of musicking? She offers personal experience insights, through her own performance practice, towards an electrified violining body. In Chapter 16, Sophie Knezic offers us a new reading and insight into the works of Janet Cardiff and Georges Bures Miller. In her analysis of the body of work concerned with the sound walk, we begin to both see and hear new forms of virtuality, created as a result of a sonic hyperrealism offered by Cardiff's voice as she narrates the listener's journey through different sites of place and experience.

In Ximena Alarcón-Díaz's Chapter 17, we see how the development of new applications to facilitate migrant bodies performing and experiencing sounds across space has led to embodied performance practices which have facilitated new modes of audience–performer engagement. In Chapter 18, placing the body at the centre of Foley sound design, Sandra Pauletto highlights an opportunity for the field and world of smart object design and interaction. For her, Foley sound is essentially a space of performing, or acting bodies, and these bodies enhance and make real all of what we see on film. Through a process she defines as "sonic implicit interaction", our relationships to smart objects can be enhanced if the processes of Foley designers are applied in the design of new smart objects.

A Note on the Times of Writing

By April 2020, with the emergence of the COVID pandemic, most of our authors were feeling very isolated, some had no access to resources to write about, and for others, their art, academic, and research practices came to a complete stop. In May 2020, we began to have conversations in collective Zoom meetings, and through a WhatsApp group we created a space for our authors to share resources and ideas. As we were, in various parts of the world, in lockdown, we wanted to offer a place for community to those of us feeling isolated and even afraid of the future. This was not an easy process given all that was happening in our lives. We also focused on the editorial process as a space to create ways to dialogue with the authors, supporting their work and creating meetings to listen to their perspectives while sharing experiences of writing, and offering feedback where necessary.

Unfortunately, during the pandemic some of our contributors were not able to continue their writing because of the impact COVID was having on their lives. The difficulty for women contributors is that many are not supported by institutions, and academic writing, for those not employed in academic institutions, is free labour which takes time, time away from freelance work, family commitments, and other jobs. We acknowledge that many of the women who had to step back did so for some of these reasons, and this is something we need to recognise as one of the many factors behind the lack of women contributing to the fields of sound, music, and performance. We want to thank those women who could not make it into our book but still gave time to the process.

Lastly, we want to thank anthropologist and artist Sarah O Keeffe Nolan for giving time to read and edit our introduction and our contributory chapter.

Notes

1 WISWOS is a network of networks whose role is to make the work of women visible/audible through a number of projects, commissions and networking events.
2 There are two links on the WISWOS website that explore what parts of the box you can work with, but only the digital learning box is still available for use: https://wiswos.com/tutorials.php; https://wiswos.com/readinglist.php.
3 For many, being self-taught meant feeling a constant sense of panic that they would be found out at any point by their male peers as not understanding the technology as fully as someone who had trained at university.
4 In this context, we mean sites of knowledge sharing, ranging from educational to performance spaces.

Bibliography

Born, Georgina, and Kyle Devine. 2015. 'Music Technology, Gender, and Class: Digitization, Educational and Social Change in Britain'. *Twentieth-Century Music* 12 (2): 135–72. https://doi.org/10.1017/S1478572215000018.

Butler, Judith. 1988. 'Performative Acts and Gender Constitution: An Essay in Phenomenology and Feminist Theory'. *Theatre Journal* 49: 519–31.

Duby, Marc, and Paul Alan Barker. 2017. 'Deterritorialising the Research Space: Artistic Research, Embodied Knowledge, and the Academy'. *SAGE Open* 7 (4):2158244017737130. https://doi.org/10.1177/2158244017737130.

Ezcurra, Mara Polgovsky. 2019. Touched Bodies: The Performative Turn in Latin American Art. New Brunswick, NJ: Rutgers University Press. https://doi.org/10.36019/9781978802063.

Jawad, Karolina, and Anna Xambo. 2020. 'How to Talk of Music Technology: An Interview Analysis Study of Live Interfaces for Music Performance among Expert Women'. In *Proceedings of the International Conference on Live Interfaces*, Trondheim, Norway, pp. 41–7. https://dora.dmu.ac.uk/handle/2086/19934.

Pagnes, Andrea (VestAndPage). 2017. 'Notes on Performance Art, the Body and the Political'. Paper delivered at *Venice International Performance Art Week*, European Cultural Centre, Venice, Italy. https://doi.org/10.22501/rc.343455.

Schneider, Rebecca. 1997. *The Explicit Body in Performance*. Hove, UK: Psychology Press.

Thompson, Marie. 2017. 'Whiteness and the Ontological Turn in Sound Studies'. *Parallax* 23 (3): 266–82. https://doi.org/10.1080/13534645.2017.1339967.

PART I
New Epistemologies of Sound

1
FORCES AT PLAY

Heather Frasch

Reflection: Notes from the Inside

I create new sounds, new instruments, new sonic objects. I combine these new things, or already existing things, together to create new forms. I set up interactions among these materials which lead to new combinations. I bring new things into the world that weren't there before.

But I don't exist in isolation. I exist within many contexts, to name a few: a society, financial systems, histories, a family, a past, a present and also a studio. My studio is filled with objects that I've collected, gathered and chosen for their sonic potential or their aesthetic quality. Ones that I've thought have some sort of potential – usually selected intuitively.

When I start to create a new piece, the starting point differs. Sometimes it starts with an abstract sonic idea, sometimes an open score, sometimes a concept or a question. Then there is a long period of exploration and experimentation. I search for the potential of what an idea could sound like. I put things together that I don't think belong to see what will happen. I try to experience my materials (physical and sonic) differently, to use them in a new or unexpected way. I play games to explore this, to get out of my habits. I challenge myself. I keep looking for new objects and sounds, new materials, new concepts … while I'm out walking my dog, exercising or food shopping. I go through my studio at home looking for forgotten objects and materials.

All in an attempt to make the abstract manifest itself in the realm of the heard, to bring something new into the world.

I experience this process, this active thinking, as an interactive network where I am not the leader, but part of a dynamic system, which includes myself, my ideas, the objects, the materials, the surrounding soundscapes, the people, the world … that surround me.

DOI: 10.4324/9781003008217-3

FIGURE 1.1 Objects in Frasch's studio in Berlin, Germany, 2017

As I experiment, I pay attention to the materials I'm using to understand what they can and cannot do, to understand what are their strengths and weaknesses. I listen to their sounds. I let them reveal things I wasn't expecting. The materials have limitations and unexpected twists. I am in collaboration with my physical and sonic materials. We are co-creating something together.

We are a network (a group or system of interconnected people or things).

They are my extended limbs. But I am not the center. We are a unified metastable bodily force, coming together and falling apart again. We are post-human (see Figure 1.1).

Thinking with Others – 1

In her book *Vibrant Matter*, Jane Bennet argues the point that 'bodies enhance their power in or as a heterogeneous assemblage' (2010 pg 23), that bodies become more as a part of things rather than alone. She uses Spinoza's notion of affective bodies along with Gilles Deleuze and Félix Guattari's notion of assemblage to theorize for 'a materiality that is as much force as entity, as much energy as matter, as much intensity as extension' (2010 pg 20) in what she calls 'thing-power'. She makes a case for an interdependent actant: one that is never alone, always interacting, cooperating and collaborating with other actants, with other forces and bodies. So that I, as the creator of new sonic worlds and instrument designs, am always in dialogue, always interacting with many materials and energies which are every bit as real, active and participatory as myself. We are co-creators.

Bennet's reading of Spinoza draws on the notion of conative bodies in order to de-objectivize bodies by breaking them down into modes, which are themselves further fragmented into what she refers to as mosaics or many simple bodies. By looking at bodies this way, as modes rather than objects, there is an active and transformative quality to their state, giving bodies the possibility to change, but also to exchange with other modes. This perspective underscores the impact that bodies have on each other. Bennett (2010 pg 24) writes:

> What it means to be a 'mode' then is to form alliances and enter assemblages: it is to mod(e)ify and be modified by others. The process of modification is not under the control of anyone mode – no mode is an agent in the hierarchical sense

Bennett expands Spinoza's notion of body and modes by drawing on Deleuze and Guattari's notion of assemblage, which she describes as non-hierarchical, 'living, throbbing confound them from within' (2010, p. 24). For Bennett, each aspect of the assemblage, from the organic to the social to the electrical, contains a force that is responsible for making things happen, for creating emergent effects which can range from a war on terror to a blackout.

Just as Bennett uses the example of a power blackout that affected nearly 50 million people in North America in 2003 to further her theory of non-human exceptionalism, where there are 'a swarm of vitalities at play' (2010 pg 32), I examine my own process of creation with instrument building and composing. Just as Bennett demonstrates how electricity, power structures and human consumption form an assemblage that has no leader, where actants are not acting alone, I too am part of a human/nonhuman inter-folding network of electronics, objects, ideas, power structures, buildings, audiences …. There are objects and materials (sensors, motors, computers, microchips, pieces of wood, glass bowls) involved(see Figures 1.2 and 1.3) There is the electricity running through the amplifiers and the transducers. There is the motion of the objects that change as the vibrational patterns shift when materials heat up. There is my deciding which objects to use depending on the performance and the composition. There is the room I play in. There is the temperature of the day, the time of the day, the audience that decided to show up depending on what else has been going on. I am co-creating with all of these elements.

There is an intentionality on my part as I carefully choose and listen to the objects and materials, trying to bring the abstract into the real, responding to how my objects are reacting when they are set into motion, thinking through the compositional underpinnings. In agreement with what Bennett writes, this intention 'is like a pebble thrown into a pond, or an electrical current sent through a wire or a

FIGURE 1.2 Image from Frasch's performance at *Post-Paradise Series*, Birmingham, UK, 2019

FIGURE 1.3 Frasch's self-made instrument, Digital Boxes, in Berlin, Germany, 2017

neural network … it vibrates and merges with other currents, to affect and to be affected' (2010 pg 32). There is a feedback loop with all these mentioned elements, including my own ability to adapt and change to situations. It is not so much that I am a 'doer (an agent)', but rather that I am 'behind the deed as a doing and an effecting by a human-nonhuman assemblage' (2010 pg 29).

Bennett (2010 pg 34) posits the question: 'If we do not know just how it is that human agency operates, how can we be so sure that the processes through which nonhumans make their mark are qualitatively different?' From my own perspective, this unclarity of creative ownership resonates with my experience. My choices, ideas and reactions are intertwined with the physical and sonic materials, the performance space, the audience, the noise coming from the street of my studio, the new energies that surround me. When I pay attention to more than myself, I experience the power of things. I feel the vibrancy of the matter that surrounds me.

Reflection: From the Inside Looking Out

Noticing the energy of the audience while maintaining my own – during the performance. Sometimes they're calm and attentive. Sometimes they're fidgety or a bit drunk. Sometimes I let their energy in, and sometimes I choose to ignore it. Always, though, I focus on locking into the rhythm of my self-made instruments, the moving sonic objects, the resulting sounds and my own internal pulse. During the performance moment, public or private, I draw deep into my own internal pacing. It's a pace that, during my everyday life, the world puts pressure on to rush ahead, always speeding me up, even if just a little bit, but usually quite a lot. The performance event is the moment to stop and block this pressure, to focus and feel my own pacing, my own rhythm.

Sometimes I clench and tense up in order to block out the energy of others and protect my own. Although I wish to relax and feel that my energy can occupy the space without hindrance from others. I wish that others would make space for quieter and lesser dominant energies to be present. Sometimes they do. Other times it makes them uncomfortable or resistant.

I strive to combine my internal rhythms with the motions and resulting rhythms of the sonic objects in action. I listen, not just with my ears, but I feel their movement with my whole organism. Our rhythms move together.

My hands know what to do during the performance from time spent doing the actions over and over again. There is a refined intimacy between my mechanics and the objects' mechanisms. My finger tips remember the feel of the energy of the objects even before they touch them. They know what the vibrating materials should feel like when things are working correctly: for example, when the electricity is at the right intensity. They quickly feel when the electricity is too much or not enough. My hands and arms know exactly how to find the very precise spot which will set the objects into motion. My hands can feel how the wood is vibrating that day and find the sweet spot. Before, during and after, my fingers feel the vibrations of the physical materials. The residue of the energy remains embedded on the tips of my fingers. I can feel the memory of the past sensations on my skin and anticipate future ones.

Thinking with Others – 2

When I perform with self-made instruments, electronics or even with the traditional flute, there is a learned affinity between my skin, my muscles and the performed physical instrument(s). I know which minute physical changes to make in order to impact the sounding vibrations. There is a trained awareness, and thus a resulting intimacy between my biofeedback and the refined motions of the physical materials. I learn(ed). My lip muscles learn(ed). My fingers learn(ed). My body changes. It remembers. My instruments are changing too, deteriorating and shape-shifting through usage. The flute becomes a little bit more worn out. The vibrating wood of a sound sculpture becomes a little bit more dented. The flux of

FIGURE 1.4 Image from Frasch's performance at *Post-Paradise Series*, Birmingham, UK, 2019

the micro-forms impacts the macro performative assemblage of human and non-human materials – affecting and affected, impacting and impacted (see Figure 1.4).

Erin Manning's work *Politics of Touch* is a dynamic exploration into the impact the senses have on a processual body, with a focus on touch, to make a case for how this perspective 'influences the way in which we articulate and live the political' (2007 pg xiii). She explores the deep impact that movement can have on qualitatively altering the body and how 'A body is never content to sit still: it must become' (2007 pg 139). Each time I perform with my instruments, each time I shift my arm or flutter my fingers, my organism is altered. New vibrations leave imprints on the skin. During the performance event, my skin, my fingers, my muscles, the objects, the electricity, the materials are interacting with each other as the sounds vibrate around and through the surfaces of the humans, air molecules and materials in the room. The entire human/nonhuman assemblage is a metastable system, always unfolding, becoming and (re)acting.

Manning explores this metastability through the notion of individuation, which she explains as a process that allows for potentiality to become realized. Manning's concept privileges the motion and transformation of bodies in relation to themselves, each other and the surrounding environments or contexts. The micro and macro forms are unstable. When one element changes, so can another. As Manning (2007 pg 93) writes:

> my matter (my energetic potential) is in-formed by a shell that never quite contains the process …. Form suggests an organization shift in the system. When matter is potentialized into a given form, a phase shift occurs. This phase shift dephases the body-as-identity, exposing the body to the effects of its reaching toward: the body becomes the multiplicity of its becoming and its having-become. Bodies are as incorporeal as they are in-formed. .. the body

becomes more than real, more than its envelope, more than the space-time of its pre-locatedness ... it is plural and unpredictable, evolving always through movements that are contingent on environments and (re)combinations.

Touch doesn't just impact and remember, it also reaches towards – it strives. For touch 'is the act of reaching toward, of creating space-time through the wording that occurs when bodies move' (Manning 2007 pg xiv). Zooming in to the tip of my finger when it touches a vibrating piece of wood, this micro point of contact sets off an unknown alteration of action and knowledge which scatters throughout the assemblage. One potentiality is engendered. There is an in-the-moment change in the body, an impact, the creation of a new memory and a potential for a new emergent future.

During a public performance, I am not alone with my sound objects. Audience members listen, or half listen, (or zone out). The vibrations sounding in the room leave their imprint on the listeners regardless of their attention. They can't help but be altered. The entire environmental assemblage is touched by the vibrations. Everything is metamorphosing. I am equally impacted by the presence of the audience as they are by me. Our muscles tense or relax, shift or concentrate. Vibrations leave a residue on our skin. They also leave a residue in our minds. We all (mis) remember what happened. Our memory remembers some things, while our skins remember others. For 'A politics of touch does not adhere to the notion of a strict interiority and exteriority. Rather it expands the chronotope of the body through a qualitative expansion of exfoliations and surfaces' (Manning 2007 pg 59).

Even something as minuscule as the tip of a finger can impact the emergent properties of Bennett's vibrant assemblage. Touch affects the past, present and future. It opens the way for more potential paths of Manning's individuation. Maybe this time, when I touch the vibrating surface, the material will be moving too quickly and I will have to react differently. Maybe this time the audience will have a unique concentration and I will be touched by something unexpected. It's not yet known. But I am ready – ready to be touched by, ready to be expanded by, ready to exchange with, the human/nonhuman assemblage of vibrating matter.

Reflection: Sitting on the Outside – Experience 1

It's a fading memory of a concert that left a strong impression on me and triggered something important. It left a spark that inspired me. It was one of those long summer Berlin nights when the well-known apartment complex on Pappelallee had a series of house concerts in different apartments since many experimental artists live in the same building. The audience wandered from apartment to apartment, then snacked on a potluck spread that was set up in the shared courtyard.

I remember it being Andrea Neumann's[1] apartment, but I could be wrong. I remember it being the first summer I moved there, in 2010, but it could have been the second, in 2011. I remember sitting in the back of the room, although I could have been standing. Even though my memory contains many holes and probably contains many inconsistencies, it's the vivid memory of Hanna Hartman's[2] performance that evening that I find important and compelling.

I remember the careful sound design created by the specific objects and materials chosen, the crunch and hiss the metallic balls made as they rolled over the ambiguous white powder (which I learned years later was potato starch). I remember that there were balls of different sizes which caused subtle variations in the sound. I remember that the ambiguity of the unknown white powder made a strong impression on me. Because it was unclear what type of powder was being used, and because it didn't have a direct narrative to its presence, I felt free to add in my own story and connections to the material. The ambiguous powder alluded to many material possibilities (talcum powder, flour, cocaine …). It was never confined to being something exact. The unclarity of the material allowed its presence to be felt stronger. With the lack of specific narrative, I could feel the energy of the material through its visual presence and feel the strength of its sonic vibrations.

The visceral memory remains – the feeling of the energy of the objects and their sounds, the vibration of their presences, with and without their sounds.

Thinking with Others – 3

We perceive objects on the stage, drawing our own personalized (historical) connections and narratives to them. As Sherry Turkle theorizes in her book *Evocative Objects: Things We Think With* (2007), there is a power that objects hold as they become our companions throughout our lives. This companionship is unique to each listener/viewer in the room. For some, there will be something specific. Maybe for one audience member at the Hartman concert, the ambiguous white powder was clearly flour and triggered a memory of a cake they baked last week. For others, maybe the white powder made them think of several contradictory elements at once. Or, as was the case with me, it captured something more unknown and evocative, or what Turkle calls 'uncanny'. Turkle describes uncanny as 'those things that are known of old yet unfamiliar' (2007 pg 8). It's almost placeable, but not quite. It alludes, it hints, but doesn't pinpoint.

Just as the human organism is touching and sensing in action, it is creating personal narratives and stories of self when observing. These human stories and connections don't need to be left out of Bennett's non-hierarchical more-than-just-human assemblage perspective. They can be part of the mix, part of the vitality, part of the power of things. But let's be sure to de-center the narrative. Not put it at the top, but keep it in the flow of motion and exchanges between forces – human and nonhuman.

Reflection: Sitting on the Outside – Experience 2

The room is dark and calm. There is a big table in the center of the room. We, the audience, encircle it. The performer, Ryoko Akama,[3] is calm and very relaxed, focused yet also at ease. Her ease is notable. One might not have known she was about to be the solo performer before she began. Then she begins. She sets objects into motion, one at a time, reflecting on a score that we don't know exists (but I learned about later). Small lamps scattered around the table obscure the objects, creating shadowy outlines, so it's mostly unclear exactly what they are.

The table seems alive. It is alive. There is motion and activity. Sounds and non-sounds. As the audience, we listen and feel, experiencing everything differently. Remembering differently. The moment is multiplied throughout the memory of the audience, broken and fragmented. We all notice something different. Important traits of the evening stand out more importantly to one than the other. And still there is a shared experience, a shared moment, a shared togetherness as we watch the relaxed performer set objects off into motion, as the table becomes alive with vibrations, motion and sounds.

I remember one strange object in particular that seemed to be a sheet of very bent metal or something that resembled that from afar. Some kind of motor is turned on underneath and it makes the material wobble and move, like a sea creature, or if there were such a thing, a mud creature. It doesn't seem to be making any specific sounds. Yet its motion is sonic to me. It implies sound with its un-sounding motions, in the company of other objects making sounds. Its strangeness alludes to abstract sounds that I imagine I hear.

I remember the moment it is turned off and then I stop focusing on it, and notice the glass bottles and the high frequencies that had been going on, which I had lost track of. I'm disappointed that it has stopped. But I'm glad the piece isn't over. I would be happy if it was never over. That it would continue on and on. And I could continue to sit and watch and feel.

But eventually, it is over. It resides in my memory. The memory changes as I change, as I (mis)remember. The memory creates an inner universe in my mind (see Figure 1.5).

FIGURE 1.5 Ryoko Akama in performance

Thinking with Others – 4

From my perspective as an audience member at the Akama concert, mundane and abandoned objects held poignant powers. There was something particular about this performance, with these particular objects, that resonated with me at that particular time. A mundane piece of metal became extra-ordinary through my eyes. I perceived something that was, and wasn't, there. It is this openness of possibility to experience, to be affected by something more than what seems to be there which in his book *Parables for the Virtual* Brian Massumi calls relationality (2002, p. 224). Massumi argues that being affected is a dynamic process of interactive change between the real and virtual. By placing a motor under the metal sheet on a table surrounded by vibrating objects, Akama gave the potential of that material to become more than just a piece of metal. From my audience point of view, the metal sheet became changed, with an unknown and indescribable something. It became alive and dynamic. It was more-than what was present. The real and the virtual became intertwined.

Massumi writes about the non-objectiveness of perception by examining the role that emotion plays in the perception of something as seemingly objective as color. He does this through an example of a scientific study that was conducted by David Katz in the first decade of the 20th century to test the effect of memory on color constancy (2002 pg 208). A subject was asked to match the blue of a certain absent friend's eyes to the red of their own lips and the color of a few other everyday objects. Massumi argues that despite the bad science with obvious flaws in the uncontrolled experiment and the oversimplification of a complex experience, the experiment shouldn't be dismissed so easily. He uses this study to observe 'the cofunctioning of affect with memory' (2002 pg 208). Massumi argues that eye color is not neutral. Color is not neutral. And memory is, of course, not neutral. Perception is not objective, but complex. Massumi (2002 pg 222) points out that:

> When remembering the color of something, or remembering a sensation, our emotional reaction highlights or emphasizes certain qualities over others …. Both the test patch and the remembered retina were certifiably blue. This much is true. But there was a singular excess in the retinal memory. This excess of effect was not attributable to any colored object. It was attributable to the uncontrolled conditions of the memory's emergence in this experimental situation. This much 'more' is also true. The interaction of the objective dimensions of blue was interfered with and modulated by a previousness of familiarity and fondness: by an unconsciously ingredient emotional charge. The viewer found the blue so fondly that it became more blue than it actually was.

This 'cofunctioning' of memory and affect, and non-objectivity of perception are as true for the sonic as for the visual that Massumi references. During that

Akama concert, the wobbly metal became strange and uncanny. I was touched by an unknown force of the presence of an odd physical metal sheet at the moment. The sheet became more than what it is. It became more than just a piece of forgotten broken metal. It became mysterious, full of unknowable potential. The objective outside and enhanced perspective on the inside become blurred. It's unclear which is 'real'. The virtual and physical exchange and transform where the cause and effect are ambiguous, what Massumi refers to as a quasi-cause (2002 pg 213). There was something about that piece of metal that transformed my perception of it. I remember it even more fondly now, as it stands out against many other instrument objects that I come across during other performances. The singularity of that odd metal becomes even more odd, more unique and captivating in my memory than it probably was in the performance.

The perception of that same piece of metal was as varied and rich throughout the performance as there were members or the audience. I was touched by this one object in particular, the metal sheet, but it's possible that some audience members didn't even notice it, or noticed other objects more, or didn't notice any and kept wishing the performance was over. There were multiple bodies in the venue feeling vibrations in multiple places of the room. There were multiple perceptions, receiving sensations differently. Certain things stood out, capturing their attention in the moment, and others didn't. Certain sounds might have seemed 'too' loud or 'too' soft to one and not to another. There was no absolute receiver. There was no one view point. There was no objective performance. The sonic moment is scattered throughout the audience members, leaving fragmented variations in their interior universes and traces on the edges of their skins. These memories themselves are alive and in flux. The memory changes as we change, modulating and unfolding. Memory is unstable. We forget. We remember. We misremember. We forget and then remember. We forget many things and remember a few others. We might remember something we had previously forgotten. We remember what was important or exciting. It stands out in our mind, but then slowly fades away over the years. The memory of the concert is as alive as the concert once was, as the presence of the object became, only in the realm of the virtual.

By adding in the virtual to the human-nonhuman assemblage we further enrich the possibility of thing-power. By considering this ability for the virtual and the real to mutually transform, and for affect to cofunction with memory, we can deepen the lens of understanding of the macro-assemblage. Still insisting to knock the human off the central role, we must just let complexity of perception and memory further enter into the picture without letting the human dominate. Rather than placing more importance on one element over another, we can still let affect impact perception and memory, which in turn impacts future humanly actions, which in turn alters the doing and the about-to-be done. The subjective perspective of the objects, the never one-sided experiences impact the evolving co-transformation of the virtual and the real. We should strive to allow the lens to be enriched while still maintaining a non -hierarchical structure.

Connecting It All Together

As we slowly zoom backwards over all these elements again, starting at the end with Massumi's examination of the complexity of perception, the instability and transformation of internal memory, then moving to the 'the eyes' of the audience and individual narratives of objects, then to the tip of the fingers with the physical and virtual vibrations, then to the electronic circuits of instrument building and extended limbs, our assemblage of human and nonhuman now contains more transformative materials and elements, more angles and sensibilities. There is the changing memory. There is the seen and the heard. There is the unseen and the unheard. There is the forgotten and the (mis)remembered. There is the overly noticed. There is the matter and non-matter quivering with vitality, impacting, informing and transforming the ever-expanding collection. This opening and enriching of perspective allows for the force of things to gain more momentum, and also allows for the sonic performance to become even more alive, to be about more than the sonic, more than the moment. It allows for the notion of performance and creation to grow and evolve inside listeners' minds, a scattered creation collaborating with a complex array of objects, energies, bodies, perspectives and memories.

Notes

1 Andrea Neumann, German musician and composer: https://de.wikipedia.org/wiki/Andrea_Neumann_(Musikerin).
2 Hanna Hartman, Swedish composer based in Berlin, Germany: www.hannahartman.de/.
3 Ryoko Akama, Japanese/Korean composer and performer based in Huddersfield, UK: https://ryokoakama.com/.

Bibliography

Bennett, Jane. 2010. *Vibrant Matter: A Political Ecology of Things*. Durham, NC: Duke University Press.
Manning, Erin. 2007. *Politics of Touch: Sense, Movement, Sovereignty*. Minneapolis, MN: University of Minnesota Press.
Massumi, Brian. 2002. *Parables for the Virtual: Movement, Affect, Sensation*. Durham, NC: Duke University Press.
Turkle, Sherry. 2007. *Evocative Objects: Things We Think With*. Cambridge, MA: MIT Press.

2
WHY SHOULD WE CARE ABOUT THE BODY?

On What Enactive-Ecological Musical Approaches Have to Offer

Lauren Hayes

What can it mean to say that musical activity is embodied? Much has been written over the last decade and beyond on the subject of embodiment within musical scholarship. Following what has often been called 'the somatic turn' that occurred around the mid-1980s within the social sciences (for the origins of this move, see, for example, Turner 2008), there has been a rehabilitation of the body as being central to understanding the various activities that comprise music making and listening. This has occurred at a variety of degrees and scales across a range of sub-disciplines. Concurrently, as sensor technologies grow cheaper and smaller, the body as a 'source' of gestural and biophysical information generation has taken a more prominent – yet not unproblematic – role within new musical instrument design that is rooted within human–computer interaction (HCI). In this chapter, I discuss how a combined enactive-ecological approach to music cognition provides a useful framework for understanding musical activity as fundamentally embodied, as well as imagining the creative possibilities that can be facilitated through technological mediation. I also examine whether practice-based research related to music, technology, and embodiment has fully grasped the social and political implications of such a turn to the body, as has been seen in other fields such as science and technology studies, and sociology.

The emerging field of enactive music cognition has gained traction in recent years as a radical alternative to traditional cognitivist strands of music psychology, as well as certain varieties of embodied music cognition, which maintain a commitment to mental representations within their otherwise body-inclusive accounts of musical activity. Coming out of research within non-traditional cognitive sciences and the philosophy of mind, the enactive approach asserts that cognition emerges from the developmental processes of sense-making and identity-forming. This depends on the ongoing affective and sensorimotor couplings that occur between organisms and their environments: the processes of living within, shaping, and being shaped by both their physical as well as sociocultural niches. A distinct, yet related, area of radical embodied cognition (Chemero 2011) that historically precedes the enactive approach is that of ecological psychology, which follows the ideas of James J. Gibson. Gibson's reformational approach emphasised the direct perception of individual organisms or animals within their environments – rejecting the need for cognitive mediation – and the strong links between perception and action. This was favoured over dominant models from the physical sciences which describe an observer-independent world (Gibson 1979/1986). Gibson's concept of affordances (Gibson 1966) allows us to re-describe the physical world by way of opportunities for action that are meaningful to particular organisms based on their capacities to perceive and act.

As somatics practitioner and researcher Jessica Rajko has pointed out, research concerning embodiment within arts practice should, itself, be embodied (Rajko 2018). These themes have been fundamental in shaping the trajectory of my own creative music practice over the last 14–15 years, from when I first started developing my own highly personalised instruments with both physical materials and computer software. But they also account for the formation of my musical identity through early piano lessons, growing up in a richly musical household, and a jagged trajectory through various genres, bands, and peer groups. In what follows, I will discuss the ways in which these ideas have allowed me to explore such perspectives within the fields of live electronic musical performance and sonic art through the use of physical, haptic, and tangible electronic and digital technologies. In each case, what is demonstrated is that the technological interventions have been important not in terms of their 'innovative' qualities per se, but rather in their ability to afford collaborative and fundamentally social approaches to music making. I situate this work alongside some recent developments within cognitive psychology that explore the implications of the enactive approach for ethics within social cognition (Colombetti and Torrance 2009), moving from the enactive concerns of the organism to an 'ethics of care' (Loaiza 2019, p2). These developments move beyond examining the action-perception of individuals in the world to more collective and dynamical group relationships (Urban 2014). I discuss where these ideas have had a continual – albeit at times implicit – influence on my creative practice. This has involved not only solo performance and group improvisation, but also working with people from a variety of communities, including children, vulnerable adults, and people with complex and profound learning difficulties. I argue that an enactive ethics of care within musical practice requires resisting the individualistic formulations and hierarchical structures that exist and are continuously reified within both academic and industry musical contexts.

What Enactive-Ecological Accounts Afford

The title of Marc Leman's 2008 book *Embodied Music Cognition and Mediation Technology* suggests a promising discussion of how an embodied – rather than purely cerebral – account of music cognition might offer up new possibilities for both understanding and 'doing' music, and the ways in which new technologies might be used within their mediation. Yet throughout the book, the representational stance is demonstrably affirmed: Leman essentially posits the human body as 'the biologically designed mediator between musical subjects and their musical environment' (Matyja and Schiavio 2013, p352). Musical meaning – per Leman's view – is 'cooked up' in the mind out of whatever has been 'received' through the sensori-motor channels. Someone with 'auraltypical' (Drever 2017, p1) hearing would, for example, detect changes in air pressure caused by the excitation of a material such as a cello string, then, passing through the apparatus of the ears, vibrations would be converted into electrical signals which transverse the auditory nerve to be perceived as sound in the brain, and finally interpreted as music. And in 'reverse', musical ideas – intentionalities that manifest firstly in the mind – are transduced back into sound, mediated by the body via materials such as musical instruments.

Leman advocates that the dynamic animations of physical interactions should be exploited within any instance of technology that 'mediates between mental processing and multiple physical energies' (Leman 2008, p.141). He suggests that such 'tools can function as an extension of the human body', and describes them as 'natural' mediators (Leman 2008, p141). While Leman's thinking points to the embodied nature of music cognition as involving processes which are distributed throughout the body, it nonetheless sits within a lineage descending from representational theories of mind (RTMs). Widely held and formalised by Jerry Fodor, among others (see Chemero 2011 for further historical discussion), RTMs ultimately argue that thoughts are dependent on the relationships between thinkers and their internal representations of objects in the world. The implications of this way of understanding musical activity and experience are not insignificant. The tendency towards the representational suggests a foregrounding of musical symbolism, most often manifested as the notation system of the musical score. Within this paradigm, the focus – particularly within research fields – can easily become narrowed around western canons, western music theory, and so on. As Mark Reybrouck notes:

> sounds, on the contrary, are the outcome of human actions. Even if they are not self-produced, they can induce a kind of (ideo)motor resonance that prompts the listener to experience the sounds as if they have been involved in their production.
>
> *Reybrouck (2005), p4*

Anthony Chemero (2011) offers a strong proposal for a radical embodied cognition that derives not from RTMs, but rather from a non-representational lineage descending from 'eliminativist' (Chemero 2011, p17) thought. Within this delineation, we see two related but distinct approaches: enactive cognition and approaches related to ecological psychology. The former stems from the work of Francisco Varela, Evan Thompson, and Eleanor Rosch (1991/2006), and the latter builds on Gibson's (1979/1986) work in visual perception. The ecological approach put forward by Gibson stresses the specificity of the perceived world to the individual organism and introduces the concept of action that is perceptually guided: 'animal locomotion is not usually aimless but is guided or controlled – by light if the animal can see, by sound if the animal can hear, and by odor if the animal can smell' (Gibson 1979/1986, p17). The physiology of the perceiving agent determines what is deemed as useful for action, and which actions are suggested by the objects or materials within its environment. The world described in this way appears very different to, for example, a bee than it does to me. Furthermore, the active processes of perception are directly coupled to the actions of the agents themselves: in my case, it is my ambulant mobility, the turning of my head, and orientation of my nose that allow me to position and reposition myself in order to perceive (smell) a flower; the bee uses flight and various orientations of a different sort. The concept of affordances emerges out of these propositions: it is a way in which to describe the world in terms of these individual perceptive capacities. Objects are perceptible by whatever actions they offer the perceiver: a flower affords sniffing (to me) and pollination (to the honey bee). We can very quickly imagine the usefulness of the concept of affordances when we extend it to the musical world. For someone with a background in jazz, piano keys would afford depressing with nuanced control. But for a toddler, they might afford bashing, and a free improvising musician may perceive the rhythmic possibilities that could emerge from running a wooden drumstick along the keyboard (what might be referred to as an extended technique). For a person with complex needs, the piano might afford an interface for expression, communication, and emotional or affective regulation (see Hayes 2015) through multivarious interactions.

While Gibson's ecological approach to perception consists of re-describing an objective world through the possibilities for action that it affords for the perceiver, the enactive approach similarly emphasises the unique physiology of the perceiving organism, but differs in that it proposes that reality is brought forth. Enactivists suggest that both cognition and the world itself co-emerge through the processes of perception and action, these comprising the ongoing sensorimotor engagement that occurs between agents and their environments. Grounded in the autopoietic – or self-maintaining – relationships (Maturana and Varela 1980/1991) between cells and environments, these ideas have not only scaled up to describe entire organisms, but also have been used to discuss larger sociocultural systems such as languages and societies. It is the historical uniqueness of its embodied existence that allows the coupled organism–niche relationship to emerge over the lifetime of the perceiving being through models which can be described and even empirically validated in terms of dynamic systems theory (Chemero 2011). From the musical perspective, the habitual experiences of one's musicking over a lifetime contribute to how one experiences and makes sense of music in any given context. This could include not only things like instrumental training, but also listening habits, concert-going experiences, participation in various musical communities, early formative experiences with sound, environmental sound, peer groups, and so on. While the ecological and enactive perspectives have fundamental differences, their commonalities have been successfully integrated by many (see, for example, McGann 2014), allowing for a combined enactive-ecological framework to be used as a powerful basis for theorising music cognition.

Social Cognition, Care, and Musicking

Hanne De Jaegher and Ezequiel Di Paolo extend the enactive perspective by highlighting the socially dependent nature of cognition. They propose that an understanding of socio-cognitive life should not simply be relegated to the domain of individuals' cognitive mechanisms within their own environments. Instead, they argue that social cognition is constructed through the unfolding interactions with others within the processes of what they term 'participatory sense-making' (De Jaegher and Di Paolo 2007, p485). Two autonomous agents are said to be 'coupled' through their face-to-face interpersonal exchanges because their interactions are spontaneously coordinated as they engage in meaning-making. Importantly, then, embodied cognition must arise out of not only purely physical or sensori-motor activity, but also through these interconnected social aspects. This takes place when we respond to and affect each other, and are simultaneously affected by the dynamic coordination that occurs through this engagement. There is perhaps no more obvious musical example of this phenomenon than what has the potential to transpire in group improvisation (see Hayes 2019 for further discussion). Giovanna Colombetti and Steve Torrance (2009) take up the work of De Jaegher and Di Paolo, relating it specifically to emotion, affect, and ethics. They suggest that emotion plays a key role in the self-regulation and adaptive processes of sense-making, and that 'the enactive approach treats cognition and emotion not as separate systems, but as deeply integrated biological, psychological and phenomenological levels' (Colombetti and Torrance 2009, p507). As we connect, we want to *feel* connected. They outline an 'inter-affective' (Colombetti and Torrance 2009, p516) approach to ethics that is not based on individualistic behavioural moralism, but rather, it asserts a collective model of sense-making where individual autonomy is both fostered and concurrently limited in favour of the autonomy of the dyad or group dynamics.

Petr Urban (2014) develops this proposal of an enactive ethics by exploring the possible kinship between care ethics and the enactive approach, suggesting that both 'attempt to rethink the concepts of autonomy, individuality and agency in a way that enables a novel reading of human relations in terms of the irreducibility of the interrelational and interactional domain' (Urban 2014, p2). He suggests that approaches such as Colombetti and Torrance's can be extended from considering face-to-face interactions to the wider domains of sociocultural institutions. Furthermore, following their navigation of individual versus collective agency, he asserts:

> a caring relationship requires a mutuality that gives birth to a domain of significance that could not have been achieved by the individuals alone. At the same time, however, what produces and sustains the required mutuality

are the various practices of agents involved in the relationship, making their autonomy also a necessary part of the game.

Urban (2015), p126

Of course, music has a long history of utility in relation to healing, therapy, communication, 'socially engaged' arts practice, and community building. Yet musicking – an active, embodied process – seen through the enactive-ecological framework can be considered *as* caring practice through an existential rather than utilitarian lens. In related work, Juan M. Loaiza (2019) extends the enactive concern of the organism – to maintain its own preservation – to social maintenance, involving an openness to the social experiences with others that enable us to 'survive'. Specifically, this framing allows notions of care to move beyond an ethics of gendered labour, behavioural morality of an individualistic nature, and the divisions between private and public life that are often foregrounded. Simplistic or detached notions of solely 'caring about' can give way to more complex, interdependent patterns of also 'taking care, care-giving and care-receiving' (Loaiza 2019, p11).

Loaiza's earlier work connects the field of enactive music cognition to the wider spheres of social musicking through some oft-cited musicological texts[1] – the works of John Blacking and Christopher Small, for example (see Loaiza 2016) – that highlight the socio-cultural-historical lenses through which musical activity can be configured. In doing so, Loaiza presents a convincing opportunity to 'move beyond the biology-culture divide without submitting to reductionism' (Loaiza 2016, p410). It is specifically this perceived split that representational accounts of embodied music cognition have failed to address, severely limiting the ramifications of embodied approaches in doing so. Loaiza and others (Krueger 2011, Hayes 2019), have furthered the appeal of Small's idea of musicking – music as a verb – through the enactive lens 'by considering musicking as a wider process and a genre of social-life' (Loaiza 2016, p411). The domains in which musical activities are seen to take place extend from networks of people, materials, and cultural institutions to the enactive cognitive domain of world/environment. In this way, an enactive-ecological framework – a radical embodied position – does not limit the body's role to one of information processing. Music, and moreover sound-based practices, can be explored without requiring to be represented in the mind, and can instead be seen as a sense-making activities beyond existing only within dominant musical discourses. This echoes the ways in which purely biological constructions of the body can often leave out historical and lived experiences. As medical history literature has documented, such refutations are often highly gendered and deeply problematic (see Duden 1998).

Mediation and Technology

Turning to the incorporation of techno-musical objects, Leman offers a discussion of mediating technologies, emphasising electronic and digital apparatuses which have the ability to 'translate' between body and mind. He points to various projects that instrumentalise the body through the parametrisation of gestural data and the encoding/decoding of kinaesthetic or biophysical information, as is common in work related to, for example, the New Interfaces for Musical Expression (NIME) research community. Yet within these frameworks, the computational theory of mind is emulated through this calculative approach to digital musical instrument design. Biological and physical 'information' is gathered or sensed, recorded, analysed, processed, and translated into sound. Furthermore, a mind–body dualism is perpetuated within this framing: the body is seen as the sensorimotor-actor and the mind as the meaning-maker. This methodology stems from the historic development of such research as emerging from HCI, rather than from musicological perspectives (see Hayes and Marquez-Borbon 2021 for further discussion). While music technologists are quick to exploit the body in this way, a consideration of what is favoured, omitted, and what is obscured within that instrumentalisation is often lacking. As we know from the work of N. Katherine Hayles, information – or rather meaning – does not readily translate between substrates (Hayles 2008), even where human bodies are concerned. Rather than simply replicating this quantification and representation of movement and physical energy, it can be more fruitful to explore the ways in which such technologies might afford collectively co-determined musical spaces to emerge through a rejection of such approaches.

As a performer, despite being demonstrably physical in the ways that I move and navigate my hybrid analogue/digital instruments on stage, there is nothing within the formalisation of 'gesture' in the sense mentioned above that aligns with how I produce sound. I do not connect together a series of choreographed discrete movements while I play. Rather, I dynamically move through various kinetic-sonic terrains in a process that might be more aligned with the notion of the cybernetic 'helms-person' navigating their ship. For example, when improvising using a 'haptically augmented hybrid piano' (Hayes 2013, p501), I fluidly explore the sonic possibilities afforded by the materials of the piano itself – metal and wood – along with an array of objects that can excite the strings – rocks, magnets, and shot glasses, for example. Moreover, my movements and the resulting sounds are structurally coupled[2] (Maturana and Varela 1980/1991) through a simple form of motion tracking. Using a repurposed games controller that tethers my hands to ground via its gloves, and which simultaneously determines a low-resolution measure of each hand's position in three-dimensional space, I am able to imagine 'locations' of expression that 'make sense' based on my own physicality in relation to the instrument (see Figure 2.1). Here, not only is my range of motion limited, but also *how* I move is haptically informed via the rudimentary 'force feedback' elicited from my wearing of the controller's gloves. The delicacy of my touch on the keyboard or the furthest reach towards the soundboard that I can achieve become sites to align with similarly precarious digital processes: deliberate instability and unpredictability within my software environment is put together with such physical bounds and thresholds. While traditional HCI research has focused on developing ergonomic relations between humans and machines, there is nothing within these frictionless interactions that appeals to me as a musician.

FIGURE 2.1 Fluid and dynamic movement is used with a haptically augmented hybrid piano, rather than discrete, choreographed gestures; images from livestreamed performance for Iklectik Art Lab, London, 2020

While much work involving music technology has converged around exploring embodiment from a purely sensorimotor perspective, other fundamental areas have been largely ignored. My own practice has been deeply informed by working with people with profound and complex learning difficulties and assisted special needs in the United Kingdom from 2006 to 2016, while working with both arts charities and local councils (see Hayes 2015, 2017b for details of some of these projects). In these scenarios, the way in which group identities are forged through the reciprocal unfolding of humans, materials, and our shared environment becomes patently evident. Devising situations that allow for collaborative musicking or designing participatory instruments provide scenarios where individuals can develop musical worlds in relation to the materials in their environments. Furthermore, these practices also allow for group dynamics or identities to emerge over time (Loaiza 2019). For example, recalling one such encounter during a session I was facilitating: all the technology I had carefully curated within the room ended up being discarded or rejected by my co-musicker; it was ultimately repurposed in favour of a wholly exploratory, participatory, and spontaneous configuration. Working from the enactive-ecological perspective of sound-based activity allows new forms of musicking to emerge through what Colombetti and Torrance might describe as this 'higher-level, autonomous dynamic of mutual exchange and coordinate response-patterns that unfold between the interactions …. Joyfulness and hope … is thus a joint product, not simply the result of an active leader and a passive follower' (Colombetti and Torrance 2009, p522).

This type of practice cannot be achieved through a centring of the development of technical objects alone. Certainly, my expertise as a musician working with digital-physical technologies has led to invitations to work with communities in dementia day care centres, assisted support needs schools, care homes, and so on, where technological interventions are called for at some point within the collaboration. However, scaffolding – to borrow from pedagogical language – and supporting how the relationships between music, people, sound, social environment, and technology develop is just as crucial in this work. This has involved a variety of methods, ranging from interview sessions, playing music from songbooks, memory games, and extended play and exploration time to ensuring that aesthetic choices neither hurt, frighten, nor over-stimulate people, rearranging and transforming the space, making cups of tea, liaising with staff, and so on. The development of collective agency through the nurturing of its dynamics is the locus of activity. Giving a sensory workshop in a day centre for adults with learning disabilities might be focused around sound and vibration, but would also involve configuring the room with attention to light, airflow, the textures and colours of the objects and materials employed, how participants are situated in relation to each other, and so on (see Figure 2.2). Again, I will stress that this process is utterly collaborative, with my role being that of facilitator rather than that of leader or instructor. Needless to say, the diachronic nature of how these types of mutual exchanges evolve can often require more engagement than may be afforded by the timelines and budgets of academic research projects. While there is arguably nothing particularly unique within the materiality of 'music technology' that ultimately distinguishes it from other musical tools and instruments, it may be its ability to afford such instances of rapid and novel socio-musical reconfiguration that has been appealing to many, including myself. For example, my early work with haptic and vibrotactile technology – used to develop my own embodied relationship with the non-tangible domain of digital audio – has since become repurposed within numerous musical workshops and projects, including within speech and hearing science research (Luo and Hayes 2019).

Loaiza (2019) proposes potential alliances of enactive-ecological approaches with feminist and queer theory, particularly in discussions of care related to modes

FIGURE 2.2 Setting up in a day centre for adults with learning disabilities with augmented fan, acoustic piano, coloured furniture, haptic listening devices, Skoog musical controller, and participants (obscured)

of oppression, the precarity of the lived body, and the vulnerability with which our identities as constituted within our relationships with others can easily disintegrate. David Ben Shannon and Sarah E. Truman's (2020) discussion of creative music practice and feminist new materialism – while not explicitly concerned with enactivist-ecological accounts – offers some further potential alliances, many of which have been explicitly addressed in my own research. For example, in adapting my live electronic performances to account for environmental instabilities – changes in concert space, loudspeaker layout, and so on – I developed a 'site-responsive' practice (Hayes 2017a, p83). Framed within enactive-ecological theory, this work is contextual and relational, non-representational, and does not seek to obfuscate the presence of myself – as a researcher, sound recordist, or performer – at a particular site. Resonances with Shannon and Truman's propositions – '(Don't separate): Imbricate! … (Don't decontextualize): Contextualize! … (Don't represent): More-than-represent!' (Shannon and Truman 2020, p6) – are evident. Yet, in discussions of enactive concern, Loaiza notes that the types of kinships afforded through musicking as I have described it do not necessarily always lead to harmonious dynamics. Furthermore, as musician and scholar Vijay Iyer cautions, in reference to numerous empirical studies, 'even an apparently impartial approach such as cognitive science is not neutral; perception is colored by race' (Iyer 2019, p760). Yet by highlighting the mutually affecting relationships that emerge through musical participatory sense-making and the affective implications of such interdependent processes, we might more readily acknowledge what ultimately is at stake within our musicking practices and reevaluate the ways in which we structure the social frameworks around us that facilitate such work.

Conclusion

As Caroline Bynum has laboured, 'despite the enthusiasm for the topic, discussions of the body are almost completely incommensurate – and often mutually incomprehensible – across the disciplines' (Bynum 1995, p5). Yet nuanced accounts of embodiment within music are important because the implications of the various approaches lead to fundamentally different trends regarding which musical activities or practices are validated and reproduced. Furthermore, as Bynum has stressed, in discussions of our histories of physicality and identity, connections to the past, the future, and ultimately death, are constantly being perturbed. While the 'somatic' or 'body' turn emerged out of critical theory and sociology of embodiment, within the electronic and digital music fields, the dominant alignment with HCI has largely not embraced the socio-political configurations of the body that such shifts made evident. In doing so, various dualisms remain generally unchallenged, including mind/body, biological/cultural, and musical/social divides. Writing on the sociology of medicine, Sarah Nettleton notes that, 'such socially created dualisms are pernicious … not only because they are false, but also because they serve to reinforce ideologies and social hierarchies' (Nettleton 2010, p51). Even while there have been numerous advances in inclusive and assistive music technologies in recent years, the enactive model of care suggests that alternative non-hierarchical models which do not involve rigid roles of 'technologists' and 'users' can lead to collective experiences that might lie beyond the imagination and time-bound limitations of what can be done within both research institutions and similarly, the music industry. Notably, these are both arenas which have favoured and been dominated by able-bodied, white, cis-male bodies functioning in highly competitive – as opposed to collaborative – domains. As elucidated in this chapter, my own research has explored and continues to explore the implications for embodied performance, improvisation, and collective sonic practice through an enactive-ecological framework, which has allowed me to care about 'the body' beyond its utility as a site for measurement. The importance of creative music practice – as embodied practice – cannot be stressed enough: as Rajko points out in her call to action, 'terms such as embodiment and embodied thinking are often discussed and analysed in writing; but if the purpose is to learn how to engage in embodied thinking, then the answers will not come from a text' (Rajko 2018, p195).

Notes

1 These works are frequently referred to in research on enactive-ecological approaches within musicology that deal with embodiment – in its broadest sense – and music.
2 While it is beyond the scope of this chapter, the idea of structural coupling is key within enactivist literature, describing the co-adaptive relationships that exist between living systems and their environments.

Bibliography

Bynum, C. 1995. Why all the fuss about the body? A medievalist's perspective. *Critical inquiry*, 22(1), 1–33.

Chemero, A. 2011. *Radical embodied cognitive science*. Cambridge, MA: MIT Press.

Colombetti, G., and Torrance, S. 2009. Emotion and ethics: An inter-(en)active approach. *Phenomenology and the cognitive sciences*, 8, 505–526. doi: 10.1007/s11097-009-9137-3.

De Jaegher, H., and Di Paolo, E. 2007. Participatory sense-making. *Phenomenology and the cognitive sciences*, 6(4), 485–507.

Drever, J. L. 2017. The case for aural diversity in acoustic regulations and practice: The hand dryer noise story. Paper delivered at *24th international congress on sound and vibration* (ICSV24), Westminster, London, 23–27 July 2017.

Duden, B. 1998. *The woman beneath the skin: A doctor's patients in eighteenth-century Germany*. Cambridge, MA: Harvard University Press.

Gibson, J. J. 1966. *The senses considered as perceptual systems*. Boston, MA: Houghton Mifflin.

Gibson, J. J. 1986. *The ecological approach to visual perception*. Boston, MA: Houghton Mifflin. (Original work published 1979.)

Hayes, L. 2013. Haptic augmentation of the hybrid piano. *Contemporary music review*, 32(5), 499–509.

Hayes, L. 2015. Enacting musical worlds: Common approaches to using NIMEs within performance and person-centred arts practices. In: Berdahl, Edgar and Allison, Jesse (Eds.), *Proceedings of the 2015 conference on new interfaces for musical expression*. (322–324). Baton Rouge, LA: Louisiana State University Press.

Hayes, L. 2017a. From site-specific to site-responsive: Sound art performances as participatory milieux. *Organised sound*, 22(1), 82–92.
Hayes, L. 2017b. Sound, electronics, and music: A radical and hopeful experiment in early music education. *Computer music journal*, 41(3), 36–49.
Hayes, L. 2019. Beyond skill acquisition: Improvisation, interdisciplinarity, and enactive music cognition. *Contemporary music review*, 38(5), 446–462.
Hayes, L., and Marquez-Borbon, A. 2021. Addressing NIME's prevailing sociotechnical, political, and epistemological exigencies. *Computer music journal*, 44(2–3): 24–38.
Hayles, N. K. 2008. *How we became posthuman: Virtual bodies in cybernetics, literature, and informatics*. Chicago, IL: University of Chicago Press.
Iyer, V. 2019. Beneath Improvisation. In: Rehding, A., and Rings, S. (Eds.), *The Oxford handbook of critical concepts in music theory* (760–780). Oxford, UK: Oxford University Press.
Krueger, J. W. 2011. Doing things with music. *Phenomenology and the cognitive sciences*, 10(1), 1–22.
Leman, M. 2008. *Embodied music cognition and mediation technology*. Cambridge, MA: MIT Press.
Loaiza, J. M. 2019. From enactive concern to care in social life: Towards an enactive anthropology of caring. *Adaptive behavior*, 27(1), 17–30. https://doi.org/10.1177/1059712318800673.
Loaiza, J. M. 2016. Musicking, embodiment and participatory enaction of music: Outline and key points. *Connection science*, 28(4), 410–422.
Luo, X., and Hayes, L. 2019. Vibrotactile stimulation based on the fundamental frequency can improve melodic contour identification of normal-hearing listeners with a 4-channel cochlear implant simulation. *Frontiers in neuroscience*, 13, 1145.
Maturana, H. R., and Varela, F. J. 1991. *Autopoiesis and cognition: The realization of the living*. New York: Springer Science and Business Media. (Original work published 1980.)
Matyja, J. R., and Schiavio, A. 2013. Enactive music cognition: Background and research themes. *Constructivist foundations*, 8(3), 351–357.
McGann, M. 2014. Enacting a social ecology: Radically embodied intersubjectivity. *Frontiers in psychology*, 5, 1321.
Nettleton, S. 2010. The sociology of the body. In: Cockerham, W. C. (Ed.), *The new Blackwell companion to medical sociology* (47–68). Chichester, UK: Blackwell Wiley.
Rajko, J. 2018. A call to action: Embodied thinking and human–computer interaction design. In: Sayers, J. (Ed.), *The Routledge companion to media studies and digital humanities* (195–203). Abingdon, UK: Routledge.
Reybrouck, M. 2005. Body, mind and music: Musical semantics between experiential cognition and cognitive economy. Trans. *Revista transcultural de música*, 9. www.sibetrans.com/trans/articulo/180/body-mind-and-music-musical-semantics-between-experiential-cognition-and-cognitive-economy (accessed 8 August 2021).
Shannon, D. B., and Truman, S. E. 2020. Problematizing sound methods through music research-creation: Oblique curiosities. *International journal of qualitative methods*. https://doi.org/10.1177/1609406920903224.
Turner, B. 2008. *The body and society: Explorations in social theory* (3rd ed.). London: SAGE Publications.
Urban, P. 2014. Toward an expansion of an enactive ethics with the help of care ethics. *Frontiers in psychology*, 5, 1354. doi: 10.3389/fpsyg.2014.01354.
Urban, P. 2015. Enactivism and care ethics: Merging perspectives. *Filozofia*, 70(2), 119–129.
Varela, F. J., Thompson, E., and Rosch, E. 2016. *The embodied mind: Cognitive science and human experience*. Cambridge, MA: MIT Press. (Original work published 1991.)

3
UNDER *MAR PARADOXO* (PARADOX SEA) AND *COASTAL SILENCES*[1]

Raquel Stolf

An assumption for this text is the methodological position *under (sob)*, which I have been investigating since my doctoral research.[2] To develop research *under the effect* of an artistic process consists of a starting plan and a crossing condition, involving a writing-*becoming* with what you write. The *under* implies an influence, but not a subservience, the *under* stands in the middle of the way, implying a relationship or articulation. Being *under the effect* of an artistic process also presupposes relationships between art and life: that is, the effect has no outline or limits established beforehand. The duration of the effect can extend to other beginnings of processes, and the process is also not something clear and exact, because the work/process that modulates writing (the work/process *under* which one writes) was produced by those who write, generating feedback.[3]

During the research project *Between the suspended word and porous listening [investigations under sound propositions]*, the process of collecting silences was initiated, involving investigations about/under proposals and experiences of silence. The first sound publication that gathered the collection of silences was *assonances of silences [collection]* (2007–2010). This publication grouped silences recorded from different contexts, on a CD with printed material, comprising "species of silences": *prepared silences; accompanied silences, silences with failure; sea floor under background noise; stacked silences*.[4] Silences that were conceived as *sound propositions*.

Since 2002, I have been investigating the construction of *sound propositions* gathered in artistic publications, which can be unfolded in installations, sound microinterventions, videos, actions, texts, and drawings. *Sound propositions* involve the participation of the body, of physical actions, and can solicit "mental acts", waiting states, and other situations, proposing modulations and listening experiences.[5] For this, sound publications involve relationships between text and sound (materially present or not), implying articulations between the record/disc as artwork (Celant 1977) and the artist's book/publication as artwork and/or space-time sequence

DOI: 10.4324/9781003008217-5

(Carrión 2011). In the construction of sound publications, their graphic and/or textual printed components are connected to what is sounding on the disc component, and the experiences of seeing-reading and hearing-listening happen under this intersection. Thus, sound publications can involve relations between audio parts (recorded on CDs, on online platforms, or broadcast in radio space, among other possibilities) and graphic, textual, and printed materials.[6]

The sound publication *mar paradoxo* is composed of printed material and two audio CDs (Figure 3.1), and involves the process of recording, proposing, writing-drawing, listening, and collecting silences[7]. In this way, *mar paradoxo* compiles and stacks *coastal silences* that surround the island of Santa Catarina, Brazil,[8] from 100

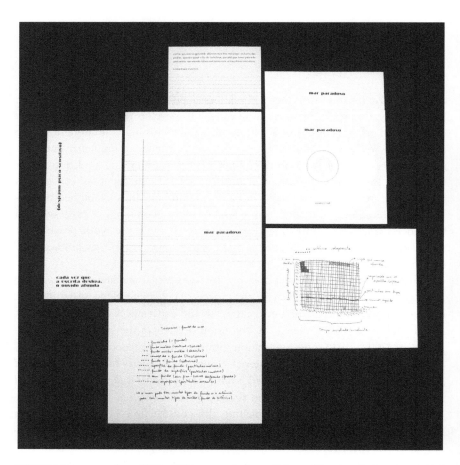

FIGURE 3.1 *mar paradoxo*, 2013–2016, general view of the publication (printed material and audio CDs)

Note: You can listen to the work at: https://soundcloud.com/marparadoxo.

Source: Image by Raquel Stolf.

FIGURE 3.2 *mar paradoxo*, 2013–2016, documentation of the process
Source: Images by Helder Martinovsky.

stretches of seabed sounds, including indications of typologies in notes-drawings from/for listening, and other materials.

The documentation of coastal silences took place along the beaches of the insular Florianópolis region, covering the north, south, east, and west regions between 2014 and 2016. I recorded *coastal silences* from jetties, sand strips, shores, stones, and grounded areas. In all, 100 audio files were recorded in places where my body could be at the limit between land/sand/stone/dock and sea. Some recordings (on beaches) involved partially entering the sea, neither diving nor swimming (Figure 3.2). All recording and editing was done on a digital recorder, and included the use of a hydrophone for underwater recordings.[9]

It was my proximity to the sea (near the island of Santa Catarina), and a deep interest in underwater *soundscapes*,[10] which catalysed the process of the publication. My process involved trying to feel, perceive, and rethink my listening for the purpose of moving different types of silences from one context to another; this included conceiving the sound publication as a kind of receptacle for a collection of silences, and the circulation of the publication in other contexts. In this sense, listening experiences constitute crucial and recurring situations in my artistic processes.

Mar paradoxo involves investigations *under* and about silence as a ceaseless murmur, also proposing the construction of fictional typologies of seabed and other types of *coastal silences* – *splashed silence, noisy silence, oscillating silence, diving silence, cloudy silence, desert silence, collapsing silence* –, denominations present in note-drawings from and for listening (Figure 3.3), presented in the printed material that forms the publication.

38 Raquel Stolf

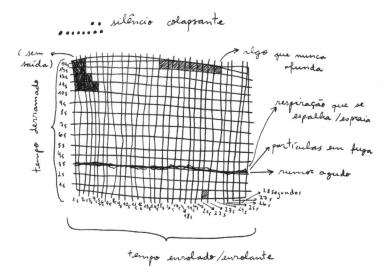

FIGURE 3.3 *mar paradoxo*, 2013–2016, detail of note-drawings from and for listening – collapsing silence, by Raquel Stolf

The construction of the sound publication has involved reflections around writing-drawing processes, and propositions of hearing and listening to silences, as well as articulations between its construction process and the collection procedure (which involves a displacement between sound, text, body, and context and intersections between writing, drawing, listening, and hearing). Collecting the *coastal silences* is thus a process between body and landscape.[11] And without the action of moving my body to an encounter with the sea, the sound propositions would not be constructed and the collection of *coastal silences* would not exist. This silent action was crucial in the process of developing the publication, just as the act of dislocation traverses the collection's procedure.

In this way, the process between body and landscape occurs under the experiences of displacement, recording, and listening (registering sound/audible silences from the floor of the sea), under the modulation of listening and editing (silences that are inseparable from listening, body-psychic silences), and under the action/gesture of writing-drawing that implies handwriting (where the body inscribes the outline of a text), the list (and its constituent relationship with infinity, in the articulation of measure and unmeasure, present in the process of listing silences), and editing. Editing is a gesture with many layers, between hearing and listening, between seeing and reading. The audio files were edited while recording, and for this process, editing involved selecting and cutting files from the moment the hydrophone touched the sea floor. Editing included cuts between one silence and another, in the construction of the 101 tracks for the sound publication, in the stacking/overlaying of all the *coastal silences*. Editing also occurred in the graphic construction of the printed material, the choice of typography[12] for the texts, and in the background of the cover (a dust jacket with folded flaps): a two-page (blank) facsimile of a calligraphy notebook.

The title of the publication *mar paradoxo* derives from a previously printed work which composes another sound publication – *FORA [DO AR]* (OUT [OF AIR]) (2002–2004) (Figure 3.4)[13] that indicates relations between word and landscape, in which the denominations *mar cozido* (boiled sea), *mar encostado* (leaned sea) and *mar paradoxo* (paradox sea) – in Portuguese, the word "paradox" suggests the word *parado* (still) – insinuates oscillations or tidal flows in the two-page facsimile of a 1996 notebook.

During the construction of *mar paradoxo*, the process of writing note-drawings from/for listening has catalysed the sound publication in different ways. As in previous sound publications, they were written-drawn during the process of listening to and listing the previously recorded audio files. Documenting this process enabled a resending of the *silences* to the reader/listener – the silence as a situation and/or state. Thus, they can be thought of as listening propositions that expand the audio files as possibilities to prolong silent situations, indicating projects of other *species of silences* (or as subtypes of *coastal silences*), creating a net of their occurrences through *seabed typologies* (Figure 3.5), for if "the sea can have many types of floor = the silence can have many types of noise (backgrounds of silence)" (Stolf 2016a).

I have previously investigated concepts, proposals, and experiences of silence that involve the possibility of the existence of sound/audible silences (silence not as an absence of sound, but implying the existence of non-senses and a constitutive paradox[14]) and of a silence that does not separate itself from listening, thought of as a situation (context) and/or body/psychic state. Among these conceptions of silence, there are also correlations between word and silence, between writing and hearing/listening.[15] To think about silence as a state of listening, as a corporal-psychic situation or way of being, implies conceiving that silence goes through the body. Silences can happen in and through the body, located psychically-corporally between inside and outside, and also in situations between body and language. Or, as Pauline Oliveros points out, "Sound impacts my body and resonates within. Sounds keep returning to me as I listen. ... We can listen in dreams. We can project sound in space or the sounding of a composition in inner space" (2019, 17). In this process, the relations between writing/drawing, hearing, and listening to silences articulate bodily experiences that probe and test a being in the world. Above all, the body is not separated from the landscape,[16] being intersected with it, composing its reliefs and voids. Listening, being an *interface* between the individual and the environment (Truax 1984, 13), can also be conceived as an opaque and alterable/sensitive canal between body and place. In *mar paradoxo*, it can be trembled, reinvented, and/or modulated, like *porous listening*, as a permeable listening:

> susceptible to the sounds around it and which at the same time actively absorbs the layers of noise, murmurs, and silences in its surroundings. In other words, it both perceives and thinks vividly of the sounds around it and tries to detail possible *assonances* between one silence and another, or possible degrees

40 Raquel Stolf

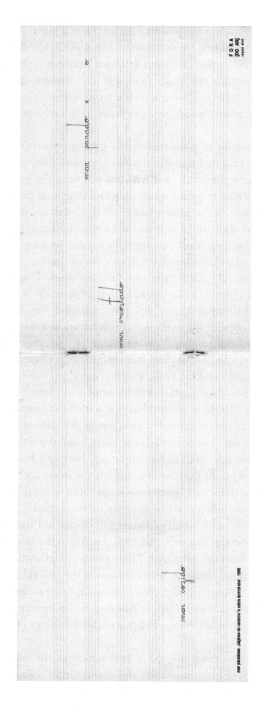

FIGURE 3.4 *mar paradoxo*, 1996, detail of *FORA [DO AR]* (OUT [OF AIR]), by Raquel Stolf

FIGURE 3.5 *mar paradoxo*, 2013–2016, detail of notes-drawings (seabed typologies), by Raquel Stolf

of kinship between noise, noise, and murmur. A porous listening is attentive to the sound layers between the nearest and the farthest point.

Stolf (2011)

In the processes of listening, collecting, recording, storing, inventing, and writing-drawing silences, there is a waiting situation, but also a repetition. Not the repetition of the same, but variations between one homonymous silence and another, between word and silence. Thus, during the recordings of silences, I perceived that there is no silence as a matrix and/or no identical *coastal silences*. Impermanent, they pulse and vibrate. They last in fleeting variations. When I hear a submerged silence, it slings and floods me.

The total duration of the double CD publication is 101 minutes, with 101 tracks. Each track is distributed/ordered by the duration of their silences, and not by the order in which they were recorded; the first track (*coastal silence 12*) lasts 11 seconds, while the last track (*100 stacked silences*) is 4 minutes and 33 seconds. Between the silences on each CD, there are no intervals, one can either dive into uninterrupted listening, with repetitions of micro-variations, listening only to brief silences, or one can listen to the stacked silences.

For Deleuze (1988), the sensation and the location of difference is an approximation: it repeats, happens, and does not crystallise. Difference is only understood by what it radiates, by what it performs, where virtuality replaces possibility, being of the order of what may happen. In the process of *mar paradoxo*, perhaps one is also looking for *infra-mince* splinters or clicks from one silence to another, in which the *coastal silences* may also be perceived as differences that happen, that survive in listening, paradoxically strange (outside/inside) and intimate (inside/outside), or that they insist, as textures splashed and blurred in the sound memory, trying to learn to remember a silence.

To do so, you also need to be in a specific position to try/test listening to, recording, and seeing-reading silences. Sometimes it is necessary to invent recording conditions or to create tricks, nets, or traps for listening.

Brígida Baltar, in her project *Collecting* series – *mist, sea air and dew*, which also features a long-playing record disc (LP) with sound recordings, dialoguing with the attempt (and need) to collect and store silences, sets out to collect what escapes. For the artist, "it has an enigmatic feeling [and a] multiplicity of senses that the mist generates.... everything can be very frightening when the mist disappears ... it is in a way an action that makes the unknown more present" (Baltar 2001, 63). The artist collects mist, sea air, and dew, and at the beginning of the work, she tried to capture and store such impalpable materials in glass containers. Over time, the action of the collection itself constitutes the proposition, an action recorded through photographs, videos, and recordings of the silences-noises of the collections, an action that can also be concatenated by other people. The LP *Coletas de neblina maresia e orvalho* (Collections of mist, sea air, and dew), seems to present to us a specie of *prepared silence*, as the minimal sonorities mix environmental sounds with electronic microtextures. On the LP cover, a small written note indicates: "[to be listened to with fewer decibels]", and the artist points out:

> There's something I discovered when I started collecting: when you get close to the mist, it's no longer there ... but further on. This also brings other meanings, something that will never be grasped ... for me, collecting mist has become almost a necessity ....
>
> *Baltar (2001, 62)*

Collecting mist or fog may involve a process in which silences are probed, requiring also a permeable, *porous listening*, which deals with "something that will never be grasped" because it is a passage. In an experience in May 1995, while walking on the Ferrugem beach (in the city of Garopaba, in the south of Brazil) on a very foggy afternoon, I recall that the sea sounded very intense. While walking, I attempted to move slowly, guided by the minimal noises within the low cloud. The mist was so thick it was not possible to see the contours of my body. When I entered the fog, I felt the sea touch my feet, but saw no horizon. I remember listening to the waves coming and going, listening to the ambiguity and oscillation of direction/position. There was no background or end in the listening, and the body seemed to be without edges.

In *mar paradoxo*, I listened to and recorded *coastal silences* as if I were touching the body in an immanent and sandy fog, or as if I were immersed in cloudiness between body/listening and soundscape. In the process of recording *coastal silences* with a hydrophone, it was crucial to perceive this state of connection as absorption, of traversing between body and place, in which I dived into a kind of interval/interstice/breath that altered and activated my listening. The experience of constructing registers or of appropriating the silences of the seabed implies an attempt to record and underline its voids and its flows.

For Clarice Lispector, "the continuous breathing of the world is what we hear and call silence" (1997, 117). Breathing happens between inside and outside, implying a double movement: breathing in and out, between collecting and displacing/dispersing. Thus, silences are a double sound life of the world, a crossing/transition between action and rest. If the world is breathing in this double and continuous movement, how can we listen and traverse this pulsating flow?

In the short story "As águas do mundo" (The Waters of the World)[17], Lispector writes about a woman's encounter with the sea:

> There it is, the sea, the most unintelligible of non-human existences. And here is the woman, standing on the beach, the most unintelligible of living beings. As a human being she once posed a question about herself, becoming the most unintelligible of living beings. She and the sea.
>
> Their mysteries could only meet if one surrendered to the other: the surrender of two unknowable worlds made with the trust by which two understandings would surrender to each other.
>
> *Lispector (2015, 337)*

The encounter happens, but I am interested in the instant before the body enters the sea, and the hesitant and dense beginning, in which "The woman doesn't know it: but she's fulfilling a courage" (Lispector 2015, 337). The woman is alone, and there is an "exiguity of the body" before the vastness of the sea:

> The salty sea is not alone because it's salty and vast, and this is an achievement. Right then she knows herself even less than she knows the sea. Her courage comes from not knowing herself, but going ahead nevertheless. Not knowing yourself is inevitable, and not knowing yourself demands courage.
>
> *Lispector (2015, 337)*

But at the same time, "The slow journey fortifies her secret courage" (Lispector 2015, 338). After the dives, the woman "wants to stand still inside the sea. So she does. As against the sides of a ship, the water slaps, retreats, slaps. The woman receives no transmissions. She doesn't need communication" (Lispector 2015, 338):

> And now she steps onto the sand. She knows she is glistening with water, and salt and sun. Even if she forgets a few minutes from now, she can never lose all this. And she knows in some obscure way that her streaming hair is that of a castaway.
>
> *Lispector (2015, 339)*

The woman "knows she has created a danger" (Lispector 2015, 339). And here I ask if this danger (and an act of a secret courage) inhabits a pause and also a wreck in the encounter between sea and body/listening, and if it is this danger-pause that resonates and spreads in *mar paradoxo*. If in "As águas do mundo" the encounter of a woman's body with the sea involves a situation of strangeness (between diving, refuge, and wreck), this state that displaces and interrogates was an incisive situation for *mar paradoxo*, present also in the concept of *coastal silence*.

In the process of constructing the sound publication, the path was also slow and there were no "transmissions of senses" (the paradox inhabits the sea of listening). In the encounters of the body/listening with/under the sea, the wreck is perhaps the probing of silences, which involves groping (listening) and testing (hearing) silences. As in the experience of entering the fog, the traversing between body, silence, and place involved a rest situation and a suspension as a submersion experience, which has altered and activated my listening.

Walking and recording on beaches also involves a relationship with a *beach-pedestrian*: there is a horizontal dimension and/or a kind of horizontal scale that can receive the body that traverses it. The beach is flat, not higher than the body. In this process (walking and recording on beaches), there is a waiting and its constitutive relationship with the *porous listening*. This implies a pause in movement, and the waiting on the body is a kind of pulsating plain of micro-events. Waiting involves a time that spreads (between inside and outside), and listening also spreads and pulses, comes and goes, oscillating and diving. And between body, text, and sound, the *coastal silences* are infinitely smaller than the extent of the sea floor, and this characteristic is what makes them also intervals for another listening, porous, bumpy, and raw[18].

Hildegard Westerkamp (2019), in her proposals for *soundwalks* (and the relationship of a body that moves and listens attentively to surroundings, composing and being able to modify them), proposes a series of reflections on the "disruptive nature of listening" (Westerkamp 2015), which can resist 24/7 activity (Crary 2014). Westerkamp (2015) points out the need for a "disruption in the sense of stopping routines, habits, unconscious gestures, reactions, and behaviors", but not necessarily involving a "violent disruption", and she suggests that:

> our listening be an ongoing practice, so present and attentive that it asserts change inside us over time, and as a result eventually in the soundscape, in our communication with others, in society at large. It is a state of ongoing attention.

Westerkamp also proposes that "The *experience* of soundwalk listening then gives us a visceral understanding of what in fact the disruptive nature of listening really is" (2015).

Thus, if *porous listening* indicates a listening position that needs the interval while trying to be a channel for the "continuous breathing of the world", it has in "disruptive listening" and slow listening a constitutive assumption. In the experiences of recording silences, there are relationships between interruption and listening, transits and stops around an island, where a body moves and listens at the edge, between sand, stone, and water, trying to record stretches of the seabed ("the most unintelligible of non-human existences", according to Lispector). At the sea floor, there are currents/flows, sand/sediment pebbles passing by, and the hydrophone-ear waiting for some attrition, friction, micro-shocks, floating percussion. In the *mar paradoxo* process, the dive occurs through listening, which receives/absorbs this incessant breathing/noise. Traversing the listening, perhaps the seabed soundscape can modulate, puncture, and decompress the body.

From a listening that pauses and oscillates, *coastal silences* can be thought of and perceived in a zone of intersections and spraying: between inside and outside – in an opening from/to a resonance space (Nancy 2007), between hearing, listening, and surroundings, always taking place in *becoming*, in a neighbourhood zone (Deleuze, Guattari 1997). *Coastal silences* are perceived on the edge, but also in the inseparability and interrelation between land, stone, sand, sea, hydrophone, recorder, body, and listening, between a counter-diving of the body on the coast, leaning against the edge from where the hydrophone dives.

If the sea never stops (but inflates, between the tides), and paradoxically, continuously flows, moving between the possibility of breath and rest, then how do we test or dig a crack (between pause and strangeness) in the listening itself?

Rosana Kohl Bines (2009), in the essay *A grande orelha de Kafka* (Kafka's Big Ear), in dialogue with a "disruptive listening", addresses the possibility of an "insurgent ear" and an escaping ear. Bines unfolds a series of reflections from a photograph of Kafka as a child, collected and investigated by Walter Benjamin:

> I propose thinking about the scope and strength of this expanded listening that Benjamin locates in Kafka's childish figure and that he will seek to cultivate as a policy of thought, betting on a kind of pedagogy of the ear, this discreet but insidious organ of the body, which works secretly, without calling attention to the escape routes that he opens and that transport the boy away from there, out of the oppressive frame. Little Kafka listens without being seen (in the act of listening). This acoustic drift swindles parental control and the effort to fix, through the eye of the camera, an immobile and embarrassing portrait of childhood. The boy escapes through the ear.
>
> *Bines (2019, 4–5)*

A divergent and dissident ear can change, moving the curves of the labyrinth. Like a kind of *stirred ear* (when the sea spreads on the sand and takes almost everything out of place), or an ear that destabilises what it hears.

In *mar paradoxo*, the hearing can doubt, with a stone (or sand) behind the ear. Moreover, the listening oscillates and does not fix itself, but it happens concretely – and there can be a relationship between the listening that diverges and a "concrete fiction" (Stolf 2016b), which passes through the body. And if the ear doubts, the body also absorbs the doubt, which can affect listening. In this way, listening, probing, and incorporating *coastal silences* involves and solicits the fissure, the hole, and the question.

Notes

1 This text presents investigations of the research project *Processes of writing/Listening of processes [articulations between voice, word, and silence in sound publications]* (2015–2021), developed at the Department of Visual Arts of Santa Catarina State University.
2 *Between the suspended word and porous listening [investigations under sound propositions]* (2007–2011) – research developed in the Graduate Program in Visual Arts of Federal University of Rio Grande do Sul, Porto Alegre, Brazil.
3 But the *over/about* may happen *under*, involving other possibilities of relationships. Researching dialogues with other processes (*about*), *under* investigations of your artistic work, or investigating dialogues *under* the about.
4 The project was developed in Florianópolis, Porto Alegre, Indaial, Blumenau, Criciúma, São Paulo, Barcelona, Madrid, and Urubici: www.raquelstolf.com/?p=467.
5 The proposals of artists such as Lygia Clark, Lygia Pape, and Hélio Oiticica, among others, are references in my processes, where the artist can be conceived as a proposer of experiences, involving also experimental practices, and participation processes (through the body, sensorial, and semantic aspects), "including proposing to propose" (Oiticica 1986, 120).
6 They can also involve propositions in dialogue with what Seth Kim-Cohen (2009) refers to as "non-cochlear sonic art", implying projects that indicate the impossibility of a sound concept without textual/discursive and/or conceptual remission, considering sound interconnected to other aspects, to any media and processes.
7 The graphic design of the printed part was made in partnership with Anna Stolf, and the publication was edited by the céu da boca label and Nave, with the support of the Elisabete Anderle Prize (support of culture from the government of the state of Santa Catarina, 2014), of which 500 copies were produced. It was launched at Espaço Embarcação (Florianópolis, Brazil) at the *Entremarés* event, with a live broadcast by Rádio Desterro Cultural: www.mixcloud.com/desterrocultural/conversas-entremar%C3%A9s-1-raquel-stolf/. Since its launch, *mar paradoxo* has been circulated at print art fairs and in artistic publications, and it was presented for listening/reading (on a shelf next to a sun lounger) at a number of exhibitions: www.raquelstolf.com/?p=3861.
8 Part of the city of Florianópolis is located on the island of Santa Catarina, on the south coast of Brazil. The city is the capital of the state of Santa Catarina, and also has a continental part. It has districts and beaches in its different regions.
9 Five *coastal silences* were recorded in 2008 with an underwater camera.
10 As R. Murray Schafer (2001) points out, the term "soundscape" refers to the "sonic environment", and "may refer to actual environments, or to abstract constructions such as musical compositions and tape montages, particularly when considered as an environment" (366).
11 In the Portuguese language, in the etymological origin of the word *costa* (coast; litoral) there is a relationship between the words *costeiro/a* (coastal), *costas* (back), *costela* (rib), *encosta* (hillside) and *encostar* (to lean) (Cunha 2007, 222).
12 Typographs used in *paradox sea*: oxygen, glacial indifference, and 20 dB.
13 Available at: www.raquelstolf.com/?p=234. In 2019, the publication was re-released digitally by Seminal Records: https://seminalrecords.bandcamp.com/album/fora-do-ar.

14 In *The Logic of Sense*, Gilles Deleuze (1998) starts from an analysis of *Alice's Adventures in Wonderland* by Lewis Carroll, among other references, in which by the path of nonsense one can reach a logic of sense. For the author, non-sense is not opposed to sense, but rather to the absence of sense. The paradox is directly related to the question of non-sense and sense itself, to the extent that the paradoxes "have as a characteristic the fact of going in two directions at the same time and making identification impossible, emphasising either of these effects" (Deleuze 1998, 78).
15 I remember the "third internal sound", indicated by Douglas Kahn, in John Cage's experience inside the anechoic chamber. The instant Cage asked himself what the sounds in the anechoic chamber would be like (the high and low noises of his own body), indicated that "he was able to listen and at the same time allow discursiveness to intrude in the experience" (Kahn, quoted in Kim-Cohen 2009, 222).
16 I am interested in thinking about landscape as an "invented concept", or a "cultural construct", as Javier Maderuelo has said, in which landscape constitutes a "group of a series of ideas, sensations and feelings that we elaborate based on the place and its constituent elements" (Maderuelo 2006, 36–38). For the author, there is no landscape without interpretation.
17 The short story "As águas do mundo" was published in the book *Felicidade clandestina* (Covert Joy) (1981 [1961]), but the fragments presented here are from the book *Complete Stories*, translated by Katrina Dodson, edited and with an introduction by Benjamin Moser (New York: New Directions, 2015).
18 A *raw listening* is a "listening that was not prepared, cooked by a context that defined it slowly and previously and was not fully planned by a situation that preceded it. Unplanned listening" (Stolf 2011).

Bibliography

Baltar, Brígida. 2001. *Neblina maresia e orvalho coletas*. Rio de Janeiro, Brazil: Author.
Bines, Rosana Kohl. 2009. *A grande orelha de Kafka – cadernos de leitura*, vol. 87/Série Infância. Belo Horizonte, Brazil: Edições Chão da Feira.
Carrión, Ulises. 2011. *A nova arte de fazer livros*. Belo Horizonte, Brazil: Ed. Andante.
Celant, Germano. 1977. *The record as artwork: From futurism to conceptual art*. Fort Worth, TX: Fort Worth Art Museum (exhibition catalogue).
Crary, Jonathan. 2014. *24/7 – capitalismo tardio e os fins do sono*. São Paulo, Brazil: Cosac Naify.
Cunha, Antônio Geraldo da. 2007. *Dicionário etimológico da língua portuguesa*. Rio de Janeiro, Brazil: Lexikon Ed.
Deleuze, Gilles. 1988. *Diferença e repetição*. Rio de Janeiro, Brazil: Graal.
Deleuze, Gilles. 1998. *Lógica do sentido*. São Paulo, Brazil: Perspectiva.
Deleuze, Gilles, and Guattari, Félix. 1997. *Mil platôs – capitalismo e esquizofrenia*, vol. 4. Rio de Janeiro, Brazil: Ed. 34.
Kim-Cohen, Seth. 2009. *In the blink of an ear: Toward a non-cochlear sonic art*. New York: Continuum.
Lispector, Clarice. 1997. *A paixão segundo GH*. Buenos Aires, Brazil: ALLCA XX.
Lispector, Clarice. 1981. "As águas do mundo." In *Felicidade clandestina*. Rio de Janeiro, Brazil: Rocco.
Lispector, Clarice. 2015. *Complete stories*, translated by Katrina Dodson, edited and with an introduction by Benjamin Moser. New York: New Directions.
Maderuelo, Javier. 2006. *El paisaje: genesis de um concepto*. Madrid, Spain: ABADA Editores.
Nancy, Jean-Luc. 2007. *Listening*. New York: Fordham University Press.
Oiticica, Hélio. 1986. *Aspiro ao Grande Labirinto*. Rio de Janeiro: Rocco.

Oliveros, Pauline. 2019. "Auralizando en la Sonosfera: Vocabulario para el sonido interno y la emisión del mismo." In Espejo, José Luis (ed.), *Escucha, por favor (13 textos sobre sonido para el arte reciente)*. Madrid, Spain: EXIT – Publicaciones de Arte y Pensamiento.

Perec, Georges. 2007. *Especies de espacios*. Barcelona, Spain: Montesinos.

Schafer, R. Murray. 2001. *A afinação do mundo: uma exploração pioneira pela história passada e pelo atual estado do mais negligenciado aspecto de nosso ambiente: a paisagem sonora*. São Paulo, Brazil: Editora Unesp.

Stolf, Raquel. 2011. Entre a palavra pênsil e a escuta porosa [investigações sob proposições sonoras]. Thesis (Doutorado em Artes Visuais). Porto Alegre, Brazil: Instituto de Artes, Universidade Federal do Rio Grande do Sul, Porto Alegre. www.raquelstolf.com/wp-content/uploads/2000/09/TESE_RaquelStolf_20111.pdf (accessed 31 May 2019).

Stolf, Raquel. 2004. *FORA [DO AR]*. Florianópolis, Brazil: Author (sound publication).

Stolf, Raquel. 2010. *assonâncias de silêncios [coleção]*. Florianópolis, Brazil: céu da boca (sound publication).

Stolf, Raquel. 2016a. *mar paradoxo*. Florianópolis, Brazil: céu da boca, Nave (sound publication).

Stolf, Raquel. 2016b. "Perguntas, anotações [sob exercícios de escrita e escuta]." *Tubo de ensaio: composição [Interseções + Intervenções]*, vol. 1. Florianópolis, Brazil: Instituto Meyer Filho, 21–30.

Truax, Barry. 1984. *Acoustic communication*. Norwood, NJ: Ablex Publishing.

Westerkamp, Hildegard. 2015. "The disruptive nature of listening." Paper delivered at *International Symposium on Electronic Art (ISEA)*, Vancouver, Canada, 18 August. www.hildegardwesterkamp.ca/writings/writingsby/?post_id=11&title=the-disruptive-nature-of-listening (accessed 11 July 2019).

Westerkamp, Hildegard. 2019. "Paseo sonoro." In Espejo, José Luis (ed.), *Escucha, por favor (13 textos sobre sonido para el arte reciente)*. Madrid, Spain: EXIT – Publicaciones de Arte y Pensamiento.

PART II

Gendered Sounds, Spaces, and Places

4
DEEP SITUATED LISTENING AMONG HEARING HEADS AND AFFECTIVE BODIES

Sanne Krogh Groth

Introduction

With two electroacoustic music (EAM) concert situations as my empirical anchor points, this chapter aims to develop a theoretical framework for defining a listening mode I call "deep situated listening". "Deep situated listening" seeks to combine two disparate feminist approaches, namely Donna Haraway's "situated knowledge" and Pauline Oliveros' "deep listening". I employ Gilles Deleuze's notion of "plane of immanence" and "affect" in order to bring out the commonalities of Haraway and Oliveros, and to relate them to the situation of the EAM concert (Haraway 1988; Oliveros 2005; Deleuze 1988).

Being present at an EAM concert, I suggest, is an occasion that invites a deeply situated listening experience that entails deep wonder about the aesthetic, affective, perceptive and performative dimensions of the music as well as situated reflection about the history, sociality and politics of the event. The genre has, since the 1950s, been closely connected to theoretical dissemination and academic practices, and the music is, as a consequence, often presented as theoretical experiments or comments on existing practices, repertoires, or writings discussing intellectual questions (not rarely grounded in continental phenomenology) (e.g. Born 1995; Groth 2014). I represent this position as "hearing heads". EAM concerts can take place in various institutions and formats, but share the features of speaker systems and technology. Using this context actively in the production consequently adds specific aesthetics to the musical performance, where the sound is not only mediated through technology, but also "mediatized", meaning that "form and material are shaped by the media, they are appearing through" (Schmidt 2011 pg 131).[1] The listeners participating in such events are mostly EAM composers working as practitioners and theoreticians, scholars of music history, theory and criticism, and professional producers, curators and music journalists. Therefore, the audience has the character

DOI: 10.4324/9781003008217-7

of a community, in which everyone is related and they depend on one another. Everyone present – whether there as a performer, composer, organizer, or listener – can easily be considered as *active participants* carrying a responsibility for the situation and the reception on behalf of the collective as well as on their own behalf. Listening in the context of EAM events is social and highly conventional, in spite of the often genre-breaking ambitions of EAM. As a result, EAM events are governed by strong conventions, including high awareness about the electroacoustics as well as the quality and placement of the speakers; a shared respect among the performers and the audience for the composer's intentions; an implicit agreement to be concentrated and quiet while pieces are being performed; and an unspoken pact to be loyal, curious and open towards the concept of a piece – at least until one finds it fair to make a normative judgment and act from this. In spite of these conventions, EAM concert spaces are far from consensual. Rather, I will claim, the concert spaces constitute a complex frame around two different listening and performance paradigms, each attended by its own understanding of aesthetics, socialities and politics.[2] I call these the "hearing heads" and the "affective bodies" paradigms, respectively. The former is well-established and dominant, while the latter is still emergent and feminist.

Passivity and empowerment

My discussion of the two paradigms extends a long and ongoing discussion of listening within EAM (e.g. Schaffer 1966; Smalley 1997; Thoresen and Hedman 2007), while my outline of the contours of a "deep situated listening" is developed in close dialogue with my own experience of specific EAM concerts. The empirical anchor points I draw upon have been essential components in the development of my theoretical argument, serving as spaces where my own bodily experiences of EAM could be taken into account.

The two EAM concert situations I will refer to took place in Tillburg, Holland in 2018, and New York City in 2011. At both concerts, I was present as a participating listener, staying in one spot throughout the whole event. I have chosen these two concerts as they were similarly curated. Both were part of academic conference programs and both sought, more or less explicitly, to engage the theoretical activities in the conferences they were associated with. I have also chosen these two EAM concerts because they, in very concrete and embodied ways, each manifest how differently two EAM listening situations can affect me. The first made me passive, while the second empowered me into action. The first invited me to act as a "hearing head", while the second allowed me to become an "affective body".

The first concert in Tillburg was programmed as part of a two-day university symposium, organized and curated by a local PhD scholar. It took place at a café-like music venue. Entering the performance space, we were met by a circle of loudspeakers placed in front of a small stage. Inside the circle, carpets were placed on the floor that appeared to invite us to immerse ourselves in the concert while sitting or lying down on them, surrounded by sound. As an introduction to one of the pieces, the composer took center stage to tell the audience that we were free to leave if we did not feel like staying throughout the duration of the piece. Then the performance began. It was both rather long and quite violent in its auditory expression, and I felt like leaving on several occasions. For some reason, however, I never did. Instead, I felt almost paralyzed sitting there on the floor, while the composer observed me from a chair placed outside the circle. The fact that I had ostensibly been given the choice to leave, but never felt I had the freedom to actually do so, made the situation even more claustrophobic and uncomfortable.

The second concert in New York took place at The Cell Theatre, a music and theatre venue dedicated to social awareness, located on 23rd Street in Manhattan. This concert was curated by the American composer Pauline Oliveros (1932–2016) as part of the annual EMS (Electroacoustic Music Studies) network conference. Here, the composers were also present, and even though I was not given an explicit invitation to leave the concert, I felt that if I wanted to leave I could. This event felt conventionally freer and more inclusive, participatory and empowering as an experience. Somehow, the two concert situations had established different kinds of affection – one brought me to passiveness and intellectual frustration, the other empowered me to action.

The two concert situations have stayed with me for years and have made me reflect upon several questions: First, why didn't I feel able to leave the Tillburg concert and what led me into this bodily passivity? Second, why did I feel positively included, and maybe even liberated, at the New York concert? Third, how does this relate to the settings, the music, the conventions and the social behaviors surrounding me? Finally, how do the specific listening situations reflect more general issues regarding affect and the performing practices of EAM?

Before returning to these questions, I will prepare my theoretical framework by turning to "affect" mainly through Gilles Deleuze's writings on philosophy of Baruch de Spinoza (1632–1677),[3] followed by Donna Haraway's notion of "situated knowledge" in combination with Pauline Oliveros notion of "deep listening".

The EAM concert as a "plane of immanence"

I will conceive of EAM concerts in what Deleuze has called a "plane of immanence" as a way of bringing out the concert situation as a dynamic and situated event. A "plane of immanence" is, according to Deleuze, not "a single substance, but rather the laying out of a common plane of immanence on which all bodies, all minds, and all individuals are situated" (1988 pg 122). Deleuze bases his theorizations on a Spinozist conceptualization of bodies which in the "plane of immanence" overcome the Cartesian mind/body problem through what Amy Cimini has described as a "re-thinking [of] the nature of substance ... everything that exists (including, of course, human minds and bodies) exists in a single, infinite substance – grounding the ontological position known as substance monism" (2010 pg 132). The bodies are mapped as a kind of geometric diagram in "longitude" and "latitude". The longitude of a body is bound to time and dynamics. It is "the set of relations of speed and slowness, of motion and rest, between particles that compose it from this point of view, that is, between *unformed elements*" (Deleuze 1988 pg 127). The latitude is "the set of affects that occupy a body at each moment, that is, the intensive states of an *anonymous force* (force for existing, capacity for being affected)" (ibid pg 127). The plan constituted by the bodies is "variable and is constantly being altered, composed and recomposed, by individuals and collectivities" (ibid pg 127–128). As time is immanent in the plane, Deleuze rightfully uses music as an analogy to understand these dynamics. It is important to underscore, especially in a chapter concerning music, that this for Deleuze is only an analogy, and not a recipe for doing analysis of musical form. Nevertheless, I see Deleuze's notion of "plane of immanence" as a useful concept for understanding listening events as it emphasizes the analytical importance of situating all objects and their mutual relations. It emphasizes:

> how it is by speed and slowness that one slips in among things, that one connects with something else. One never commences; one never has a tabula rasa; one slips in, enters in the middle; one takes up or lays down rhythms.
> *Deleuze (1988 pg 132)*

Listening always happens in the middle of something else, in media res. Deleuze reminds us that the listening body is a mode of being affected, it is dynamic and situated, it is shaped by its surroundings' circumstances and it can be anything: "it can be an animal, a body of sounds, a mind or an idea; it can be a linguistic corpus, a social body, a collectivity" (ibid pg 127).

The "plane of immanence" helps us grasp the experience of an EAM concert in a way that reaches beyond conventions, meanwhile also embracing them: the overcoming of the mind/body problem invites a reflection that can both be rooted in more conventional intellectual knowledge and combined with a bodily experience of the piece. The adoption of a situated and dynamic definition of the "affective body" opens a kind of analytical perception that exceeds a static focus on the composer or performer, and invites us to pay attention to the changing dynamics *between* various bodies such as composers, performers and audiences as well as to those of sound, lightning, technology, scenic setting, venue, sociality, politics, aesthetics and ideology.

As a term, "affect" provides us with a framework that helps to highlight the bodily experiences of the concert event without ignoring the scholarly knowledge about production, musical form, technology and aesthetics. Deleuze distinguishes between two sorts of affections. One springs from the affected individual and is defined as *actions*. The other originates outside the individual and is defined as *passions*. A body's capacity for being affected manifests as a power of *acting* if (it is assumed to be) filled by active affections, but it can also be *acted upon* when filled by passions. If we are filled with passion in a meeting with a body that we do not agree with, our power of acting becomes diminished or blocked. Conversely, when we meet a body whose "longitude" and "latitude" agree with our own, we are affected by joy and we sense an increasing power of acting. In other words, we gain and lose empowerment in the given situation.

As noted by Sarah Ahmed, "passion" and "passive" both have their roots in the Latin word for "suffering" (*passio*). With this in mind, Ahmed argues that:

> To be passive is to be enacted upon, as a negation that is already felt as suffering. The fear of passivity is tied to the fear of emotionality …. To be emotional is to have one's judgement affected: it is to be reactive rather than active, dependent rather than autonomous.
>
> *Ahmed (2015 pg 2)*

Finding her argument in feminist philosophers, Ahmed states that as emotions are associated with women "who are represented as 'closer' to nature, ruled by appetite, and less able to transcend the body through thought, will and judgement" (ibid pg 3), this negative association with passiveness "works as a reminder of how 'emotion' has been viewed as 'beneath' the faculties of thought and reason" (ibid) and thereby also as a subordination of the feminine (and the body). Later in my analysis, I will claim that Ahmed's reasoning can be found in my reaction to the concert that I was unable to leave: Instead of being empowered, I was being *acted upon* and brought to passiveness; meanwhile, I was also encouraged to *act* (by leaving the concert). This caused a frustrating contradiction: I was set in an emotional state of passiveness – meanwhile, this very same passiveness was denied in the situation, as I was expected to act against it. Implicitly, I was not given the choice to stay and accept being uncomfortable with the piece.

Hence, the listening approach towards which I am aiming is one that takes emotions, affections, passions and actions into account, trying to avoid a normative judgment embedded in them. The Spinozist approach, as sketched out above, opens up an ethics that encounters affection manifested as joy or sadness (Deleuze 1988 pg 19), empowerment and disempowerment. I aim at an in-situ reflection on my concert experiences, a reflection that builds on the dynamics of affects, actions and passions from the bodies present – even though they do not fit the preprogrammed and canonic ideals of the conventional listening strategies, behaviors and ethics. I suggest a listening analysis that focuses not merely on the "hearing heads" of the concert event, but one that is also attentive to the "listening bodies". I call this type of analysis "deep situated listening".

A feminist perspective

In addition to its inspiration from the Spinoza/Deleuze/Ahmed perspectives, a "deep situated listening" approach draws on a combination of Donna Haraway's terms "feminist objectivity" and "situated knowledge", and on Pauline Oliveros' notion of "deep listening".

Over the years, Haraway has continuously explored how best to approach knowledge from a non-universalist perspective by highlighting how all knowledge is "situated". Extending previous writings, Haraway's most recent book, *Staying with the Trouble* (2016), reminds us to focus on what is present, and even though times can be troublesome, not to stick to imaginary futures. She reflects upon the troubled histories of science and knowledge by returning repeatedly to the "ubiquitous figure … SF: science fiction, speculative fabulation, string figures, speculative feminism, science fact, so far" (ibid pg 2) – all SF stories from our troubled times are "crocheted together" into an intriguing narrative. The aim is manifold. It encourages us to listen to the diversity of voices and bodies, some of which we might not yet understand. It encourages us to make kin with a broad variety of multi-species beings. It suggests we need to "compost" our knowledge in organic constellations in order to act in the current situation: "to make trouble, to stir up potent respond to devastating events, as well as to settle troubled waters and rebuild quiet places" (ibid pg 1).

Whereas resonance can be found in the theories of Deleuze as presented above, Haraway takes an explicit feminist position. In her earlier writings, Haraway describes "situated knowledge" as a feminist scientific knowledge paradigm:

> The Moral is simple: only partial perspective promises objective vision. [… Feminist objectivity is about limited location and situated knowledge, not about transcendence and splitting of subject and object. It allows us to become answerable for what we learn how to see. … The science question in feminism is about objectivity and positioned rationality.
>
> *Haraway (1988 pgs 583, 590)*

Haraway uses a thorough reflection on "primate vision" (2018/1989) as a metaphorical entrance to her formulation of the feminist knowledge paradigm. Seeing, Haraway argues, is not a divine sense that provides synoptic clarity. Like other primates, humans always see from a particular place. There is no God's point of view. In a feminist knowledge paradigm, seeing is always situated and a result of our primate nature. Objectivity is aimed for through the partial and local. Knowledge is aimed for through "seeking perspectives from those points of view, which can never be known in advance, that promise something quite extraordinary, that is, knowledge potent for constructing worlds less organized by axes of domination" (1988 pg 584–585). Objects of knowledge should be treated as actors and agents, and never serve "as slave to the master that closes off the dialectic in his unique agency and his authorship of 'objective' knowledge" (ibid pg 592). It is a knowledge that embeds a political awareness, the community rather than the individual, and one that seeks a non-dichotomous, non-universalist and non-hierarchal, diverse and inclusive diagram of knowledge.

Haraway's point that seeing is always situated can readily and fruitfully be applied to hearing and listening. Listening is also, by the very embodied nature of our primate ears, always situated. Listening, like seeing, is also dependent upon the technological and historical longitudes and latitudes of the situation. As Haraway reminds us:[4] "Histories of science may be powerfully told as histories of the technologies. These technologies are ways of life, social orders, practices of visualization.

Technologies are skilled practices" (1988 pg 586) Haraway continues the situating of technology with rhetorical questions adding further, partial perspectives to the technologies of vision:

> How to see? Where to see from? What limits to vision? What to see for? Whom to see with? Who gets to have more than one point of view? Who gets blinded? Who wears blinders? Who interprets visual field? What other sensory powers do we wish to cultivate besides vision?
>
> *Haraway (1988 pg 587)*

What goes for seeing also goes for listening: it is situated by embodiment, technology and histories of power. Later in the chapter, I will return to these questions, for they are highly relevant in the context of EAM concerts, which always occur in a close relationship with technology and instruments, embodiment and histories of power. I will rewrite Haraway's questions to the sense of sight, to let them fit the perspective of listening in order to embed them in my analysis of a concrete concert experience, and thereby situate my knowledge in this specific situation. The questions will in this context not only serve as metaphorical and rhetorical guidelines, but also as concrete, analytical questions that can lead towards new knowledge and reflections on listening paradigms.

Deep situated listening

What struck me when I worked with this rewriting of Haraway's questions from seeing to listening was that they almost turned into a text score, encouraging me to follow the questions in the actual listening situation. In particular, Haraway's rewritten questions when applied to music functioned like a text score by the American composer Pauline Oliveros (2005). My chain of association here is not an aimless stream of consciousness, but a thread leading me directly to the empirical analysis of the concert in New York, curated by Oliveros as part of the annual EMS network conference.[5]

As an international platform for academic discussions of EAM, most attendees at these conferences are composer-researchers, but musicologists and musicians present and participate too. The initial initiative for the EMS network stems from EAM research environments in UK and France. Its aesthetic and ideological roots can be traced back to the 1950s EAM experiments, and especially to Pierre Schaeffer and his Groupe de Recherches Musicales. Because of this heritage, discussions of phenomenology and perception, reduced and acousmatic listening, analysis and categorization of sound objects, along with new technologies and multiple speaker systems, were not surprisingly also popular conference papers that year.[6] In addition to academic papers, the conference series also presents a concert program with a variety of EAM performances with corresponding aesthetics to the presented papers. In this context, a full day with presentations and a concert curated by Oliveros stood out as quite unique. As one of the pioneers at the San

Francisco Tape Music Centre at the beginning of the 1960s, Oliveros' relationship and connection to the EMS network was obvious. Meanwhile, her later work and the development of "deep listening" has less obvious connections (Oliveros 2005). In an interview with me after the concert, she explained her relation to Schaeffer's ideas this way:

> I believe that Schaeffer's work is very important and interesting, but it is not what I am talking about at all. He is a reductionist. He is reducing listening into a particular way. I am studying the faculties of listening or the intentional processes of listening, which is the ability to focus, open, receive and expand. I call this "inclusive listening" and I call focus, "exclusive listening". I believe that Schaeffer was talking about exclusive listening, but not ambient, or open, or global. The interplay between those … are very important as we live our lives.[7]

Oliveros' "deep listening" is not limited to musical practices or just listening to EAM; rather, it embraces and is relevant in all aspects and situations of listening and living. After all, the idea of "deep listening" as a practice did come out of a musical situation, namely the recording of the album *Deep Listening*:[8]

> it is called so, because of the nature of the recording experience, which was in a cistern with a 45 second reverberation time. In this particular place the reverberations are almost the same, and you could hardly tell the difference between a reflected sound and a direct sound. So, playing in that environment was a new kind of challenge. It got me to understand that the space is as much a part of the instrument as the instrument making the music. It was not only listening to what you were playing, it was also listening to how the space was playing. So, this we called "deep listening".[9]

Over the years, "deep listening" has become an educational program training specific, bodily listening practices, combined with a more overall life practice and philosophy. With Oliveros' social awareness and social engagements, "deep listening" is not only listening to the actual resonances or reverberance of a space, it is also a feminist "deep listening" to society, to minority voices, to diverse socialities and politics.

The concert in New York was an example of this, as the second of two in a series called *Stretched Boundaries* (Tucker 2016 pg 181; Oliveros 2016 pg 184–185). Oliveros had curated the program, presenting music with and by performers and composers some of whom had physical disabilities. Oliveros' event demonstrated how they brought this into their musicianship, but also how each had found a way to deal with their physical challenges through various technological means:

> The objective … is to include artists with disabilities in more mixed-abilities public concerts and presentations to bring this population forward and also

to bring artists without disabilities into contact with artists they might otherwise miss in an ableist culture.

Oliveros (2016 pg 185)

The concert opened with the energetic piece *Play the Drum*, by young students from the Abilities First School, a school for children with disabilities in Poughkeepsie, New York led by Leaf Miller. Oliveros told me about her choice of these performers:

> It is important that these kids get to perform in front of an audience in New York. When will they ever be invited to do that? We made a context for them to do that. I think that is important, because I think that is inclusive. It opens up new thoughts and new pathways, and new possible collaborations for making music.[10]

The audience gathered that afternoon were the conference participants: professors and lecturers, doctoral students, prominent composers and performers from most regions of the world, all with a professional interest in music technology, some in music aesthetics, a few in music history, and perhaps a handful showing interest in social questions related to the genre. The opening piece was followed by Neil Rolnick's *Mono Prelude*, reflecting his sudden hearing loss in one ear. Next was Deborah Egloff's *Prometheus*, with the performer David Whalen, a quadriplegic, using a JamBoxx (mouthpiece controller) to make music and visual illustrations. After that, Clara Tomaz's *Deviations and Straight Line* addressed speech impairment, with the voiceless artist herself singing through an electronic device. Finally, there was deaf-born Christine Sun Kim's work *Binary Reality with a Delay*, which explored her perception and auditory communication.

Even though the concert happened nine years ago, I still recall it vividly (maybe also because I have occasionally revisited it when introducing students to the work of Oliveros). My memory of it is also vivid, I think, because this was not only highly memorable, with its introduction to new technological solutions and non-normative perception modes, but also because it was a surprising and joyful event that affected me deeply and planted a special vibrance in my body. The opening drum piece by the young performers had an especially strong impact on me. Oliveros (2016 pg 185) recalls it this way:

> The musicians in the Play the Drum Band played like professionals and received an ovation from the audience of sophisticated electro-acoustic artists, technologists, and listeners. They were a hit. They had never had an experience like this. Their performance in the second *Stretched Boundaries* concert succeeded in showing them, their fellow performers, and the audience that they are musicians.

The noise of a tight drumming rhythm hit us before we saw the performers. I remember it as an almost shocking – but nevertheless pleasant – surprise, and a most welcome contrast to the intellectual presentations and discussions at the conference. From being a "hearing head" in the conference space, I now transformed into a situated deep "listening body".

During the conference, I would present a paper that reflected my own position as a fairly young historian researching the history of Swedish EAM. My educational training had placed me within a knowledge position and listening practice that were shaped by the (masculine) discourse of acousmatic listening (e.g. Schaeffer 1966; Smalley 1997; Thoresen and Hedman 2007) and musical/performance analysis (e.g. Auslander 2004; Sauter 2000). Because of this, I would almost automatically pay attention to the acoustics, the musical structure and aesthetics, the performer's skills and appearance, and to the overall politics and contexts while sitting in the concert hall. At the time (2011), I was becoming increasingly aware of the non-symmetrical perspectives in the discourses of EAM concerning gender and center/periphery, but this was as far as my thoughts on diversity went at the time. There is no doubt that the concert disrupted my knowledge situation by bringing a novel and critical perspective to what I already implicitly knew.

The opening, the drumming sound, planted itself in my body with surprise and *affect*, and, I believe, I hardly had time to stabilize the situation with an intellectual reflection before the concert started. In the words of Spinoza and Deleuze, I was filled by (what I experienced as) *joyfulness* that eventually led to a feeling of *action*; or, in other words, I became empowered through a deep listening situation. The performers who appeared behind this and the rest of the concert's production of music and sound opened me towards a questioning of my normative understanding of perception and listening. I was not engaged as a "hearing head", but was invited to participate as a situated and deep "listening body". Together with the overall concept of the concert (i.e., providing a performance platform for musicians with disabilities), this framing of my appearance also led me to situate and question my existing and normative knowledge on listening. Nine years later, I can now use Haraway's work to conceptualize and re-formulate what was then a spontaneous and affect-full experience. My reformulation of Haraway's questions explores in the situated nature of listening what Haraway sought to ask of seeing (after Haraway 1989 pg 587):

> How to listen? Where to listen from? What limits to listening? What to listen for? Whom to listen with? Who gets to have multiple voices? Who gets muted? Who listens with no perspective? Who interprets the auditory field? What other sensory powers do we wish to cultivate besides listening?

In combination with the conference, the New York concert to me became a subversion and critique of a listening paradigm that has its roots in a masculine Western European tradition: a tradition of science that tends not to position its scientific objectivity, but to claim it as a universal truth. By reflecting on Oliveros' intentions, ideologies and practice with "deep listening" through the concepts of Haraway's "situated knowledge", I have now made space for an alternative conceptualization of the EAM concert. It is an alternative that is rooted in feminist thinking and that differs by taking affective, bodily and situated knowledge perspectives into account.

Situated listening and what to do with passion and passiveness

Finally, I can now return to the problem introduced earlier, namely: why didn't I leave the concert in Tillburg, even though I wanted to and had even been invited to leave? As explained at the beginning of the chapter, this Tillburg concert also took place in an academic context as an evening event curated by the same person who had organized the two-day seminar. There were a limited number of people at the concert. I was older and had matured, and my academic status had increased. So, one would think, I could have left if I had wanted to. But still, during the concert I became mentally and physically paralyzed, and neither able to engage with nor leave the concert space.

If we take the Spinozist–Deleuzian perspective on this listening situation, we might say that I was met by a *passion* that filled or *affected* me with *sadness*, which led me into *passiveness* or *disempowerment*. And as Ahmed's writings have highlighted, the emotions and affective states of passiveness have been associated with the feminine and ascribed a lower value than those of action. Through my reflections two years after the concert, I found that it was not the music itself that made me uncomfortable. Instead, my passiveness and the feeling of gradually being disempowered affected my experience of this concert. The (male) composer had encouraged the audience to leave, to *act*, if any of us did not enjoy the piece. But I could still not leave. Leaving a musical piece was, to me, not only to act against conventions, but also to act against my own curiosity. I had, after all, travelled a distance from Copenhagen to participate in the event – to agree and disagree, and to challenge or find new knowledge positions. Although I believe he did it with good intentions, the effect of his suggestion that I should leave if I was not *affected* with joy by the piece was to restrict my emotions and behavior in a masculine direction that I did not feel capable of enacting. The apparently free choice was an encouragement to stand up and actively act against conventions, and to explicitly show whether I was with or against the piece. I instinctively felt it necessary to stay listening to the piece, to pay attention to, through careful listening, the aesthetics, whether or not I enjoyed the work. I was scripted into a particular masculine kind of action pattern that was not mine. Even though I struggled to find a resonance with the work, I attempted to gain an understanding of the sound, its technological intentions, ideology, politics and perhaps its sociality. After years of careful analytical research, through the readings and works of Haraway and Oliveros, I can now ask: what kind of rationality was at stake here, and how was its positioning to be understood? How were the knowledge production and the aesthetics to be situated? How could I "compost" the meeting, and organically digest it with my previous experiences and existing knowledge? At the time, these questions were not possible, as they were overshadowed by the aesthetic, political and gendered conventions of the event.

Instead of engaging actively, I felt guilty and weak while listening, as my displeasure while staying was not an approved behavior. Having the composer observing the audience outside the circle of speakers from a God-like position only served to disempower my listening.[11] As a result, I became paralyzed by being affected by a passion that finally turned into passiveness and despair.

Concluding remarks

In this chapter, I have introduced to the notion of "deep situating listening" – of how it can be achieved and lead to empowerment, and how it can be disrupted, and then lead to disempowerment. "Deep situated listening" is a listening practice and ideology acknowledging that the notion of the "body" exceeds human beings to include technology, space, politics and sociality as well as histories of gendered and other forms of power. The bodies through which we experience our listening are situated in their own rational positioning, and they are to be perceived as dynamic. They never act solely, but have an impact on one another, as they are able to affect and be affected by the situation. I wish to underline that the various bodies are not contributing to the situation, but they *constitute the situation* as a whole.

"Deep situated listening" is an analytical attempt to democratize the study of music reception by allowing more actors in. In the concrete case of the EAM concert situation, I tried to do so by acknowledging aspects and actors of the concert event that are often suppressed in the "hearing heads" approach to music reception analysis. The "hearing heads" approach to listening has little time and no language for the conventions of the concert event, for the gendered dimensions of invitations to act, for the hierarchies and power structures that are built into the spaces of concert events and into the scenic arrangements of the space. A "deep situated listening" approach, it is important for me to state, does not pretend to be a substitute for the knowledge already existing within the tradition of EAM. Rather, "deep situated listening" is a complement to the "hearing heads" approach by composting and organically bringing out the historical longitudes and latitudes of listening that remain hidden in the "hearing heads" approach. This feminist perspective is an intentional and political attempt to bring in an analytical openness towards and awareness of other voices and histories that a "hearing heads" approach does not expect to hear. The "deep situated listening" approach is able to identify multiple listening positions that exceed the "ideal" and universal listener of the "hearing head" approach. A "deep situated listening" allows us to meet and composite the bodies of sound that do not cohere with our own.

Acknowledgments

Thanks to Philip Dodds and Nils Bubandt for providing me with their perspectives and comments on this work.

Notes

1 Author's translation.
2 A similar aim with a focus on sound art can be found in Groth and Samson (2017).
3 For further discussions on Deleuze, Spinoza and music, see Thompson's (2019) development of the music's ethico-affective ambivalence and Cimini's (2010) application of Spinoza's ideas in an analysis of the piece of Xenakis.
4 For the logic of the argument, I will in this section not move further into the differentiation of listening and hearing, but stay with the term "listening", as I am here mostly interested in the conscious act, and not the physical ability of hearing.
5 For the full program, please visit www.ems-network.org/ems11/concert.html.
6 The Schaefferian tradition has been continued in the UK, where Denis Smalley's spectromorphology and the development of the speaker system BEAST has had a significant influence on the UK EAM scene.
7 Interview with the author, June 15, 2011. The interview was initially made with permission for publication as an audio report at Seismograf.org, but due to the sound quality, it was never published at the time.
8 For a thorough analysis of the album, see Stewart (2012).
9 Interview with the author, June 15, 2011.
10 Ibid.
11 For a further discussion of the performing composer's role in contemporary music, see Groth (2016).

Bibliography

Ahmed, Sara. 2015. *The Cultural Politics of Emotion*, 2nd edition. Edinburgh, UK: Edinburgh University Press.
Auslander, Phillip. "Performance Analysis and Popular Music: A Manifesto". *Contemporary Theatre Review*, 14, 1 (2004): 1–13.
Born, Georgina. 1995. *Rationalizing Culture: IRCAM, Boulez, and the Institutionalization of the Musical Avant-Garde*. Berkeley, CA: University of California Press.
Cimini, Amy. 2010. "Gilles Deleuze and the Musical Spinoza". In *Sounding the Virtual: Gilles Deleuze and the Theory and Philosophy of Music*, edited by Brian Clarence Hulse and Nick Nesbitt, 129–144. Burlington, VT: Ashgate.
Deleuze, Gilles. 1988. *Spinoza: Practical Philosophy*. San Francisco, CA: City Lights Books.
Haraway, Donna. "Situated Knowledges: The Science Question in Feminism and the Privilege of Partial Perspective", *Feminist Studies*, 14, 3 (1988): 575–599.
Haraway, Donna. 2016. *Staying with the Trouble: Making Kin in the Chthulucene*. Durham, NC: Duke University Press.
Haraway, Donna. 2018/1989. *Primate Visions: Gender, Race, and Nature in the World of Modern Science*. New York: Routledge.
Groth, Sanne. 2014. *Politics and Aesthetics in Electronic Music: A Study of EMS – Elektronmusikstudion Stockholm, 1964–1979*. Mainz, Germany: Kehrer Verlag.
Groth, Sanne. "Composers on Stage: Ambiguous Authorship in Contemporary Music Performance", *Contemporary Music Review*, 35, 6 (2016): 686–705. doi: 10.1080/07494467.2016.1282650.
Groth, Sanne and Kristine Samson. "Sound Art Situations." *Organised Sound*, 22, 1 (2017): 101–111. doi: 10.1017/S1355771816000388.
Oliveros, Pauline. 2005. *Deep Listening: A Composer's Sound Practice*. New York: iUniverse.

Oliveros, Pauline. 2016. "Curating Stretched Boundaries, the Concerts". In *Negotiated Moments: Improvisation, Sound, and Subjectivity*, edited by Gillian Siddall and Ellen Waterman, 184–185. Durham, NC: Duke University Press.

Sauter, Willmar. 2000. *The Theatrical Event Dynamics of Performance and Perception*. Iowa City, IA: University of Iowa Press.

Schaeffer, Pierre. 1966. *Traité des objets musicaux: Essai interdisciplines*. Paris, France: Éditions du Seuil.

Schmidt, Ulrik. "Music and Design: Phil Spector and Soundscapes Mediatization", *K&K*, 39, 111 (2011): 127–150. doi: 10.7146/kok.v39i111.15760.

Smalley, Denis. "Spectromorphology: Explaining Sound-Shapes". *Organised Sound*, 2, 2 (1997): 107–126. doi: 10.1017/S1355771897009059.

Stewart, Sharon. "Listening to Deep Listening", *Journal of Sonic Studies*, 2, 1 (2012). www.researchcatalogue.net/view/261881/261882 (accessed 5 October 2021).

Thompson, Marie. "Spinoza and Musical Power," *Textual Practice: Spinoza's Artes*, 33, 5 (2019): 803–820. doi: 10.1080/0950236X.2019.1581686.

Thoresen, Lasse and Andreas Hedman. "Spectromorphological Analysis of Sound Objects: An Adaptation of Pierre Schaeffer's Typomorphology", *Organised Sound*, 12, 2 (2007): 129–141. doi: 10.1017/S1355771807001793.

Tucker, Sherrie. 2016. "Stretched Boundaries. Improvising Across Abilities". In *Negotiated Moments: Improvisation, Sound, and Subjectivity*, edited by Gillian Siddall, and Ellen Waterman, 181–184. Durham, NC: Duke University Press.

5
THE FIELD IS MINED AND FULL OF "MINAS"

Women's music in Paraíba – Kalyne Lima and Sinta A Liga Crew

Tânia Mello Neiva

Contextualizing the subject

I am a non-white cis woman from São Paulo (south-eastern Brazil), living in João Pessoa (north-eastern Brazil) since 2011. I have worked with dance, theatre and experimental music since 2009, and engaged in performance art with my own art collective. My postdoctoral research (2019–2021) focused on two interconnected issues that had emerged during my PhD programme: the importance of technology as a means of production,[1] and the low representativeness of women in the experimental music scene in north-eastern Brazil. My goal was to analyse what the women in the city of João Pessoa were doing musically, whether and how they used technology, whether they thought about issues such as racism, sexism, colonialism and capitalism, and how these issues appear in their trajectories and works. I sought to map and give recognition to the musical production of women in João Pessoa from a decolonial and Marxist feminist perspective, particularly those with an openly progressive political bias.

One of the most unequal countries in the world (Organisation for Economic Co-operation and Development Brazil, 2018, p.6), Brazil is marked by huge regional disparities, in which the south-east is the dominant region (Oliveira, 2018). The prevailing narrative is that everything produced in the country's large economic centres such as those located in the south-eastern region is superior to the cultural production of the poorer areas. This undermines the visibility, recognition and remuneration of artists from poorer regions.

Another important characteristic of music in general is that it associates masculinity with ideas of production and, conversely, femininity with reproduction. Lucy Green (2001) refers to this process of stigmatization, invisibility and marginalization of women's music and the affirmation of female stereotypes in music as

DOI: 10.4324/9781003008217-8

"musical patriarchy". Creation and creativity are considered to be production activities and associated with the idea of rationality and genius, and therefore the male, while musical performance is linked to reproduction, and thus to the feminine. As a result, women have historically been assigned the stereotypical roles of singers, music teachers and interpreters of certain instruments such as the piano (Green, 2001; Lane, 2016). In the urban musical context of João Pessoa, many women deal with musical patriarchy on a regular basis.

As part of my postdoctoral research, I interviewed 12 women musicians via YouTube. The goal of this project, which I called "Jornadas Sonoras" (Sounding Journeys), was to get to know the artists living in João Pessoa whose productions and careers are not only artistic, but also progressive, feminist and political.[2] The artists I interviewed were: Luana Flores, Sandra Belê, Del Santos, Clara Bione, Val Donato, Maria Alice, Angela Gaeta, Maria Juliana, Harue Tanaka, Teresa Cristina Rodrigues, Raab Catarine and Glaucia Lima.[3] Some work with typical music styles from north-eastern Brazil such as *forró*, *coco* and *maracatu*, to name a few; others work with rock, electronic and pop, and yet others, classical music. Some are singers, while others are instrumentalists and most are composers. Some have pursued a formal education in music, and others have not. All declared that their city's music scene was sexist and racist to the point that they have had to scream to be heard at certain moments of their lives. Moreover, all said that many of their male colleagues underestimated them and that they had been discriminated against by people from southern and south-eastern Brazil.

Most interviewees reported difficulties in making a living from music and artwork, which obliged some to work as teachers, in local courts, as broadcasters etc. All produced music using technology, ranging from WhatsApp to share musical ideas to digital recorders to produce beats and electronic music. In this context, the concept of technology is quite broad.

Luana Flores, for instance, is a beatmaker, music producer, composer, DJ and a lesbian. In her music and performance, she highlights her sexuality, her gender identity (cis woman) and her place of origin (João Pessoa). She has gained visibility not only in João Pessoa, but also on the national scene.[4] Flores says that her performances question stereotypes associated with the idea of femininity. In addition to including her sexuality in everything she does, she raises the issue of gender identity by asserting herself as a cis woman. For Flores, this statement is important because she does not fit the stereotype of femininity due to both her physical appearance (haircut, clothes etc.) and non-normative sexual orientation (lesbian), which are not associated to normative femininity.

Flores commented on the predominance of artists from the south who have greater visibility on the national music scene. In her music, she emphasizes the strength of the north-east, which some may see as contradictory since she mixes traditional culture with new ones. She dialogues with a "futuristic aesthetic".

Like Luana Flores and the other women musicians I interviewed in 2020, Kalyne Lima and her band Sinta A Liga Crew (Feel the League Crew) are examples of woman musicians fighting to occupy all possible spaces in an adverse national

FIGURE 5.1 Luana Flores
Source: Image by Kio Lima.

context dominated by a highly sexist culture. In João Pessoa, the music scene featuring women in different music niches – such as electronic,[5] percussion,[6] hip hop and rap,[7] among others – is on the rise. This is the context in which Kalyne Lima and her group live, write music and perform.

Hip hop is also a north-eastern woman's thing

Kalyne Lima is one of the founders of the hip hop group Sinta A Liga Crew and the author of *O Campo Minado* (2016) (The Minefield), an autoethnography in which she discusses female participation in the hip hop scene in Paraíba.

Hip hop has been gaining visibility in Brazil since the 1980s, primarily in the city of São Paulo, where the movement first emerged. According to Lima (2016, p. 17), female participation in Brazilian hip hop began in 1988 with Sharylaine Bakhita from São Paulo, the first woman to record a rap song in the country (in *Collection Consciência Negra*, Vol. 1). In a tone of denunciation, Lima (2016) states that although the hip hop and rap scene grew throughout the 1990s in João Pessoa, female participation was rare and barely accepted.

The typical outfit worn by rappers during their performances consists of baggy Bermuda shorts and shirts, caps, chains and sneakers (Cirino, 2012, p. 130). Common gestures in rap performances are singing while keeping their necks stiff and bouncing up and down and moving their arms and hands to the beat to emphasize certain lyrics. Rocha, Domenich and Casseano (2001, p. 82) argue that in hip hop circles, there is greater acceptance of female participation if women perform as break dancers rather than rappers. In this case, they usually wear slim-fitting clothes instead of the loose-fitting ones worn by men, as we will see later in the analysis of

FIGURE 5.2 Kalyne Lima
Source: Image by Amadeus Araújo.

a video clip of the Sinta A Liga Crew, in which I compare typical rappers' outfits to the attire the band adopted.

Originally from the outskirts of João Pessoa, Kalyne Lima got involved with rap and hip hop when she was a teenager. With Miguel Nery, she created the group Raw Reality in the early 2000s. As the group did not have their own DJ equipment, they created their own percussion instruments (tambourines, rattles etc.) and developed a language capable of appropriating elements of popular north-eastern Brazilian music and mixing them with hip hop. The group developed into a social movement called the Raw Reality Street Culture Social Project, which educated children and young people from poor neighbourhoods (Lima, 2016, p. 71).

According to Lima, the group's incorporation of Brazilian percussion instruments and rhythms to adapt reflects the true nature of hip hop, which constantly evolves together with the reality in which it is inserted. In relation to gender, early in Lima's hip hop career, she assumed a male "poetic persona" for the lyrics she wrote (Lima, 2016, p. 72).

In 2003, Lima joined artist Julyana Terto to create the first female rap group in Paraíba: AfroNordestinas. One year later, the group won the Revelation Award at the *Para Todas as Tribos* (For All Tribes) MPB-SESC Festival. AfroNordestinas played an important role in the constitution of a female rap and hip hop scene, which began to grow in João Pessoa, albeit timidly, in the late 2000s. In 2007, the group received the award for Best Female Demo at *Hutúz*, the biggest hip hop festival in Latin America.

Hip hop was gaining strength in other parts of the north-east at that time as well. In 2007, the *Second Hip Hop Meeting in the Northeast* was held in João Pessoa; Kalyne Lima was the organizer. This time, issues on the feminist and women's agendas were at the forefront throughout the entire event to compensate for problems women artists faced in the previous year's event, where women were given almost no space to speak (Lima, 2016).

Due to her growing involvement in women's issues in the Paraíba and national hip hop movements, Lima was invited to become a member of the Central Única das Favelas (CUFA, the Central Union of the Favelas) in 2008. In 2009, in recognition of her work, she was awarded the "Women Making History, Heritage of the City" title at João Pessoa City Hall. Then, in 2010, AfroNordestinas released their first CD (Lima, 2016, p. 75). In 2012, Lima was admitted to study journalism at the Federal University of Paraíba. During this period, the artist put all her musical duties on standby to concentrate on her studies. In my interview with her, she emphasized how important obtaining a degree was to her as someone who had studied in a public school in a low-income area and started working when she was 14 years old.

After finishing her degree in 2016, Lima resumed her activities with AfroNordestinas. That same year, the first concert by a nationally renowned rapper, Karol Conka, was held in João Pessoa. After a lengthy negotiating process, the opening act for the concert was a group of local rap and hip hop women, from which Sinta A Liga Crew was born.

Sinta A Liga Crew is composed of Kalyne Lima,[8] Camila Rocha[9] and Preta Langy.[10] Priscila Lima (graffiti artist) and Giordana Leite (dancer) also appear in the

FIGURE 5.3 Sinta A Liga Crew, from left to right: Priscila Lima, Preta Langy, DJ Guirraiz, Giordana Leite, Camila Rocha, and Kalyne Lima

Source: Image by Marcelo Rodrigues.

video clip that I analyse in the next section. In 2017, they released their first CD, *Campo Minado*.

Campo Minado (Minefield)[11]

The song "Campo Minado" was composed in 2016, the same year that Kalyne's book with the title *O Campo Minado* was published. The CD was released a year later, in 2017, and on January 22, 2018, they launched the official video clip.

In the video clip, the women wear a mixture of pop diva and dominatrix outfits, and their performances feature typical hip hop references. The video starts with the camera zooming in on a pair of bright black combat boots on a fluffy grey rug. Someone puts the boots on and gets up from the sofa. An electronic keyboard introduces a riff that will be played throughout the video clip. In the next scene, a woman's hand with black fingernails and a fingerless glove puts a microphone into a black purse.

After this brief introduction, suggesting that a woman is getting ready to sing, Camila Rocha appears, singing the song. She is wearing camouflage leggings and her upper body is covered with black tape arranged in a kind of geometrical pattern. Her hair is short and bleached.

Preta Langy is the next woman to sing. She is wearing a short, long-sleeved, black see-through fishnet shirt over a black top that reveals her belly, a black spike necklace and, like Camila, camouflage leggings.

After Preta, Kalyne takes over singing. Kalyne is wearing a short camouflage dress, black fishnet pantyhose with long black socks (over her knees) and a black lace garter belt. Black straps (probably from lingerie) can be seen through her dress's neckline.

All three are wearing heavy blue makeup around the eyes, black eyeliner and lipliner, and glittery silver lipstick. They are also wearing spiked shoulder pads, black fingerless fishnet gloves and black combat boots. Their clothing and makeup are a mixture of military, punk and dominatrix references, and set the tone of the group's outfit and visual identity, which was created by the visual artist and fashion consultant Nanda Bechara. The outfit dialogues with references of pop divas such as Madonna, Lady Gaga and Beyoncé.

The lyrics of "Campo Minado" were written by the three artists, who alternate singing the verses in the album recording, the video clip and in live shows. They sing two choruses together. Both in the video clip and live shows, during the second chorus, they perform a choreographed sequence and the audience is expected to sing and dance along with them. The video clip focuses on whoever is singing at the time.

While singing, all three artists move their arms and heads to the beat. They often bend into squat positions, walk around the stage while marking the beat, and sometimes kick and jump. They also interact with the audience. The rehearsed choreography consists mainly of a movement where they shake their arms, turn around 180

The field is mined and full of "minas" 71

FIGURE 5.4 Image from the videoclip of Sinta A Liga Crew – "Campo Minado"
Source: www.youtube.com/watch?v=M_Qfh7E-7qk.

degrees and make a gesture that suggests they are looking off into the distance. They also shake their hips, bend into squat positions and point to their vaginas.

The entire performance – the way they act and dance and their outfits – is staged to illustrate the message in the song's lyrics (see Table 5.1).

Some considerations

The concept of "musical patriarchy" was developed by Lucy Green (2001) to refer to formal musical education contexts. Although neither Lima nor the other members of Sinta A Liga Crew have pursued a formal education in music, Lima's trajectory and the issues raised by the group in "Campo Minado" confirm that this concept also applies to their context.

For Green (2001, pp.58–62, 76–83), women's actions in the music world are mediated by public exposure, which reinforces the tendency to associate women with nature (as opposed to men, who are associated with culture). Such an association fosters behaviour or practices that emphasize signs of femininity rather than the codes that are – supposedly – essentially musical. As a result, the focus is on women's bodies, which are eroticized, sensualized and commercialized, and women are disassociated from practical creativity and intellectualism, as can be seen in the area of music creation, for example.

In the case of Lima, her work in hip hop and the limited participation of women in this scene demonstrate how certain fields of music are considered inappropriate for women. For example, she stated that before AfroNordestinas, she used to assume

TABLE 5.1 Lyrics and form of *Campo Minado* – Portuguese and English

Form	Campo Minado (Portuguese)	Minefield (English)
1st verse Camila Rocha	Mina girando, mina rimando, mina riscando, mina pintando	Minas [a mine and a girl] spinning, minas rhyming, minas scratching, minas painting
	O campo está minado pra quem anda vacilando	This is a mined field for those who are messing up
	Cuidado mano, porque eu tô te focando	Careful bro 'cuz I'm focusing on you
	Se eu mirar no preconceito você vai sofrer o dano	If you aim your prejudice at me, you will suffer the damage
2nd verse Preta Langy	Sinta A Liga Sinta o clap Sente o peso, do Nordeste	Feel the League Feel the clap Feel the weight, from the north-east
	Várias minas, que dominam, do mic até o cap	Several minas [girls] who dominate from the mic to the cap
	Vou chegar chegando, com meu pensamento insano	I'm coming full force, with my insane thoughts
	Não dou "back-to-back" pra fingidores de malandro	I don't give "back-to-back" for fake bad boys
3rd verse Kalyne Lima	E é nessas fitas, que a gente parte pra cima, diversidade que ensina, conceito que contamina e a rima que disciplina, colada com as outras mina, eu tô com as trapa, eu tô com as trans, to com quem respeita a vida	And it is in these [contexts], that we rise up, diversity that teaches, concept that contaminates and rhymes that discipline, stuck together with the other minas [girls], I am with the "trapa", I'm with the trans, I'm with whoever respects life
Chorus part 1 All together	Eu tô com as mana, tô com as mina, tô com as mona, tô com as gay	I'm with the sistas, I'm with the minas [girls], I'm with the monas [women], I'm with the gays
	Em terra de machocrata quem se desconstrói é rei	In the land of machocrats, the one who is deconstructed is king
	Se o corpo é meu é minha lei	If the body is mine, it is my law
	Em terra de machocrata quem se desconstrói é rei	In the land of machocrats, the one who is deconstructed is king

Chorus part 2
Twice
All together
  with a dance
  choreography
	Deixa as garotas brincar,
	É o poder, aceita porque dói menos.
	Deixa as garotas brincar,
	De longe falam alto, mas de perto tão pequeno
		Let the girls play,
		They have the power, accept it because it hurts less
		Let the girls play,
		From far away they speak loudly, but up close, they're so small

TABLE 5.1 Cont.

Form	Campo Minado (Portuguese)	Minefield (English)
4th verse Camila Rocha	O comando é feminista, só com mina terrorista Se tu der algum deslize jogo teu nome na pista Se não quero não insista Tenho pra mais de mil sista Só cumade* cabulosa, não tem macho que resista	The command is feminist, only with terrorist minas [girls] If you slip up, I'll put your name on the track If I don't want to, don't insist I've got over a thousand sistas Only the best partner, no macho can resist
5th verse Kalyne Lima	Eu sou a neta da bruxa que a fogueira não queimou Minha pisada sinistra é no compasso do meu flow Eu desconjuro tua força Tua língua virou forca Os machos tremeu na base, quando as mina se juntou	I'm the witch's granddaughter that the fire didn't burn My sinister stride is the rhythm of my flow I exorcize your strength Your tongue has become a noose The machos trembled at the base when the minas [girls] got together
6th verse Preta Langy	Caminhando, planejando Mundão vou conquistando Jogaram pedra, falam merda e agora estão me olhando Por que hein? Sei que escondido você aperta o play Pra escutar meu som e mais de uma vez	Walking, planning I'm conquering the big world They threw rocks, talk shit and now they're looking at me. Why, huh? I know that you secretly press play To listen to my music and you do it more than once
	Chorus part 1 *They sing all together*	
	Chorus part 2 *Twice* *They all sing together while doing a dance choreography*	

Note: * *Cumade* is the same as *comadre*. The term has various meanings in Portuguese, the most common one being "godmother", and also a midwife assisting a woman with childbirth. *Comadre* in the sense here refers to a kind of sisterhood, which is the more common use of the word in Brazil, especially in not very intellectualized contexts. The lyrics suggest that the women are part of a sisterhood, and not of the elite and thus, "real" people.

the persona of a man to write and sing her lyrics, using adjectives or nouns in the first-person singular of the male gender. We can relate this to the idea of gender coloniality proposed by Maria Lugones (2008). Lugones highlights that patriarchy cannot be dissociated from racism and capitalism, as gender coloniality was created by the colonizers when they saw other ways of living and relating to others. Due to their racism, they saw the people living in the territories that we call America today as inferior, and sometimes not even human. They were unable to understand the relationships between indigenous men and women, which were not based on power and disputes. For Lugones, this was how gender coloniality was born. In their performances, Lima and the women of the Sinta A Liga Crew use the image of pop divas, the dominatrix and other symbols in a context where they are not expected. They get out of the "normative box" of their local context and assume symbols from another normative box – that of a "pop diva".

The lyrics of the first verse of "Campo Minado" (see Table 5.1) affirm the work of women artists or "minas" (girls/women) who operate in different areas. The field is "mined" in the sense that it is both occupied by "minas" (girls/women) and ready for an explosion if any "male behaves badly". The lyrics of the first stanza also touch upon the situation in north-eastern Brazil. The women in the song are not "minas" from just anywhere, but from a region that has historically suffered discrimination, received fewer incentives and less financial support, and is invisible at various levels, even in the area of academic production, for example. The song's lyrics are about how this feminist struggle has a ballast to support it: "I have more than a thousand sistas ... I'm the witch's granddaughter that the fire didn't burn". They thus recognize an ancient struggle, characterized by a lot of pain and resistance, that women have been waging over many centuries. It also talks about the broader feminist agendas that recognize trans people as essential to the struggle.

In "Campo Minado", the artists show how the issue of the representativeness of women can positively transform a context when they suggest that the rap scene is being occupied by many women, and this inhibits men from engaging in sexist behaviour. This can be seen, for example, when they sing:

> If you slip up, I'll put your name on the track
> If I don't want to, don't insist
> I've got over a thousand sistas.

If we see representativeness not only as women's presence in specific spaces, but as their actions in these spaces, it is how they occupy these spaces (quality), and not so much the number of spaces (quantity), that matters. Thus, occupation can be decisive for establishing a fairer and less violent music scene: by occupying and increasing the visibility of the actions they take to confront sexism, these women transform the field positively. They fight to prevent setbacks from happening, while setting an example for other women. Another example of their capacity to transform the music scene is the fact that the *Hip Hop Meeting in the Northeast* began incorporating women's demands into its second edition in 2007. This helped secure the space that the women had won by confronting and overcoming strong resistance from the men.

In relation to the idea of musical patriarchy, the Sinta A Liga Crew's performance contests the stereotypes of the historically male-dominated fields of music creation (composition), rap and hip hop, as well as the sexualized image of female performers. When they put on a piece of women's clothing such as a "garter belt" (symbol of sensuality and eroticism) and play the dominatrix role, they are saying that they are in control. By performing in this attire, they are able to debunk various stereotypes. First, they show that women *do* have a place in hip hop; in their performances, the symbolic femininity of the "garter belt" is detached from the element to which it is normally associated: women as sex objects. They play with the symbols of heteronormative sexuality to question the role and meaning traditionally assigned to them. When they appropriate these symbols, it is as if they are saying that they can rhyme, dance, sing, paint graffiti and expose themselves in public however they want without being objectified. By doing so, they give new meaning to these symbols.

The band uses some of the patriarchal symbols and strategies that Green (2001) denounces as sexism, such as their outfits, which portray a sexual and erotic image of the female body. According to Green, such exposure is typical of musical patriarchy because it objectifies the female body. However, for the band, it means empowerment and control of their lives, choices and artistic careers. They put performance and discourse together with this kind of sexualized outfit to denounce sexism, LGBTQIA+ phobia, racism, internal colonialism and many other forms of discrimination and social injustice. Contradiction permeates the universe of the character of the dominatrix, who uses the elements that have historically relegated women to the role of sexual objects as the basis for her power. Therefore, the band breaks with the idea that for a woman to be recognized as a composer, she must abdicate her supposed femininity. They assume a type of femininity that explores a sexualized image of power and that does not submit, but rather dominates others.

Regarding the issue of internal colonialism, Lima perceives the ethno-racial and class inequalities between Brazilian regions and points out that her work does not receive the same attention and visibility that artists from the south and southeastern regions get, nor is its circulation as widespread. This is explicit in her discourse when she presents herself as a north-eastern feminist woman from the periphery. Recognizing that north-eastern artists do not have the same opportunities, Lima takes conscious action to strengthen the north-eastern hip hop scene. It is thus no coincidence that she produced the second *Hip Hop Meeting in the Northeast* in Paraíba and wrote a book on female performances in João Pessoa's hip hop scene.

In my analysis of Kalyne Lima's trajectory and her work as part of Sinta A Liga Crew, I sought to exemplify disruptive bodies, lives and stereotypes. May they serve as an invitation to engage in further reflection and mobilization, which are direly needed, especially in times of the proliferation of fake news, the weakening of democratic institutions and the worsening of social inequality in the country. For me, they serve as a source of inspiration and learning:

The field is mined for those who hesitate. And the field is minado!

Notes

1 For the selection of my subject, I did not make an aesthetic choice in relation of the kinds of music studied.
2 The interviews were scheduled according to the feminist agenda: in August and September, – lesbian and bisexual visibility months, respectively – I only invited lesbian and/or bisexual artists to participate. In October, I brought the issue of maternity to the agenda to contest the commercialization of Children's Day by inviting only artists who were mothers. As November 20 is the Day of Black Consciousness in Brazil, I only interviewed black artists that month.
3 The interviews are available at: https://youtube.com/playlist?list=PLGEub5wbJvQyi9 wcrCjh1kyjhbIbbWWDx. An online discussion on the project "Sounding Journey" during the Symposium *Out of the Bubble*, which was part of the programme on discourse during the *Dystopie Sound Art Festival 2020* in Berlin and Brazil, is available at: https://youtu.be/rM_fzLmrHJE.
4 In 2019, she was selected to do an artistic residency at Red Bull Station in São Paulo. In 2020, she won the "artistic revelation" *SIM São Paulo* (São Paulo Music Week) prize and was interviewed for the important rock magazine *Rolling Stone*. To listen to her music and watch her video clips, go to: https://open.spotify.com/artist/5QnMVhi34lc uj6iaOrMuXv or www.youtube.com/c/luanaflores.
5 Such as Luana Flores, Katarina Nepomuk and Deborah Malacar, to name a few.
6 Del Santos, the all-women percussion group As Calungas, Angela Gaeta, Priscila Fernandes and others.
7 The Sinta A Liga Crew women's, Jessica Caetano, Bixarte and others.
8 Kalyne Lima is a rapper and journalist and works at Central Única das Favelas (Central Union of the Slums), which is her main job.
9 Camila Rocha is a rapper, visual artist and hairdresser, the latter being her main source of income.
10 Preta Langy is a rapper, and works as an eyebrow designer and hairdresser together with Camila Rocha.
11 *Mina* is Portuguese for "girl". "Campo Minado" is a reference to both a minefield and a field full of girls; the artists associate the two to suggest that both are dangerous.

Bibliography

Cirino, Andréa Cristina. 2012. Rap Enquanto Performance: Um Evento de Comunicação e Expressão Musical. *ETD – Educação Temática Digital* 14, 2, 126–139.

Green, Lucy. 2001. *Música, Genero y Educación*. Translated by Pablo Manzano. Madrid, Spain: Morata.

Lane, Cathy. 2016. Why not our voices? *Women and Music: A Journal of Gender and Culture* 20, 96–110.

Lima, Kalyne. 2018. *O Campo Minado: Livro Resultado de Trabalho de Conclusão de Curso do Curso de Jornalismo da Universidade Federal da Paraíba*. João Pessoa, Brazil: independent publication.

Lugones, Maria. 2008. The Coloniality of Gender. *Worlds* and *Knowledges Otherwise*, 2, 1–17.

Organisation for Economic Co-operation and Development Brazil. February 2018. *Relatórios Econômicos OCDE Brasil*. Available at: www.oecd.org/economy/surveys/Brazil-2018-OECD-economic-survey-overview-Portuguese.pdf.

Oliveira, Ana Luiza Matos de. 2018. Crise amplia desigualdades regionais no mercado de trabalho. Fundação Perseu Abramo – Partido dos Trabalhadores, 28 February. Available at: https://fpabramo.org.br/2018/02/28/crise-amplia-desigualdades-regionais-no-mercado-de-trabalho/.

Rocha, Janaina, Domenich, Mirella and Casseano, Patrícia. 2001. *Hip Hop – a Periferia Grita*. São Paulo, Brazil: Editora Fundação Perseu Abramo.

6
WORKING WITH *WOMENS WORK*
Towards the embodied curator

Irene Revell

Prologue: unboxing Oliveros

The verb *to curate* has never been in wider circulation, its current sense stemming from within but appearing in countless instances well beyond contemporary art (Balzer et al. 2015). At its heart is the figure of the *curator*, 'typically immaculately dressed, well-spoken and with a pleasing personal style … the right kind of personality' (McRobbie 2015). Amongst this proliferation is a growing field of curating within sound and music. Whilst explicit use of the term 'curator' in a music context seems to begin in the 1990s (McKeon 2021), its origins may be traced to earlier decades, though there is only recently a growing literature on the wider topic. This chapter adds to the latter, and argues for a form of *embodied* curating that here emerges from the specific challenges of curating historical text-based performance scores – especially through the prism of a feminist score anthology, *Womens Work* (1st issue 1975, 2nd issue 1978) – that, in short, inserts the curator's own active body, amidst others, into the heart of the work. My focus here is on textual instructional works that stem from the 1960s and 1970s and have in general terms already been the subject of ongoing interest within and beyond exhibition-making, yet rarely has this activity been critically appraised nor alternative means for sharing such works developed. Moreover, there is a marked proliferation in the use of textual instructional performance scores in contemporary practice that renders these questions timely.[1] This chapter has two orientations in this regard: a discussion of how one might work as a curator with these kinds scores, and in its conclusion, the implications of such *embodied* curatorial practices that I argue these works imply and which may be resonant amidst a wider field of work that shares their live social materiality, especially, though not limited to, sound and music performance.

DOI: 10.4324/9781003008217-9

I came across *Womens Work*, co-edited by Fluxus artist Alison Knowles and composer Annea Lockwood, and the main focus of my own work as a curator over recent years, as a result of an earlier encounter with composer Pauline Oliveros' text score *To Valerie Solanas and Marilyn Monroe in Recognition of Their Desperation* (1970).[2] The context here was the touring exhibition *WACK!* at MoMA PS1, New York (2008), the first survey of the feminist art movement of the 1970s. I was utterly compelled by the Oliveros work's title and implications, but frustrated by my attempts to read the two lengthy pages of textual instruction: peering over a small vitrine, both physically and mentally exhausted at the end of a vast group exhibition, not even an ideal condition for reading the printed document, let alone understanding what the piece might sound like. As a curator, the obvious conclusion was to arrange a performance of the work. I realized this project some years later with sound artists Cathy Lane and Lee Ingleton in the context of our *Her Noise: Feminisms and the Sonic* programme at Tate Modern in 2012, with Oliveros as keynote speaker. I then became involved in a filmed iteration of the work that artist friends Pauline Boudry and Renate Lorenz made the following year having independently encountered the score in the *WACK!* exhibition and heard tell of our London performance. These enfolding encounters set a series of challenges to me as a curator, the more obvious of which is the potentials and limits of the exhibition format, with its corollary call for live performance. Less obvious is the slow realization during these and further examples I will go on to discuss that it is the process of performance, the negotiation of the score by the performers and others engaged in staging the performance, that holds some of the richest encounters with the work: at least in the case of text instruction, that leaves significant elements open to interpretation and negotiation. I assert that this processual, social and inevitably thoroughly embodied group experience presents the greatest challenge to the curator's mediation of such works, whether in attempting to incorporate elements into either of the paradigms of exhibition or performance, or in thinking through this processual 'in-between' as its own format.

In the first section, I give an account of my work with the *Womens Work* score anthology to explore the wider curatorial challenges, potentials and limitations of the paradigm of exhibition-making. The second section offers a counterpoint: my workshop series *These Are Scores* began as a means to develop a related live performance programme that organically emerged as a curatorial format in itself, offering a sense of this embodied group negotiation that occurs between reading a score and any final performance. These workshops became my preferred format for sharing these works as a curator whilst placing new and specific demands, as host or convener, on my own body's active presence within my curatorial work. Ordinarily, the curator herself is physically separate from the artwork(s) that she is presenting, aside from the 'exhibition tour' or 'introductory talk', and then always with clear distinction. Moreover, these glimpses are separate from the invisible work of curating, the process by which the project has come to pass. Rarely, if ever, are the curator, her body and her work immersed, entangled, physically, in the work she is presenting, for all the porous boundaries that this might imply[3] – as it is in the case of such a workshop. In the third, concluding section, I take up the challenges of the workshop, this live social medium, as a medium of curating and the foregrounding of the curator's own body and the labour of curating at the centre of the presentation of the works. This chapter ultimately argues for what I call the *embodied curator*, who may be found in the midst of the work, not so much the sounding curator, but the curator embodied in sounding work. My understandings of embodiment here are foregrounded in philosopher Karen Barad's framework of *agential realism*, where matter and meaning are iteratively performatively co-constituted in 'a posthumanist, performative understanding of the materialization of bodies' (Barad 2007, 34). Speaking from the field of body studies, Lisa Blackman articulates this Baradian approach to bodily materiality as 'based on conceptions which emphasize the lively, agencial capacities of matter at all scales ... replac[ing] the psyche (often equated to subjectivity) with a more entangled and distributed conception of materiality, which introduces non-human agency into being and becoming' (2021, 89). I contend that the embodied curator exists through these iterative enfolding encounters with texts, bodies, their sound and movement, in time and space that parallels the open-ended life many of these works might lead through their iterative live performance. In turn, this chapter's writing embraces these understandings in order to speak of my own repeated encounters with these materials and their physical, embodied negotiations – not only embodied in a very literal way, as workshop host in the conclusions of this work, but throughout the years of process that I describe, as a body accumulating knowledge from these multiple encounters, rather than a singular, linear institutional engagement with history.

Exhibition as (lively) expanded publishing

Slow Runner

Womens Work, co-edited by Alison Knowles and Annea Lockwood and self-published in New York, began life as a magazine project that would amount to two issues, in 1975 and 1978, the former a booklet of textual instructional scores, the latter a fold-out poster with 25 contributors in total, spanning disciplines of composition, fine art performance, choreography, painting, video art and astrology.[4] Most scores are open to any performer; some are more abstract or esoteric; many don't necessarily engage a public audience; some are larger-scale or more ambitious; relatively fewer require trained dancers or musicians, though most have sonic elements if not physical movement, amongst them being widely known works such as composer Mieko Shiomi's *Spatial Poem* (1965–75) and Annea Lockwood's *Piano Transplants* (1966–2013), as well as some written specially for the collection.

If working with the Oliveros score *To Valerie Solanas and Marilyn Monroe in Recognition of Their Desperation* seemed to invite speculation that the textual, instructional performance score might hold potential as a feminist medium, then an affirmative answer seemed to come in the form of *Womens Work*. As mentioned earlier, I first encountered *Womens Work* through research on this topic towards an exhibition project, *Slow Runner* (held in the Badischer Kunstverein in 2013), a group exhibition that explored Oliveros' feminist philosophy of music which was commissioned alongside the premiere installation of the eponymous Boudry/Lorenz work. Here I displayed the two original issues of *Womens Work* sent by Annea Lockwood herself, alongside a series of facsimiles of individual pages – at this point, there was only one copy in any European institutional archive/library, in Denmark. Even as I was arranging the display, it seemed to have failed to convey the excitement that flowed through me from the materials: modest and monochrome, the vitrine felt unimaginative and, again, mute. My only resolve was to provide an additional complete facsimile copy which visitors could physically leaf through and read themselves whilst sitting in chairs next to the display: a small act of comfort and generosity.

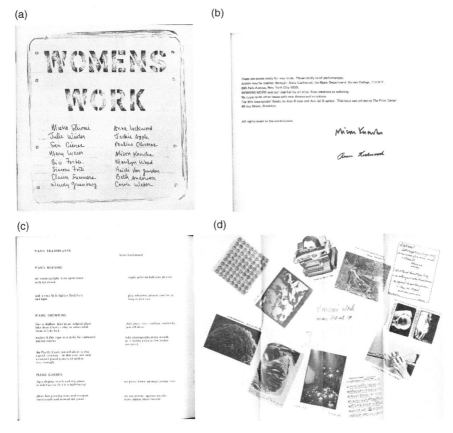

FIGURE 6.1 (a) *Womens Work*, first issue (1975) cover; (b) *Womens Work*, first issue (1975) colophon; (c) Annea Lockwood's *Piano Transplants*, first issue; (d) *Womens Work*, second issue (1978)

Words to be looked at and actions to be performed

For all that this first attempt at exhibiting *Womens Work* felt a disappointment, I note now that the exhibition format had been crucial in my repeated physical encounters with these historical materials. Were it not for the *WACK!* exhibition, I might not otherwise have encountered the Oliveros score; in turn, I learned of the existence of *Womens Work* because of its inclusion in an archival exhibition at MoMA, New York, and then only through curating my own exhibition project. My initial impulse was to feel cynical about the placement of the Oliveros score in the vitrine, seemingly a fetish for ephemera that abstracts and even alienates the work from its performance, its sound and music, its confluence of bodies in time and space, its vital embodiment. Yet this underestimates the visual-textual power of such scores, the important modes of looking and reading, themselves no less physical acts. As historian Liz Kotz insists of the post-Cagean *event score*, they are 'inseparably words to be looked at and actions to be performed' (2007, 9). For all their limitations, these encounters also speak of the exhibition's potential in sharing these materials that might otherwise be confined to the domain of archives or rare booksellers, functioning as an expanded form of publishing that might in turn proliferate their live performance(s) – where the curator has physically inserted the score into the 'path' of the exhibition visitor, bringing this material to different audiences, to those that would not have encountered the work initially, nor would seek out those archives. Any genealogy of artists' publications of performance scores would surely underline the importance of their visual, printed form. And in one widely known example, John Cage's *Notations* (1969), co-edited with Alison Knowles, there is moreover an implicit argument for the exhibition of scores: the book itself is just one outcome in a more ambitious project to collect the manuscripts from which the published excerpts derive into a museum collection for any number of future exhibitions (Kim, 2013). Here I am underlining that the exhibition of these performance scores as visual or reading material by curators has not only occurred retrospectively, but rather, that exhibition may be a mode explicitly sought by practitioners harnessing this potential. The operative question then might be how best to exhibit such scores: how to convey aspects of their live, processual nature; how to include live performance?

Recent curatorial engagements often explore the duality highlighted by Kotz. In particular, the past decade has seen a trend for the linkage of archival displays with a live performance programme, often within the same galleries. Excellent examples that have added to my own thinking include the daily live dance works of Trisha Brown included in the Barbican's *Laurie Anderson/Trisha Brown/Gordon Matta-Clark* (2011) exhibition curated by Lydia Yee, and numerous projects at Raven Row, London termed 'Live Exhibitions' where regular performances formed part of the core of the exhibition, including Catherine Wood's *Yvonne Rainer: Dance Works* (2014) and Jason Bowman's *In Case There's a Reason: The Theatre of Mistakes* (2017). These present a luxurious opportunity for the galleries to 'come to life', evidently relying on exceptional institutional support. Although it is beyond my scope here to draw out any example in detail, I suggest these also tend to present a compromise between programming at a frequency where most visitors to the gallery will experience something live, and the aura of the one-off event. Whilst unquestionably a generous intervention into the static gallery display, performance within the 'white cube' almost inevitably absorbs some of this static ambience, risking the rendering of performance, human bodies, as gallery objects. Thinking about sound performance more specifically, curator Lina Dźuverovič (2020) has described the secondary 'entertainment' value afforded to sound performance in the gallery. Moreover, composer and curator Chiara Giovando (2017) further articulates this fundamental spatio-temporal mismatch even more cynically in the specific case of music: 'it's a technical issue —it often sounds a certain way (very echoic) – but also a conceptual one: against the silence of the static, music can't help but become manipulative'.

The *Documenta 14* exhibition (held in Kassel in Germany and Athens in Greece in 2017) included historical textual and graphic scores as one of its major thematic strands, though it notably diverged from the aforementioned trend, presenting one-off performance events. Most compellingly, the curatorial team of *Documenta 14* took certain score-based structures into the conception of the working processes of the exhibition itself: Jani Chrisou's notion of a *continuum* as the basis for collaboration between artists, curators and exhibition workers, and Cardew's notion of *unlearning* as central to the overall exhibition's title, *Learning from Athens* (Folkerts 2017). Seeking to set these score-based practices in dialogue with the exhibition's own curatorial practices registers a significant intention towards working with this 'process of performance', albeit one that in this instance is not readily available to those outside its operations, that is to say, exhibition visitors.

ORGASMIC STREAMING ORGANIC GARDENING ELECTROCULTURE

To return to *Womens Work*, I was able to redress my earlier disappointment with a further exhibition project, ORGASMIC STREAMING ORGANIC GARDENING ELECTROCULTURE (Chelsea Space, 2018), co-curated with Karen Di Franco. Here *Womens Work* and Di Franco's respective research materials, artist Carolee Schneemann's performance text *Parts of a Body House* (1957–68), were brought together as a framework for an intergenerational dialogue between these historical scores and five contemporary art practices that work between the page and the body with text, sound and performance (Beatrice Gibson, Ghislaine Leung, Roy Claire Potter, Charlotte Prodger, Tai Shani). Here the acoustics and relatively small galleries, in line with Giovando's thinking, led us to an entirely separate, stand-alone performance programme in the 'black box' at LUX, Waterlow Park. And in the gallery we worked with the Schneemann text, and scores from *Womens Work* by Alison Knowles, Annea Lockwood and composer Mieko Shiomi in this form of expanded publishing: working closely with the architecture of the space to produce modes of reading that centred the comfort of the bodies of our audience, often in relation to seating; with a designer, we enlarged many scores to

FIGURE 6.2 *ORGASMIC STREAMING ORGANIC GARDENING ELECTROCULTURE*, Chelsea Space (2018), installation view: Annea Lockwood, *Piano Transplant no 1* (1966) and Carolee Schneemann, *Parts of a Body House* (1957–68), re-set by Matthew Appleton

the scale of the gallery walls, in some cases re-setting for wider legibility. Younger works also contributed to this human scale, including Ghislaine Leung's conceptual score *Colour Hides the Canvas, Moulding Hides the Frame* (2013) that instructs painting the entirety of the gallery's picture window with live yoghurt, softening the natural light and creating a more intimate atmosphere where visitors are no longer visible to the public outside; and Aine O'Dwyer's performance recording of Annea Lockwood's prepared piano, *Piano Transplant No 1* (1966), played back via transducer on the piano itself, sparse yet warm punctuations of the room's space-time, literally resonating through the wooden archive. Linking the historical scores with contemporary practices was also a conceptual means to 'enliven' their readings, bringing them into dialogue with these younger works in an intimate physical immediacy: 'a kind of proliferative energy that suggests an ongoing conversation about histories, materials and acts of making and un-making' (Morgan 2018, 81). In the midst of contemporary works and outside of fusty vitrines, for me these efforts presented these scores in means that were as 'lively' as possible, if not conventionally live: an approach that embraced its own limitations.

Live materials: the workshop as curatorial format

The introductory page (see Figure 6.1(b)) of the first issue of *Womens Work* begins: 'These are scores ready for you to do. Please notify us of performances' (Knowles and Lockwood 1975).

If *Notations* makes an argument for the exhibition of scores both on the page and in physical space, then the *Womens Work* publication additionally invites performance. As I argue in detail elsewhere, this generous insistence on performance marks the feminist potential in this project, offering the scores for direct and immediate use and bypassing music publishing institutions, their permissions and fees (Revell 2022). Co-editor Annea Lockwood asserts that 'these are live materials … you look at a score, you do it' (Lockwood 2017, 121). If the exhibition projects I describe in the previous section were forms of expanded publishing, bringing this otherwise little-known, rare magazine project to new audiences, then the ultimate conclusion would be to re-publish the collection: something that I undertook in collaboration with New York publisher Primary Information in 2019, publishing a new facsimile edition that includes both issues. Yet from the point of view of the curator, this conclusion of sorts does not fully address such an insistence on 'live materials', performance. I had always envisaged convening a multi-disciplinary performance group that would workshop the numerous scores in the collection, culminating in an ambitious programme of live performance – what I saw as the ultimate goal of my work with *Womens Work*.

However, in attempting a prototype workshop, these ambitions fell starkly into question. An invitation to lead a workshop with Margate-based music improvisation group Athelstan Sound presented an opportunity to begin to tentatively think through this group process. Yet, in re-reading the works contained in *Womens Work* in preparation – that is to say, beginning to negotiate their performance – I came to more fully appreciate how heterogeneous they were in spite of their shared medium of textual instruction and overlapping communities of practice. Whilst, as above, all are emphatically intended for some form of performance, I wanted to work out which works in the collection we might be able to physically perform within the scope of a two-hour workshop: for some, like Oliveros' hand-written *Sonic Meditation*, this seemed feasible; others would need more preparation or performance time; others were more ambitious still, such as Annea Lockwood's own *Piano Transplants* (see Figure 6.1(c)). Workshop-planning aside, it became almost immediately obvious that the notion of one large-scale performance programme (albeit over several days) was an impossible fantasy with too many diverse works to be pragmatically feasible, never mind conceptually appropriate. Yet what happily emerged was that sharing these works in the format of a workshop – group reading, discussion and performance – sparked precisely the same kinds of processual encounters and thick embodied understandings that had emerged from the aforementioned instances of staging performances of Oliveros' *To Valerie Solanas and Marilyn Monroe in Recognition of Their Desperation*. In their textual, instructional form, these scores share a potential that extends from their group publication into these group workshop situations; it is this social exchange that might be the live part that all these works can share together, beyond their adjacency in print.

Taking its title, *These are scores*, from *Womens Work*'s introductory sentences, I went on to develop this workshop series that functions as a means for sharing the collection and its scores with a public, with more than ten iterations to date in a range of art, music, public and academic contexts. In brief, I split the time into two parts, 'reading' and 'performance', echoing Kotz's duality, though most importantly

FIGURE 6.3 (a) preparing photocopied scores from *Womens Work* for *These are scores*, Sounding Bodies, Copenhagen (2018); (b) 'reading', *These are scores*, Art Research Work conference, Zurich University of the Arts (2017); (c) 'performing', *These are scores*, Chelsea Space, London (2018)

with discussion straddling both. In the first part, we break into smaller groups, each with a different selection of the text scores from the first issue of *Womens Work*; each group is free to make their own way through any, or all, of their scores, reading and discussing. When the smaller groups feed back, we come to a consensus about which works we will focus on in the time we have for the second part, according to what has been of most interest: this might be performance of one or more of the scores, usually with discussion about the works' arrangement, and often repetition and modification. One of the most revelatory aspects of these workshops is the extent to which the works come to life in these group situations simply through reading and discussion, and where very often performance already begins spontaneously whilst 'reading'. The same and different works attract interest each time; profound questions often arise from the works and beyond, such as how far can we take our own interpretation before the performance is no longer the authored work?

In fact, the workshop, as a live, social, group format, feels immediately resonant with some of the group work and performance contexts through which these works and their 'scorers' emerged: Pauline Oliveros' Women's Ensemble, the Sonic Arts Union (Mary Lucier), Sounds Out Of Silent Spaces (Knowles, Lockwood, Ruth Anderson, Julie Winter), Experimental Intermedia Foundation (Elaine Summers), and doubtless others.[5] In a 2017 public in-conversation with writer Frances Morgan, composer Mary Jane Leach made a striking comment on her experiences of score-based performance in group rehearsal situations: 'We would spend probably 80% of the time discussing the score.' Hearing Leach's anecdote – albeit not one of the *Womens Work* contributors, though speaking of an overlapping period in New York – would come to crystallize my understandings that the workshop format in certain profound senses reproduces aspects of these historical group-working and/or performance contexts. In her appositely titled article 'Producing Situations: How Performer-Curators Are Rethinking Roles and Formats' (2020) musician, curator and researcher Heloisa Amaral discusses her own experiences of opening up the rehearsal space, and even within that the decision-making processes, to a wider public audience. This approach is highly resonant with my own use of the workshop to share these materials, though in Amaral's examples the orientation is still towards a final public performance(s) as ultimate outcome. Rather, whilst a few of the iterations in my series did culminate in performance for an additional audience, I am here proposing the workshop as a means to an end in and of itself.

This is not to say that such a workshop format would in any way supersede the value of staging performances of any individual work. Rather, it might be particularly valuable for seeking to present a broader sense of such works and their processual nature, a 'group show', as it were – or indeed, to explore works already grouped by their publishing, such as *Womens Work*. What I am proposing is a format that offers a compelling means to render the looking/reading of score-based works communal and discursive, whilst offering some sense of the negotiation of their live process that would otherwise not be easily accessible in any final performance, outside of the approaches Amaral outlines – a synthesis of key aspects of exhibition and performance brought together in this third paradigm. I am not suggesting that the idea of a workshop as a curatorial format is anything new *per se*: this seems perfectly in line with the notion of the *curatorial* that understands an expanding field beyond the exhibition itself, and particularly the *educational turn* within that (Martinon et al. 2013). Yet where a curator might ordinarily include a workshop in a wider programme, perhaps with an artist commissioned to lead it, what is distinct here aside from the specificity of score-based performance works is that these workshops are essentially stand-alone events in themselves where the curator *also* acts as workshop convenor or host, roles that effectively coalesce, inserting the physical presence of the curator into the heart of the activity, and largely condensing the curatorial labour into the time-frame of the event.[6] In the next, concluding section, I will discuss what for me has been the most immediate repercussion: the implications this format has on the figure of the curator, its multiple demands on my own bodily physical presence, suggesting what I term the *embodied curator*.

Hosting live social volumes: towards the embodied curator

Salomé Voegelin has compellingly proposed the paradigm of *volumes* for the curation of sound-based works in gallery space (Voegelin 2019, 46–7). This offers a potentially Baradian understanding of the three dimensions of the gallery as a host to the combined works, visitors and everything else contained within. For Voegelin, this might pertain acutely to sounding works that literally fill the room, 'touching' other works. I find this intervention crucial in thinking through the implications this has for the medium of curating itself in light of my own shifting understandings: the shift from thinking through the rigid architecture of institutions, gallery walls, vitrines (and their institutional time-scales) to the simpler yet more dynamic index of their volume. Taken further, the concept of volume might offer itself to re-imagining such institutions; a re-imagining that is crucially within the terms of the works themselves. My own development of the workshop as a curatorial format for sharing these score-based performance works with others, albeit emanating from specific performance histories, might share in this challenge of the medium of curating and might exist precisely in such volume(s), where the literary sense of the word functions aptly here too. If Voegelin's notion of *volume* accounts for sounding works more generally, then I further propose the additional qualification of the *live social volume*. Here it is the curator herself who produces, or holds, this live social volume through her own physical presence as host, the *embodied curator*.

In what I have described, I see the workshop as a means to encounter these works through directly exploring the scores in this group process where my role as host is to provide the smallest yet decisive amount of structure to enable this exchange, not to necessarily pour in my own knowledge nor act as a focal point. Though I acknowledge that my own physical presence as host is not neutral by any means, and I believe this is a format that could be readily replicated by others (and for other forms of experimental scores, or other works altogether), there is no doubt that the personality and temperament of the host will affect the feeling in the room. I am a university-educated white middle-class person whose first language is English, and also a relatively introverted, queer, disabled person – all factors that affect my outward presence in these contexts.[7] As host, my ambition is not to become a unilateral authority, but rather to facilitate this group exchange, the authority flowing from the materials, the scores themselves, through me as host and between us all. I propose that the *embodied curator* pushes beyond singular outcomes (the exhibition, the performance) altogether. For Karen Barad, agency is not a property of fixed 'things', but rather a *doing* and a *becoming* that occurs through the co-constitution of matter and meaning in its iterative performativity (2007, 178). I suggest that the embodied curator is agent precisely through this *doing and becoming*; not a unilateral presenter of works or knowledge in time and space, but rather one conduit through which these group encounters with works might flow.

Yet nevertheless, my own physical body is suddenly intrinsically present in this more social, intimate role: an entanglement which is a decisive shift in the figure of the curator. Here I am not *presenting* the works at a distance, a safe activity for any curator who has conviction in their choices: no longer wearing white gloves to place archival copies of scores in vitrines nor introducing an evening with Pauline Oliveros safely behind a lectern. Instead, I am physically 'turning up' – *being present myself* – in multiple contexts with a rucksack of photocopied scores to be shared out by hand, invariably wearing clothes for comfort not prestige. In committing to this format, I was almost inevitably pulled outside of my 'comfort zone' and pulled into the 'work'. That is to say, my work became the work of negotiating performance, hosting this process in collaboration with everyone in the room. Work that has an initial structure, two hours, two halves etc., but also takes on improvisation, responding to changing conditions, not least the emotional labour, the physical stress, of hosting any such group, moments of uncertainty, anxiety and clarity, elation. Here the medium of curating is decisively live and social, flowing through my own body as host, as embodied curator.

With small groups and the commitment to several hours, the workshop, as a case in point, is an intensive format that is not easily 'up-scalable'. Yet this intimate, human scale might also be a relief. Although in my case emanating from a long-standing engagement with the materials, any given workshop or similar event does not demand of the curator complex preparation, bureaucracy, fundraising, organization. Physically turning up with my clutch of scores requires a discrete and modest commitment of time, energy and budget where the largest part of the curatorial labour is contained within the time and space of the event itself – that is to say, the main work of curating is happening live in the room, not, as would usually be the case, almost entirely prior to any presentation of work. It thereby offers a tightly boundaried format that would suit the many of us who struggle with the ever-increasing demands of 'keeping up' in the art world for all kinds of reasons (Dźuverovič and Revell, 2020). Whilst engendering these new demands on the curator's embodied presence – from *presenting* to *being present* – the notion of the *embodied curator* also produces a significant opportunity to re-think curating on a scale that is commensurate with human bodies, their capacities, needs and desires – a format that allows autonomy for the curator to work within and beyond institutions, and might be applicable to an array of other situations that share a live, social material.

Notes

1 Two recent examples include John Burtle and Elena Mann's text score collection *Propositional Attitudes*, and the currently touring *Soundings: An Exhibition in Five Parts*, co-curated by Candice Hopkins and Dylan Robinson, which asks, 'How can a score be a call and tool for decolonization?'
2 I discuss this work with the Oliveros score, and give a more detailed historical account of the *Womens Work* project in a forthcoming article (Revell 2022).
3 There are of course exceptions to be made here too, notably the case of artist-led institutions more generally, and in particular, certain histories within conceptual art.
4 Contributors to the two issues: Beth Anderson, Ruth Anderson, Jacki Apple, Barbara Benary, Sari Dienes, Nye Ffarrabas (participating as Bici Forbes), Simone Forti, Wendy Greenberg, Heidi Von Gunden, Françoise Janicot, Alison Knowles, Christina Kubisch, Carol Law, Annea Lockwood (also included as Anna Lockwood), Mary Lucier, Lisa Mikulchik, Ann Noël (included as Ann Williams), Pauline Oliveros, Takako Saito, Carolee Schneemann, Mieko Shiomi, Elaine Summers, Carole Weber, Julie Winter and Marilyn Wood
5 The Women's Ensemble was founded by Pauline Oliveros at University of California, San Diego, and met weekly in her home in the early 1970s with some public participatory performances. Sonic Arts Union was a touring multimedia performance group

comprising Mary Ashley, Robert Ashley, David Behrman, Shigeko Kubota, Barbara Lloyd, Alvin Lucier, Mary Lucier and Gordon Mumma. Sounds Out of Silent Spaces was a group founded by Phil Corner and Julie Winter which hosted performances of members' group works in 1970s New York. Experimental Intermedia Foundation is a space and non-profit organisation founded in the late 1960s in New York.

6 Here I would like to posit a connection to curator and theorist Bridget Crone's notion of the 'sensible stage', with its insistence on separation and immersion at once, with an inherent reflexivity (Crone 2013).

7 Not least as the works in question are text scores that are almost all in the English language, though in one workshop in Paris this advantage was overturned by a consensual decision to conduct the discussions in French, putting me, with my far-from-fluent French, suddenly at a disadvantage.

Bibliography

Amaral, Heloisa. 2020. "Producing Situations: How Performer-Curators Are Rethinking Roles and Formats." *OnCurating*, 44: 23–30.

Balzer, David. 2015. *Curationism: How Curating Took Over the Art World and Everything Else*. London: Pluto Press.

Barad, Karen. 2007. *Meeting the Universe Halfway: Quantum Physics and the Entanglement of Matter and Meaning*. Durham, NC: Duke University Press.

Boudry, Pauline, and Renate Lorenz. 2013. *To Valerie Solanas and Marilyn Monroe in Recognition of Their Desperation*. Installation with Super 16mm film/HD, 18 mins.

Burtle, John, and Elena Mann, eds. 2018. *Propositional Attitudes*. Los Angeles, CA: Golden Spike Press.

Cage, John, and Alison Knowles, eds. 1969. *Notations*. New York: Something Else Press.

Crone, Bridget. 2013. "Curating, Dramatization and the Diagram." In *The Curatorial: A Philosophy of Curating*, edited by Jean Paul Martinon, 207–213. London: Bloomsbury.

Džuverović, Lina. 2020. "Is The Honeymoon Over? The Tumultuous Love Affair between the Museum and the Arts of Sound." *Circuit: musiques contemporaines*, 30, 1: 11–23.

Džuverović, Lina, and Irene Revell. 2020. "Lots of Shiny Junk at the Art Dump: The Sick and Unwilling Curator." *Parse*, 9. http://parsejournal.com/article/lots-of-shiny-junk-at-the-art-dump-the-sick-and-unwilling-curator/.

Folkerts, Hendrik. 2017. "Hendrik Folkerts – Keeping Score: Notation, Embodiment, and Liveness." Recorded 11 September 2017 at Villa Romana, Florence. Audio 49:56. Radio Papesse. https://radiopapesse.org/en/archive/lectures/hendrik-folkerts-keeping-score.

Giovando, Chiara, Andrea Lissoni, Fionn Meade, and Eric Namour. 2017. *Making Room For Sound*. Interview by Michelle Fiedler. Mexico City, Mexico: Buró-Buró.

Kim, Rebecca Y. 2013. "A United Front: John Cage and the Foundation's First Decade." In *Artists for Artists: Fifty Years of the Foundation for Contemporary Arts*, edited by Eric Banks, 60–81. New York: Foundation for Contemporary Arts.

Knowles, Alison, and Annea Lockwood, eds. 1975. *Womens Work*, 1. New York: self-published.

Knowles, Alison, and Annea Lockwood, eds. 1978. *Womens Work*, 2. New York: self-published.

Kotz, Liz. 2007. *Words To Be Looked At: Language in 1960s Art*. Cambridge, MA: MIT Press.

Leach, Mary Jane. 2017. "In Conversation with Frances Morgan." *Kammer Klang*, Café Oto, London, 5 December.

Lockwood, Annea. 2017. "You Look at a Score, You Do It." Interview by Irene Revell. *Cesura//Acceso*, 2: 118–126.

Martinon, Jean Paul, ed. 2013. *The Curatorial: A Philosophy of Curating*. London: Bloomsbury.

McKeon, Ed. 2021. "Making Art Public: The Curatorial as Musical Praxis." PhD dissertation, Birmingham City University.

McRobbie, Angela. 2015. "Is Passionate Work a Neoliberal Delusion?". *Open Democracy*, 22 April. www.opendemocracy.net/en/transformation/is-passionate-work-neoliberal-delusion/.

Morgan, Frances. 2018. "Review (On Site) of *Orgasmic Streaming Organic Gardening Electroculture*." *The Wire*, 415: 81.

Oliveros, Pauline. 1970. *To Valerie Solanas and Marilyn Monroe in Recognition of their Desperation*. Baltimore, MD: Smith Publications.

Revell, Irene. 2022. "Speculating on the Feminist Performance Score: Pauline Oliveros, *Womens Work* and Karen Barad." In *Performing Indeterminacy*. Cambridge, UK: forthcoming special issue of Contemporary Music Review.

Voegelin, Salomé. 2019. *The Political Possibility of Sound*. London: Bloomsbury.

7

TEJUCUPAPO WOMEN

Sound mangrove bodies and performance creation

Luciana Lyra

Warning-manifesto

This text was woven with the fabric of performative writing (Lyra 2020) and consists of a documentational intention and a poetic-literary aspiration, immersed in an artistic-academic investigation that has subjectivity as its compass. Penned from a first-person point of view, the text plays with the writing, a *collage* of impressions and experiences, a juxtaposition of images that unveils my artist-researcher self. This is reflected by the deep dive that occurred when I immersed myself within the acting style of the performers of the community theater of Tejucupapo, a small district in the North Forest of Pernambuco, Brazil. There I absorbed its unique kaleidoscope of bodies and sounds.

It is important to highlight that the hybrid writing style of this chapter, elaborated under the sign of performance, is intimately linked to what I have experienced. It introduces new methodological designs disconnected from common models that constitute formal academic structures under the rule of rationalist, patriarchal, white, heteronormative thinking.

Over the red thread of time that articulates the year 2011, when I completed my PhD in Performing Arts,[1] which relied heavily on my experience in Tejucupapo, and the year 2020, when I can still hear the echoes of that fundamental experience, I developed an autonomous writing style. This allowed me to emancipate myself as an artist-researcher and guided me towards the backyards, the *terreiros*,[2] the ancestors, and the Other, creating friction between art and life and legitimizing authorial voices.

This chapter is divided into sections named after terms from music and literature, indicating its transdisciplinary nature. Composed of a prelude, three movements, an interlude, and an epilogue, it also presents three important concepts elaborated after my initial experience in Tejucupapo: *artethnography*, *mythodology in art*, and *f(r)iction*

DOI: 10.4324/9781003008217-10

artist. Experienced as practices in the performing arts, here they work as dynamos for the creation of bodies and sounds.

Tejucupapo in prelude

The mangrove forest lies sunken in nature's womb. Half earth, half sea, tidal waters in motion, tropical humidity, submerged. Among the standing dense tangle of roots reaching for the sun, lagoons, inlets, a mouth of brackish muddy waters, saline soil of decomposing matter, a world of essential activity going on silently and voluntarily below ground to support a portion of our planet.

Feet dive into that womb, calloused hands grasp its roots, making it hard to distinguish what is hand, what is forest. Armed with small knives, women harvest oysters that feed hungry bellies. They go about their daily offering ritual in silence, bearing the triple oppression of gender, race, and social class on their bodies. One can hear the sounds of those famished stomachs building tunes with each stroke of the *pandeiro*[3] and the *ganza*[4] that move hips and create strong beats in the *terreiro*.

There is a place where the ecosystem still prevails, where the beach becomes mud. That place is called Tejucupapo, where, symbolically, my mother and perhaps all mothers were born. I am made from this mud, black as earth. I am elusive. Every thought, every day, takes me back to Tejucupapo, to the swamp where these women came from. My ancestry, women made out of *tejucu*,[5] their thick hair intermingled with a horse's mane, their legs spread apart over the animal's back like amazons (Felinto 1992). Their strength comes directly from nature.

Tejucupapo is an estuary of female power, a battlefield and a place of struggle in Goiana, Pernambuco, Brazil. This is where, during the Dutch occupation of the Brazilian Northeast region, which lasted from 1630 to 1654, a conflict that became known as the Battle of Tejucupapo took place. It was the first known conflict in Brazilian history with female participation, an episode with almost no documentation, excluded from official accounts. Armed with sticks, stones, and chili pepper water, the women of Tejucupapo subdued their Dutch enemies, creating the

FIGURE 7.1 Tejucupapo mangrove forest, 2007
Source: Author's private collection.

FIGURE 7.2 Dona Biu de Vinuca, an oyster gatherer from Tejucupapo, working, 2008
Source: Author's private collection.

mythical image of the female warrior in the region, an image that has stood the test of time and spread through space.

It was there that in the 1990s, Luzia Maria da Silva, a nursing assistant at the community health center, along with other women of the village, turned the fight of their ancestors into restored history through theater. She wrote and directed a play called *A Batalha das Heroínas* (The Battle of the Heroines), having the women of this small district in the North Forest of Pernambuco as protagonists, "actresses" cast among housewives, civil servants, farmers, and oyster and shellfish gatherers. In the theatrical production, they bring their own lives to light (Bezerra 2004).

By way of the theatrical version of the 1646 battle, performed from 1993 to 2019, everything that is rustic, poor, and rural becomes admirable, fierce, and utopian, and emerges at Monte das Trincheiras (Trenches Mountain), where the 16th-century heroines defeated their enemies, now a performing stage. The village's old town trembles with the dance, bodies, gestures, gaze, sounds, noises, smells, tastes, extravagance, ruins, and vertigo of the play. Between rehearsals and performances all through the month of April, destitute women take the lead in their ancestors' fight, being fueled by their masks and offering these same masks the possibility of a new magical incantation through their performance.

In 2006, after going through a performing experience with the myth of Joan of Arc, the heroine, getting an MA in Performing Arts from UNICAMP in 2005, and reading *Tejucupapo: História, Teatro, Cinema* (Tejucupapo: History, Theater, Film) (Bezerra 2004), I came across the women of that district in Goiana and quickly identified similarities between my performance of Joan of Arc and *A Batalha das Heroínas*. This close connection seemed to have three aspects in common: both plays shared the same basis, the myth of the female warrior; performing experiences articulated both past and present through imagery; and the actors' masks had an eminent individual, self-referring origin.

Artethnography in three movements and an interlude
Movement I: Sounds and bodies of the mangrove forest

I arrived in Tejucupapo for my first *artethnographic*[6] field action as a researcher on April 27, 2007. The sun had opened its eyes early in the morning to take me to the edge of the mangrove forest where my generous guides were waiting. They had been summoned by Dona Luzia days before. At the harbor, at a distance that did not seem that great, I could see the twisted trunks that formed the bottom and constituted those muddy waters of a slightly dark green. Suddenly, when I looked over the vegetation, I was somewhat startled. Between sunbeams, shadows, and the majestic sound of the wind, I caught a glimpse of three women beneath monumental coconut trees with basins on their heads and a little girl in their arms. They also carried buckets in their hands and oars on their shoulders like crosses. They were the women of the mangrove forest, humming softly a song that I could not recognize.

Dona Zinha, the oldest of them, had a deep, firm voice and seemed to stare at me through slits. I could not look at her directly. I kept turning away, but wanting to find her gaze. Her birth name was Maria do Carmo, and she was a beautiful black lady who walked barefoot, had a scarf on her head, and possessed a silent wisdom. Her rough hands would guide me through the mangrove forest of Tejucupapo. Labyrinthine hands, marked by the sun and time, pointed the way through the twists of the vegetation. More energetic and talkative, Ediana, or Mo, Dona Zinha's daughter, introduced me to the magical universe of the mangrove forest with youthful joy. She was the one who told me about the local fauna and flora, the one who carried Vitoria, the little girl, in her arms. Vitoria, or India, was 3 years old and liked inviting me into the tide. Speaking seemed very difficult for her. Nonetheless, she would break into invented songs from time to time.

Nuca came right behind her sister Mo. Both were almost the same age. Her birth name was Edilene, and she was exceptionally pretty. Although she had a stern disposition, her beauty called attention for its unusual balance. She had an interesting combination of both harsh and fine features that gave her a roughly delicate air. She was also said to be India's mother, even more so than her sister. Nuca's green eyes resembled a battlefield. Her black skin glistened in the sun, a black skin of strong contrast. She did not talk much, but when she did, she was always firm.

From the harbor where they were all waiting, I could see the strong torso of a 16-year-old boy immersed in the tidal waters. Dona Zinha called him over. He was another of her children. Although his birth name was Evandro, everybody called him Neguinho due to his boyish perkiness and his dark skin. He was the one who brought the boat to the shore, propelling it for the slow journey. The boat, called "Heroínas" (Heroines), now carried our small group of women. The women of Tejucupapo slowly unveiled the interior of the mangrove forest with the rhythmic sound of the oars in the water. The calm, dark tide of mud seemed to keep secrets

FIGURE 7.3 Tejucupapo mangrove forest and oyster gatherers, 2008
Source: Author's private collection.

and mysteries that the *pescadeiras*, the gatherers themselves, kept, the same way they cultivated oysters and shellfish which would feed them and their families. The mangrove forest seemed to be like a mother to them, welcoming them by reaffirming the power of nature for their livelihood, and at the same time, moving away, showing them how firm, hard, and cutting it could also be. Researcher Maria Angélica Freire, for example, observed that for the *pescadeiras*:

> The mangrove forest is like heaven and hell at the same time. It is just like heaven due to the fact that, when push comes to shove, it presents all its nourishment possibilities and serves as a meeting spot where friends and acquaintances can forget about their lives of poverty and hardships for a moment and share a little of themselves with each other. It is also just like hell because they consider their work repulsive and leave their vanity behind to deal with all the filth and smell of the mud. In the end, after three hours of hard labor, the final product is sold for an extremely low price.
>
> *Freire (2000, p. 45)*

Unexpectedly, Dona Zinha burst out of her silence, making me leave my own thoughts behind. Her voice warned me that everything in Tejucupapo begins and ends in the mud of the mangrove forest. According to her grandmother, the Dutch reached the village through a path under the swamp, digging a tunnel straight there from the Fort of Itamaracá.[7] The women rejected those men and made them go back to where they had come from, from the mangrove forest to the sea.

I was moved by the connection of those women with the mangrove forest. Images were powerful and important to them, giving them a bodily, palpable, material outline. The mangrove was alive and told stories, moving them at the core of their bodies. Geographically speaking, mangrove forests serve as nurseries for the sea, where several marine and estuarine species reproduce and develop. These are different forests; they are forged in an environment with a combination of salt and fresh water, protected from sea waves, and grown on soft and muddy soil.

The mangrove forest is a transition between water and dry land. It is drenched by numerous small canals every day, flooded loudly by the tides. It was as if the mangrove forest nourished those women, feeding them their physical and imaginary meal. They had a strong bond with the swamp, with its murky water, its twisted, tangled roots. It was as if they were merged in nature, like root-bodies involved and invaded by mother-water, grounded on the muddy soil, in a permanent and integrating process that made them heroines who beat their own war drums.

I was deeply immersed in my watery thoughts when Dona Zinha announced we were returning to the harbor. I was startled by the sound of birds chirping at the end of the afternoon. I did not know what time it was nor what part of the mangrove forest we were in; on each side, the vegetation looked the same in its natural variation. I was certain that I had lived in extended time during the trip through the insides of Tejucupapo and taken a mythical journey lulled by the sweet music of silence, murmurs of women and children, water sounds, and animal noises, one that I would take on many other occasions after that.

Movement II: Sounds and bodies of the festivities

Epiphany, January 6, 2008. Kings night. Almost 8 o'clock at night. Several people were waiting in a *terreiro* in Tejucupapo. About an hour before, people started gathering there. I had just arrived, guided by Zinho, an openly gay young *pai de santo* of Umbanda, Dona Luzia's right-hand assistant in the planning of the district's cultural events.

Dona Luzia was already positioned next to the musicians, talking to the local people with her grandson Gabriel on her lap. In front of the musicians, boys and young men danced in a separate group, following the strong rhythm. Suddenly, with the change of pace, the oldest women formed a circle and started a *ciranda*, followed by the stomping and clapping of *coco de roda*. Dona Luzia observed quietly. Since she had joined the Evangelical Church,[8] she did not dance, drink or party anymore; she just planned and produced the events.

Ciranda and *coco de roda*, dance and music that are part of the June festivities in Brazil,[9] are performed throughout the year in Tejucupapo, including during the period right before Carnival. These manifestations have always been part of celebrations in the colonial-era sugar cane mills of the area. It is said that the enslaved people used to huddle in the *senzalas*, big houses where the enslaved Africans were grouped together, and dance by thrusting their navels back and forth while clapping. These movements followed the sound of the drums, the *ganzas*,

FIGURE 7.4 Women of Tejucupapo backstage during *A Batalha das Heroínas* (2008)
Source: Author's private collection.

FIGURE 7.5 *Ciranda* music and dance in Tejucupapo, 2008
Source: Author's private collection.

and the high pitches of women's chants, and displayed a type of sensuality that resembled the coming and going of the tides, the movements of the daily grind in the farms and mills, and the ancestry of African music and dance.

After almost an hour of *ciranda* and *coco*, the small crowd grew around the musicians. I saw men, women, and children of all ages watching the dancers, chatting among themselves or simply wandering around, enjoying beverages and typical dishes, especially those made from corn and cassava. The full moon was shining in the night sky while I was having fun with the community, dancing and trying to keep up with the verses of the nearly unintelligible songs.

Dona Luzia was a strong supporter of local dance and music manifestations, of which *A Batalha das Heroínas* was the most important. The play existed not only due to the unique drive of the community leader who had turned the story into a theatrical production, but also because a warrior spirit animated that leader and reverberated within other local women in a collective experience, reaffirming the need for traditional manifestations. *Ciranda* and *coco de roda*, led by female *mestras* (masters),[10] also promoted a thriving experience. Hand in hand, stomping their feet on the floor and joining their navels, those women exorcised the evil spirits of domestic violence and social neglect, giving their gender a new meaning.

To gaze into history and theater, as I did in Tejucupapo, taking part in the traditional manifestations of the village, implies establishing an important relationship, especially when examining the textuality of those manifestations through their images, movements, and sounds. To that extent, it is a matter of understanding that community theatrical fact as an extensive and complex network of dynamic and

FIGURE 7.6 *Coco* in Tejucupapo, 2008
Source: Author's private collection.

multiple relationships that moves through and overflows from history in splendid diversity. Through *A Batalha das Heroínas* and other traditional manifestations in Tejucupapo, metaphors, allegories, and other elements come together to concoct a significant landscape, articulating a way of thinking and acting, a worldview, and its numerous historiographies.

Movement III: Sounds and bodies of the theater

April 29, 2009. That afternoon, framed by an unexpected rainbow, I witnessed the beautiful and rustic *A Batalha das Heroínas* in a state of *participant observation*, in line with Wacquant (2002).[11] I realized that I was watching a production that could be described as a direct heir of the theater of the people, which could be called a *theater of the margins*, that is, one that is not part of an official and privileged art circuit.

A familiar voice came out of the speakers. It was Dona Luzia's recorded voice that narrated the episode of the battle of Tejucupapo with some epic music in the background. While the recording played, the action took place according to markings that had been carefully defined during rehearsals that had happened throughout the entire month.

Farmworkers cleared the bush while women began selling shellfish, oysters, and coconut *pixaim*,[12] just as they do in everyday life. At a surprising moment, a horse neighed and took over the scene, with a man on its back announcing that the Dutch had just arrived in the district, going back in time with that performance.

Gunshots, lines, screams, and resounding music constituted the landscape of sounds of the 50-minute play that unfolded under the open sky. Over the layer of sounds, characters from the distant 17th century were impersonated by local women. However, those personifications did not seem to equate to the incarnation of a fictional mask or the embodiment of a character, as researcher Maria Angélica Freire (2000, p. 22) states:

> Particularly the women who embody crucial historical figures in the fight against the Dutch, such as Maria Camarão, report that when they are about to go on stage, they are overwhelmed with such emotion that they feel like the historical figures themselves, their ancestors. They feel as if they embody their spirits.

In the midst of this network of knowledge, Richard Schechner (1985, p. 4) discusses how performers of different ritual experiences and theatrical traditions do not try to hide their bodies behind masks. The transformation that audience and performers go through is deeply connected to a relation between masks and bodies that is capable of producing a liminal state. Through masks, the women of Tejucupapo perform their own history/story in a poetic manner, ritualizing themselves. What is uncovered behind, below, and above the masks may be extraordinary.

In fact, in *A Batalha das Heroínas*, the acting is not similar to that of traditional theater; it is more like consecutive transformations, open to the possibility of actors

FIGURE 7.7 *A Batalha das Heroínas* (2007)
Source: Author's private collection.

leaving their masks and resuming their own social personalities, using the masks of the play as motivating forces in their daily lives. According to Freire (2000, p. 22):

> In everyday experience, the reality of Tejucupapo has shown us how the woman who was visited and praised by D. Pedro II on December 7th, 1859 continues to guide the community. Not even the lack of formal education, extreme poverty, and lack of opportunities can wane the fighting spirit of those local women. Some of them believe that their strength comes from the blood of Maria Camarão that runs through their veins, the great heroine of the battle of Trincheiras.

From that perspective, the acting process of *A Batalha das Heroínas* is based on the ritualization of the particularities of the actors and the development of their personal and social skills, not on the performance of fictional roles. As reasserted by Carlos Carvalho, a stage director from Pernambuco:

> There, theater plays a social role and serves as an element to promote education. The theatrical production of Tejucupapo is essential for that society to understand itself. They talk about their own lives. The citizen-artists adapt and play their own history on stage.
>
> *quoted in Bezerra (2004, p. 64)*

When the performers experience the lives of female warriors in *A Batalha das Heroínas*, I assume that they act as *f(r)iction artists*, that is, they perform in the gaps between what is fiction and what is real, between themselves and the characters, their bodies in constant flow and transformation, reverberating several experiences, thus creating the possibility of a social action that could bring change, switching between the self and its counterparts. Researcher John Dawsey (2005), who has coined the term *f(r)iction* in the field of the Anthropology of Performance (Turner 1988), reminds us that the performers in social rites go into:

> a subjunctive way ("as if") of placing oneself in relation to the world, causing clefts, shedding light on the fictional dimensions of what is real, and subverting the effects of reality of a world that is seen in an indicative mood, not as moving landscape, full of possibilities, but just as it is.
>
> *Dawsey (2005, p. 170)*

Interlude

Between that first contact in 2007, when I could hear the loud sounds of the nature of Tejucupapo, the festivities of 2008, and the experience with the local community theater in 2009, I took several other field trips to the area over a five-year period. Those journeys led me to put together an orchestra of sounds that evoked the women of Tejucupapo, their work in the inlets, their festivities, their bodies in motion, and their theater.

My experience with numerous artistic activities in the community and my studies in the Anthropology of Performance and the Anthropology of the Imaginary (Durand 1990) inspired me to strengthen the concept of *f(r)iction artist* discussed earlier, as well as to develop the concept of *artethnography*, which serves as a device that promotes interaction between artists and communities. These communities are defined based on the personal dynamics of the artists in the creation process (Lyra 2013, p. 33).

Artethnography empowers the imagination of a common collective *ethos* capable of transforming, reinforcing, or even breaking ties of unity, allowing groups to reconstitute their identities by experiencing stories about themselves in a kind of collective autobiography, which necessarily stems from particular echoes and drives within the artists.

Inspired by my relationship with the women of Tejucupapo, I wrote and produced a play called *Guerreiras* (Warriors) between 2009 and 2010. The play was a collaborative endeavor with the actresses who traveled to the community with me several times. Intimately woven into *Guerreiras* was the music of Alessandra Leão,[13] which mirrored the fieldwork/ethnographic experience. The musician reminds us that:

> To create the soundtrack, I based my compositions on the sounds of the drums, *bombos, ganzas* and voices of the *coco*, the *cavalo marinho* and the *ciranda*, typical manifestations of the North Forest of Pernambuco, leaving some

room for some "new" rhythms of the region, such as *brega*. But what would these songs discuss? What would these women say? Days in Tejucupapo, days of conversations, mangroves, many realities, several different times, endless stories. Days in Recife and São Paulo. Days with the actresses, many other stories, myths, legends, natural sounds, images, objects, shapes... Themes started emerging, *Guerreiras* began revealing itself, voice, text, movement. The soundtrack tries to serve the plot in a way that is closely related to each character and the mythology behind them.

Alessandra Leão, quoted in Lyra (2010, pp. 28–29)

Still on the creation of the soundtrack, the music director adds:

It was not difficult to engage in exchanges for the creation of the soundtrack, because that is how I usually work; I base my work on themes. But it was challenging, because that is not a traditional way to create soundtracks. Going to Tejucupapo was a turning point for me. The elements of the soundtrack have a lot to do with the imaginary of the community.

Alessandra Leão, quoted in Lyra (2010, pp. 28–29)

Considering Ryngaert's perspective (1998, pp. 69–70), in *Guerreiras*, the ties between lines, music, images and movements connected the text to contemporary ideas of playwriting. In a close dialogue between music and sound, theatrical conventions of a realistic nature were broken, pushing back the limits of what is "representable" and promoting greater freedom and abstraction.

FIGURE 7.8 *Guerreiras* (2010), written and directed by Luciana Lyra, showing actresses Viviane Madu, Simone Evaristo, Cris Rocha, Katia Daher, and Luciana Lyra on stage

Source: Author's private collection.

FIGURE 7.9 *Guerreiras* (2010), written and directed by Luciana Lyra, showing actresses Katia Daher and Viviane Madu on stage

Source: Author's private collection.

During the writing/staging of *Guerreiras*, *artethnography* found a privileged place in the invocation of polyphonic and fragmentary universes, typical of the activity of the community in nature and in its theatrical production, which does not consider the text as the main mediator of meaning. Naturally, I understand writing/staging as an inseparable pair within the creation process of *Guerreiras*:

> The materialization of the crossroads proposed by the text took place on the stage. The text, in turn, was produced based on the crossroads of performed actions. Like the ouroboros, the process was translated into the continuity between text and staging, self-fertilization. *Guerreiras* was translated into a performative text, that is, one that is originated by the performance itself, while creating it and making it possible.
>
> *Lyra (2011, p. 152)*

Artethnography does not look for cultural authenticity nor attention to the technical details that form a kind of cultural grammar that tries to interpret symbols. The writing of the experience, in the field, manifested itself in the performance (writing/staging) of *Guerreiras*, which is why it is intrinsically uncertain, partial and incomplete.

Epilogue: Network of practices for performance creation

My experience with *Guerreiras* and my observations in my PhD and postdoctoral research gave rise to several performances between 2010 and 2020. All of them were based on a network of practices that ended up stimulating the shaping of what I call a *f(r)iction artist*. *Artethnography* led to the development of another creative practice related to it, *mythology in art*.

Mythodology in art is a group of ritual and existential games that fuels the theater. I ended up experimenting with it on pedagogical processes at the universities I work at (the State University of Rio de Janeiro, the State University of Santa Catarina, and the Federal University of Rio Grande do Norte), as well as in the context of art and theater companies and collectives in a number of cities throughout Brazil.

In another work, I argue that *mythodology in art* is an heir of Durand's idea of mythology. It is the result of an *artethnographic* experience, a possible avenue for the artists to throw themselves at the *f(r)iction* between life and art in the investigation of the soul, beginning with themselves, to animate the world. Myths are fundamental. Elements of the *mythodology in art*, they open the questions of life to personal and culturally imaginative critical thinking. They mitigate the desire to get to know the other without getting to know the self and promote the understanding that the main obstacle to get know the other is exactly the anxious and fearful desire to meet him/her (Lyra 2015, p. 18).

More than an attempt to implement a method, the work with *mythodology in art* reveals intentions of the contemporary thought to reestablish image and myth as propelling springs of self-recognition. It also acknowledges performance as a ritual way of manifesting these images as incentive to a theater that is committed to restore the role of myths in the world.

After *Guerreiras* (2009–2010), I wrote and directed several plays, such as *Homens e Caranguejos* (Men and Crabs, 2012), *Salema* (Salema Porgy, 2012), *Obscena*

FIGURE 7.10 Actress Simone Evaristo in *Guerreiras* (2010)
Source: Author's private collection.

FIGURE 7.11 Scene from the play *Pour Louise ou a desejada virtude da resistência* (2016), direction and dramaturgy by Luciana Lyra

Source: Author's private collection.

(Obscene, 2015), *Cara da Mãe* (Their Mother's Face, 2015), *Fogo de Monturo* (Surprise Element, 2015), *Quarança* (2016), *Therèse* (2017), *Yriadobá* (2018), *A Bárbara* (The Barbarian, 2018), and *Bia Boa* (Nice Bia, 2019). They were all part of a group of writing/staging creations that drank from the *mythodology in art* fountain and were stirred up by *artethnographic* experiences, shedding light on matters which revolved around women, feminine archetypes, and feminisms that guide women's struggle in Brazil.

Heavily marked by music and the body, all the work mentioned above goes back to that initial experience in Tejucupapo in some way. In the creation process for these plays, sound and body dynamics tried to respond to the stimulus of games and rituals, as in the theater and traditional manifestations in Tejucupapo. The perspective of a game/play was the starting point for the bodies, which were lulled by the sounds of songs and drums that marked the pulsation of the movements with the rhythm.

In these productions, we defined the body as a physical structure that moved around with feet on the ground, rooting itself, forging a strong relationship with the ground, or as an affective structure that nurtured memories, exhibiting signs of symbolic nature and expressing its experience as a human being. We always looked at the movements of the body in this context. With *artethnography* in mind, we glanced at bodies within these creative processes that moved according to what affected them, not the other way around. In the creation of these productions, we experienced time – the time of waiting, immersing, listening, and being available to something outside ourselves, so that an experience could actually take place. The time to open ourselves and listen was always part of the process.

Tejucupapo women **107**

FIGURE 7.12 Scene from the play *Homens e Caranguejos* (2012), direction and dramaturgy by Luciana Lyra

Source: Author's private collection.

FIGURE 7.13 Scene from the play *Salema – sussurros dos afogados* (2012), direction by Luciana Lyra

Source: Author's private collection.

Like the women of Tejucupapo who took part in *coco* and *ciranda*, performing in unison with the environment, the sound, the movement, and the body, I tried to encourage the artists involved in the productions mentioned to work the response of their bodies to their themes and contexts, reverberating what affected and moved them, mirroring their personal and social experiences, fomenting acting through playfulness, not through planning and building a scene. This way, sounds and movements that made up the play emerged from a poetic experience of the body, which served as a platform for inventiveness, integration, and freedom.

In the sound manifestations and theatrical production of Tejucupapo, acting is a stage for experiences. On stage, sound bodies of the mangrove forest are transfigured. I tried following the lessons I learned with the community in my theater endeavors, encouraging artists to articulate themselves and their symbolic, memorial confluence, including an array of sounds shared in experiences in a context of otherness. In a continuous dialogue between the I and the other lies the intention to make the kind of transformative art that aims to promote change in everyone involved in a creative process, a performing art that serves as a meta-commentary on the hardships and conflicts of life and art, functioning as an interpretive reorganization of social and artistic experience.

In the rhythmic strokes of different times and spaces, I can hear the echoes of history and the women who weave it. I look at the past not to live it again, but to rediscover myself and reinvent the present. I am taken back to Tejucupapo, to the battle against the Dutch, to the theatrical production of that community and everything that has sprung from it. I am led to a world of possibilities, knowing that I am whole and carrying both a warrior and a sweet woman inside me. *You shall pass, you shall pass, and our flag shall stay!*

Notes

1 PhD in Performing Arts, completed in 2011 at the State University of Campinas, in São Paulo, Brazil. Under the title *Guerreiras e Heroínas em Performance: Da Artetnografia à Mitodologia em Artes Cênicas* (Female Warriors and Heroines in Performance: From *Artethnography* to *Mythodology* in the Performing Arts), the research was supervised by Professor John Dawsey of the University of São Paulo and funded by the São Paulo Research Foundation.
2 A wide dirt area outdoors where traditional celebrations take place.
3 A percussion musical instrument consisting of a wooden frame with goat or synthetic skin stretched over a rim holding metal jingles. It is widely used in a number of Brazilian music and dance forms.
4 A percussion musical instrument used in samba and other Brazilian music styles. It is a type of rattle, consisting of a metal or plastic cylindrical tube filled with sand, cereal grains, or small beads.
5 The mud that constitutes the mangrove forest in Tejucupapo, Pernambuco, Brazil.
6 Related to the concept of *artethnography* developed by Luciana Lyra. *Artethnography* is the complex intertwining between artists and contexts of otherness, so that this polyphonic interweaving of experiences fuels the performance.
7 A beach on the north coast of Pernambuco, Brazil.
8 Tejucupapo is a *quilombo* area, an old community settlement founded by escaped enslaved Africans in colonial Brazil. The area was also home for indigenous people in the past. Due to that fact, many artistic traditional forms descending from these groups arose in the region. They were historically colonized by the Catholic Church, and by the

Evangelical Church later on. In suppressing behaviors of non-white bodies and their cultural, creative, and traditional activities, the Catholic Church and the Evangelical Church have deemed them minor and negative.

9 In a large part of Brazil, as the Northeast region of the country, traditional manifestations are grouped in three cycles of festivities: Carnival, June, and Christmas. June festivities are in line with the winter solstice for the Southern Hemisphere, the longest night of the year. It is a way to celebrate the natural cycle and organize the community for the end of a time and the beginning of another with a new crop.
10 In the Brazilian Northeast area, artistic traditional manifestations, such as *cavalo marinho*, *maracatu-rural*, and *pastoril*, are led by men, whereas *ciranda* and *coco de roda* are led by women.
11 The method adopted by ethnographer Loïc Wacquant creates the possibility of a "participant observation", in which the observer becomes an experimenter, while experimentation turns into a means to observation. It is also an attempt to capture and restore the dimension of the body, commonly deemed secondary in investigations, to the theoretical and methodological level.
12 A typical local dish.
13 Alessandra Leão is a composer, singer, and percussionist from Pernambuco, one of the founding members of Comadre Fulozinha. Since 2006, she has launched her successful solo career and released several solo albums. In 2019, she released the album *Macumbas e Catimbós*, nominated for the Latin Grammy. See www.alessandraleao.com.br/.

Bibliography

Bezerra, Cláudio (ed.). 2004. *Tejucupapo: História, Teatro, Cinema*. Recife, Brazil: Editora Bagaço.
Dawsey, John Cowart. 2005. Victor Turner e Antropologia da Experiência. *Cadernos do Campo* 14, 13, pp. 163–176, 2005. DOI: 10.11606/issn.2316-9133.v13i13p163-176. Available at: https://repositorio.usp.br/item/001514226. Accessed 31 August 2021.
Durand, Gilbert. 1990. *Mito, Símbolo e Mitodologia*. Lisbon, Portugal: Editorial Presença.
Felinto, Marilene. 1992. *Mulheres de Tijucopapo*. Rio de Janeiro, Brazil: Editora Nova Fronteira.
Freire, Maria Angélica Almeida de Miranda. 2000. *Associação Heroínas de Tejucopapo*. Final paper, Graduate Certificate in Association and Cooperative Movements. Recife, Brazil: Federal Rural University of Pernambuco.
Lyra, Luciana. 2010. *Guerreiras: Texto Teatral e Trilha Sonora Original*. Recife, Brazil: Brascolor editora.
Lyra, Luciana. 2017. *Dramaturgia Feminista: Fogo de Monturo & Quarança*. São Paulo, Brazil: Giostri Editora.
Lyra, Luciana de F. R. P. de. 2005. *Mito Rasgado: Performance e Cavalo Marinho na Cena in Processo*. Thesis for Master in Arts. Campinas, Brazil: Art Institute, State University of Campinas.
Lyra, Luciana de F. R. P. de. 2011. *Guerreiras e Heroínas em Performance: Da Artetnografia à Mitodologia em Artes Cênicas*. Dissertation, PhD in Arts. Campinas, Brazil: Art Institute, State University of Campinas.
Lyra, Luciana de F. R. P. de. 2013. Da Artetnografia: Máscara-Mangue em Duas Experiências Performáticas. Report, Postdoctoral Fellowship in Anthropology. São Paulo, Brazil: University of São Paulo (unpublished).
Lyra, Luciana de F. R. P. de. 2014. Artetnografia e Mitodologia em Arte: Práticas de Fomento ao Ator de F(r)icção. *Urdimento – Revista de Estudos em Artes Cênicas* 1, 22, pp. 167–180.

Lyra, Luciana de F. R. P. 2015. Mitodologia em Arte no Cultivo do Trabalho do Ator: Uma Experiência de F(r)icção. Report, Postdoctoral Fellowship in Performing Arts. Natal, Brazil: Federal University of Rio Grande do Norte (unpublished).

Lyra, Luciana de F. R. P. 2020. Escrita Acadêmica Performática … Escrita F(r)iccional: Pureza e Perigo. *Urdimento – Revista de Estudos em Artes Cênicas* 2, 38, pp. 1–13. DOI: 10.5965/14145731023820200033. Available at: www.revistas.udesc.br/index.php/urdimento/article/view/17759. Accessed 31 August 2021.

Ryangaert, Jean-Pierre. 1998. *Ler o Teatro Contemporâneo*. São Paulo, Brazil: Martins Fontes.

Schechner, Richard. 1985. *Between Theater and Anthropology*. Philadelphia, PA: University of Pennsylvania Press.

Schechner, Richard. 2002. *Performance Studies: An Introduction*. New York: Routledge.

Turner, Victor. 1988. *The Anthropology of Performance*. New York: PAJ Books.

Van Gennep, Arnold. 2006. *Os Ritos de Passagem*. Petrópolis, Brazil: Editora Vozes.

Wacquant, Loïc. 2002. *Corpo e Alma: Notas Etnográficas de um Aprendiz de Boxe*. Rio de Janeiro, Brazil: Relume Dumará.

PART III

New Methodologies in Sound Art and Performance Practice

8
LOOKING FOR SILENCE IN THE BODY

Ida Mara Freire

Body and Performance

> I clung to my anger for a long time – it was very hard to let go of – but when I began to give it up to the Silence around me, my fingers, as if of their own accord, began to weave. Like the girl in the story Arwhal had told me, in finding my own Silence I was finding my own power – of transformation. As I wove, I talked and laughed and sang; I cursed, and I swore. All to myself. And then I wove some more and came to understand how Silence could speak and be silent – how Silence could be filled with noise and also be still. And finally, I understood what Arwhal meant – that Silence does not always mean the absence of sound, because in all that sound – of my own voice – I was able to find and hear my own Silence. And I was ashamed – of how much I had resisted the wisdoms Arwhal had offered me in presenting me with a chance to find my own Silence.
>
> Philip (2003)

Weavers of Existence is a performance and an essay on freedom. This is a solo with a duration of approximately 25 minutes, created in 2013 at the same time as this chapter was originally written. A creative process involved four elements present in South African dance performances: dance, song, storytelling, and spirituality. The performance has already been presented several times in events in academic and artistic contexts: *Fazendo Gênero 10*, Merleau-Ponty in Florianópolis, Brazil; *II PIBID Theater National Meeting* – Uberlândia, Brazil; I Week of Black Awareness at Instituto Federal Catarinense, Rio do Sul; the *USP Conference in Physical Education and Sport*, session on "Body, Rite and Performance", Centro de Artes, Santa Catarina State University; and the exhibition *Web of Affections*. In this chapter, I interlace threads of the black women's lives that are tied to the thread of my life. With the free threads

FIGURE 8.1 One step
Source: Image by Marina Moros, 2013.

of Zezé Motta's[1] songs and of philosopher Hannah Arendt's[2] writings, I weave this text-existence. In reading the essays and poems of Marlene NourbeSe Philip, not only am I inspired to resist the bonds of cultural hegemony, but also to transcend them, creating possibilities of writing that links the dynamics of the speech with the dynamics of the action, to compose a text that is moved sometimes as dance through space, other times as a song, rhythm for the time.

In the search for the understanding of my existence, this is how writing happened: traces in space, traces of human landscapes, daily records in pencil and paper. But between not seeing and being seen – the difference experienced, studied whether in skin color, in the female condition, in the spiritual trajectory – became dance, word, and today is presented as a danced word. I dance, I write, I weave words with frayed threads of the flower of the womb of my ancestors, my great-grandmothers. I search my memories, and in the corporeal memory I decipher the pain, I find the root of the violence, I observe the fear, I distil the happiness, I decorate the sweetness, I dive in the peace, and I know the freedom. From this creative process, I begin again to investigate, to seek silence in my own body. But how did I get to that point?

I was writing the text *Weavers of Existence* to participate in a contest, *Black Women Tell Their Stories*, when words appeared on my body, asking for movement. My training in dance started when I was approximately 23 years old, and as soon as I finished my graduation I took jazz classes, workshops, and courses in theatre and somatic education offered in university extension projects. Then I started to practice Afro ballet in a private dance school, and auditioned for and started to participate in the African dance group Freedom, Song and Dance. Over these four decades, I have practiced and studied dance in its different systems, styles, and modalities. When working with contemporary dance, I have sought to research the codes of

FIGURE 8.2 The sound of silence
Source: Image by Silvana Macedo, 2019.

improvisation in traditional dances, for example: Arab dance, African dance, toyi-toyi, capoeira, flamenco, tango. This research has helped me to create dance with movements that come from an origin, a place, a people, marked by their history and experiences. To dance, I go to the yard, I need to walk, put my feet on the ground. I walk. The movement of walking requires rhythm, compass. Dance comes. It is not just any dance, it is toyi-toyi.

"Ukuzabalaza", popularly known as "umzabalazo", are the meanings of toyi-toyi in South African communities that signify "stand firm, refuse to give way or resist". In other words, it is a political dance that the apartheid government could not control. Present during national protests in the 1980s, it was accompanied by libertarian songs and shouts of political slogans. Over the years, toyi-toyi dance proliferated throughout the country and became more sophisticated, and developed with a varied number of steps and body movements. Toyi-toyi is danced in unison, with movements determined by words and rhythm. Dancers can raise their knees high, in a military style, or articulate them as in a ritual, depending on the song. Toyi-toyi was born as a movement that influences the community, becoming part of its culture and a political expression (Twala and Koetaan, 2006).

For the most oppressed black people in South African society, the melody of liberation songs and the dance of toyi-toyi become an important way to escape the harshness of life in the township. The repeated pace of toyi-toyi causes everyone to put out the toughness faced during the apartheid government. There are many toyi-toyi songs that deal with the emotions of individuals involved in the struggle for better living conditions. These songs illustrate and explain the situation in which people find themselves. When dancing toyi-toyi and chanting songs and slogans, they believe that their feelings are expressed.

Van Schalkwyk (quoted in Gray, 2004), a researcher on the themes of freedom songs, recalls that people participating in the liberation movement across South Africa, sang the same freedom songs, even though they were not familiar with the language of song. It is worth remembering that we are talking about a country with more than 96 native languages, of which 11 are official. The accompaniment of the song rhythm helped to unify the oppressed people and to provoke the apartheid government. As an Afro-Brazilian dancer living in Cape Town in 2011, I realized that as South African people danced toyi-toyi, they accessed the same information and communicated with the same performance.

During the performance of *Weavers of Existence*, I dance toyi-toyi. From my body in silence the word appears in my mouth as a song. I take a stone in my hand, I hide myself, I'm scared. But someone calls me. Come fight with us. I'm not alone. We are many girls, boys, black bodies. Listen to the song! We go, walk, march and dance, sing, pray, cry, beg. We listen to the song from our heart. How can I describe the voice that sings "Spread your wings over me, Lady Liberty?"[3] That song I repeat as a mantra at the bottom of my heart. The unmistakable voice of the singer and actress Zezé Motta, contralto, velvety, stuffed like the aloe vera leaf, curative, medicinal. Like your naked black body, free. One of the first black nudes I saw in the cinema. I mirrored her small breasts, recognized mine. I learned to be free, as well, in the nakedness of my being. A voice that sings about freedom also sings about pain:

> I get this pain
> Or this pain must die
> The pain that teaches us
> And the desire not to have
> Suffer from more than anything
> We need to learn
> I scream and let go
> I need to learn
> Heal that tear or ignore any being
> I'm still cheating or cheating on my life
> Because when I'm in love it's like suffering
> I die of loves
> I need to learn
> I get this pain
> Or this pain has to die.
>
> Eu fico com essa dor
> Ou essa dor tem que morrer
> A dor que nos ensina
> E a vontade de não ter

Sofrer de mais que tudo
Nós precisamos aprender
Eu grito e me solto
Eu preciso aprender
Curo esse rasgo ou ignoro qualquer ser
Sigo enganado ou enganando meu viver
Pois quando estou amando é parecido com sofrer
Eu morro de amores
Eu preciso aprender.
"Dores de Amores", Luiz Melodia (1978)

In this chapter, I intend to describe how an unexpected phrase expressed during the performance impelled me to become a witness to those who can no longer use their own voice to express the pain.

Looking for Silence

Reading and studying the work of NourbeSe inspires me to pay attention to the words that inhabit the body. I met her in summer 2006 in Toronto, on a study trip where I attended the *World Dance Alliance Conference*. In writing to my wise friend Lera Philip, who lived in London at that time, I said that there was a lot of similarity between London and Toronto, and that only her gentle company was missing. She replied that she had a cousin in Toronto called NourbeSe. And few days after contacting NourbeSe, we met each other, and she with her generosity helped me to know a little about Canadian culture. And for me, the most important thing, at that moment, was when she presented me her work.

NourbeSe is an award-winning Afro-Caribbean writer. At the beginning of 2020, she won the PEN/Nabokov Award for International Literature. At first, what most caught my attention in her work was the fact that she shared an experience with silence in the Christian meditation tradition, which I was starting to practice at that time. But in her first email, she challenged me to find a sacred sound for everyone who is not a Christian. On 7 September 2006, she wrote:

> Ida:
>
> Greetings! How are you? Have you settled back in and are now back to classes? I did call you on your last day here, but you must have already left – that was the day when everything had gone crazy at the airports.
> It was such a pleasure meeting and talking with you. Lovely, indeed.
> Ida, I do think you should keep on working on find a word for those of us who aren't Christian. Maybe the orishas will help. I think it's important that we find a sacred sound that connects with that large force and that is not bound to Christianity, so do keep thinking and praying about it.

> Am about to leave for a couple of weeks to work on my poetry ms – will remain in Canada but am going to the Cornwall area-about 4 hours from Toronto.
>
> My best to you,
>
> NourbeSe
>
> "Art is not a mirror to reflect the world, but a hammer with which to shape it."
> Vladimir Mayakovsky

This was the first of many emails NourbeSe sent me. In this correspondence, we talked about personal, family, and professional projects, and on 18 January 2007, I wrote:

> NourbeSe,
>
> How are you, my dear friend? Many Thanks for your e-mail and words. I am here! Keeping on … Living in my new house, waiting my baby, enjoy the summer days. I am very glad to meet you. Maybe I back to Canada if I win the award from the embassy. This could be good, to have the opportunity to see you again. I hope everything is fine with you.
>
> Lot of Love,
>
> Ida

We exchanged information about our creative processes and study trips. On 22 January 2007, she wrote:

> Dearest Ida:
>
> How wonderful to hear from you. You have been in my mind, and I was going to be writing to you to wish you all the best for the New Year, but you beat me to it. I do hope you can make it back to Toronto because I would love to continue talking with you. I went to a dance conference held here this weekend gone – The International Association of Black Dance – IABD – I thought of you and your work on dance and the blind many many times. The next conference will be held in Texas next year, so maybe you can see if you can attend. It is a US organization which held its annual conference outside the USA for the first time ever ….
>
> The poetry manuscript I am working on is really moving well and I am happy about that. It is challenging work – very hard at times but worthwhile because I am learning so much from it.
>
> Anyway, dear Ida, I do hope you are feeling better, and that life brings you much joy in this coming year. This is my year according to the Chinese horoscope – the year of the pig and my birthday is in a couple of weeks – February 3rd. I want to celebrate it in the Caribbean – don't know why, but

that is important. I would like P. to come with me, but he says he can't afford it – he is looking for work and as of the end of February his settlement ends – he was laid off and had a year's salary as a settlement.

Anyway, even if I have to do it alone, it is important enough to me to do it. I want to go to Guadeloupe which is the home of a now deceased poet – Nobel laureate, St John Perse. His work has meant a great deal to me in my writing life and there is a museum there about him. Will keep you posted on it.

My heart goes out to you in your grieving, and I send you much love and support,

NourbeSe

Then, on 11 August 2009, I wrote to her:

NourbeSe!

I am so thankful for you sent me your wonderful Zong! I don´t have many words to tell you about my feeling. But I have something to say about your beautiful work: Congratulations! It is a pleasure to read it. The way you linked law, poetry and history was fantastic …

I enjoy having your picture, too.
I will write to you as I finish to read the book…
Meanwhile I say again thank you!

Axé!

Ida

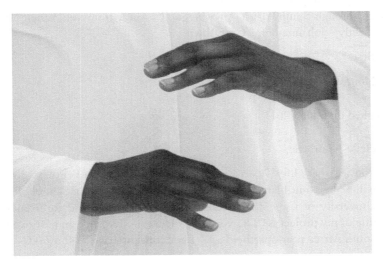

FIGURE 8.3 Touching the invisible

Source: Image by Marina Moros, 2013.

In the summer of 2011, I travelled to South Africa with my 6-year-old daughter to develop postdoctoral research. In my hand luggage, M. NourbeSe's book would be my map to guide the steps in the discontinuous journey in search of silence in my own body.

On 3 June 2011, I wrote to her:

> Dear NourbeSe,
>
> How are you my dear friend. My daughter and I are living for one year in South-Africa. I brought with me your book Looking for Livingstone: An Odyssey of Silence.
>
> I am trying to think about an aesthetic of silence, from dance, from body, from blindness, you are here with me...
>
> Lot of love,
>
> Ida x

I heard from her on 4 June 2011:

> Dear dear Ida:
>
> So very good to hear from you! How long have you been in South Africa and what are you doing there? Questions questions! Am happy to hear you have Livingstone with you – he did missionary work in that part of the world, you know. By the way, do you have my latest work, Zong!? Do let me know and if you don't will send you a copy.
>
> Would be wonderful to meet in South Africa. I have a couple of families I help to support in Swaziland and would like to visit them and one has to go through South Africa. Anyway, good to hear from you. Where are you exactly – Johannesburg? Cape Town?
>
> Best,
>
> NourbeSe

I replied on 6 June 2011:

> Hello NourbeSe,
>
> You see, that's life. We arrived here in Cape Town, 4th February 2011 and will be here until January 2012. I am a visiting scholar in School of Dance, University of Cape Town, researching about dance and forgiveness, the title of my project is "The voices of silence: body, dance and forgiveness in South Africa post-apartheid …". I am concentrating in the TRC – Truth

and Reconciliation Commission; it is interesting because I am finding many art works related to this subject, but not in dance.

Yes, the Livingstone is here with me. I also received the Zong! It is possible to buy it here because I would like to give it to the Director of the Dance School, who I am working with. And how are you? your family? Let me know if you would like to visit us …

Warm regards,

Ida

I heard from her again on 30 November 2013:

Dear NourbeSe,

Hope you are well. Yesterday I watched Zong! collective reading, I would like to be present, will be an extraordinary experience.

Here, the performance in the Museum, I dance for the spirits, only one of my students comes. Friday afternoon, end of the semester … other reasons.

But I captured the attention about the Zong! and by Facebook, I posted some fragment of the book and some pictures, from the performance "Weavers of Existence" inspired in your poems, the university site shared the events in the news. Last week in the meeting of the university press the editorial board was enthusiastic to translate Zong! So, I think everything is in the right place and time.

With my best wishes,

Ida

On 25 October 2015, I wrote again:

Dear NourbeSe,

How are you? Step by step I am creating a new life, spending the time writing, reading, in silence, dancing, taking care of my daughter and my mom, and cooking …

In November here is the month of Black Consciousness, and this year I was invited to give a talking and I will talk and dance about your work, not only Zong, but the title is also "Body, Space and Memory in the Poetics of Silence of M. Nourbese Philip".

Hope this could demonstrate how much I appreciate your work,

With my best wishes,

Ida

She replied on 27 October 2015:

> Dear Ida:
>
> How wonderful to hear from you! And even more wonderful to hear of what you're planning to do. Marvellous! It is synchronous but November 29th, 2015, will be the 4th anniversary reading performance here in Toronto and I am in the process of preparing for that. I didn't want to ask you again since you had said that you were spending time reflecting and having made changes in your life. I have made contact with a Brazilian sister, E.T. – she is a professor but also a capoeirista and I've asked her if she would do a performance in resonance with us. If, of course, you were moved to make a gesture of resonance, I would be delighted, although it is enough that you're doing something on my work.
>
> I very much like the idea of Black Consciousness vis-a-vis Black History. Wonderful.
>
> Best,
>
> NourbeSe

What is mirrored by this exchange of emails is the maturing of a friendship between two black women who are linked by the search for silence in the body, manifested in the creative processes of their artistic works. The section will present some traits of NourbeSe's work that were fundamental to identifying the voices of silence in the study trip during the post-doctorate in South Africa and its unfolding in the elaboration of the corpographies' creative process.

Dance as a Witness.

> hold we to the centre of remembrance
> that forgets the never that severs
> word from source
> and never forgets the witness
> of broken utterances that passed
> before and now
> breaks the culture of silence
> in the ordeal of testimony.
> in the history of circles
> each point lies
> along the circumferences
> diameter or radius
> each word creates a centre
> circumscribed by memory… and history
> waits at rest always
> still at the centre
>
> *Philip (1993)*

FIGURE 8.4 Stillness
Source: Image by Silvana Macedo, 2019.

Does the body forget? This was the question I asked when walking the streets of Cape Town hand in hand with my daughter, then 6 years old. After living in South Africa for a year, in February 2012 we returned to Brazil and I started writing about the experience. I wonder what the body remembers? What my body remembers from that time spent walking on South African land? Remembrance and forgetfulness are the elements that make up the narrative of my body memory.

How did dancing become a witnessing experience? Perhaps this searching of silence in the body began when I was still in my mother's womb, occupying without knowing the place where I testified her pain. Before I was conceived, my mother had lost a 10-month-old daughter. And it was this memory that was awakened in me when I performed the sentence that was not written on paper, but was silenced in my body.

> My pain is the pain of a dead child.

Those words came out of me, accompanied by a raspy, plaintive, suffering voice. I was squatting, immersed in the depths of body and soul, interpreting a reading of a mental flow during the *Weavers of Existence* performance. Those words were not written in the text I was reading. After listening to them, I placed them in my body, and I remained silent.

Dance is linked to freedom, because when dancing, my body that inhabits the movement transmutes into gestures of searching for myself in the bodies that are there, dancing with me. In the same free action of dancing with others, they configure the power to preserve the act, the gesture, the repetition. But my desire to continue the dance causes me to invent, making the creation of the moment arise, with the same effort, the interruption of a gesture that begins in another. In this creative moment, in the pause of the act of breathing, in the silence between the heart rhythm, lurking, in the breach of thought and in the crack of the heart, an ambience for forgiveness is installed. And in this space between reason and emotion, where some realities tend to persevere in being, this corpography is created and a field of freedom is drawn on the body itself.

By sharing the corpographies of that time and South African space, I check the traces of a dance's steps left on me.

The "corpography" can resemble the "biographemes" created and defined by Roland Barthes, such as "I like certain biographical traits that, in the life of a writer, enchant me as much as certain photographs; I called these traits 'biographies'; Photography has the same relationship with history as the biographeme with biography" (Barthes, 1980: 51). Here, I look for a moving writing which articulates in a displacement of the gesture that writes for the gesture that dances, in the same way that the dance moves towards a writing that denotes the marks of steps, lapses and flashes of a body memory. In the manner of Barthes (1980), corpography has the same relationship with body memory as photography has with history, and the biographeme with biography. Once you have awakened a bodily memory, creating a corpography involves three elements with their respective three basic steps: (1) silence, to listen carefully; (2) word: to write with the senses; (3) body: to dance with the heart.

This creative process starts with paying attention in the silence in the body. South African researchers Christine Anthonissen (2006) and Fiona Ross (2006) show themselves to be on this path when they assume the attitude of paying attention to what is not said, but is expressed by facial expressions, gestures and body language, the interrelation between words and silence. Interested in studying how memory is mediated by language, they highlight the role of creative thinking and the ways of reconstructing the South African people to deal with conflict and difference on a national scale with splendid sensitivity. Fiona Ross suggests the need to renew the notion of attention to be a witness of pain and its wounds marked in memory, and still identifies the subtlety and the limitation of language in the face of the pain experienced or remembered.

The time lived on South African land makes me perceive body, pain, and memory as a puzzle game that deserves sensitive attention to study it. I learnt by reading Philip, Anthonissen and Ross that affirming pain is also questioning certainties and doubts in the face of one's own pain or that of others. But to deny the other's pain is not an absence of thought, but an absence of sensitivity. For sensitive attention is to recognize the constraint of testimony and the way in which word and convention operate in the constitution of speech and silence. It means being aware of the limits of academic claims. Remember that when studying about suffering, it is necessary to respect that something escapes, and sometimes it even distances us from the inaccessible and foreign truth. At this moment, I assume how dancing, writing, and meditating can favor an exercise of otherness, of sensitive listening to oneself and the other.

Pause. Again, the body is still to remember. Attention. Discern to forget. Silence to forgive. Dance to understand. It is this writing about silence and memory. Pause and forgiveness. Dance. Body. Words. Do they make sense to you? My hand writes like this, at risk, does not outline the letters, streak fills the space between the lines. I write above the line, I don't want to touch it, I leave it intact from someone else's streak. For these words expressed here, my lyrics were not in vain.

The experience of writing and dance have been expanding my understanding about my existence as an African-Brazilian woman in a hostile world. Paying attention in the national South African post-apartheid body dancing toyi-toyi, I learnt the power of the song in the communication and creative expression. This boosted me to create the corpographies. The dialogue with Marlene NourbeSe Philip inspired me to resist, to transcend, and to listen to the language of silence and become a witness to those who can no longer use their own voices to express the

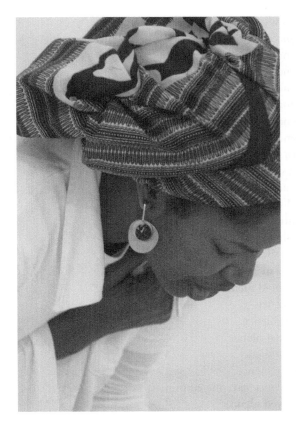

FIGURE 8.5 Inner silence
Source: Image by Marina Moros, 2013.

pain. An attention that demands an intertwining between words, silence, absence, and awareness of the cultural conventions that intervene and shape them. Paying attention is delicate, it is a profound effort against the limit of culture. It is a call to action, a return to the very things about seeing and hearing yourself and the other. As a dancer witness, I searched and found silence in and between bodies.

> Rough silence, which shaves the ear to the point that it cannot hear anything.
> You really want to hear a word. Silence.
> No voice.
> Nothing is expressed.
> Contained air.
> Nothing comes out.
> In the voice: the silence of the unspoken words.
> Sacred or poorly said.
> The silence of fear.
> The silence of pain.
> The silence of revenge.
> The silence of resentment.
> The silence of remorse.
> The silence of anger.
> The silence of love.
> The silence of the wound.
> The silence of disappointment.
> The silence of frustration.
> The silence kept.
> The torn silence.
> The lost silence.
> The found silence.
> The tied silence.
> The frustrated silence.
> The harsh silence.
> The gross silence.
> The heavy silence.
> The measured silence.
> Infinite silence.
> The cried silence.
> The shouted silence.
> The lonely silence.
> The empty silence.
> The full silence gave me emptiness.
> The betrayed silence.
> The silent silence.
> The verbalized silence.
> The forbidden silence.

The dancing silence.
The buried silence.
The choked silence.
The fought silence.
The difficult silence.
The silence of shame.
The shame of silence.
Silence.

Notes

1 Zezé Motta is a renowned Afro-Brazilian actress and singer.
2 Hannah Arendt (1906–1975) was a German political philosopher of Jewish origin.
3 Translated from the song "Senhora Liberdade" by Nei Lopes.

Bibliography

Anthonissen, Christine. 2006. The language of remembering and forgetting. *Journal of Language and Politics* 5.1:1–13.
Barthes, Roland. 1980. *A câmara clara: notas sobre fotografia*. Rio de Janeiro, Brazil: Nova Fronteira.
Gray, Anne-Marie. 2004. The liberation songs: an important voice of black South Africans from 1912 to 1994. *Journal of Education* 33.1: 85–102.
Philip, M. NourbeSe. 1993. *Her silence softly breaks*. London: The Women's Press.
Philip, M. NourbeSe. 2003. *Looking for Livingstone: an odyssey of silence*. Toronto, Canada: Mercury Press Fiction.
Ross, Fiona. 2006. Linguistic bearings and testimonial practices. *Journal of Language and Politics* 5.1: 111–124.
Twala, Chitja and Koetaan, Quintin. 2006. The toyi-toyi protest culture in the 1980s: an investigation into its liberating and unifying powers. *South African Journal of Cultural History* 20.1: 163–179.

9
OUR BODY IN #SONICWILDERNESS & #SOUNDASGROWING

Antye Greie-Ripatti (AGF/poemproducer)

through listening, interacting, collaborating, playing, connecting, employing one's body with technology, exploration of existing soundscapes forms a new audio-body practice. a collaborative site-specific application. rethinking composition body tek[1] of body and space and time. looking into audio as material. a bodily material self as sonic-corporeality. as in fluid zoning between human resonance and the world we inhabit. permeation. someone said audio permaculture. re-imagine questions of the body in sound. #

#sonicwilderness participants are asked to explore the multiple body problem: resonance, source, vibration, relation. the wildness of sonic bodies.

via experimental narration #sonicwilderness sessions are examined.

AGF facilitated #sonicwilderness interventions in locations such as remote Finnish tundra, Indonesian agricultural spaces, Vietnamese public space, Berlin Reichstag's meadow, Latvian post-war scenario. focus on incorporating sonic feminisms and networking possibilities for marginalized lives.

imagining a sound (practice) that is growing. {#soundasgrowing} a way of composition that is aligned with your own growth and time line

the body in #sonicwilderness is placed. moved into. it is social, practical, relational, off grid, moving around. deliberately off-civilised, like slow functional movement in relation to space, but not custom. the music is played – it touches, communicates, or wants to (interact) with the environment either is indifferent (or helpful) and changed … important is to neglect what is expected.

like *Blueberry techno*, a score created in the project {score 2015}

the body is engaging, in contact with outside-offness – it can be grass, mud, branches, stone, berries, bark, moved water flowing, waves making rhythm, announcing a beat.

DOI: 10.4324/9781003008217-13

#sonicwilderness & #soundasgrowing   129

FIGURE 9.1 Hanoi Leninpark, 2018
Image credit: #sonicwilderness.

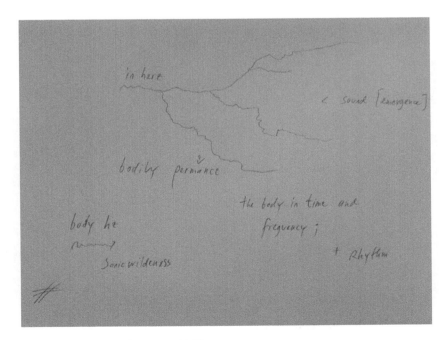

FIGURE 9.2 *Blueberry techno* score, 2015
Source: #sonicwilderness.

bodily permeance
the body in time
sound emergence
frequency, rhyme
rhythm and –ess
body in hz – a solidicity

≈≈≈≈≈> #sonicwilderness

so a body, the body, is our body, a shared body. like collective consciousness the body is the body is bodies into ONE body, we are one body. a collective body exceeding entity and we move independently and together. like freedom.

{music is the highest form of sharing says the late wonderful sci-fi writer Ursula Le Guin in her visionary utopian novel *The Dispossessed*}

un-pattern your body from normality, behaviour that is judged and learned. allow wildness of sonic bodies. listening, interacting, collaborating, and playing together with sound.

any sound that can be found by exploring these spaces and develop methodology and technology in collaborative site-specific sound exploration.

rethinking technology, compositional technology … looking into audio as material considered sustainable, compose as if growing, composting … re-using

FIGURE 9.3 Carsten Stabenow, Berlin, 2017

Source: #sonicwilderness.

sounds and taking care of it, as well as software and the technology surrounding etc.
#soundasgrowing
   "the body as data"
consent and "existing while in public":

   {x} body problem
   the girl who screams,
   look calm holding
   the collectif.wild-body

   sonic feminisms
   and networking possibilities
   female: pressure network

   {The Universal Right to Breathe (Achille Mbembe)}

   to go outside
   to move freely

   and hum, make a sound,
   resonate in space,
   a capability to offer

   the voice as part
   of the unique body to carry tune

   through the eye of the needle
   to be forced to swing intimately
   with one's resonance in space and time and group

   one's own life –
   our life on Earth with others
   (including viruses)

   decomposition of bodies
   the object body
   a machine body
   a digital body
   an ontophanic body.
   pollen, spores, and mould.

   we have never learned
   to sound with all living species
   community – or rather the in-common

FIGURE 9.4 A line of women in the rice fields
Source: #sonicwilderness.

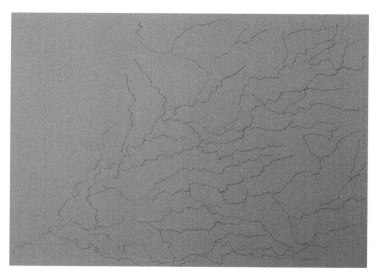

FIGURE 9.5 *Blueberry techno* score, part 2, 2015
Source: #sonicwilderness.

FIGURE 9.6 Samiland, 2015
Source: #sonicwilderness.

"a line of women in the rice field,
sonifying the mathematics
of labour, rows, mud and space" #nusasonic
#feministsonictechnologies

having a unique encounter with others
the possibility of sharing unconditionally
drawing from it something absolutely intrinsic,
a thing uncountable, incalculable, priceless

over the cracks
literally everything must be reinvented
starting with the source/ power …

{the battery is the message says Samir Bhowmik}[2]

social. listening like reading the room
but there is no room, there is sky, sometimes
abandoned architecture or an inner-city park

nurturing and preserving
across the interface of xxx

the earth is still here
through the digital

FIGURE 9.7 Sonic wild
Source: #sonicwilderness.

      the body of flesh and bones
      the physical and mortal body
      will be freed of its weight and inertia
      the end of this transfiguration

      before this virus
      breathing and human resonant bodies
      shares breathing. absorption of oxygen
      and release of carbon dioxide

      ungrounded

      our common ground
      belongs
      to human and other

      being in the biosphere
      carrying small technoscience

      as portable resistance

      like laying in a creek
      and jam with compositing wood

#sonicwilderness & #soundasgrowing **135**

FIGURE 9.8 Hanoi
Source: #sonicwilderness.

>   between those who dream
>
>   this sudden
>   unforeseen and unpredictable
>   sings
>
>   treeing
>   tuning to the frequency of the tree
>   being with the tree
>   a melting attempt to overcome body
>   not take from the tree
>   not as an extractivist practice
>
>   : {sonic} TREEing
>   like para-consciousness
>   communication, frequency meditation
>   like "giving each other strength"
>   type of {silent} calibrating
>
>   a collective meditation in hz (frequency)
>   #blindsignal
>
>   what men have built
>
>   when poured concrete
>   against shores and on top
>   of habitat

FIGURE 9.9 Skibotn session, Caspar Ström, 2015
Source: #sonicwilderness.

    ruins of infrastructure
    resonance

    a bunker and the reverb
    waves crashing
    in rhythms of space time

    :if the score
    is a potential

    of what can happen
    a future possibility

    applied to the lines
    like mycelium
    linked with the fungi
    of our bodies

    the inter-territory of
    our matter
    in reference to
    radical mycology {Peter McCoy}

suggests
sound as GROWING

initiating connections
growing into
frequency
falling the trails of
nutrition

Outro

the #sonicwilderness practice as an active practice, moving body in space and changing space via collaborative vibration. over the years it has led to many collaborations in sound and music, friendship, time spent musicing and building networks across cultures.

it has influenced organizing with the feminist organisation and international electronic arts network female: pressure[3]

it has led to network building and composing of the recent project rec-on.org – next-step collective practice for musicians and sound artists to … grow into territories … online or irl. while materializing and teaching #sonicwilderness … the image or concept of growing sound #soundasgrowing instead of "notating, coding, improvising within rules, like rhythm and harmony" extends to sound related and political participation.

If we grow sound in time, life itself is the time to make a sound, so life is the composition!

FIELD CAMPS #sonicwilderness
sonicwilderness: https://nusasonic.poemproducer.com
#sonicwilderness: http://soccos.eu/blog/detail/sonicwilderness
#russula: http://soccos.eu/blog/detail/russula-camp-blueberry-techno
#residence: http://soccos.eu/blog/detail/are-we-exchanging-culture
#SAMA: www.uniarts.fi/en/blogs/sama-sound-art-sonic-arts/feedback-session-boat

thank you to everyone who contributed to #sonicwilderness

Notes

1 traditional environmental knowledge
2 http://samirbhowmik.cc/
3 www.femalepressure.net

10

WHAT MAKES THE WOLVES HOWL UNDER THE MOON?

Sound Poetics of Territory-Spirit-Bodies for Well-Living

Laila Rosa and Adriana Gabriela Santos Teixeira

#Breathing in
We know how to dance, intuitively.
I invite us to awaken this power,
Here and now,
Orbiting with the stars,
Reborn with each Moon,
As everything is alive.[1]

Inaê Moreira

What does "Sound Poetics of Territory-Spirit-Bodies for Well-Living" mean? How can we sound and voice our bodies towards a decolonial, anti-racist healing path, Abya Yala feminism and Sonology[2] for Well-Living? How can body and performance inform immersive sound spaces and performance practice throughout a composition, recording and video made with a lot of intimacy and freedom (free improvisation), even over the long distance between Vale do Capão, Brazil[3] and London, UK? By understanding artistic production *as* knowledge production, can our bodies in sound be regarded as a new feminist and decolonial epistemology of sound (or a gendered and racialized soundscape), video making and performance practice?

It is important to highlight that we have observed some of the academic and artistic productions within the field of sonology in Brazil that are focused more exclusively on the scope of artistic and academic creation. However, this is still a mainly white, male, academic, middle-class, heteronormative, cisgender and southeastern field, which reflects the racial and social inequalities between the Northern and Southern regions of Brazil. On the other hand, at Federal University of Bahia, Salvador, Northeast, we have "Feminaria Musical: Research Group and Sound Experiments",[4] as a space for the co-creation of a sonology for Well-Living. Thus, the sound experiments by women become sound-musical poetics and feminist artivism as an expression of decolonial feminist epistemology.[5]

Our sonology for Well-Living is born from the horizontality of co-creation from our bodies, voices and the available sound elements, which can be acoustic or not, and which do not necessarily pass through electronic or electroacoustic music, as commonly present in research and sonology groups in Brazil. We understand that the technical configuration itself excludes those who do not own it, either due to specific technical knowledge or due to access (or lack thereof) to specific equipment. For us, the experimental is born out of the experiment, the body, the voice, the feeling, the intuition, the memory, the exchange, regardless of specific technical devices.[6]

Regarding the theoretical approach on Feminist and Situated Knowledge (Haraway, 2000), we quote our own studies as a feminist and decolonial goal/desire in performance, sound, sonology and aurality: Laila Rosa's Masters and PhD research (2005 and 2009) on gender, race and sexuality in Brazilian African-Indigenous sacred music in Candomblé and Jurema religions (Rosa, 2005 and 2009). Both works are inspired by sacred and non-Western feminine acustemologies that present ancestral and diverse materialities of sound, body and performance. They are very contemporary, extrapolating (and sounding out) patterns of gender, sexuality, race, ethnicity, social class and generation for the Well-Living of people and communities historically and socially subordinated by structural racism and heterocispatriarchy. On the other hand, Adriana Gabriela presents her research on Theatre and Performance of Sacred Feminine for healing. She is also co-creating women's performatic and empowering rites, showing how Afro-Brazilian Goddesses have much in common with a feminist and black decolonial Sacred Feminine (Teixeira, 2016).[7]

By this, *Praying to the Goddess*, or *Rezo para a Deusa*,[8] is a prayer, a meditative, feminist artivist audiovisual and intuitive[9] piece that is strongly engaged to answer the questions above. It is inspired by the approach of "Well-Living" by the Black Women Parade (2015), as well as, "Territory-Body-Spirit", by the Indigenous Women Parade (2019).[10] This political agenda makes the wolves in us howl under the moon and co-create, while we heal and write together. By doing that, we ask for guidance from the Oracle of the Goddess' Deck, by Amy Sophia Marashinsky (2007). Also, this *prayer* helps us to build new methodologies for composing, co-creating in sound making and performance, embracing the wolves and witches we are.

As a creative process (or intuitive guidance), we present our poems, images, paintings with menstrual/moon blood[11] and embodied sound: breathing, silence and Tibetan meditation singing bowl, voicing and singing ancestrality as a shamanic and Peruvian *Icaro* healing chant sounds, playing the *rabeca*,[12] sounding traditional and contemporary, in both Portuguese and English, with our very Brazilian accent. Thus, a four-hand, experimental, poetic sound and audiovisual piece of healing and revolution is born, in times of pandemic. It departs from the thinking and co-creating of two Brazilian feminist artivists: both cis and bisexual women, one mestiza, one black. We are interested in understanding/being aware of and expressing our decolonial existence and desire through sound and video making as experimental and healing paths.

This experimental writing is also born from the theoretical and political approach of amefricanity, or *amefricanidade*, by Lélia Gonzalez (1988); gender and intersectionality and black feminism by bell hooks (2019) and so many others;[13] Abya Yala Feminism by Francesca Gargallo (2012);[14] Gloria Anzaldúa's borderline and Chicano lesbian thought (2000) and so on. Those authors reaffirm the importance of recognizing voices and writings as personal narratives. They also recognize "other" forms of a non-linear flow *as* knowledge. To poetize and sonorize this writing from our bodies, African sacred thought, Makota Valdina Pinto (2013), Abya Yala shamanic tradition,[15] Yoga and Veganism (Oberom, 2015) traverse us. Finally, Lorena Cabnal[16] (2010) helps us understand our artistic/artivist work from a territory-spirit-body or body-feeling perspective. Composing an artistic communication that inspires Well-Living can be revolutionary, especially in these challenging times of illness of the soul, physical body and Planet that is the COVID-19 pandemic.

We are talking about a poetic and embodied sound experiment that is born from our territory-spirit-bodies and the geographic places where we are currently situated in this pandemic context. Sound, word and movement weave a virtual and dynamic encounter. This captures our trajectories, desires and directions in the journey of a feminist artivism that involves bodies and healing, in the composition of this video art, where the video element is essential for the work's own conception (Sharp, 2013).

Finally, we believe in the relevance of raising our text-experiment and video art as a prayer to Mother Earth, because we are in the world and trying hard to be aware of it. The World in us. At this point, we are re(X)isting, as transfeminist Viviane Vergueiro (2015) proposes. We think. We write. We compose. We perform. We heal. We connect with our ancestors. Those who came after us. Those who will come after us. And so many others. It is time to rethink communication in its many ways. We also speak about both an internal and external time for deep listening.

> Our writing flows in sound poetry.
> We invite you to pass through the portal.

#experiment: *The Lunar Howls of Wolves*

As *Wolf women*, we begin this experiment howling song, sound, listening, viewing, feeling and poetry. In the first place, this is about our connection with the cards from the Oracle of the Goddess (Marashinsky, 2007). Laila took out a card and we started our poetic-sound and performance experiment. Gabriela's card was the pre-Hellenic Goddess *Eurynome* (Greece), which invites us to open up to the conscious healing ecstasy of dance and creation. Gabriela associated yet another card, the card of the Slavic Goddess *Vila*, a mutant who invites us to heal through dancing and changing form, in connection with the elemental beings of nature; Laila's card, on the other hand, was the Hindu Goddess *Shakti*, who summons to cosmic and tantric orgasm, a profound re-energization of being. Based on our cards, we gave birth to poems, paintings and a sound experiment, co-creating a decolonial and feminist Abya Yala sonology for Well-Living, which means giving birth to the stories that need to be told, played, sung and sounded, to be heard and healed. Stories and sounds historically remained invisible and unheard.

Wolves # diary: the oracle of the Goddesses – the cards

Gabriela:… it has to do with the cards of the Goddesses Vila and Eurynome … dancing the various forms, nature, totality, the healing ecstasy … I had cramps, I hummed … I hummed, feeling blood and words … for healing. So, the proposal now would be for you to bring the howl of your moon … whatever is born there, Shakti or whatever is going through you, as an act of listening, connection and improvement. I will be active all day today. I reserved tomorrow to write and concentrate. I am still banza,[17] but strong and feeling purposeful. Let's feel it. The words were born from this concentration with the listening of the womb. kisses, beautiful flower.

Laila: What a beauty! I will be inspired by these words to put them in the text! Chaos here, but I am strong and purposeful, too!

#The Oracle of the Goddesses: The Cards

Gabriela's Card 1: *Vila – Shape Change*
Gabriela's Card 2: *Eurynome – Ecstasy*

> **Dancing With the Goddess Vila**
> Aê Aê …
> The vein of your life
> Runs sacred in bloom
> Within the sea
> Within the being
> Every drop of love
> Divine and sacred blood
> Come, cleanse me with love
> Reborn
> It unfolds
> All the wealth of being
> Hey …
> For a flower to sprout firm
> For firmness to sprout from a flower
> a flower
> must be free
> must be light

> must live with love
> Cure comes
> Healing will
> Heart follows in peace
> my chant has power
> the power to be reborn
> Moon Blood
> Blood of light
> Eternal Venus in love
> Womb of peace
> Belly of love
> This flower will be reborn
> Flower comes
> Flower goes
> Serene bloom
> Within the heart
> Within the immensity
> All wealth of being …
> *Adriana Gabriela*

The Goddesses *Eurynome* and *Vila* communicate both a healing and creative dimension. Both are representations of vital and winged dancers. The Goddess *Vila* is dance, it is mutation, it is full nature and it can also be the arrow of death. Healing by movement. She is the fluidity and expanded perception of the unity of being. *Vila* is transformed into a poem as a sacred drop of blood. She is also healing and firmness of flowering. The Goddess *Eurynome*, on the other hand, speaks of pleasure, of the ecstasy of living which comes from releasing pain and consciously opening ourselves to ecstasy. While writing this text, we realized that we were menstruating together. On the same day and same crescent moon. Connected wolf-women.

In our journeys for healing the fragmentation of our bodies and the heritage of the capitalist and utilitarian body, we understand menstruation as an important vital cycle. It is one door for self-knowledge and empowerment, as an experience of being, flesh, blood, belly-listening. It also integrates a deep listening to our (dis)harmonies. The commonly painful body, during the menstrual period, can be transformed into an ecstatic body, a pleasant and meditative body for enjoyment, that is: a source for its own artistic medicines. When the womb breathes, sings and speaks, suffering is diluted, from the deepness that is silence, mystery and uterus, the gourd of creation; there are answers towards Well-Living.

We believe in a corporeal feminism. According to Elizabeth Grosz (1994), "every body is marked by the history and specificity of its existence", making it possible to build a biography of this body that is individual and social, covering everything from accidents to illnesses to its own functioning, preferences, movements, habits, postures, behaviors, among others:

> Every body is marked by the history and specificity of its existence. It is possible to construct a biography, a history of the body, for each individual and social body. This history would include not only all the contingencies that befall a body, impinging on it from the outside – a history of the accidents, illnesses, misadventures that mark the body and its functioning; such a history would also have to include the "raw ingredients" out of which the body is produced – its internal conditions of possibility, the history of its particular tastes, predilections, movements, habits, postures, gait, and comportment.
>
> *Grosz (1994, p. 142)*

Lorena Cabnal helps us to recover our "body territory" as a daily struggle:

> Recovering the body to defend it from the structural historical attack that threatens it becomes a daily and indispensable struggle, because the body territory has been a territory disputed by the patriarchalists for millennia, to ensure its sustainability from and on the body of women.
>
> *Cabnal (2010, p. 22)[18]*

By doing that, we understand that when we are sharing thoughts and feelings about our menstruation experiences, we also include female bodies that do not menstruate, in their cis and transgender diversity. We consider that menstruating is material and physical, but also poetic and energetic, regarding the memories from our "subtle body", a concept from Yoga's subtle anatomy or physiology:

> Emotional aspects are forces of vibrating energy that are formed in the astral body, and are expressed in the physical body. In this astral dimension, thoughts, especially those charged with emotional intensity, can take shape with their own characteristics and remain energetically charged within the individual's astral body, without the individual being aware of it. These "thought forms" are fickle and behave fickle. They can be the cause of the imbalances manifested in the physical body, and, thus, the ways of treating diseases could take into account the energetic and magnetic aspect of this subtle body, and treat the individual with energetic or vibrational therapies ....
>
> *Moura (2013, p. 47)*

To consider the body's material and subtle dimensions is to heal. During the writing process, Laila underwent two surgical procedures to treat a borderline ovarian tumor that manifested itself for the third time in her previously abused and sexually assaulted body. It is a body that tells its own story through the journeys of many pains. From the perspective of the subtle body, the ovaries are located in the second *chakra*, the *Svadistana Chakra*, which is related to the energies of the sacred feminine and masculine. This energy is present in all bodies, regardless of gender identity. Finally, it is time to call for a rebalancing of our belly, our center of power, with the Goddesses' imagetic, archetypal and energetic support. Painting with menstrual blood becomes a tool for self-knowledge, acceptance and healing.

#Dancing With the Goddess *Shakti* – energy

Bleeding and giving birth to *Shakti*
My sacred blood reveals
Delicate pigments,
light and healing.
They are pigments-fragments-I.
Body-earth petals in bloom.
Uterus in bloom, I snaked.
Lunar Shakti.
Mermaid singing.
It's me, snake.
They are the blessings of Oxumaré,
Ewá,
Vital energy,
Sacred Kundalini.
Tantric.
Shakti dancing to cosmic bliss.
The sunshine,
The brightness of the moon,
The brightness of the stars.
Laila Rosa

The Goddess *Shakti* is vital and creative energy, the source of creativity, cosmic ecstasy, renewal. She is also the nectar, cosmic serpent, the *Kundalini* that crosses and aligns all the *chakras*, energy centers of our physical and subtle bodies:

> Within each human being there is a network of nerves and sensory organs that interpret the external physical world. At the same time, within each of us there is a subtle system of channels (*nadis*) and energy centers (*chakras*) that take care of our physical, mental, emotional and spiritual being.... At the base of the spine, in the triangular bone called the sacrum (ancient civilizations knew that there is something sacred about this bone) lies the most subtle spiritual energy, dormant in most of us, called Kundalini.[19]

Shakti is *tantra*, power and vitality. Body-earth-uterus in bloom. Lunar. Mermaid singing. Archetypes of the *orixá Oxumaré*, African Yoruba God of the rainbow and the serpent, brother of *Ewá*, Goddess of the arts and of the evening, rivers, the secret and sacred forests, and also of the serpent (Prandi, 2001).

What Makes the Wolves Howl under the Moon? **145**

FIGURE 10.1 *Lunar painting 10.1: Uterus in flower, I snaked*, by Laila Rosa

FIGURE 10.2 *Lunar painting 10.2: Lunar Shakti, Siren's chant*, by Laila Rosa

 # Praying to the Goddess

Our experimental audiovisual piece *Praying to the Goddess*, or *Rezo para a Deusa*, tries to sound healing and Well-Living through four main sound steps:

a) Goddesses – our voices: 1. a chant/lullaby for the Goddesses *Vila* and *Eurynome* – Gabriela sung it based on the poem she wrote; 2. Laila – translating Gabriela's poem into English, interacting with her chant as an echo; 3. poem dedicated to *Shakti – Kundalini, Ewá*[20] by Laila in both Portuguese and English. Goddesses are sounding at once, which means different mythological traditions inform several possibilities of feminine archetypes. Dance. Prayer to the blood-moon and to the moon. Flower. Reborn.
b) *Shakti, Kundalini*, Tibetan Meditative Bowl – Voicing and sounding meditation and healing: 1. Laila breathes, sings and interacts with Gabriela's voices, with glissando, inspired by shamanic healing voicing, *Icaro* singing, exploring the low and high voice borders as a prayer and also an Om mantra, the primordial sound; 2. Tibetan Meditative Bowl – light, shining and meditative. Heal *Shakti* means heal sacred feminine. Energy. *Tantra. Kundalini*. Chakras. Subtle body. Awareness. Silence. Deep listening. Love.
c) *Rabeca* – voicing female body and the Mother Earth: 1. Laila plays the *rabeca* – as a popular and traditional instrument, it sounds old, ancient. It means the body. Mother Earth. Conflict. Blood. Pain. Illness. Activity. Glissando. Pizzicato. It creates another sound ambience. Contemporary. Contemplative.
d) Electronic basis: sounding pandemic. Something else. We do not know. Expectation. Anxiety. Movement. Encounter. Illness. Healing.

By sounding all of these, we have our video art, sharing personal images from our personal and artistic folders. Our faces. Bodies. Families. Sacred. Artistic/artivist journeys. Images we have made during our recent journeys through Brazil, Mexico, Peru, Angola, England and France. We intend to learn how to work with the Goddesses *Eurynome, Vila* and *Shakti*, opening a path for flowering with this meeting. The messages that have been addressed to us are: learning how to change shape with *Vila*, paying attention to possible rigidity and stagnation. Dancing and being danced by each being (spiritual, human and non-human), the whole and the nature around us. The mystery of life and its impermanence is manifested in nature.

Creation is a challenge and a game. It has the limits of materialities not always available and the greatness of improvisation. To create without perfectionism and with flexibility is always to create with what we have. To create carefully, with the desire to see the unexpected be born and accept that time makes its cuts. It is easy to lose the sense of time while going through the night, playing with colors and shapes, with rhythms and sensations. We use images of our paths as women around the world, internal and external, things, symbols, affections, actions that are important to us. It is noteworthy that in this part of the process there was some irritability… let it go. Breathing and breathing to find the flow. The process itself is a great teacher, and a result is just one part of this broad learning of creation in motion.

#Breathing out

We take a feminist and cosmological approach for Well-Living our body-territories as strategies to get out from the human domination of nature and all non-human beings, the speciesism. We call for *Ahimsa*, the yogic and vegan principle of non-violence (Oberom, 2015). We also enjoy a conscious ecstasy with *Eurynome*. We release the attachment to toxic behaviors, thoughts, repetitions of emotional narratives of pain that contract the belly and life. We ascend to the dance of pleasure, to the flow of a body that celebrates, pulsates and sings life, assuring ourselves the right for Well-Living.

Living, contemplation, internal rhythms, cycles, the cultivation of our harmony. Our own healing, of our *body-territory-spirit*, is also the healing of the Earth, love to the Earth. Singing, dancing, eating and loving are fundamental principles of integral nutrition, spiritual connection and community fellowship. Thus we pray – we bless, we sing like singing-poetry; thus we create, with the refinement of tranquil perception.

With *Shakti*, we seek to release the belief that the constant demands and practices of life push us hard, bore us and disconnect us from our center. Activating the awareness that, in constant re-energizing, everything flows, even in challenges and pains, because there is cosmic energy in abundance available. As a wizard friend would say: "The tools are available, just take ownership of them instead of succumbing."

At this point, we reaffirm health and awareness in times of crisis, health and awareness in difficult times, health and awareness for good. We, humanity, hurried inhabitants of this planet, insist on neglecting the voices of the Earth, the other voices among us and present in nature. Our dance, our song is an evocation of noise-knowledge, ruin-knowledge, crawling-knowledge, wind-knowledge, continuous flow-knowledge that inhabits our ancestral memory, and also knowledge that is alive and present in numerous practices, lives, communities, peoples, several existences. We receive the invitation to dance daily with life in a harmonic way. The practice of art is a fruitful support for this well-living, well-dreaming and well-doing, keeps us healthy and healing, offers us health to "constantly sing to life", despite any regrets, to insist in just being, proposing to love and live, transmit and communicate, as the *body-territory-spirits* that we are, voices of healing, voices of Life.

We do not need a perfect tuning, a state of perfection, a metric that is difficult to match or elaborate languages. Through free and intuitive improvisation, sacred feminine, body performance, video art and interdisciplinary approaches, we are trying to reach this place "beyond skill acquisition" as Lauren Hayes (2019) pointed out.

Sensitivity and intuitive embodied knowledge[21] will be our note, in the way of expression, yes and no, by expanding and reaping the wrong. We want to see the key in which we are all one, a philosophical concept that makes me love you, whoever you are. May it produce love between us, and help us to expand our sciences, to expand experiences of freedom, to heal all kinds of fears of saying, creating and being. We want to take it easy, and we also want you to feel free to elaborate paths for creation and writing, to bring your voice to the flights of your existence and experience, of your most delicate and divine, divine being.[22]

As goddesses, we are, we dance and we sing for them, with them and from them. We want to wake up with the voices of nature, with the simplicity of a celestial speech that is also ground, root, black, indigenous and subaltern, because it outlines everything and the center. It is the womb, the waves that keep flowing in and out of the belly of the world territory. We want to wake up with the bird that teaches, with the flower that teaches, the trees, herbs, each being, each finger, thread, link, wing, saliva and tooth, with the organism that we are, with the teachers of the teachers, the various faces and manifestations of Mother Nature.

We want the pleasure of creating and writing to run through us; it will run through us. Also focusing on the subsidy of this freedom for the creation of knowledge through narratives, sounding and performing that value our paths and ways of articulating sensitive ideas. That is why we cherish our bellies. That is why we sit naked on the Earth. That is why we sing to the red waters and receive songs from them. That is why we are cyclical like the Moon. That is why we howl. As my mother (Whose mother? Ours!), my mother's mother and my mother's mother's mother used to say, "I will not die quietly". So I howl, then I create ... and vice versa.

Wolves # writings # break

Gabriela: I'll write to you. Starting the work. In the bubuia[23] of connection we go. The goddesses in us. Scripture with love and conscience.
Laila: Come on. Trust me I trust you. Go forward delicately, with courage, gratitude and faith in art, in us. The goddesses in us always. So it is.
Gabriela: We have everything. To Heal and Create also involve recognizing this wealth of medicines which is being a woman, in its most diverse forms.

We breathe here.

Break.

Silence.

Pranayama.[24]

Notes

1 "Sabemos dançar, intuitivamente. Nos convido a despertar essa potência, aqui e agora, orbitando com as estrelas, renascendo a cada lua, como tudo que está vivo" (Moreira, 2020, p. 4).

2 According to the Brazilian composer Valéria Bonafé, "the notion of sonority is not circumscribed in a theory of composition where sound is usually taken as "a thing" or as a parameter. On the contrary, sonority will be considered as a more holistic idea, always aiming the integration of elements in the compositional plan" (Bonafé, 2016, p. 174). Isabel Nogueira and Leandra Lambert also present "some reflections about feminist epistemologies, sound creation and the gendered allocation of space", talking about "the creative process and discussing its relations with feminist epistemologies"(2016, p 135). Finally, Rodolfo Caesar includes de field of Ethnomusicology, which is important to us: "For some time, *Sonologia* (sonology) was polarized between 'hard' and 'soft' sciences, thus trying to adopt a trans-disciplinary attitude, something that seldom materialized. … Since then, we started to deserve sympathetic attention and established connections with another group that grew up inside Music Faculties: ethnomusicology" (Caesar, 2016, p. 306). On the other hand, Steven Feld (1990) proposed the concept of *Acustemology*, for understanding acoustics *as* epistemology, while Ana Maria Ochoa Gautier (2014; 2006) presents her brilliant research on Aurality, for understanding listening and knowledge in Colombia and Latin America. For Gautier, sound and listening is politics. We specially follow her steps on this matter.
3 Chapada Diamantina National Park, Bahia, Brazil.
4 Coordinated by Laila Rosa with the collaboration of students, scholars and artists, including Adriana Gabriela (Unicamp), Jorgete Lago (Pará State University), Francisca Marques (Federal University of Reconcavo in Bahia), Isabel Nogueira (Federal University of Rio Grande do Sul) and others, since 2015.
5 Since 2012, the group has produced intensely, both academic and artistically. We also conduct a pioneer research on feminist epistemologies in music in Brazil and female composers in Salvador, Bahia (Rosa, 2012). Besides that, we have worked on and co-created collaborative actions with black, indigenous and LGBTTQI + communities and their social movements.
6 Perhaps for this reason, we are not regarded as a feminist artivism group in the field of experimental music or sonology in Brazil, although we are a feminist experimental sound group that have worked since 2012. We have not really attended such spaces; we hardly see ourselves represented by them, with restricted exceptions of some artists and researchers.
7 We also mention the Research Group Feminismos del Abya Yala (UACM), coordinated by Norma Mogrovejo (Mexico), of which Laila Rosa is a member, coordinating the project "*Encuentro Sagrado con si misma/Sacred Encounter with oneself*: women, body, voice and sound experiments from elsewhere". It was part of her oneyear reasearch as Visiting Scholar and Artist in Residence in the USA, Mexico and Peru (2018–19). In 2020, during the COVID-19 pandemic, this project became "Listening to yourself and the world: introduction on gender studies, ethnic-racial relations, body and sexualities in music", with several guests from Brazil and Latin America. See: www.facebook.com/feminariamusical/posts/3297791000340762 and https://youtu.be/cQB8RqgHPl4.
8 https://vimeo.com/595453500.
9 According to Inaê Moreira's proposal (2020).
10 Both parades took place in Brasília (Brazil), and protested for civil rights such as life, health and territory.
11 For *menstruation* we use the term *moon*, under a sacred feminine and shamanic approach from Abya Yala (Latin America).
12 Brazilian fiddle.
13 Carla Akotirene (2018); Djamila Ribeiro (2018); Oyeronké (2004).
14 When compiling the thoughts of several women from Abya Yala (Latin America).

15 Especially Mexican and Peruvian.
16 A Guatemalan Xinka-Maya indigenous communitary and feminist artivist.
17 Feminine variation for the term *Banzo* "a word that, according to Nei Lopes, in the *New Banto Dictionary in Brazil*, originates in the language *QUICONGO*, *mbanzu*: thought, remembrance, and in *QUIMBUNDO*, *mbonzo*: longing, passion, hurt. For him, "Banzo is a deadly nostalgia that affected black Africans enslaved in Brazil" See: www.geledes.org. br/banzo-um-estado-de-espirito-negro/.
18 "Recuperar el cuerpo para defenderlo del embate histórico estructural que atenta contra él, se vuelve una lucha cotidiana e indispensable, porque el territorio cuerpo, ha sido milenariamente un territorio en disputa por los patriarcados, para asegurar su sostenibilidad desde y sobre el cuerpo de las mujeres" (Cabnal, 2010, p. 22).
19 See: www.sahajayoga.org.br/index.php/sobre-a-meditacao/area-de-aprofundamento/15-corpo-sutil.
20 A female African *orisha* from Yoruba tradition.
21 Inaê Moreira, *Dança Intuitiva* (2020).
22 bell hooks, *Vivendo de Amor* (2010); Thich Nhat Hanh, *How to Love* (2015).
23 Etymology: from Tupi *mbe'mbuya*. "1. *Bubuiar* act or effect, boating; 2. Bubble; 3. Light and floating thing. Voiceover: *Bubuia*: floating with the current."
24 "Yoga breathing technique that brings mind control, de-stress and revitalizes – and whose benefits are already scientifically proven. ... The word 'prana' has several synonyms in different cultures: chi, ki, vital energy, breath of life, breath .... That is, it is what feeds life, in addition to the physical body. ... Yama means, roughly speaking, path. The term refers to the rules of ethical conduct that make a true yogi" (www.ecycle.com.br/3394-respiracao-pranayama).

Bibliography

Akotirene, Carla. 2018. *O que é interseccionalidade? Coleão feminismos plurais*. Rio de Janeiro, Brazil: Editora Letramento.

Anzaldúa, Gloria. 2000. "Falando em línguas: uma carta para as mulheres escritoras do terceiro mundo." *Revista Estudos Feministas*, 8(1), pp. 229–242.

Bonafé, Valéria. 2017. "The experience of sonority: the dangers of a journey into the unknown." In: *Sonologia 2016 – Out of Phase: Proceedings of the International Conference on Sound Studies*. São Paulo, Brazil: Nusom – Research Centre on Sonology, pp. 174–175. Available at: www.eca.usp.br/sonologia.

Cabnal, Lorena. 2010. *Feminismos diversos: el feminismo comunitario*. Madrid, Spain: ACSUR. Available at: https://porunavidavivible.files.wordpress.com/2012/09/feminismos-comunitario-lorena-cabnal.pdf.

Caesar, Rodolfo. 2017. "Closing words." In: *Sonologia 2016 – Out of Phase Proceedings of the International Conference on Sound Studies*. São Paulo, Brazil: Nusom – Research Centre on Sonology. Available at: www.eca.usp.br/sonologia.

Carneiro, Anni de Novais. 2019. Feinária musical: saúde, arte, afetividade e educação no contexto da Universidade Federal da Bahia. Doctorate thesis, Postgraduate Program in Interdisciplinary Studies on Women, Gender and Feminism. Salvador, Brazil: Faculty of Philosophy and Human Sciences, Federal University of Bahia.

Carvalho, Ellen. 2015. Aioká – breve estudo sobre corpo e gênero no canto popular. Final course paper, bachelor's in Popular Music – Song. Salvador, Brazil: Federal University of Bahia.

Costa, Alexandra Martins. 2017. "Palavra Preta", "Som das Binha" e "Sonora" – espaços de mobilização e fortalecimento da produção musical de mulheres de Salvador. Master's dissertation, Postgraduate Program in Interdisciplinary Studies on Women, Gender and Feminism. Salvador, Brazil: Faculty of Philosophy and Human Sciences, Federal University of Bahia.

Faur, Mirella. 2001. *O anuário da Grande Mãe: guia prático de rituais para celebrar a Deusa*, 2nd edn. São Paulo, Brazil: Gaia.

Feld, Steven. 1994. "From ethnomusicology to echo-muse-ecology: reading R. Murray Schafer in the Papua New Guinea Rainforest." *Soundscape Newsletter*, 8. Available at: www.acousticecology.org/writings/echomuseecology.html.

Feld, Steven. 2015. "Acoustemology." In: D. Novak and M. Sakakeeny (eds.), *Keywords in Sound*. Durham, NC: Duke University Press, pp. 12–21.

Gargallo Cellentani, Francesca. 2012. *Feminismos desde Abya Yala: ideas y proposiciones de las mujeres de 607 pueblos en nuestra América*. Bogotá, Colombia: Ediciones desde Abajo.

Gautier, Ana Maria Ochoa. 2006. "Sonic transculturation, epistemologies of purification and the aural public sphere in Latin America." *Social Identities*, 12(6), pp. 803–825.

Gautier, Ana Maria Ochoa. 2014. *Aurality: Listening and Knowledge in Nineteenth-Century Colombia*. Durham, NC: Duke University Press.

Gomes, Francimária Ribeiro. 2017. Trânsitos musicais e comunicação popular: experiências de protagonismo de mulheres negras em Cachoeira, BA. Master's dissertation, Postgraduate Program in Interdisciplinary Studies on Women, Gender and Feminism. Salvador, Brazil: Faculty of Philosophy and Human Sciences, Federal University of Bahia.

Gomes, Rodrigo Cantos Savelli. 2016. "Os percursos da etnomusicologia feminista nas últimas quatro décadas: uma visão de dentro por Ellen Koskoff." *Revista Estudos Feministas*, 24(2), p. 292. Available at: https://periodicos.ufsc.br/index.php/ref/article/view/44621.

Gonzalez, Lélia. 1988. "A categoria político-cultural de amefricanidade." *Tempo Brasileiro*, 92/93, pp. 69–82.

Grosz, Elizabeth. 1994. *Volatile Bodies: Toward a Corporeal Feminism*. Indianapolis, IN: Indiana University Press.

Haraway, Donna. 1988. "Situated knowledges: the science question in feminism and the privilege of partial perspective." *Feminist Studies*, 14(3), pp. 575–599.

Hayes, Lauren. 2019. "Beyond skill acquisition: improvisation, interdisciplinarity, and enactive music cognition." *Contemporary Music Review*, 38(5), pp. 446–462.

hooks, bell. 2010. "Vivendo de amor." Portal Geledés. Available at: www.geledes.org.br/vivendo-de-amor/.

hooks, bell. 2019. *Erguer a voz: pensar como feminista, pensar como negra*, translated by Cátia Bocaiuva Maringolo. São Paulo, Brazil: Elefante.

Lago, Jorgete Maria Portal. 2017. Mestras da cultura popular em Belém-PA: narrativas de vida, ativismos culturais e protagonismos musicais. Doctorate thesis, Postgraduate Program in Music. Salvador, Brazil: Federal University of Bahia.

Marashinsky, Amy Sophia. 2007. *O oráculo da Deusa: um novo método de adivinhação (The Goddess Oracle)*. São Paulo, Brazil: Ed. Pensamento.

Moreira, Inaê. 2020. "Dança intuitiva: corpas em movimento, ciclos lunares e ancestralidade." Available at: www.inaemoreira.com/dan%C3%A7a-intuitiva.

Moura, Soraia Maria de. 2013. A percepção da fisiologia sutil na prática do yoga. Master's in Education dissertation. Campinas, Brazil: State University of Campinas.

Nhat Hanh, Thich. 2015. *How to Love*. Berkeley, CA: Parallax Press.

Nogueira, Isabel and Lambert, Leandra. 2017. "Strana Lektiri, voicing and cut-up tragedy: some reflections about feminist epistemologies, sound creation and the gendered allocation of space." In: *Sonologia 2016 – Out of Phase: Proceedings of the International Conference on Sound Studies*. São Paulo, Brazil: Nusom – Research Centre on Sonology, pp. 135–140. Available at: www.eca.usp.br/sonologia.

Oberom. 2015. *Vegan yoga: o ashtanga yoga de Patanjali sob a perspectiva vegana*, 2nd revised and updated edn. São Paulo, Brazil: Editora Alfabeto.

Oyewùmí, Oyèrónké. 2004. *Conceituando o gênero: os fundamentos eurocêntricos dos conceitos feministas e o desafio das epistemologias africanas.* Translation of *Conceptualizing Gender: The Eurocentric Foundations of Feminist Concepts and the Challenge of African Epistemologies. African Gender Scholarship: Concepts, Methodologies and Paradigms*. CODESRIA Gender Series, vol. 1, pp. 1–8. Dakar, Senegal: CODESRIA.

Pinto, Valdina Makota. 2013. *Meu caminhar, meu viver*. Salvador, Brazil: Secretariat for the Promotion of Racial Equality, Government of the State of Bahia.

Prandi, Reginaldo. 2001. *Mitologia dos Orixás*. São Paulo, Brazil: Companhia das Letras.

Ribeiro, Djamila. 2017. *O que é lugar de fala?* Belo Horizonte, Brazil: Letramento.

Rosa, Laila. 2005. Epahei iansã! Música e resistência na nação Xambá: uma história de mulheres. Masters in Music – Ethnomusicology dissertation. Salvador, Brazil: Federal University of Bahia.

Rosa, Laila. 2009. As juremeiras da nação Xambá (Olinda, PE): músicas, performances, representações de feminino e relações de gênero na jurema sagrada. Doctorate in Music thesis. Salvador, Brazil: Federal University of Bahia.

Rosa, Laila. 2019. "Trânsitos e conexões sagradas, feministas e musicais de *Abya Yala* entre Brasil e México." *Revista Brasileira de Estudos da Homocultura*, 2(3). Available at: www.revistas.unilab.edu.br/index.php/rebeh.

Rosa, Laila and Nogueira, Isabel. 2015. "O que nos move, o que nos dobra, o que nos instiga: notas sobre epistemologias feministas, processos criativos, educação e possibilidades transgressoras em música." *Revista Vórtex*, 3(2), pp. 25–56.

Rosa, Laila, Iyanaga, M., Hora, E., Silva, L., Araujo, S., Medeiros, L. and Alcantara, N. 2013. "Epistemologias feministas e a produção de conhecimento recente sobre mulheres e música no Brasil: algumas reflexões." In: Isabel Nogueira and Susan Campos (eds.), *Estudos de gênero, corpo e música*, vol. 3. Porto Alegre, Brazil: Associação Nacional de Pesquisa e Pós-Graduação em Música.

Santos de Jesus, Bruna. 2017. Mulheres no reggae? Das epistemologias feministas ao reggae no cenário soteropolitano: experiências de mulheres e música. Final course paper, bachelor's degree in Gender and Diversity Studies. Salvador, Brazil: Federal University of Bahia.

Santos de Jesus, Bruna. 2021. As cantautoras de reggae em Salvador/Bahia: a música como ponto de partida. Master's dissertation, Postgraduate Program in Music. Salvador, Brazil: Federal University of Bahia.

Sharp, Willoughby. 2013. "Videoperformance." *eRevista Performatus, Inhumas*, 1(6).

Silva, Mara Ariana. 2019. Raperas sudacas: a poética amefricana e mestiza sapatão na América Latina. Master's dissertation, PostgraduateProgram in Interdisciplinary Studies on Women, Gender and Feminism. Salvador, Brazil: Faculty of Philosophy and Social Sciences, Federal University of Bahia.

Teixeira, Adriana Gabriela Santos. 2016. Mulher no palco: ritos poéticos teatrais de iniciação ao feminino sagrado. Master's dissertation, Postgraduate Program in Performing Arts. Salvador, Brazil: Federal University of Bahia.

Vergueiro, Viviane. 2016. Por inflexões decoloniais de corpos e identidades de gênero inconformes: uma análise autoetnográfica da cisgeneridade como normatividade." Master's dissertation, Institute of Humanities, Arts and Sciences Professor Milton Santos. Salvador, Brazil: Federal University of Bahia.

11
DISPATCHES
Cartographing and sharing listenings

Lílian Campesato and Valéria Bonafé

Invention and sharing of listening

In this chapter, we will present one of the actions we undertook as part of Microfonias: Invention and Sharing of Listening,[1] a collaborative project, both practical and speculative, which we started in 2017. This project aims to investigate listening experimentally, with meaningful openness to creative practices. The emphasis on the experimental process is what moves us in this research-creation project towards new modes of knowledge. In our project, we start from the premise that 'knowledge is invented in the escape, in the excess' (Manning 2016, 38), which implies crafting techniques and methods that favour displacements and create the conditions to escape what is already known. Our methodology has been based on conversations (between us and other artists) that later become material for analysis and discussion. The project implies a challenging exercising of alterity through which it is possible to experiment oneself in the other and at the same time the other in oneself (Campesato and Bonafé 2019). The other, here, is the outside-of-the-subject, the social other, things, technologies, nature, all that which produces effects on our bodies. At stake is the readiness for an experience of listening that effectively opens itself to the *outside*, to virtualities and multiple mediations, and which stirs the emergence of complex networks of listening with significant potential of expansion (Campesato and Bonafé 2019).

When we began the *Microfonias* project, we connected more on the basis of resonances than by identification, as our artistic practices point to different techniques, media, resources and musical scenes.[2] What we had in common was the desire to build an alternative environment for research and artistic creation where we could invent ways of acting based on our own experiences. This environment was crafted throughout the meetings and modulated by a particular ethic. This ethics is, to a large extent, defined by the long interaction and the regularity of the

DOI: 10.4324/9781003008217-15

meetings, as well as by a relationship with the work that goes beyond objectivity and productivity, blurring the boundaries between what belongs to the personal sphere and what constitutes itself as research and work interest. As a result, we see the emergence of a space of trust that welcomes vulnerabilities and a dynamic that does not run over the time of creative imagination. In our project, we create new possibilities by putting in contact our biographies, artistic practices and individual investigation. Added to this is the fact that this environment was created by the encounter between two women, being therefore deeply modulated by it. This is reflected in the creation of particular modes of existence, language and knowledge, taking us to the field of feminist epistemologies (Rago 2021, 131).

Our trajectory until this point includes three actions. The first was developed in 2017–18, and started with recorded conversations analysing our own creative processes.[3] The second one took place in 2019, and integrated into our process the work of Brazilian artist Janete El Haouli (1955–), where we worked on the basis of recorded testimonies.[4] In our third action, beginning in 2020, we propose maintaining an artistic correspondence between both of us through conversations, extrapolating the verbal dimension, that unfold by means of poetic language, exclusively on an aural, imagetic and affective plane. Even if each of these three actions have their particularities both in terms of research focus and methodology, they interweave and compose a broad project dedicated to the poetics and politics of listening in the field of musical and sound creation. Our actions could be described as experimental practices destabilizing hegemonic forms of listening and discourse while pointing towards a *feminist politics of listening*.[5] In this sense, we have exercised different listening practices, which appear as a consequence of our interest to reflect on the complexities inherent in processes of *sharing listening*. This interest has led our project to unfold in a relational perspective, constituted especially around the idea of *conversation*:

> Conversation implies interaction, mutual action shared between different bodies. Interaction in a conversation is not tied to a simple to and fro between well ordered interlocutions. It is flux. Not the sum of I and the other, but the *passage* from one to the other. It is *between*, in the interval that both repels and attracts the agents.
>
> *Campesato and Bonafé (2019, 53)*

If the conversation implies interaction between different bodies, the quality of the interaction needs to be questioned: what is it that really constitutes the *passage* between bodies in a conversation? In our experience, listening is central in responding to this question. During a conversation, it is the availability to listen to the other which ends up modulating what is said. It is a listening presupposing both the capacity to be affected and to affect, a listening which is present affectively. In a conversation, this presence may include oral manifestations – a question, a commentary, some sort of interjection – or even a bodily gesture, a gaze, a nod. But it also may be exercised silently by simply maintaining an open channel of listening.

This allows to surface that which is frequently silenced in written discourses, in interviews or conferences. The situation, context, things, events also play a part in building encounters. It is in the heterogeneity of mediations that the conversation opens space for error, stuttering, noises, for affects, for that which is veiled, the unsayable and the inaudible.

The three actions created in these last few years build on an understanding of conversation as a process dealing with and investigating that which is between the lines. Be it through the relation between presence and alterity implicated in the conversation, the testimony or non-verbal correspondence, be it through the necessary displacement to navigate through the voice or through the poetics of another artist, singularities are triggered, actualizing in particular ways the multiple assemblages (material, affective, contextual, human, nonhuman) accumulated in the experience of listening.

In this chapter, we will concentrate on the analysis of our most recent action, taking place in the context of the COVID-19 pandemic. This action is based on asynchronous and non-verbal conversations between both of us. The conversations are neither oral nor written. Instead, we sent each other small compositions, sonic miniatures, audiovisual impressions created especially for this conversation and which could be understood as artistic testimonies of our bodies, our 'listenings', our lived experiences. However, the analysis presented in this chapter is not restricted to artistic objects created in the context of this action. What is under analysis is listening in relation to what is listened to. By analysing this action, we want to show in what way relations emerging from listening transcend the place of the physical body, as well as sound as a vibrational entity. Our analysis seeks to highlight the relational and multimediated nature of the body (Rolnik 2018) and sound (Born 2019), which also constitutes the very nature of listening.

Our analysis path involves a circuit of relations that freely navigates through three instances: artistic objects, textual production of what we call *affective reports from listening*, and the creation of a *fiction-score*. This circuit and the particular way in which it develops reveal a kind of map, a cartography of our listening. Through this cartographical movement, we seek to share not only what we hear, but how our listening navigates.

Dispatching listening

The action we started during the pandemic consists of non-verbal and asynchronous conversations taking place in the form of an artistic correspondence, which we simply called *Dispatches*. A dispatch may be a sound miniature, a montage of images, a video, a small composition or any other sort of artistic production. It is dispatched without any kind of contextualizing message other than the title. It is important to note that the dispatch has a specific address. The recipient isn't the general public, but one of us. After receiving it, a personal listening adventure begins, together with the creation of another dispatch, moving the process onwards. The emphasis on the term 'dispatch' is related to our interest in the process of addressing the other as well as in the movement of passage established between us through our listening. A dispatch is an inscription of a singular listening urging on another listening.

In this section, we analyse two specific dispatches: *sky-only, a vertigo*, an archive sent by Lílian Campesato to Valéria Bonafé on May 8, 2020, and *or-life (impulse 1 and impulse 2)*, a set of three archives sent by Valéria Bonafé to Lílian Campesato on May 20, 2020. Both dispatches have an audiovisual format and involve recording, editing and digital processing of sound and video. Here, our main strategy for analysis[6] is the production of two affective reports from listening, dedicated to each of the dispatches. The dynamic used to produce the reports involves listening to the received dispatch and, based on this experience, producing a possible narrative about this listening experience in the form of a text. These are reports written in poetic language and undertaken as a sort of register of the assemblages perceived during a specific listening. These reports work as testimonies of our listening: the situation in which we listen, the images we create, our memories and subjective impressions. The way these reports are carried out reflects our desire to experiment with the construction of narratives based on sensible experience. Just as in a conversation or testimony, they favour openings towards the other while establishing multiple networks of listening between different agents.

Before moving on to affective reports from listening, we present what we call a *fiction-score* of the *Dispatches* action. This fiction-score synthesizes our action in the form of an artistic proposition. It explains the fundamentals, dynamics, ethics and desires involved in the action, functioning as an invitation to other people who may want to practice it. The fiction-score also brings a preamble that contextualizes the moment in which the action was created, highlighting the impact of social isolation resulting from the COVID-19 pandemic on the course of our project and, consequently, on the creation of this action. It is also important to mention that this fiction-score was prepared after the creation of some dispatches. It did not, therefore, operate as a prescriptive score, in which idea precedes action. Rather, the fiction-score is a later inscription of what we experience in our collective practice. In this way, our fiction-score also integrates our process of analysing the *Dispatches* action and reflects our desire for involving other people in our listening experiences. Through the reports and the fiction-score (in addition to the artistic pieces themselves), our listeners-readers – you – are invited to listen to our and your own listening.

Fiction-score

Dispatches, a proposition for sharing listening[7]

For two or more resonating agents

A virus is a micro-agent placed at the limit between the living and the non-living. It differs from other living beings as it does not possess a cellular structure or its own metabolism, and depends on a host to survive and reproduce. In 2020, a strange state of mind took hold of the planet. Isolation, masks, extreme asepsis. The age of an accentuated separation of bodies. Avoid sharing: the same air, the same surface. Avoiding contact with other skins; sterilization of touch. But the ear is also tactile. The voice of the other comes through the air, touches my eardrum – that very thin skin membrane vibrates and reacts. Listening is a transmission and contact. It needs a host and it is only in it that it survives, resonates. Listening-virus.

fundamentals

- the dispatch is any type of artistic production especially created and addressed to someone
- the exchange of dispatches constitutes a *conversation* of an artistic nature
- the *agent* is someone who wants to participate in the conversation

dynamic of the conversation

- agent A creates a dispatch and sends it to agent B, who starts the conversation
- after receiving the dispatch, agent B creates a new dispatch and delivers it to agent A, moving the process along
- the operation is repeated while there is the desire to continue the conversation
- more than a linear question-and-answer dynamic, the proposition is to gradually compose a cloud of dispatches that work throughout the conversation as a virtual field of memories and accumulated experiences and through which agents may traverse freely

ethics of the conversation

- act freely on the received dispatch, give continuity or promote breaks in the flow of the conversation, always look to sustain the relation between the listening of the received dispatch and the process of creation of the new one

suggestions to share listening

- don't bar ideas, don't block impulses, don't interrupt flux, don't get stranded with limiting technical issues
- open up to vulnerability, deobstruct access to fragilities
- give way to the unsayable and the inaudible
- don't run time over

Two affective reports from listening

The first affective report

Written by Valéria Bonafé from listening to *sky-only, a vertigo*, sent by Lílian Campesato to Valéria Bonafé, May 8, 2020.

When I received Lílian's first dispatch, it was almost 60 days since I had last left my house. I live in the city of São Paulo, in a house surrounded by buildings on all sides. Plunged into the middle of them, I have an oasis, a garden, with a large tangerine tree and three fructiferous shrubs, allowing me the company of some species of birds. Throughout the day, the chanting of the birds is diluted in the human and nonhuman sounds of a vast metropolis: the sounds of engines, honking, sirens coming from the avenue, the roaring accelerations of the hurried motorbikes working for delivery companies, the noise of police helicopters regularly flying over a favela close to where I live, the barking dogs, the neighbourhood's buzzing, the incessant noise of new buildings being built, which don't stop rising during the pandemic. Even if isolated inside the house, the sounds composing my quarantined sound landscape don't allow me to forget that I am one of the bodies inhabiting one of the ten most populated cities in the world, which is also one of the epicentres of the pandemic in Brazil and the world, and in that month of May, an epicentre of 'panelaços'[8] against the current Bolsonaro government.

The link for the dispatch arrived in my email box in the early hours of May 8. Like a child waiting anxiously for the arrival of a very special present, I was in a mix of curiosity and enthusiasm. But in receiving the link, I felt the situation demanded a certain preparation – mine and of the environment – for me to 'unwrap' and find out what was, after all, the first dispatch I was receiving from Lílian in our new experimental action together. I decided to wait. I passed all day prolonging with pleasure that state of suspension, of openness to the unknown. As if it were possible to hold back a little the flow of time and freeze a micro-particle of an instant prior to any actualization, that unattainable point which is the plenitude of a field of virtualities. In the folds of my memory and in the midst of my affects, my imagination groped for infinite possibilities from the incessant loop implanted in me from the moment I read the filename: 'sky-only, a vertigo.mov'.

Contrary to the experience of other people, my isolation during the pandemic hasn't been solitary or allowed time for myself. Having a small baby who demands exclusivity, of my gaze, my listening, my body, it's only after she's asleep that the rhythm of the house changes and I have some time to be alone. Late at night, sat in front of the computer, in the dark, with headphones, I was ready to finally only listen (alone and exclusively) to sky-only. Besides my state of total availability, the setting and technological gear involved helped me open myself to a space of immersive fruition. The blacked out room made the screen magnetize my gaze, whereas the closed-back over-ear headphones (with excellent noise isolation) sucked in the totality of my listening. There I was released from the surrounding world, wholly open to the aesthetic experience.

A black screen. I hear a sonorous landscape, plenty of birds, insects, the wind. But I also hear her footsteps, her breathing. She had told me she'd be travelling to Ubatuba, a coastal city 250 km from São Paulo, to try to take the edge off the quarantine pressure. Differently from me, she lives in an apartment, without a garden, birds, a place to take in the sun, being only able to see a snip of the sky through the window (as she told me a few times). What I hear seems to be her walking in the wilderness. I feel happy for her. Noises of the equipment, taps on the microphone. Faced with a recording full of traces, where a body and its performance make themselves intentionally present, I take hold of myself as a confidant of her listening, now inscribed in audiovisual media. She invites me to walk with her and listen to her listening. A complex entanglement between nature, bodies, subjectivities and technology *traverses my ears. Or rather, only one of my ears. The exclusivity of the left-ear channel begins to disturb me: why is it all condensed only on one side? Could it be some sort of problem with my device? I check, and everything is running well. I then ask what her intentions could be: an uncommon field recording listening proposition? A conceptual provocation? Would she be trying to tell me something with this? Is she reserving the opening of the right ear for some sort of special moment? I begin to hear the depth of the silence in my right ear. My body splits in two, a sensation of incompleteness, of an absent presence.*

After around two minutes of acousmatic mono listening, already sensing myself in the midst of Brazil's Atlantic Forest, my eyes are invited to participate in this walk: greens appear, the gradations of colour, the intensities, the shining of the sun (see Figure 11.1). An exuberant forest overflowing life. But the horizon is not on the eyeline. Drawing my gaze towards the sky, she shows me the forest in an ascending movement, from the ground upwards, sliding and spinning uninterruptedly between the wide treetops, composing a complex and extensive web of branches and ramifications. I become aware of the musculature of the neck, shape up my posture. Besides the intense shifting of the camera, some techniques of editing and montage – altered speeds, overlaps, transparencies, slight lags – contribute to a vertiginous narrative outline. Disorder, frenzy. In the midst of the rhythmic liveliness of layers of sounds and images, my senses confound themselves, and all of a sudden my memory retrieves the image of my placenta – hyper-ramified life interface connecting and sustaining the flux between the inside and the outside. I blend the green with a red membrane and add to the sound landscape the mark of another body: the heart of a foetus. Moved, I add to the sound inscriptions of animal-bodies, of a human-body in movement, of the machine-body recorder, the memory of the accelerated pulse of an unknown-body yet to be born, placed at the threshold between the living and the non-living.

This complex, heterogeneous entanglement of assembled mediations, actualized in the moment of listening to sky-only, *placed me in an interesting perceptual tension. The tension emerged from a very stark contrast between the outside and the inside. Initially,* sky-only *transported me outside (of the isolation, of my city, of my routine, of my body) with the help of triggers throwing me inwards (the night, solitary listening, the dark, headphones). But then, by placing myself outwards in the middle of the rainforest,* sky-only *took me towards very intimate visual, sound, bodily, affective memories. Just like a placenta, my listening oscillated simultaneously between the inside/outside and the outside/inside: the outside inside me, the inside outside me. The pandemic, the city, the isolation, the solitude, the dark, the headphones, the colours, the forest, the sky, the sun, the chanting of the birds, her steps, her breathing, the*

  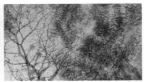

FIGURE 11.1 Three frames of *sky-only, a vertigo*
Source: Personal archive. Available at: www.microfonias.net/dispatches.

noises of the recording, the left channel, the arboreal ramifications, the speeds, the lags, the rhythms, the placenta, the heart: the set of things, of material and immaterial processes, human and nonhuman, assembling a singular listening.

Another blackout. Black screen, the sound landscape remains, her body remains. Six or seven minutes of the video have passed. In the dark, I focus again exclusively on listening. I – finally – sense the right channel open, and immediately after, I hear her voice: 'May fourth, two thousand and twenty … eight in the morning …'. What for someone else would have been nothing other than documentary information to me opened an immense field of meaning. I know her routine and know that hour in the morning is rather early for her. She too is the mother of a young girl. I understood immediately that, just as I had to do to be able to listen to her, she too had to find time to be alone. A desired solitude. Again the universe of motherhoods actualized in my listening of her dispatch. Maybe it'll take some years for both of us to be able to talk about anything – even when there are no words uttered – without maternity traversing our conversation. Or maybe not even then it'll be possible. We are also assembled by the vertigo of motherhood.

The second affective report

Written by Lílian Campesato from listening to or-life (impulse 1 and impulse 2), sent by Valéria Bonafé to Lílian Campesato, May 20, 2020.

It was from the corner of a room, real close to the window covered by protective screens, that I interacted with the external world from the apartment where I live with my partner and our 3-year-old daughter. An apartment in a high building surrounded by many other buildings in a neighbourhood whose population is six times larger than that of the city I was born in, 802 km away. In the miniscule trajectories between rooms, I could accompany voyeur-like the changes in the sound landscape of this place throughout day and night. I didn't know if the birds and their chanting increased in quantity, if the sounds of the city were a little less intense, or if my listening was more attentive. Today, it all seems like fiction. Besides the birds' melodies, the whining of mosquitoes, the noise of the neighbours'TV and of the delivery motorbikes, every night the neighbourhood also voiced the political polarization that took hold of Brazil in general and São Paulo in particular. From my window would leave and enter the cries, 'Out with Bolsonaro', 'Murderer'. But you could also hear 'Lula thief', or in Portuguese, 'Petralhada',[9] in the midst of the sounds of banging pots and pans echoing from the buildings.

After a few months of social isolation, we had already experienced the vertigo of freedom in our first trip to the coast after the beginning of the pandemic. On our return to São Paulo, and after our first encounter dedicated to this experimental action, I avidly awaited reencountering Valéria. Something difficult to explain put me in a state of excitement which easily made me abstract the uncountable layers of mediation implied in that virtual encounter. I had only just started to become aware that the world I knew and the relations I had established would never be the same again. I felt my body more and more stranded to the ground, more and more delivered over to the force of gravity. But I always turned to that corner in the room, sat down, with a body stationed in front of a laptop, its small built-in camera, earphones plugged into the P2 outlet of my sound card, connected to a video call software package. This was my phantasy *environment, of strangeness between what was and was not conscious, between what I could and could not hear, between what I could and could not say. In these virtual interactions, so natural nowadays, not even in the domain of simulacra are we ever able to look in the direction of the person we're talking to. Perhaps it's due to the extreme level of abstraction that we are led to believe that such a simulacrum of interaction is a 'conversation'.*

With the first dispatch I received from Valéria, 15 days before the second one, I had solitarily prepared the listening context and been able to give the dispatch the fruition time it asked of me, choosing to listen, pause, return, listen many times, close my eyes, go through the little piece I had awaited with such expectation following my own criteria and without anyone around. But with the second dispatch we were both sat in front of our laptops with the camera on, in an uncanny situation, me listening for the first time, and she observing me on the other side of the call. We listened to the three small videos of or-life (impulse 1 and impulse 2) *only once and in sequence. While I watched the videos during a quick six minutes, the video call remained open the whole time. I was the one who had suggested watching the video before beginning the conversation of that encounter on May 20, 2020. Still, I quickly regretted the suggestion. The level of tension was high. My attention oscillated too much and did not obey my command. I feared not being able to understand, cohere with the dispatch in the way I wanted. Yet, as soon as the videos stopped playing and I began thinking out loud about that experience, I quickly became aware of a sort of simultaneity with time during listening. I became conscious of a temporal multiplicity and realized myself listening to my own listening in the moment I was listening. It was like navigating an overlap, like a net connecting another time and another place to the here and now.*

The first thing I do is read on the screen two words separated by a hyphen: Life-humanity. I ask myself if it is the name of a session or if I'm trying to create meaning from the words. Soon they vanish and I make the effort to listen to a really low sound when, all of the sudden, the surprise. I started smiling when I recognized those sounds. The sound gesture, sliding granularly, of Japu's unmistakable chant was there, all at once, clear: it was my recording which was now appearing in Valéria's dispatch. The same exuberant sound landscape of the Atlantic Forest. It led to many surprises, made me smile and provoked in me a certain awkwardness. I started remembering, forming images, feeling a mix of affection and anxiety. Initially, I did not understand that the sounds were growing and panning from right to left. Wow! Could it have been an intentional construction using my mistake in sending her a version of sky-only, *a vertigo exclusively for the left channel? Really? But what I'm aware of in my left channel is an opaque sound, apparently highly processed, with a highly rhythmic character. It wasn't the shiny landscape filling the harmonic spectrum. It coincided with the moment the images began to move, with the part where the shot of the trees moves from the ground upwards. As soon as I recognized my own video, I perceived the blur making the transition towards the red. A filter transforming and mixing that image triggered in my body an uncanniness, a strong noise, difficult to explain. All of this happened in only two minutes. Again I feel the time of listening overlapping a multiplicity of simultaneous layers.*

Impulse 1 lasts only 60 seconds, but it is what unveils the uncanniness I had felt, that I had already experienced. Close-up, an image reappears with red stains. It is a placenta stamped on paper (see Figure 11.2)! And immediately I am sure that the opaque and rhythmic sound I heard with plenty of processing and edition was a foetus's heart. My shoulder falls, my mouth opens and releases a sigh. I am taken from the present to the past, I return to the sensation of gestation, I remember giving birth. I smile, deeply moved!

Impulse 2 starts. Now it is a cut from the take of the leaves of the cacao tree filmed close-up and in movement. They are in the original colour, at a slightly altered speed. I see an image with Valéria appear, her hand in a smooth swing, with the red filter. It was as if she were dancing with those leaves, like a fragment of an idea of freedom that is inside us. It seems Valéria was there with me, dancing with me, strolling silently. There's no sound produced, but I don't stop listening to the birds, the cardiotocography, to something unsayable. I open myself to the lightness of the movement of her hands, stretch my back, breathe in deeply and wait for the fade out.

I return to the abstract and metaphorical window of the video call, I have to look at her and say something. I feel safer with a bunch of mediations. How impossible it is to face someone in that environment, have a conversation as if I were talking to myself.

Making our own listenings audible

What happens when we make ourselves available to share our listening? Can we express to the other what we experiment with our own bodies? What emerges from this effort of sharing? In our collective experience, sharing processes of listening through relational actions – recorded conversations, the work with audio testimonies, dispatches of an artistic nature – has allowed us to unpack and reflect on ethical, poetic and political questions implicated in listening. After all, how do we perform our listening? To what extent do we have control of that experience? What do we hear, and what do we silence? Which forces make up our listening? These are some of the questions raised by our practice of artistic correspondence – *Dispatches* – and which have helped us displace the reflection on listening to the field of its production, to lived experience, performance, invention.

The *Dispatches* action results in a circuit that allows us to cartograph and share our listening. This circuit involves creating an artistic object to be sent to someone, listening to the artistic object received from someone, creating a report after listening to that artistic object, and reading a listening report produced from this encounter with the object. By creating a new dispatch, we not only listen to our experiences and those of our bodies, but try to make them audible to the other person. While receiving a dispatch, we open ourselves to the other, listen to their

FIGURE 11.2 Frames of *or-life* (left), *impulse 1* (centre) and *impulse 2* (right)
Source: Personal archive. Available at: www.microfonias.net/dispatches.

experiences, their bodies, their listening process, weaving into this openness the listening of our own experiences, our bodies, our listening process. By producing what we call affective reports from listening, we propose to cartograph and share our listening experience of the pieces through textual construction of sensible narratives. Through these reports, we can follow the movement of listening, how it navigates, where it goes.

An artistic object is always an open event, a field of virtualities. Even if each dispatch carries a series of choices and inscriptions, in contact with the other it will be actualized again, always in a singular and unpredictable manner. This multimediated listening experience is not given in the abstract sphere of the subject, but in the body, outside-the-subject, in the lived situation. Here, we consider the body as a place crossed by a set of experiences and which is constituted by multiple relationships that go beyond the borders between subject and object, I and other, conscious and unconscious, human and nonhuman (Rolnik 2018, 53–54). Similarly, sound is also understood here as a relationship – that is, as a phenomenon that emerges from a constellation of multiple mediations that involve mental and bodily, material and affective, individual and collective, human and nonhuman elements and processes (Born 2019, 198).

In the affective reports, we transpose more objective descriptions of our listening situations and open ourselves to a complex set of mediations, which includes sensations, images, memories. What acquires stronger emphasis and becomes more meaningful is what appears in the form of tangible traces, crops up between the lines, looms in what we thought to be irrelevant, the existence of which passed unnoticed. Considering listening as an *embodied act of thought* (Souza-Lima et al. 2021, 30), we seek in our reports to touch upon what is not easily expressed in words, but which nevertheless we know to be real because it concerns what is alive in ourselves and outside of us (Rolnik 2018, 53).

Finally, this action makes us realize the noise implied in the listening experience, what escapes or appears between the lines. What remains from this collective exercise of cartographing and sharing are traces of listening experiences, effects produced precisely on the basis of ambiguities, hesitations, openings. In our non-verbal conversation, we amplify the force of noise, of that which is between the lines and which, after all, constitutes the entirety of the listening experience.

Notes

1 www.microfonias.net.
2 Valéria Bonafé is a composer, and her work has a wide circulation within the so-called concert music circuit. Her practice is characterized by processes that take place mostly in deferred time and by a strong presence of musical writing. Lílian Campesato is a composer-performer, and her work has a wide circulation within the so-called experimental music circuit. Her practice is characterized by processes that take place mostly in real time and by a strong presence of improvisation. We both understand *listening* as

one of the main foundations of our artistic practices. Besides, our collaboration has been strengthened around listening.

3 This action resulted in designing what we call *conversation method*, in an extended debate on listening. On the basis of heterogeneous reading materials from the fields of sound studies, anthropology, psychoanalysis, philosophy and feminist studies, our discussions on listening moved into the field of subjectivity and prompted us to take on the idea of *self-listening* as an important first operator in our project. See Campesato and Bonafé (2019).

4 In this action, we deepened a debate on the construction of discourse and (self-)narratives. We also developed a methodology for analysis based on sharing our listening impressions through the production of what we call *affective reports from listening*. The action resulted in the production of a script for an imaginary piece. Whereas in the previous action we focused on the idea of self-listening, in this action we looked for the development of mechanisms to share listening as action, performativity, leading us to the idea of *listening networks*. See Bonafé and Campesato (2021).

5 We have maintained the horizon of a feminist politics of listening in view since the beginning of our project. More recently, we synthesized this commitment in the following way: 'In this project, the focus is on how women listen to themselves, understand themselves, express themselves. At stake, therefore, is a project committed to exercising a feminist politics of listening, which values random aspects, apparently insignificant, yet intimate, singular, in the desire to build an alternative history, counter-discourses to the dominant ones in the field of artistic creation' (Bonafé and Campesato 2021).

6 The way we understand analysis in our project differs from approaches focused exclusively on the object (music, sound) or the listener. What interests us is to work with an analytical approach that focuses on the *relationship* established between the listener and what is listened to. In our project, the analytical exercises aim to address not the object or the subject, but the listening experience, in its multimediated nature.

7 A Portuguese version of this fiction-score was published as part of a compilation of artistic propositions (verbal instructions, texts, infographics) created during the COVID-19 pandemic. See Campesato and Bonafé (2021).

8 Translator's note: *Panelaços* are a means of peaceful protest where people bang on pots and pans and shout political slogans from the windows of their homes.

9 Translator's note: The Portuguese translation for the Beagle Boys is 'Irmãos Metralha'. In May 2016, the very month when President Dilma Rousseff's impeachment process (or 'rite' as it is strangely described in Brazil) reached the Senate, Reinaldo Azevedo, a right-wing Brazilian journalist, coined the term *petralhada*, alluding to the Beagle Boys, to designate Partido dos Trabalhadores politicians and affiliates.

References

Bonafé, Valéria and Campesato, Lílian. 2021. 'Many voices, resonating from different times and spaces': a script for an imaginary radiophonic piece on Janete El Haouli. *Feminist Review* 127 (Sonic Cyberfeminisms): 141–149. DOI: 10.1177/0141778920969598. https://journals.sagepub.com/doi/10.1177/0141778920969598 (accessed: 25 August 2021).

Born, Georgina. 2019. On nonhuman sound: sound as relation. In: *Sound Objects*, edited by James A. Steintrager and Rey Chow, 185–210. Durham, NC: Duke University Press.

Campesato, Lílian and Bonafé, Valéria. 2019. La conversación como método para la emergencia de la escucha de sí. *El Oído Pensante* 7: 47–70. http://revistascientificas.filo.uba.ar/index.php/oidopensante/article/view/7543 (accessed: 25 August 2021).

Campesato, Lílian and Bonafé, Valéria. 2021. Envios. In: *32 instruções para escutar n(a) pandemia*, edited by Rui Chaves and Fernando Iazzetta. São Paulo, Brazil: Berro.

Manning, Erin. 2016. *The minor gesture*. Durham, NC: Duke University Press.

Rago, Margareth. 2021. Epistemologia Feminista, gênero e história. In: *As Marcas da Pantera: percursos de uma historiadora*, edited by Margareth Rago, 129–145. São Paulo, Brazil: Intermeios.

Rolnik, Suely. 2018. *Esferas da Insurreição: notas para uma vida não cafetinada*. São Paulo, Brazil: N-1 edições.

Souza-Lima, Henrique, Germano, Gustavo, Campesato, Lílian, Esteves, Lúcia, Mapurunga, Marina, Bonafé, Valéria and Reis, Vicente. 2021. Between control and more-than-human events: the listening experience in the light of speculative pragmatism. *AM Journal of Art and Media Studies* 24: 29–39. DOI: 10.25038/am.v0i24.419. https://fmkjournals.fmk.edu.rs/index.php/AM/article/view/419 (accessed: 25 August 2021).

12
APPLYING FEMINIST METHODOLOGIES IN THE SONIC ARTS

Listening to Brazilian Women Talk about Sound

Linda O Keeffe and Isabel Nogueira

Introduction

As female researchers within the sonic arts and music technology, our perspectives have been shaped by a strong engagement with feminist studies and feminist practices (Isabel is based in Brazil, and Linda in Ireland and the UK). We have worked to develop together a new type of sonic arts practice shaped by feminist theory and practices since October 2017.

In early 2017, we began a lengthy dialogue about our relationship to space, mediated by sound, and how listening, as a practice, alters that relationship. This included the way sound can create a sense of belonging or exclusion. Between early 2017 and July 2018, we began to share recordings of the soundscapes we were located in: Porto Alegre, Brazil and Lancaster, UK. The soundscapes included voice-over narration, where we examined our feelings about sharing a listening experience, whether sounds in a place triggered feelings or memories, and more importantly, where and when, as a woman, we could or could not listen or record safely. This then began a process of considering the body of a woman at the centre or locus of the experience of listening. We examined our bodily perceptions as we move through different environments, and our reactions to certain sounds such as large groups of men chatting or shouting, loud sounds, sounds which we define as aggressive, intrusive or invasive of our hearing space, and what we define as positive soundscape/listening experiences. This led to observing ways we might shift our movement and location when we detect a sound that made us feel uncomfortable or unsafe. These reflections led us to think about our practice as female field recordists, composers and performers, and whether the sounds we heard in our everyday lives might impact on our creative practices. What and where did we feel safe to record, what instruments, tones, timbres or words might we use in performances, the way we work with space in the creation of installations, and what

DOI: 10.4324/9781003008217-16

unconscious affects might shape our conceptual processes? In this way, we began to explore the definition and interpretation of the concept of gendered soundscapes and how we might find a way to transform or challenge that relationship to our sonic environment.

Following on from these months of shared findings, Isabel introduced Linda to the work of Brazilian poet Clarice Lispector, in particular her poem 'Se eu fosse eu' (If I were me). The key tenets of this poem relate to the sense of knowing oneself and then presenting that truthful version of yourself to the world, expecting that at first you will be rejected. For us, the conceptual theme represented a new turn in our practice: what does it mean to be oneself, to present a true version of the self in our performance and practice personas? If we could be ourselves, not afraid of the soundscape, not afraid of being attacked, or feeling excluded in certain public spaces, who would we be? It also included the idea that how we might make sound or music could be more truthful if we felt less judged and more accepted in the very masculine world of the sonic arts and music technology.

In our response to 'Se eu fosse eu', we asked what is required to undo these assigned gender norms, find new gender identities, and create a performance work that challenged how we had worked in the past. In developing this concept as a form of practice-led methodology, we designed an approach that would involve a participatory form of research engagement. We would work with different groups of women to explore listening, performing and composing from a gendered ear view, also exploring whether sounding has become a political and personal act for women. The focus would be from the Brazilian context, a site which Isabel felt was radically underexplored within the field of sound, music and equality. In April of 2018, we began a collaboration with the dance collective ECOAR Group, located in São Paulo, working with the choreographer Marilia Velardi. 'Se eu fosse eu' became the theme for both the dance performance and our composition and sound design process. We included the voices of the dancers and choreographers in our work, which premiered in São Paulo in August 2018. This work would be the first stage of developing our methodological approach to a feminist listening practice and would shape our engagement with other sonic arts and performance collectives, and within the many discussions and workshops we had with female-identifying and non-binary composers and sound artists in Brazil.

Sound and Gender

Gender roles have evolved over time, and whether related to religious, socio-cultural, economic or sexual norms, how we perform our assigned gender roles alters in response to these external changes. Yet what remains is the same binary identity of female/male *difference*, one that we must continue to perform, because those 'who fail to do their gender right are regularly punished' (Butler 1988). In our work, we want to examine how the female body constitutes a listening body in a space, one that has written into it both the political, the body which is shaped by the constituent parts defined by society, and the personal, the 'I' and the 'we' experience, where what is felt by the individual and the group of female bodies listening and performing in space is understood as a phenomenologically shared and understood experience.

Developing Our Methods

In advance of our Brazilian collaboration, we began to explore soundwalking as a feminist method. This involved sharing a reading list and talking about our experiences working as a sound artist (Linda O Keeffe) and composer performer (Isabel Nogueira). We began by examining the origins of the soundwalk and how we had used it in our individual practices.

For us, the central tenet of the soundwalk is the focus on attentive listening to familiar spaces, addressing underlying assumptions about a soundscape, and making the familiar, unfamiliar. Equally, soundwalking can raise awareness about how space design, which shapes the soundscape, can influence both our perceptual and physical relationship to a place. For other soundwalking experiences, where sites are narrated for the walker, the experience is focused on attuning the body to particular experiences of space either from the past or imagined futures, and these walks are again about highlighting how sound can shape our experience of a place (Westerkamp 2012).[1] However, walking and listening to explore gendered soundscapes has a very different and more defined motivation. With this in mind, we planned and developed a set of routes that would take us through very distinctive environments, from public parks to industrial sites, back streets and construction areas, shopping districts and large roadways. The goal was to examine, within an urban space, the very different sound zones that might be perceived as locationally and sonically gendered. In Brazil, there is also the long and problematic history of racial exclusion and segregation connected to both enslaved Caribbean and African populations alongside the colonisation of native Brazilians. This means that the concept of the soundscape and place belonging becomes a far more complex process to examine. In developing the soundwalks, we adapted elements of Pauline Oliveros' Deep Listening Method that we would explore with our participants in advance of the soundwalk – sound as both a gendered and racialised experience linked to space design (Stoever 2016; Steinskog 2018; Thompson 2017). We also wanted the walkers to note how they felt about the sounds they heard, to explore what effect listening has on their embodied connection to different spaces.

What Makes a Feminist Methodology?

A feminist methodology is concerned with the construction of new knowledge and often located within a grounded theory approach, as the goal is first and foremost in the production of social change. Interviewing is one of the most 'frequently used data collecting methods in Women's Studies' (Ikonen and Ojala 2007), and is seen as pivotal within social studies of collecting the woman's point of view.

Since the early days of feminism, there has been a movement to challenge and transform methodological approaches and epistemologies of social science research – a long-term goal of challenging the production of knowledge.

Key to these challenges is a concern with power relations between the researcher and the researched. Feminist researchers look to find ways to empower the researched through emancipatory methods. The emancipatory process is 'the placing of control in the hands of the researched, not the researcher' (Oliver 2002, 18); it is allowing the researched a type of ownership of the knowledge they produce. Feminist methodologies argue that we must take into account 'the observer's standpoint, a direct challenge to universality and objectivity' (Schwartz-Shea 2006, 89). In several participatory projects undertaken by Linda, a key principle has been to hand over the tools of research to the participants, to give them ownership of both the data collection and a place within its analysis or presentation, particularly when the outcomes are creative (O'Keeffe 2015; O Keeffe 2017). Isabel's work with black communities in Brazil is shaped by an examination of feminist and post-colonial methodologies which explore processes of inclusion and participation through music production. In developing a feminist methodology, it is necessary to make central the concerns of 'the interests and desires of our societies' most economically, socially, and politically vulnerable groups' (Harding and Norberg 2005, 2). We wanted to adapt and use elements of this process through our engagement with artists, composers and researchers who took part in our focus group workshops.

Soundwalking as a Feminist Methodology

The goal of the feminist soundwalker is to examine space through an embodied approach, using listening as the primary sensory engagement, as listening often reveals the hidden contexts and meaning of place. In our soundwalks, we identified a number of sites to bring walkers, sites that were very much designed spaces, from public parks to high streets, backstreets, laneways and major thoroughfare's. The choice of walks was also based on our participants' familiarity with and relationship to the area: we wanted to bring them through spaces they used on a regular basis.

The design and expected use of place is located within traditional patriarchal systems – 'Architecture, the arts, and other spatial practices have never been neutral' (Schalk, Kristiansson, and Mazé 2017, 13) – and require an intersectional approach to challenge traditional notions of spatial use as well as the long-ignored engagement with our perceptual relationship with sensory space. In other words, we live and operate in spaces that rarely include the voices of the marginalised or excluded in their design. Although these groups, the primary users of public spaces, often find ways to adapt or alter spatial use through the creation of sensory cultures and social practices, if redevelopment occurs, it is that sensory map, created to overlay the public space and give ownership to the users of that space, that becomes erased. Mags Adams (2009) has used soundwalking to bring designers, urban developers and architects through spaces prior to design projects so that they might have an understanding of the spaces they intend to redevelop or reconstruct. This method presupposes a disconnect with the everyday use of space by designers, planners and city managers, who in the main tend to be middle-class men. If we consider what we know about positions of power, we can make a supposition that most organisational hierarchies are dominated by men. This means men have significant control over the design of both public and private space, places that are primarily occupied by women, children, the elderly and the excluded.[2]

In the design of our soundwalk, we created a set of discussions beforehand with our participants that explored the notion of gendered sounds, gendered perception of soundscapes and gendered listening. The different groups of women argued for and against sound as gendered, and explored how listening might be framed from living within a machismo culture within Brazil. Through our focus groups, and in advance of our soundwalk, our listeners began to think about how they would pay attention to sounds from these perspectives while walking, including any memories that might arise as a process of this reflection and analysis. They argued that it was necessary to be as open to sounds as possible, to not enforce ideas of gender in advance of listening in place. This then became the basis of the gendered listening soundwalks. Lefebvre argues that the traditional model of exploring space is one of a body occupying an empty space. This places the space and the body as 'indifferent' to each other, therefore 'anything may go in any "set" of places' and again 'any part of the container can receive anything' (1974, 170). However, a soundwalking method encourages listeners to pay attention to familiar spaces and locate 'synchronized and

FIGURE 12.1 Listening during a soundwalk in Porto Alegre, Brazil, August 2018

regularized sound that follows social patterns and activities' (O Keeffe 2015, 12). Our soundwalkers were walking familiar spaces, but listening and paying attention differently: they were no longer passive, but active listeners. Through the soundwalk, they began to think about the impact certain sounds might have on their bodies, their relationship to place, and further, their relationship to sound.

This iterative process of developing the soundwalks with our participants is shaped by the participatory process; 'feminist researchers have long advocated that feminist research should be not just on women, but for women and, where possible, with women' (Doucet and Duignan 2012). In soundwalking methods conducted by O Keeffe (O Keeffe 2015; 2017; 2014), all participants take a key role in listening, walking, mapping and discussing place and space. The soundwalker is not new to a space; rather, they already have a connection, one that is embodied through historic, socio-cultural connections, and in some instances, economic ties. Through advanced discussions with soundwalkers, we can begin to unpack the relationships and assumptions they have about space design and their soundscapes.

Working with Women in Porto Alegre

Our first set of workshops began in the city of Porto Alegre on 6 and 7 August 2018 at the art space Galeria la Photo, we titled the workshop 'Resonating the Female Body in Space'. We brought a collection of women together who worked across a broad spectrum of fields and disciplines in sound and music. This included audio engineers, traditional musicians, composers, those who worked from bedroom studios using synthesis, or those constructing home-made digital instruments. The group also consisted of transgender participants, very much identifying as women in sound, but also wanting to be recognised as transgender because of the experiences they have, which are unique to their lives as women existing in a patriarchal, homophobic and anti-trans society. This two-day workshop would include an introduction to the history of soundwalking, deep listening and sound mapping, a soundwalk through the city, a mapping exercise and a performance. The workshop also included a one-hour focus group discussion which examined their relationship to the everyday soundscape, as well as a remembered soundscape, and what brought them to sound or music. We were also very interested in exploring their relationship to technology in their practice. As in the UK (Born and Devine 2015), music technology is very much a masculine space in Brazil: few women train in music technology courses, and it is seen as a space occupied by and for men. For a number of our participants, the only way to work with sound and technology is to teach yourself or learn from a male friend or partner:

> I asked my mother to do an electrical course at SENAC. I searched for it and I said 'I wanna do this course,' and she said 'It's gonna be all men, you're not gonna do it.' So it stopped, then, my interest ....
>
> *focus group participant*

Sound and technology in performance spaces in Brazil are very male-dominated. Although women are regularly invited to venues as both artists and audience, they are definitely in the minority. In our discussions with a number of women, most recalled early childhood stories, songs and actions that very much framed the divide between men and women as intrinsic and biological. This then impacted on their relationship to music and sound, what instrument they chose to use, where they would study, and how they would perform – but also their place as a woman in a space which they see as inherently male. For one participant who had a male child, the responsibility of raising a boy in this world became extremely stressful:

> there's a song in Brazil that's saying ... 'Woman who is a bully / who is going to have a boy / what is the destiny / what will he / will be / when will he grow / nananana,' the music is just that, and then comes 'there will be war yet / no.' That's all it's all about. And it's saying it's going to have a war, because war is men's stuff. And I listened to this music a lot, I cried a lot, because, well, because I felt a lot of responsibility for having a boy, to make a boy not be sexist and, I don't know, all these things, it taught me, no, touched me, and this music is like 'it's going to have a war, we're still in the war,' I don't know. So, when you say about technology and relating this to men, I remember so much of my feelings about men's stuff and men's world. I don't know, all this, all the time, I'm thinking about this progress and I think it's so interesting how far we were in technology and all these big, big buildings, all these things, and this was built mostly for men, women are so in a second place on these big constructions.
>
> *focus group participant*

For another, being raised as a boy before they transitioned led them to reflect on how gendered technology was seen in the family home, particularly as it related to music:

> I think, listening to your side of the story and my side of the story being so different, because, just because of the fact that I was raised being perceived as a male and I performed male gender roles for a while. But I ended up now playing electronic music mostly because I spent my entire life using the computer, it's the language I was used to. And I wasn't afraid to ask because I never had experiences where people were condescending or things like that, and I think that's solely [due] to the fact that, you know, they thought 'Oh, it's a boy playing with his toys, with his computer.'
>
> *focus group participant*

They talked about how their sister was told to learn the piano and to not use or play with their brother's technology even though she had expressed an interest in learning how to use it.

Following on from the morning's discussions, we then undertook our soundwalk. Both Linda and Isabel led the group on a slow walk through a number of sites. At five-minute intervals we would stop, set a timer for three minutes, spread out, close our eyes, and listen (see Figure 12.1). Walkers could also collect objects on the walk which they felt resonated with their experience and could be used in the next part of the workshop, which was the creation of a sound map. This soundwalk took approximately one hour, and ended with some breathing and stretching exercises as well as a quick debrief on how everyone felt, before returning to the studio. Often after a silent soundwalk, listeners can find it difficult to talk, sometimes there is tension in the body from slow walking and deep listening which makes it necessary to slowly move back to normal talking and normal walking practices. Our participants then created a series of memory maps using paper, drawing materials, physical objects collected on the walk, and text to describe their experiences. On the second day, we began with a discussion on the history of the graphic score. Using the maps as inspiration, the group worked on creating a graphic score using drawings, objects, voice and texts for its realisation. We then created a group performance. Some key concepts that emerged in our discussions following these practices were how certain sounds, timbres, music, things they defined as noise did in fact feel gendered. One composer suggested that her move to noise music in performance stemmed from a belief that she would only be permitted opportunities to perform if she 'sounded' like the men who performed in the new music collectives. Both Linda and Isabel attended a concert later in October of the band of one of our participants. Before a performance, she spoke to the audience about our workshop and how it inspired her to create a new work, using sounds, notes and styles she had never used before, feeling they hadn't belonged to her.

Engaging with Women across Brazil

In late August, we began a series of discussion sessions with a local female-directed and female-only Batuca group. The founder, Biba Meira, had worked as a jazz drummer for most of her musical career and wanted to encourage women to participate in what is normally a male-dominated performance space. We attended one of their practice sessions, and after it, over home-cooked food, we chatted about the role of women in music, their experiences performing in public, how their family saw them as musicians, and how their sound might be different to other Batuca groups. For some, being a part of this group, this way of learning and performing together, was a form of empowerment, of learning about equality:

> I think I learned a lot with Batucas, not just on the drums, because I evolved a lot on other instruments with Batucas, and also evolved through the other women there, because I knew feminism was about equality between men and women, but I hadn't realised how powerful women were together, you know? How beautiful and genuine that is ….
>
> *Batuca band member 1*

FIGURE 12.2 Biba Meira conducting the group in August 2018

Having the opportunity to be part of the performance spaces, to participate in Carnival, to be thought of as musicians and performers, had other unforeseen impacts:

> We started playing with the street ensembles there as well. The empowerment that the girls taught me helped me a lot. For example, some time ago I would never show my legs because I thought: 'I have big hips, I have cellulite ….' – No! We are all equal, we are all women, of different ages, different lifestyles, of everything, but our sorority is stronger. Even though I enjoy hanging out with men, I think variety is healthy, but having a group just for women and realising that this competition doesn't exist, that these women are here to welcome you, it's really transformative to the participants, it's amazing, we've known each other for not that long, and yet we have such a…
> Such affinities ….'
>
> *Batuca band member 2*

We realised in the conversation circles with these women the strength and power of listening, that many of our stories, limitations, perceptions and feelings of incapacity are shared by other women.

FIGURE 12.3 Chatting with Batuca performers over food, August 2018

On 20 August, we developed a workshop for girls (aged 14–16) at Odyla Gay da Fonseca school (this was part of the project Girls and Science, from the Federal University of Rio Grande do Sul). Some of the activities replicated the work we had done at Galeria Photo, but this time we were focused on education spaces. Our work with these young women included the gendered listening soundwalk, a talk on the practice of deep listening, a discussion about women, sound and technology, and the creation of sound maps. This workshop included the participation of the sound artist Rebecca Collins. We also had a focus group session with the teaching staff in this state-run mixed school, exploring themes about gender, race and class within the Brazilian teaching sector. This was incredibly informative to our research, as it exposed the absence of tools for educators who wished to explore and expand what they could teach in their own classrooms.

Over the course of three months working in Brazil, we created a series of discussions about the research we were undertaking and the impact this was having on our practice. We travelled to Rio de Janeiro, São Paulo and Manaus, covering approximately 4,500 km in this period. Our trip to São Paulo included the performance of our sound design commission *If I were Me* at Espaço Nucleo, for the Research Group in Body and Art Studies dance collective developed by the choreographer Marilia Velardi. On 27 August, we participated in the Brazilian Association of Music Investigation Conference, in Manaus (in Amazonas). We presented a paper about feminist epistemologies in the sonic arts at the first Gender and Music symposium held by this conference. We also ran a number of concerts, symposiums and workshops on peer-to-peer learning for women.

Conclusion

Prior to the research, we imagined there would be a change in our relationship to our bodies, but we could not have imagined what this change would be. Our process was iterative, meaning that themes would emerge through our discussions and creative engagement with different women. There were common or shared themes that emerged in our workshops, talks and even within performances, such as trauma, family histories, gendered relationships to public and private space, problematic attitudes to women in the arts and education, and the treatment of women of colour and trans women. These themes made us feel uncomfortable, and the way we opened up and shared together was new. We had no previous experience of working together on all these fronts, and each of us had a specific need, whether for rehearsal and preparation time or for ideas on how to conduct the workshops and lectures. For us, a key part of our collaboration was to constantly talk to each other. This constant dialogue allowed us to organise the workshops, respond and adapt to new situations, and plan the many artistic performances and concerts over three months; this meant our collaborative approach became a very intense and transformative experience for the both of us.

We understand that there is a loop, a circularity, between teaching, artistic practice and where we present our work outside the university. So we sought to inhabit these places and perceive in our bodies what was changing, how we transported these experiences and things learned from one place to another. The development of different activities during the residency brings an important element that characterises women's work: the plurality and accumulation of roles. Green (1997) talks about a separation between the work done by women in the field of music, and here we extend this conception to the field of sound arts and sonic arts. According to Green, there are certain areas and spaces of music that are seen as more acceptable for women, such as singing, teaching and playing some instruments, whereas spaces of technology, the studio, audio engineering, computer music and coding are not seen as spaces typically occupied by women. Within these dynamics, our proposal was to develop peer-to-peer learning approaches, to encourage women to develop new skills and new methods of making. For us as performers, we wanted to overcome innate fears around spontaneous and improvised performance opportunities. In our discussions with different women, they stated that whether in performance or education spaces, women are underrepresented in key roles. This links to an understanding that it is part of the patriarchal logic that women have a lapse of confidence in their own abilities, always living in the logic of not being good enough, not enough. According to Crasnow (2020), 'feminists are united in urging recognition of the social contexts in which' research takes place and 'knowledge is received'. As more women enter a field of knowledge, whether in the arts or sciences, it becomes increasingly apparent where the gaps lie in supporting their contributions and engagement with those spaces.

From the understanding of the body as a place of meaning construction, but mainly of the body as a locus and mediator of learning, experiences and possibilities, we understand that it is necessary to de-territorialise in order to build a new process of reterritorialisation. At the same time, cultural constructions of gender senses are not only manifested consciously, but also unconsciously. We agree with Suely Rolnik (Rolnik and Preciado 2018) when she argues for an insurrection of the unconscious to escape the cafetinistic processes of gender coloniality. In this process of accessing the constructions of unconscious processes, art is a privileged space for constructing sense making, it is something that you learn by doing, where the creation of methods is constantly tested, retested and validated.

We realised through our collaboration and working with different women's groups, that sharing our skills, listening and talking to each other, gave us a sense of empowerment, of no longer feeling isolated. This brings us back to the work of Clarice Lispector, 'Se eu fosse eu', by examining how we might be true to ourselves, how we trigger processes of estrangement and enchantment, which allows us to think differently from the way we were taught.

Notes

1 See Sophie Knezic's Chapter 16 in this book on Janet Cardiff and Georges Bures Miller; see also the work of Hildegard Westerkamp for narrated soundwalks.
2 In this instance, the excluded are dependent on the socio-cultural space being examined, so excluded could include race, class, religion, gender, or all of these attributes if examined from an intersectional perspective.

Bibliography

Adams, Mags. 2009. 'Hearing the City: Reflections on Soundwalking'. *Qualitative Researcher* 10: 6–9.

Born, Georgina, and Kyle Devine. 2015. 'Music Technology, Gender, and Class: Digitization, Educational and Social Change in Britain'. *Twentieth-Century Music* 12 (2): 135–72. https://doi.org/10.1017/S1478572215000018.

Butler, Judith. 1988. 'Performative Acts and Gender Constitution: An Essay in Phenomenology and Feminist Theory'. *Theatre Journal* 49: 519–31.

Crasnow, Sharon. 2020. 'Feminist Perspectives on Science'. In *The Stanford Encyclopedia of Philosophy*, edited by Edward N. Zalta. Palo Alto, CA: Metaphysics Research Lab, Stanford University. https://plato.stanford.edu/archives/win2020/entries/feminist-science/.

Doucet, Brian, and Enda Duignan. 2012. 'Experiencing Dublin's Docklands: Perceptions of Employment and Amenity Changes in the Sheriff Street Community'. *Irish Geography* 45 (1): 45–65. https://doi.org/10.1080/00750778.2012.698972.

Green, Lucy. 1997. *Music, Gender, Education*. Cambridge, UK: Cambridge University Press.

Harding, Sandra, and Kathryn Norberg. 2005. 'New Feminist Approaches to Social Science Methodologies: An Introduction'. Signs: Journal of Women in Culture and Society 30 (4): 1–7.

Ikonen, Hanna-Mari, and Hanna Ojala. 2007. 'Creating Togetherness and Experiencing Difference in Feminist Interviews – Knowing in a Post-Standpoint Way?' *Graduate Journal of Social Science* 4 (2): 80–103.

Lefebvre, Henri. 1974. *The Production of Space*. Hoboken, NJ: Wiley-Blackwell.

O'Keeffe, Linda. 2015. 'Thinking Through New Methodologies. Sounding Out the City with Teenagers'. *Qualitative Sociology Review* 11 (1): 6–32.

O Keeffe, Linda. 2014. '(Sound)Walking through Smithfield Square in Dublin'. Sounding Out!, 10 February. http://soundstudiesblog.com/2014/02/10/soundwalking-through-smithfield-square-in-dublin/.

O Keeffe, Linda. 2015. 'Memories of Sound: Socioeconomic, Community and Cultural Soundscapes of Smithfield, Dublin from the 1950s'. In *Auditory Culture Reader*, edited by Les Back and Michael Bull, 2nd ed., 217–28. Oxford, UK: Berg.

O Keeffe, Linda. 2017. 'Performing the Soundscape with Third Age Adults: The Derry Soundscape Project'. *WI Journal of Mobile Media* 11 (1): 24.

Oliver, Mike. 2002. 'Emancipatory Research: Realistic Goal or Impossible Dream?' In *Doing Disability Research*, edited by Colin Barnes and Geof Mercer, 15–31. Leeds, UK: The Disability Press.

Rolnik, Suely, and Paul B. Preciado. 2018. *Esferas da inssureição: notas para uma vida não cafetinada*, 1st ed. São Paulo, Brazil: N-1 Edições.

Schalk, Meike, Thérèse Kristiansson, and Ramia Mazé, eds. 2017. *Feminist Futures of Spatial Practice: Materialisms, Activisms, Dialogues, Pedagogies, Projections*. Baunach, Germany: Art Architecture Design Research.

Schwartz-Shea, Peregrine. 2006. 'Judging Quality: Evaluative Criteria and Epistemic Communities'. In *Interpretation and Method: Empirical Research Methods and the Interpretive Turn*, edited by Peregrine Schwartz-Shea and Dvora Yanow, 1st ed., 89–113. New York: M.E. Sharpe.

Steinskog, Erik. 2018. *Afrofuturism and Black Sound Studies: Culture, Technology, and Things to Come*. Palgrave Studies in Sound. London: Palgrave Macmillan. https://doi.org/10.1007/978-3-319-66041-7.

Stoever, Jennifer Lynn. 2016. *Sonic Color Line: Race and the Cultural Politics of Listening*. New York: New York University Press.

Thompson, Marie. 2017. 'Whiteness and the Ontological Turn in Sound Studies'. *Parallax* 23 (3): 266–82. https://doi.org/10.1080/13534645.2017.1339967.

Westerkamp, Hildegard. 2012. 'Soundwalk Practice: An Agent for Change?' In *The Global Composition: Sound, Media and the Environment*, edited by Sabine Breitsameter and Claudia Soller-Eckert, 55–70. Darmstadt, Germany: Fachbereich Media.

PART IV
The Body Technology

13
THE SENSUALITY OF LOW FREQUENCY SOUND

Cat Hope

Introduction

When people describe physical effects of sound frequencies, it is usually about the experiences of extremes: a piercing high tone, a pounding low beat. However, sustained low frequency sound has the capacity to induce what could be considered a sensuous listening experience, created by the conscious sensing of vibrations in the body. Studies have shown that very low frequencies can be experienced through our skin in addition to the ears (Yamada et al. 1986, 21), providing an opportunity to re-evaluate listening and its relationship to our bodies.

The effects of low frequency sound have been understood and engaged in music throughout history. Drumming in passage graves in the Neolithic age generated extremely low sounds as a technique to alter consciousness (Devereux 2001, 45), and some large concert organs feature pipes that emit low frequency sounds intended to stir religious congregations into feeling closer to their God (Angliss 2003, 139). The low-pitched instruments of the classical music tradition, such as the tuba and double bass, were often used to reinforce and stabilise harmony. More recent developments in electronic music have revolutionised our experience of low frequency sound by amplifying ranges previously inaudible to the human ear. This has seen these sounds used to boost effects in movies, reinforce beats in dance music, and create an arrival point for the ubiquitous 'drop' in recent commercial music. However, some artists are manipulating low frequency sound in music compositions to deliberately create 'vibration-sensation' (Trower 2012, 9), where audiences can experience a more embodied listening experience.

DOI: 10.4324/9781003008217-18

Low Frequency Sound and the Sonic Body

A quick overview of very low frequency (VLF) sound maybe useful here. VLF sound is considered to be below 200 Hz, and includes the so-called 'inaudible' range of infrasound, which for humans, is below around 20 Hz.[1] It is a frequency range most often discussed in the context of acoustic science when addressing noise control and sound pollution regarding wind farms or traffic (Leventhall 2003), urban myths (Swezey 1995), and weaponry (Goodman 2012; English 2016). In music, VLF is most often discussed in the context of popular dance tracks, usually in terms of its role in reinforcing the beat, or as the foundation of high-volume amplification experienced in dance clubs, raves, or outdoor concerts, where the bass frequencies can often be heard from much further away than other frequency ranges (Jasen 2016; Fink 2018). When VLF sound is in the infrasonic range, the nature of the sound changes: a note played as a long, smooth tone will be reproduced as 'rough' and irregular (Yeowart 1976, 41). A closer examination of VLF in broader music contexts is only just starting to appear, as electronic music continues to develop, and the effects of VLF sound on the body are now well documented. VLF can vibrate parts of the body, creating physical effects such as, unconscious vibration in the eyes, causing vision blurriness and apparitions (Tandy 1998, 321). It can vibrate specific internal organs and bones, with vibrational therapies that use VLF claiming health benefits (Ruan et al. 2008). A subtle approach to reception occurs when VLF is experienced in the body by 'listening' through the skin. This offers a different physical reception to sound in music to that only experienced via the ear. Julian Henriques (2003) uses the term 'sonic body' in an attempt to theorise this sensory experience of bass, where the body acts as a sensate actor between nature (our bodies) and culture (music). Kendall Walton uses the term 'somatic perception' to explain the way VLF sounds 'not only come to us, but are experienced as being inside us' (Walton 2012, 124). These frameworks provide an opportunity to create sensation-orientated responses to music where VLF is present. These responses can be applied via compositional approaches, as well as performance (including playback techniques), some examples of which will be discussed in this chapter.

The term 'sensuous' is often used when discussing the phenomenology of sound, applied to listening experiences considered erotic (Trower 2002; Craig-McFeely 2016) and embodied (Voegelin 2010; Eidsheim 2015). The sensuous represents a level of attention toward the senses more broadly, taking 'it all in' (Lynne 2019). Psychologist Alphonso Lingis claims 'sensuality is an irresponsible responsiveness to pleasure and discomfort' where 'someone presents [themself] disarmed, denuded, needing nothing from me, surrenders [themself] to me' (Lingis 2007, 2).[2] This points to a giving over of the body to a physical sensation. This sensation can be considered and designed by a composer or performer. When listening includes the body beyond the ear, this sensual attention becomes part of the musical listening experience. The presence of VLF sound in music can turn the listeners' focus away from an intellectual or emotional response engaged directly through the ear to the brain, to one where the physical sensation and attention via the skin and core of the body is a more active aspect of the listening experience. These concepts provide an opportunity for a truly sensual experience of music, where the sound's interaction with the body becomes part of musical experience.

VLF sound can be engaged in a broad range of unique compositional approaches in both acoustic and electronic music. VLF sound in acoustic instruments is experienced at very low volumes compared to other frequency ranges. In addition to instruments developed specifically to extend frequency ranges of established counterparts, such as the sub-contrabass flute and the octobass,[3] common acoustic instruments can produce VLF sounds. Performance techniques that enable the sub-harmonic of a note to sound can be employed, yet due to their low volume, are unlikely to stimulate any identifiable physical response. Instruments such as the double bass, piano, and bass clarinet can create VLF in their frequency range, and we could argue that it is the timbral quality of notes in these ranges, rather than their physical impact, that could be described as sensual. However, once these sounds are amplified, a physical response can emerge as a result of extended frequency ranges being rendered audible.

Acoustic instruments are characterised by natural decay, breaths, bow changes, or repeated strikes to sustain ongoing sound. Electronically produced sounds can provide much longer, uninterrupted durations, and synthesised sounds can reach lower ranges of audible sound with additional amplitude. Amplification of VLF sound requires appropriate equipment such as powerful amplifiers and large subwoofers. It can also be generated by bespoke sound reproduction systems made as part of installation artworks. It is important to note that amplification does not necessarily result in very high volumes – rather, it enables the sound to be experienced by humans (Hope 2009, 51). High levels of amplification can create sudden and intense dynamic contrasts, with changes of volume and pitch register. Amplification of VLF sounds can result in radical sensorial alterations for listeners. These large amplifiers and speaker stacks can even be thought of as the new great organs: enormous generators of powerful sound designed to transport congregations of listeners. The listeners' sensate 'responsiveness to pleasure and discomfort' is realised, and as composers and performers engage with this expanded range of frequencies, they can create music that can physically caress their listeners at one turn and startle them at another.

Just as with any other audio range, VLF can be used singularly or as part of a more complex combination of frequency ranges in varying timbres and musical ideas. The unique timbres of electronically reproduced low frequency sound create the opportunity for the development of new materials from established compositional methods. The results obtained by the creation and manipulation of recordings and electronically generated sounds in VLF ranges are further expanded when combined with unamplified acoustic instruments. In addition, the sound of the reproductive equipment can be included. For example, the sound of air being shifted in front of a large subwoofer speaker operates in a similar volume and timbral range to very low wind instruments. These applications have the capacity to supplement auditory perception in critical ways (Walton 2012, 125).

What follows is a discussion of three artists' methods for engaging VLF sound in a range of different compositional and performance Works. The theoretical approaches described so far are explored in a variety of techniques and applications to create a range of possibilities for sensate listening experiences.

Power-Induced Sensuality in the Work of Thembi Soddell

Australian sound artist Thembi Soddell works with large amplification systems in solo live performances and installations experienced by audiences in complete darkness. Soddell requests this darkness as a tool to erase their physical presence as a performer, encouraging listeners to focus on the sound – not the performance – of the music. This creates an experience for listeners that could be described as somewhere between live performance and installation, drawing a strong connection between the two forms in the artist's own output. Soddell's installation *Held Down, Expanding* (2018a) takes the form of a listening booth, where participants enter a dark room that leads them to focus on how sound interacts with their personal space, intensifying a sensate reception to it. A similar approach is taken in Soddell's live performances, where the stage is visibly removed from audiences, leaving only a few LED lights flickering on the amplifiers or sound card in the distance. Yet this approach does not downplay the importance of the live performance: the live opportunity provides a gateway to access these large amplification systems and listening spaces where these sounds can be heard at their best in a collective listening experience that embraces the ephemeral energy of performance.

Soddell's music is characterised by dramatic changes in volume: sharp dynamic cliffs where a very loud sound seems to leap into the air, rumble beneath, or suddenly disappear to reveal a quiet, thin, and fragile sound beneath. As a listener at these events, I have found myself suddenly exhaling involuntarily in these moments. Gradual introductions into audibility using extremely slow, evolving crescendos and textural complexity make these 'sonic shocks' within the consistent stream of sound all the more powerful. Suddenly stripping sounds back to sparse worlds, or suddenly intensifying them, creates a dramatic listening experience that Soddell uses VLF ranges to define. The listener's body feels very present in the walls of sound that fill the entire space. Soddell engages VLF ranges to create important contrasts with very quiet sounds, often in conjunction with high frequency extremes. This very low sound – and its removal – gives many of these sudden high volume and density shifts their power. Soddell (2018b) describes these extremes as emotional tensions: 'These experiences are ones of extremes and emotional intensities; the tensions between horror, beauty, rage, desire, confusion, love and perceptual annihilation.'

Tension is often discussed in the theoretical analysis of tonal music as an opposing force to the release of dissonance in cadential harmonic movement (Cazden 1980). However, Soddell's music evokes tension – and release – with the new dynamic means afforded by high-powered amplification, putting the importance of harmonic movement into the background. This creates a dramatic listening experience: the music reaches out and grabs you; it is confronting, but enthralling. Whilst Soddell outlines the compositional imperative as driven by emotion, the reception is largely physical, creating a state that 'extends the possibilities for how we are embraced and engulfed by the acoustics we encounter' (English 2018). Sensate experiences are created as a way to control the reception of the emotional intensities used to design them. Audiences inhabit a languishing, velvety pool of VLF sound that makes a sudden cut or escalation all the more exciting, creating a sensual experience that traverses an intense warmth in one moment, and a sudden exhilaration in another. Repeat listening leaves one waiting on edge for the next shift, but still getting caught out whilst honing in on the texture of the almost inaudible opposite.

Soddell collects recordings of performances of vocal, electronic, and instrumental sounds as materials from which to build compositions. These are made specifically for the project at Soddell's request, and are manipulated in a way that renders them mostly unrecognisable in the final work. It is an approach that creates an interesting, subliminal loop back to instrumental performance in these somewhat abstract electronic works, and they are the basis of Soddell's unique timbral range. For the works on her album *Love Songs* (2018b), contributing artists were approached to perform a 'perceptual collapse' on their instrument for their contribution to the album. 'Perceptual collapse' is a concept adapted from Canadian mental health advocate Mark Henick, who uses it to explain his experience of depression and suicidality (Henick, 2013). An 'experiential framework' is created to analyse and represent states of psychological distress using sound (Soddell 2019, 1), where five stages of 'perceptual collapse' that link experience with sonic articulation are created: emotional weight, perceptual disorientation, temporal expansion, experiential paradox and protective disrupture (ibid., 15). Soddell articulates the importance of these stages in both the lived experience of mental illness as well as the process of making music by noting that they create a 'cycle of composition and analysis grounded in understanding my lived experience of perceptual collapse' (ibid., 84).

These recorded contributions from performers do not necessarily feature VLF sound ranges in their original form, and Soddell subjects them to a process of sampling and manipulation that is further nuanced in live performance. Soddell explains how 'emotional weight can be embodied in sound through metaphors such as low frequency sound representing heavy emotions, or through creating sounds with strong downward force' (ibid., 157). This 'downward force' is an example of how VLF can be conceptualised as part of a compositional method, and is discussed further later in the chapter.

The music videos created for three of the five tracks on the *Love Songs* album reinforce the sensual nature of these works. Created by Vanessa Godden, the videos feature intense closeups of the lower half of a face. In the video for one track, 'Erasure', shiny black goo oozes from a mouth in a frame where only the mouth, nose, and neck are visible, as can be seen in Figure 13.1. This physical material appearing to come from inside the body highlights the sensate internalisation of sound, almost illustrating a removal of the sound from the body. It emerges as

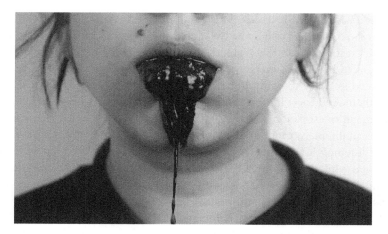

FIGURE 13.1 Video still from Vanessa Godden's video for Thembi Soddell's track 'Erasure', from the *Love Songs* album

a continuous dark mass – reiterating the slow, dark, and amorphous elements in the music.

In a rare notated work by Soddell, *your sickness is felt in my body* (2014), electronic sounds are combined with six acoustic instruments as a fixed media part. This 12-minute composition is created using the same foundational compositional approach as *Love Songs*, that of collecting materials from contributors to create the electronic part. Each of the six musicians performing the piece are asked to send a recording of a performance in response to a phrase provided by the composer. *your sickness is felt in my body* comprises one consistent, slow crescendo mirrored in an escalation of textural density. Together with the fixed media part consisting of VLF sounds as well as higher-pitched, continuous noise, an evolving source of consistently building tension is created. The unamplified acoustic instruments are eventually completely subsumed by the powerful playback produced through an amplification system featuring a large subwoofer speaker, ensuring the production of VLF sounds. There is a sudden cut at the end, revealing a small, eerie, yet delicate sound tail lasting for some seconds, performed on the bass flute. The airy, empty sound is almost a statement of its futility, whilst simultaneously reminding us of an alternate sensuality in the human breath as it peters out. The sonic similarity of the breathy flute sound to the gentle movement of air generated by the activated subwoofer speaker cone can be heard with careful listening. As a performer of the bass flute in the Decibel new music ensemble premiere of this work, I experienced the loud, built-up sound as exhilarating and strangely chilling, highlighted by the contrast created when it was removed to reveal to lone flute part. This is in line with some experiences ascribed to VLF, such as chills and tingling (Van den Berg 2008, 235). The acoustic instruments/contributors feature live in the performance itself, creating specific fine details that are eventually subsumed by the electronic playback part. The volume differences between the electronic and acoustic sound worlds remind us simultaneously of the power of amplification and the fragility of low frequency acoustic sounds. The combination of the electronically modulated VLF with the acoustic instrumental timbre creates a new kind of sound world, underpinned by sensate experience.

The tensions and contrasts enhanced by Soddell's compositional engagement of VLF ascribes different dimensions to the sensuality of the listening experience, where the low frequencies create a definite physical response using sculptural compositional techniques – where walls of high volume materialise and vanish from softer fragile pools of sound, creating a 'state of heightened vulnerability and bodily awareness' (McIntyre 2012, 50). The gravitas, disorientation, warmth, and exhilaration of this music goes beyond the tropes of 'noise' and 'discomfort' often associated with the experience of VLF, to a more complex and sensuous relationship with sound.

The Delicate Sensuality of Low Frequency in the Work of Marina Rosenfeld

Marina Rosenfeld is a New York-based artist with an expansive practice that includes turntablism, installation, and art music composition. Perhaps best known for her work with teenage girls in pieces such as *Sheer Frost Orchestra* (1993) and *Teenage Lontano* (2008), Rosenfeld maintains a unique sensitivity to low frequency sound, evident in her installations and turntablism in very subtle, understated compositional ways. As a turntablist, Rosenfeld often utilises dub plates for source material.[4] Artists in the jungle, reggae, grime, and dubstep music scenes often use these collectable records in their music, sought after for inclusions not found on commercial releases. In Rosenfeld's performance *The Accompanists* (2007), the crackle of static and needles shifting across unstable grooves characteristic of turntablism are present. However carefully controlled, intermittent low tones of the recorded tracks, and low thuds created by deliberate nudging of the turntable body and stylus arm have a strong presence. These sonic features create a thread of soft VLF sounds through the work, highlighting the dub plate 'singularity and fragility' (Rosenfeld n.d.). Rosenfeld's live turntable performances have a wonderful delicacy and deftness of touch in direct contrast to more mainstream turntablism approaches. Her manipulation of records, turntables, and associated components create a playful, fleeting manipulation of VLF sound that disrupts the more conventional role of low frequency as a heavy, dramatic, or beat reinforcement tool. These are delicately sensual works.

Rosenfeld also performs the turntable as an instrument in chamber music ensembles. I performed bass flute in the 2011 performance of *WHITE LINES* (2003–) with the Decibel ensemble, together with bass clarinet, viola, cello, guitar, drum kit, and Rosenfeld on turntables. The VLF soft, whispery string bowing occupies a surprisingly similar sound world to that of record static, and Rosenfeld draws these sounds out of the instruments in this performance. Her slowing down of records on the turntable mirrors the glissandi on acoustic instruments, and often descends into inaudible VLF ranges. Subtones created by the multiphonic effects possible on the wind instruments meld with Rosenfeld's low taps of the turntable, as do gentle taps on the bass drum using soft mallets. These similarities between the turntable and its acoustic counterparts operating in the acoustic volume range create a low frequency parameter on the cusp of audibility. Similar approaches are used in Rosenfeld's live turntable performance on the CD release *theseatheforesthegarde* (Rosenfeld 1999), which opens with a very quiet, steady, low hum, creating a unique frame for sounds laced with the static, skips, and crackles characteristic of turntable performances. Just as Soddell manipulates contributions performed by others, Rosenfeld de-identifies original material by manipulating it into her own sonic designs, with VLF sound providing a subtle yet important compositional tool.

Rosenfeld's most significant exploration in VLF sound reproduction is *Cannons* (2010), a three-movement work composed for four large, resonating 'bass cannons' and ensemble (percussion, viola, cello, and the composer on turntables) in a resonant space. The cannons are custom made for the piece from steel pipes of 1, 3, 5, and 7 metres long, fitted with subwoofers at one end and installed in a large space alongside two full-range speaker horns that are used to amplify the turntables. The cannons are capable of reproducing VLF with fidelity even in the infrasonic range, and create vibrations that can be experienced in the bodies of the audience members and the performing musicians alike. Rosenfeld amplifies sounds specifically composed for the work through these pipes, creating a sparse, delicate, and playful spatial work. Like her turntable performances, Rosenfeld's *Cannons* does not feature exclusively low frequency sounds, but when they are in the foreground, they are warm, round, and often playful. Sounds often descend in long, smooth glissandi, sliding through the hearing range and landing briefly into sensate ranges – a compositional tool mirrored in the acoustic instrument parts. Contrasting with these instruments, the cannon sounds seem strangely more natural – whilst also otherworldly – often in playful conversation with the acoustic instruments. The tones often break up somewhat, identifying them as being in the infrasonic range, and other times they sneak in and out of audibility.

The VLF generates some similar effects to that experienced in Soddell's work. Sometimes, the air movement generated from the speaker is audible, resembling whispers, creating a surprising intimacy. At certain points, the acoustic instruments become consumed by the electronic sounds produced by the cannons, and at other points the cannon VLF melds with acoustic sound to create new timbral qualities. Again, low tones are never used as percussive or harmonic support, but as an integral and sometimes even melodic part of the compositional fabric. Using a similar approach as taken in *WHITE LINES*, the turntable bridges these timbral connections. The engagement of what Soddell calls 'downward force' as a compositional technique is also employed, but in very different aesthetic. Rosenfeld's engagement with VLF ranges is more slippery and elusive. However, both engage VLF ranges to invite close listening, rewarded with sensual outcomes across tentative,

FIGURE 13.2 A photograph of the performance space in Rosenfeld's *Cannons* installation, Midland Railway Workshop, Western Australia, 2010
Source: Photo by Cat Hope.

suggestive sound worlds that innovate the way that VLF ranges are manipulated in compositional processes.

Whilst Soddell engages large amplification systems to enable her VLF sound propagation in live performance, Rosenfeld designs her own bespoke system for the electronic sound transmission in *Cannons*, as seen in Figure 13.2. Both reflect the requirement for facilities beyond a standard 'concert' amplification provision for the VLF propagation. Soddell uses a stadium-size amplification system for her performances, and Rosenfeld presents bespoke systems as part of the installation design in *Cannons*. Both approaches enable a broader distribution of the VLF sound, which tends to be much less directional than other frequency ranges, thus intensifying the audience experience.

Timbral Sensuality in My Own Compositions

My own work traverses notated composition and improvised performances where the exploration of VLF sound is a central concern. My notated compositions engage VLF sound both sonically and conceptually. In the literal sonic sense, I have a series of works that feature VLF sine tones alongside acoustic instruments in chamber music works. Frequently used in acoustic measuring tests, sine tones are often referred to as 'dead tones' (Goeyvaerts, in Sabbe 2005, 244). My works aims to demonstrate that these tones have their own timbral and sensual application that is highlighted when combined with acoustic instruments. The tones I use are always below 100 Hz, and I call them subtones. Compositionally, they are treated as another instrumental part in the ensemble and are balanced in volume to acoustic instruments during performance – using a subwoofer speaker to ensure VLF audibility. The compositions explore the way we experience the timbre of subtones in various acoustic ensemble configurations.

Works such as *Shadow* (2016), for two string instruments and subtone, see the acoustic instruments weave in, out, and around the subtones, with the aim of creating new ways to experience the colours of these instruments when foregrounded by this warm, low, oscillating tone that is experienced physically by the listeners. The subtones thread in and out of the acoustic sounds across very long durations – the piece progressing slowly, simply, and quietly – the subtone and acoustic colour becoming increasingly similar despite the difference in frequency range. The string players are asked to play without vibrato and to make bow changes as unnoticeable as possible, to mirror the uninterrupted electronic subtone. These long durations of sound draw the listener into a focus on the colour and detail of the sound itself, where the absence of pulse obscures the passage of time, and the quality of the sound becomes the focus of listening (Demers 2010, 95). This listening focus reveals a warm, sensual exploration of the sound foregrounded by these durations and the subtle glissando movement that provides the only pitch movement in the piece. The rich harmonic overtones created by the bowing of the strings coalesce into the subtone, in a similar way that occurs in the performance of Rosenfeld's *WHITE LINES*. At times, the acoustic instruments are subsumed into the tone, as in Soddell's *your sickness is felt in my body*.

In *Tone Being* (2016), for tam-tam and subtone, the acoustic instrument can reproduce sounds closer in frequency range to the subtone, and an excerpt of the score is shown in Figure 13.3. The tam-tam physically swings after being struck, its slow movement back and forth mirroring the pulsating waves created by combined subtones emitting from the subwoofer speaker placed nearby. This is a compositional attempt at a physical mirroring of sound waves, bringing elements of installation into the live performance of this notated work. The deep ring and shimmer created when the instrument is struck with a soft mallet decays quite quickly, leaving the core sound of the instrument to be subsumed into the subtone. The electronic sound continues on well after the decay of the tam-tam has faded away. This is a reversal of the process Soddell applies at the end of *your sickness is felt in my body*. It is difficult to hear exactly when the tam-tam sound stops, as its timbre becomes similar to the subtone during this process of its volume decay, confusing the identity of the electronic and acoustic sounds. The vanishing high frequency shimmer fades away to unveil the interplay of low acoustic and electronic sounds, the sensual experience gradually revealing itself to the listener.

The use of sine tones in modern compositions is not new (see works by Chiyoko Szlavnics, Maryanne Amacher, Alvin Lucier, La Monte Young, and others). However, an exclusive focus on subtones across multiple chamber music configurations is unique, providing new insights into the ways different combinations of acoustic instruments can integrate into electronic sound to create sensual listening experiences. Whilst tones may well be used in compositional aspects of

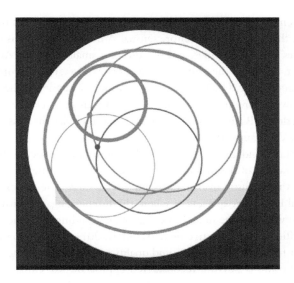

FIGURE 13.3 Screenshot of the animated notation score for Cat Hope's *Tone Being* (2016). Original in colour

both Rosenfeld's and Soddell's work, they are not presented in such explicit and exposed ways, or treated in such a similar compositional way to acoustic instruments. They are engaged to extend and enhance the VLF experience of these works to enable sensate listening.

My solo improvised electric bass noise performances use large, powerful valve bass amplifiers driving multiple 15-inch subwoofer speakers in the production of the sound. In conjunction with a range of effects pedals, this creates a specific timbral palette focused on the VLF aspects of the bass guitar sound, as subwoofer speakers do not produce other higher frequency ranges produced by smaller speakers. As a result of amplifier build and design, these amplifier/speaker combinations create a very different, noisier 'colour' than those used in concert settings. Elongated VLF sounds are again a feature of these performances, created using sampling and looping effect pedals. The bass guitar tone is coloured by the effect pedals, using a range of different distortions, delays, and a downward octave shifting effect – effectively overlaying the bass guitar sound with a 'synthesised' version of itself, operating like the subtone in the works above, melding into a complex but singular sound world.

These performances subvert the role of the bass guitar by removing it from its standard engagement with a percussion section to reinforce the beat or foundational harmonies. The performances generate VLF sounds that fill the room in a similar way to Soddell's sounds, the timbral qualities of the bass highlighted and exposed without other instruments around it. The guitar itself is recontextualised soloistically, as is the music itself. Feedback is an important element of these performances, created and controlled as a melodic device alongside heavy distortion, growling sounds, and droning bass interrupted by percussive attacks. It resembles the sine tones mentioned earlier, and bass feedback is characterised by a lower frequency range that is warmer and more sensual. A double bass bow is used to create sustained tones from the strings, and the use of a small handheld AM radio with inbuilt speaker, held over the guitar pickups, creates a low, uninterrupted, sustained sound of untuned static. The foundational harmonic structure of the instrument is extended – lower in frequency, but more adventurous in its colour range, creating a 'sensory overload' (Radio Static Radio n.d.) that includes the sensual experience created by the VLF ranges themselves.

In these notated and improvised works, the compositional focus is firmly focused on how explorations of the timbre of low frequency sound interact with other frequency ranges in acoustic instruments and effects such as feedback. This in turn creates sensual listening experiences where the listener engages with the music in more intimate ways that are linked to sensation, responding to music as both a 'surface of intensities and an affective field' (Braidotti 2011, 24). Improvisation enables the performer to follow ideas and sound qualities that emerge as the work unfolds, whereas compositions provide reconsidered approaches to similar elements. The amplified low frequency sounds – as subtle caresses in the quiet composed works, or the all-consuming, vibrating waves of the solo improvisations – create sensual listening experiences facilitated by the VLF experience.

Conclusion

The focus on VLF sound in composition and performance practices reminds us of how the experience of music remains firmly rooted in the senses (Austern 2002, 1). A focused and deliberate control of VLF sound in composition creates new ways of making and thinking about sensuous listening worlds. The stark cliffs and visual void of Soddell's live electronic performance, the playful gurgles and murmurs of Rosenfeld' dub plates and cannon speakers, as well as the timbral explorations of my own music, provide different exemplars of this technique, and evidence a range of approaches to the sensual. Each of these projects produces results where VLF sound highlights the sensory nature of listening to the point that it becomes sensual. The entire body becomes an inextricable mechanism for understanding the musical material as a sensual experience. These are musical ideas that snap us alert, wash over us, caress, and weave around our other senses. They both demand and consume attention from the listeners' body. Whilst the power of electronic amplification enables sounds that would be impossible to experience otherwise, acoustic instruments can interact with these sounds to foreground and combine with timbres that create innovative new sound worlds. A sensuous sonic body is an integral part of a new way of engaging with music and its rewards.

Notes

1 Infrasound refers to sound beyond the range of human hearing. However, infrasonic frequencies can be heard at high amplification levels (Hope 2010).

2 This quotation has been slightly altered, from 'himself or herself' to 'themself' to reflect a more up-to-date approach to pronouns.
3 The sub-contrabass flute extends the range of the standard C flute by two and a half octaves. Similarly, the octobass extends the range of the double bass by an octave.
4 A dub plate is an acetate LP record used by studios to test recordings prior to making a full run of vinyl.

Bibliography

Angliss, Sarah. 2003. Infrasonic – Summary of Results. London: Soundless Music Infrasonic Project. https://content.instructables.com/ORIG/FNG/5J5C/H9K2FIZK/FNG5J5CH9K2FIZK.pdf (accessed: 16 March 2022).

Austern, Linda Phyllis. 2002. Introduction. In *Music, Sensation and Sensuality*, edited by Linda Phyllis Austern, 1. New York: Routledge.

Braidotti, R. 2011. *Nomadic Subjects: Embodiment and Sexual Difference in Contemporary Feminist Theory*. 2nd edition. New York: Columbia University Press.

Cazden, Norman. 1980. The Definition of Consonance and Dissonance. *International Review of the Aesthetics and Sociology of Music* 11(2): 123–168.

Craig-McFeely, Julia. 2002. Seduction by Cultural Stereotype in Seventeenth-Century England. In *Music, Sensation and Sensuality*, edited by Linda Phyllis Austern, 199–319. New York: Routledge.

Demers, Joanna Teresa. 2010. *Listening through the Noise: The Aesthetics of Experimental Electronic Music*. New York: Oxford University Press.

Devereux, Paul. 2001. *Stone Age Soundtracks: The Acoustic Archaeology of Ancient Sites*. New York: Sterling Publishing.

Eidsheim, Nina Sun. 2015. *Sensing Sound: Singing and Listening as Vibrational Practice*. London: Duke University Press.

English, Lawrence. 2016. Friday Essay: The Sound of Fear. *The Conversation*. https://theconversation.com/friday-essay-the-sound-of-fear-65230 (accessed: 12 August 2020).

Fink, Robert. 2018. Below 100 Hz: Towards a Musicology of Bass Culture. In *The Relentless Pursuit of Tone: Timbre in Popular Music*, edited by Robert Fink, Melinda Latour, and Zachary Wallmark, 104–105. Oxford, UK: Oxford University Press.

Godden, Vanessa. 2018. *Erasure* [music video]. https://vimeo.com/250207640.

Goodman, Steve. 2012. *Sonic Warfare: Sound, Affect, and the Ecology of Fear*. Cambridge, MA: MIT Press.

Henick, Mark. 2013. Why We Need to Talk about Suicide. TedXToronto. www.youtube.com/watch?v=D1QoyTmeAYw (accessed: 2 August 2020).

Henriques, Julian F. 2003. Sonic Dominance and the Reggae Sound System Session. In *The Auditory Cultural Reader*, edited by Michael Bull and Les Black, 471–472. New York: Berg.

Hope, Cat. 2009. Infrasonic Music. *Leonardo Music Journal*, 19: 51–56.

Hope, Cat. 2010. The Possibility of Infrasonic Music. Doctor of Philosophy thesis, Melbourne, Australia: RMIT University, unpublished.

Hope, Cat. 2016. *Shadow* [music composition]. Los Angeles, CA: Material Press. DOI: 10.26180/5cda1bd41b1a8.

Hope, Cat. 2016. *Tone Being* [music composition]. Los Angeles, CA: Material Press. DOI: 10.26180/5cda0c5c12ac6.

Hope, Cat. 2019. *Cat Hope Improvised Solo Noise Performance* [music performance]. Melbourne, Australia: Substation.

Jasen, Paul C. 2016. *Low End Theory: Bass, Bodies and the Materiality of Sonic Experience*. New York: Bloomsbury Publishing.

Leventhall, Geoff. 2003. *A Review of Published Research on Low Frequency Noise and Its Effects*. London: Department for Environment, Food and Rural Affairs.

Lingis, Alphonso. 2007. Contact: Tact and Caress. *Journal of Phenomenological Psychology*, 38(1): 1–6.

Lynne, Gia. 2019. Sensual Isn't the Same as Sexual: The Practice of Pleasure Extends beyond the Bedroom. Salon. www.salon.com/2019/05/22/sensual-isnt-the-same-as-sexual-the-practice-of-pleasure-extends-beyond-the-bedroom/ (accessed: 1 August 1 2020).

McIntyre, Sally Ann. 2012. The Sound Already Present. *RealTime*, 111: 50.

Radio Static Radio. n.d. Cat Hope Review, Rochester. www.cathope.com/noise-and-improvisation (accessed: 4 July 2020).

Rosenfeld, Marina. n.d. *My Body*. www.marinarosenfeld.com/my-body (accessed: 25 November 2020).

Rosenfeld, Marina. 1993. *Sheer Frost Orchestra* [music composition]. www.marinarosenfeld.com/the-sheer-frost-orchestra.

Rosenfeld, Marina. 1999. *theseatheforesthegarde* [sound recording]. Los Angeles, CA: Charizma, 003.

Rosenfeld, Marina. 2007. *The Accompanists* [music performance]. Philadelphia, PA: Institute of Contemporary Art. https://fractalmeat.wordpress.com/2012/04/30/marina-rosenfeld-the-accompanists (accessed on: 23 August, 2021).

Rosenfeld, Marina. 2008. *Teenage Lontano* [music composition]. www.marinarosenfeld.com/teenage-lontano.

Rosenfeld, Marina. 2010. *Cannons* [music installation]. *Totally Huge New Music Festival*, Midland Railway Workshops, Perth, Australia. www.marinarosenfeld.com/cannons (accessed: 2 August 2020).

Rosenfeld, Marina. 2011 *WHITE LINES* [music performance]. Perth, Australia: Perth Institute of Performance Arts. https://decibelnewmusic.com/videos/white-lines-by-marina-rosenfeld/ (accessed on: 12 August 2020).

Ruan, Xiang-yan et al. 2008. Effects of Vibration Therapy on Bone Mineral Density in Postmenopausal Women with Osteoporosis. *Chinese Medical Journal*, 121(13): 1155–1158.

Sabbe, Herman. 2005. A Paradigm of 'Absolute Music': Goeyvaerts's N°.4 as 'Numerus Sonorus'. In Revue Belge de Musicologie/Belgisch Tijdschrift voor Muziekwetenschap, 59: 243–251. www.jstor.org/stable/25485985 (accessed: 12 August 2020).

Soddell, Thembi. 2014. *your sickness is found in my body* [music performance]. https://vimeo.com/114104431 (accessed: 1 May 2020).

Soddell, Thembi. 2018a. *Held Down, Expanding* [sound installation]. Abbotsford Convent, Australia: Liquid Architecture. https://liquidarchitecture.org.au/events/held-down-expanding (accessed: 20 August 2021).

Soddell, Thembi. 2018b. *Love Songs* [sound recording]. Red Hill, Australia: Room40: RM491.

Soddell, Thembi. 2019. *A Dense Mass of Indecipherable Fear: The Experiential (Non)narration of Trauma and Madness through Acousmatic Sound*. Doctor of Philosophy thesis. Melbourne, Australia: RMIT University. https://researchrepository.rmit.edu.au/esploro/outputs/doctoral/A-dense-mass-of-indecipherable-fear/9921864093201341 (accessed on: 4 August 2021).

Swezey, Stuart, ed. 1995. *Amok Journal – Sensurround Edition*. London: Amok Books.

Tandy, Vic, and Lawrence, Tony R. 1998. The Ghost in the Machine. *Journal of the Society for Psychical Research*, 62: 360–364.

Trower, Shelley. 2012. *Senses of Vibration: A History of the Pleasure and Pain of Sound*. New York: Continuum.
Van den Berg, Frits. 2008. Low Frequency Noise Can Be a Phantom Sound. Paper delivered at 13th International Meeting on Low Frequency Noise and Vibration and Its Control, Tokyo, Japan, 21–23 October.
Voegelin, Salomé. 2010. The Critical Agency of the 'Avatar-I': Accessing the Silence of the Inaudible. *Four By Three Magazine*. www.fourbythreemagazine.com/issue/silence/accessing-the-silence-of-the-inaudible (accessed: 10 August 2020).
Walton, Kendall L. 2012. Two Kinds of Physicality in Electronic and Traditional Music. In *Bodily Expression in Electronic Music: Perspectives on Reclaiming Performativity*, edited by Deniz Peters, Gerhard Eckel, and Andreas Dorschel, 114–129. New York: Routledge.
Yamada, S., Watanabe, T., Kosaka, T., Negishi, H., and Watanabe, H. 1986. Physiological Effects of Low Frequency Noise. *Journal of Low Frequency Noise, Vibration and Active Control*, 5(1): 14–25.
Yeowart, Norman S. 1976. Thresholds of Hearing and Loudness for Very Low Frequencies. In *Infrasound and Low Frequency Vibration*, edited by W. Tempest, 37–64. London: Academic Press.

14
CYNOSURIC BODIES

Susie Green and Margaret Schedel

Introduction

As music technologists who often work with dance, we have used a variety of methodologies, including autoethnography, to research computer interfaces that translate human motion into sound. Our use of the word "cynosuric" in the title was chosen as an archetype with a multiplicity of meanings inherent to the material. Cynosure is the ancient Greek name for the star Polaris, also known as the North Star. In the northern hemisphere, it appears as fixed in position in the constellation of Ursa Minor, while nearby stars seem to revolve around it, making it an external reference point for navigation. In ancient Greek, *kynosoura* means "the dog's tail"; its very name implies embodiment. We have organized the chapter into three sections, contextualizing a number of case studies in which human anatomy is translated into data and individuals are interpolated into computational systems. "Hand as Body" serves to scale focus, centering yourself as a cynosure. Throughout the chapter, you will find miniature interactive handography (hand-choreography) exercises featuring the hand as a metaphor for the body. The section "Body as Pieces" reflects the etymology of cynosure referencing the body. It features works that used and customized systems to accurately inscribe the mechanics and intentions of the subject and technology used. In the section "Pieces as Practice", the navigational aspect in the phrase "let the cynosure be your guide" serves to highlight examples of practice-based research/ pieces by composers, technologists and performers that strive to overcome the implicit biases built into interactive systems. Finally, we conclude with the section "Manifesto", which amplifies the cruciality of understanding how a system measures a body and its workings. It brings to light a system's own limitations, capabilities, and adaptability with a view towards evolving its accessibility across the full spectrum of individualized bodies. Ultimately, by placing the body at

DOI: 10.4324/9781003008217-19

the cynosure of research/epistemologies/practices, we point to culture, power, representation, and social equity.

Hand as Body

As an introduction to embodied cognition—the philosophy that our bodies, and even our environment can enact knowledge and the concept that our brains are not the only site of thinking—we begin with Merleau-Ponty and Smith's *Phenomenology of Perception*. In this thought experiment, focus is drawn to the hand as both experiencing touch and simultaneously performing the act of touching:

> I can, with my left hand, feel my right hand as it touches an object, the right hand as an object is not the right hand as it touches: the first is a system of bones, muscles, and flesh brought down at a point of space, the second shoots through space like a rocket to reveal the external object in its place.
> *Merleau-Ponty and Smith, 105*

We invite you to perform the above as preparation for the handography exercises available online (see Figure 14.1). Feel free to physically use your hands, visualize them in your mind, or adjust to embrace your own abilities to gain an embodied understanding of the concepts we explore. We encourage you to translate our handography exercises to other parts of your body, adapting your cynosure to understand divergent artistic impulses. This adaption acts much like the Adaptive Use Musical Instrument (AUMI), which enables users with extremely limited voluntary mobility to interact with a computer through movements they can control "such as breathing and eye movement" (Finch et al., 2). To address diverse learning styles/abilities/accessibility options, we've included photos and a weblink/QR code leading to short audio/video instructions, beginning with *Perception* (see Figure 14.2).

We were inspired to shrink the body's kinesphere down to the hand to create handography exercises, influenced by movement theorist Rudolph Laban's Multidimensional Model, choreographer William Forsythe's Improvisation Technologies lecture, and the concept of "marking" in dance. Forsythe unpacked Laban's concept of the kinesphere, an imagined scaffolding that surrounds the body

FIGURE 14.1 QR code for www.susiegreen-music.com/handography
Source: Susie Green, 2020.

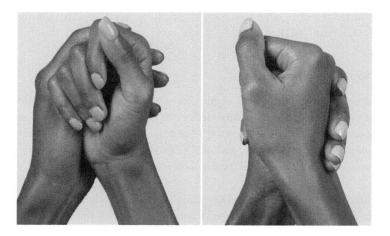

FIGURE 14.2 *Perception*
Source: Susie Green, 2020.

and holds the shape of all possible movement by and around that body (Laban, 10), to reveal a fractal of kinesphere iterations "that change size, multiply, fragment, collapse and disappear swiftly" (Baudoin and Gilpin). Just as Forsythe used these smaller scales to expand options for new choreography, dancers often shrink their own kinesphere, reducing the movement of a routine, taking smaller steps or lower kicks, even substituting hand gestures for full body motion to mark movements while memorizing new combinations of choreography. These reductions "facilitate real-time reflection, while saving energy, avoiding strenuous movement … without the mental and physical complexity involved in creating a phrase full-out" (Kirsh, 17). Throughout the chapter, the handography will increase in complexity. We start with very simple exercises and interactive systems focused on the hand, and progressively add adjacent body parts and other embodied systems and technologies, mirroring this chapter's expansion.

The hand may arguably be the locus of transformation of body gesture into sound when playing an instrument; however, for this chapter, our focus is on movement in itself—not instrumental techniques. We unpack "interfaces as translators" (Johnson, 14) of movement into sound. We have made sure to reference both hardware and software of interactive systems, much as embodied cognition recognizes both the hardware of the body and the software of the brain as sites of cognition and knowing. For example, commercial infrared (IR) motion-detection devices such as the LeapMotion and Kinect both bundle hardware and software to use an interface to track the body.

The LeapMotion was made specifically for the hand, while the Kinect is used for full body tracking. Both define an agent's bodily motion, allowing marker-less motion capture where:

> a human body is represented by a number of joints representing body parts … each joint is represented by its 3D coordinates. The goal is to determine all the 3D parameters of these joints in real time to allow fluent interactivity and with limited computation resources.
>
> *Zhang, 6*

Both systems use continuous IR transmission paired with spaced out IR receivers, allowing software to calculate the likely location of joints to build a 3D representation of the skeleton. Currently, both interfaces are unable to maintain consistent mapping if the body occludes (blocks) itself or is occluded by another body. The software running behind the scenes assumes a universally placed center point from which a virtual skeleton, of the hand or the body, is built upon in order to map potential movement. This general assumption can cause issues when attempting to track and map bodies in motion that do not share this cynosure. Not all centers of gravity on a human body are the same, especially when that body is in motion; each person's kinesthetic center is highly individualized.

Miller Puckette and Kerry Hagan, collaborating as "The Higgs whatever", use a LeapMotion controller in *Who Was That Timbre I Saw You With?* (2018). They wrote custom software in Pure Data as a hand gesture-to-timbre converter, mapping the "shape of the human hand to timbre (considered as a collection of entangled parameters" (Puckette and Hagan, 1). Schedel has watched multiple performances of this work, and made the following observations: the piece uses two LeapMotion controllers, and in general, each performer uses a single hand above the controller nearest to them. The resultant sound is clearly related to the performers' movement. Occasionally, one performer reaches over to interact with the other's controller. This instantly doubles the input on that interface, creating a distinct difference in the quality of sound. By playing in each other's space, they became entangled with one another's mapping and sound while the pas-de-deux-like nature of the encounter creates a miniature interactive dance/gesture/instrument environment.

The kinesphere of each individual's hand varies depending upon its range of motion, length/size/number of fingers etc. The following handography, *Multi-Dimensional Isolation* (see Figures 14.1, 14.3, 14.4 and 14.5), will guide you to discovering your own hand's kinesphere through motion. It will also help you gauge your range of motion and limitations while considering how you would tailor any technologically mediated elements that use movement in composition and performance. Discovering our limits can reveal adroitness within our range of abilities which can be useful when utilizing/creating interactive interfaces.

Body as Pieces

In the previous section, the hand was used as a case analysis for the body. Now we bridge from body parts in motion to the collective movement of the whole body. Take, for instance, American Sign Language (ASL), a 3D language where meaning

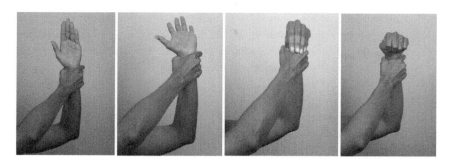

FIGURE 14.3 *Multi-Dimensional Isolation*
Source: Susie Green, 2020.

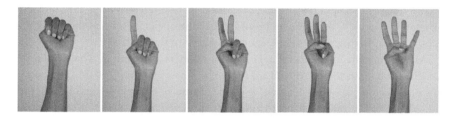

FIGURE 14.4 *Multisequence, thumb in*
Source: Susie Green, 2020.

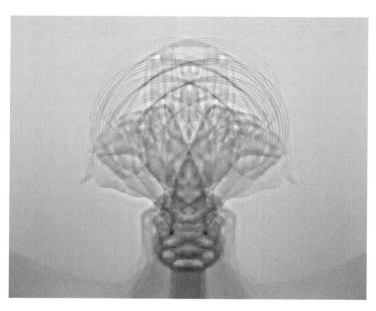

FIGURE 14.5 *Kinesphere of the Hand*
Source: Susie Green, 2020.

is transmitted with nuance through the whole body and is not limited to the hands (Christina Whitehouse-Suggs, personal communication, July 2020). Researchers have been working to create systems using gloves, cameras, or IR sensors to translate individual signs into audible words. However, ASL is a voice in and of itself, where the face, body, shape, and speed of motion between signs is as much a part of the communication as dynamics are in heard speech and music. This is also true when using sensors and capture systems to interpret the essence of expression of the embodied voice in motion (Winters, 401). The expression of a unique body through dance and/or movement is best done when interfaces are tailored to the ways in which the subject actually moves. Here we look at a sample of works and interactive systems that consider the body in motion. Although interfaces cannot perfectly capture the full spectrum of under/overtones expressed, they can be used to augment human artistry through interactivity. We use Birringer's definition of interactivity as a:

> collaborative performance with a control system in which the performer-movement or action is tracked by cameras or sensors and thus used as input to activate or control other component properties ... [allowing] performers and computers to generate, synthesize and process images, sound and text within a shared real-time environment.

The translation from sensor input to sensible output is called mapping (Naccarato and MacCallum 2016, 1), and is the main decision point in interactive systems—deciding what numbers coming in will be associated with what audiovisual output.

Since the 1970s, several systems for tracking dance have been developed. These interfaces can be divided into three groups: inside-in systems—sensors placed on the body to track the body; inside-out systems—sensors placed on the body to track the environment; and outside-in systems—sensors placed in the environment to track the body, such as the LeapMotion or Kinect (Mulder). For an overview of the history of interactive dance systems, please see Wayne Siegel's well-researched chapter "Dancing the Music: Interactive Dance and Music" (Siegel). One fascinating early interactive system not covered by Siegal is Erkki Kurenniemi's 1971 DIMI-O or Optical Organ, used to create the *DIMI Ballet*. It was an outside-in optical video synthesizer which made music based on a digitized image system consisting of a video interface that contained organ sounds, memory, and video circuitry, which allowed notes played through a keyboard synthesizer to be displayed visually on a small television screen. The graphical notation, resembling modern-day MIDI, was saved in the interface's memory, and played back or manipulated by various controllers. A video camera connected to the interface captured the dancer's image in real time; when their image interacted with the graphical notation on screen, notes sounded (Green-Mateu, 29).

An example of both an inside-in and inside-out system used for interactive dance is Geoffrey Wright and Charlene Curtiss's *Instrument of Balance and Grace* (1993). An interdisciplinary team (including Schedel) taped sensors to Charlene's arms to measure the extension of her elbows, mounted potentiometers on the wheels to measure rotation, and developed a new custom ultrasonic sensor, created in collaboration with Johns Hopkins/NASA's Applied Physics Laboratory, that was mounted under the carriage to measure tilt; all of this data was sent wirelessly to a computer. One of the first gestures in the piece had Charlene raise her arms to ring a bell. She also had to accelerate on her wheelchair to move into the next movement phrase, which included a tight spin. When she propelled her wheelchair forward by bending her arms and extending them, it caused a misfire in the computer program and the bell would ring. One possible solution to correct this misfire would have been to change the choreography or the resultant interaction, but everyone felt that the choreography and the proposed sonic interaction were the strongest way of opening the piece. The team brainstormed many solutions, but had no way of determining if Curtiss's arms were pointed up or down without adding another sensor, and the wireless interface couldn't transmit another channel of data. The first attempt to rectify this was to only allow the bell to ring if the speed was high enough, but different size stages made creating a static cutoff point based on speed impractical. By observing Charlene closely, Schedel realized that the dancer didn't bend her elbow in all the way when engaging the wheels, and suggested that she could fold her arms close to her body and then extend them to trigger the sound. The programmer created a gate that only allowed the bell trigger if the arm sensor was below a certain threshold of 200 milliseconds before the extension. By understanding how the sensors worked, what was possible with the software, and what was integral to the choreography, Schedel was able to create a solution that worked technically and aesthetically. *Instrument of Balance and Grace* used Curtiss's unique physical characteristics as a starting point, and technology was used to extend her capabilities (Geoffrey Wright, personal communication, July 2020). The piece ends with her performing virtuoso-like movements that caused her to hurl her body out of the chair to extend her spirit beyond both physical and technical limitations.

We like Garland Thomson's definition of disability as "the attribution of corporeal deviance—not so much a property of bodies as a product of cultural rules about what bodies should be or do" (Garland Thomson, 73). The final pose of *Instrument of Balance and Grace* shocked the audience because Curtiss broke the rules about what a person in a wheelchair should be able to do. Specifically, "disability scholars have rejected the idea that a person who uses a wheelchair "'is' disabled" (Phelan, 322); indeed, Curtiss noted that she has "greater movement and speed in her chair than any dancer limited by movement of legs alone" (Curtiss, quoted in McKerrow). A system designed to track the maximum speed of an able-bodied person would not be able to quantify Curtiss's movement accurately.

Much as Forsythe fragmented the kinesphere, in recent years "the body has been transformed from the universalized white, heterosexual, middle class male norm, to 'bodies,' a fractured series of subjects seeking agency through multiple identifications, to the cyber subject, threatening the body with no body at all" (Parker-Starbuck, 40). Ideally when designing embodied interactive systems, "integrations with technology [will be] more than an innovative performance practice, they [should] serve as a springboard for the development of a vocabulary of technological language through which to better understand a diverse range of bodies" (ibid., 67). Throughout the 21st century, technologies have become more efficient, components have become cheaper, sensors have become smaller, and wireless technologies have become faster, more reliable, and draw less power. Combined with open-source software and internet tutorials, these changes mean more people than ever before can create and customize interactive systems—we do not need to design for a single sample-size body.

In 2014, Patricia Alessandrini and Frieda Abtan created *Mondgewächse*, an audio-visual performance with ShareMusic & Performing Arts' In:fluence Ensemble and inclusive performance artists. It was the result of a collaborative workshop where the artists' varied abilities became the scaffolding for the design of three distinct interfaces: the mouth-organ, shadow puppet, and the feedback membrane (Alessandrini and Abtan). The agency of the performers was fully honored and "fluidity of roles/functions in the decision-making process, such that the binaries of user/designer and creator/performer (were) blurred" (ibid., 1). Peter Larsson, a longtime member of and performer with ShareMusic, helped design and play the mouth-organ played in *Mondgewächse*. It was born out of Larsson's desire to create colors corresponding to sound. After consulting Clarence Adoo, a professional trumpet player who had extensive experience using the digital wind instrument HeadSpace, the team tailored a system that translated Larsson's head movements and lip pressure to create music and control pitch, timbre, notes, and amplitude. "It was the first time I felt free musically because I don't have to use my hands, my limitations. I could use my head … to explore and create music without limitations," Larsson said in an interview at the *International Conference on New Musical Interfaces* in 2020 (quoted in ibid., 2). He went on to advocate for electronic, digital, technology-driven instruments to be considered as legitimate instruments in otherwise "classical" environments. Access to workshops like these is important for performers and designers alike to create a space and dialogue when actualizing instruments, performances, interfaces, and narratives that center non-standard bodies to explore embodied expression.

Although Siegal and Jacobsen wrote these words over two decades ago, they still hold true:

> an artistic choice must be made as to which aspects of movement are to be charted … which interface is ultimately chosen will depend not only on artistic needs but on other, more mundane factors such as availability, cost, and dependability.
>
> *Siegel and Jacobsen, 29*

We advocate for the addition of equity and inclusion to the list of factors taken into consideration when choosing a system or sensor for interactivity because many commercial systems do not work on people with disabilities or differently shaped bodies. Similar issues occur with the use of inexpensive energy expenditure sensors, which have issues with tracking users with darker skin or tattoos (Scherbina et al., 2). To circumvent these issues, systems discard data through:

> noise reduction and normalization of data leading to an erasure of context, as well as normalized interpretations and representations of bodies … [and] when we remove all divergent behavior from a bio signal, because it does not meet our expectations of how the body usually acts, or should perform, we delimit our capacity to observe bodily differences.
>
> *Naccarato and MacCallum 2017, 5*

It is possible to create systems that can be customized to observe and interact with all bodies.

Pieces as Practice

The following are examples of practice-based research/works by music/tech composers/performers specializing in dance, embodied practices, methodologies, and processes. The observations and subsequent adaptations each made while creating these pieces below highlight collaboration with sensors, systems and the users/performers involved. Furthermore, we bring attention to the fluid boundaries between human and technology by discussing technology as performer and human as technology while considering the peripheral concepts of culture, power, representation, and social equity.

Inter-Act

In Green-Mateu's audio/visual installation *Inter-Act* (2017), participants' movements were captured by a Kinect1515 and mapped to music and visual effects via the Synapse and Ableton software packages (Green-Mateu, 47). To begin the experience, Green-Mateu stood with arms out, elbows bent, and hands up so the system could recognize and lock the mapping skeleton onto her body. When another person showed interest, she invited them to stand in front of her in locking-position and transferred skeletal mapping to their body. They were then able to control their experience projected on a large concave screen and heard over a surround system with the option to pass on the control by occluding themselves behind the next player. A diverse range of individuals with differing body types, sizes, and abilities participated and passed the skeleton on to one another. This early version of motion capture was used to test a one-size-fits-all model to compare with more tailored approaches as part of Green-Mateu's research into technologically mediated dance and movement mapping strategies. Although the mapping was exactly the same for each body, the range of motion from person to person changed, causing interesting and differentiated sounds and visual effects.

The Kinect has also been used in clinical settings. Schedel worked on a project sonifying the gait of people with Parkinson's Disease, a neurodegenerative disease that often presents with involuntary quivering movement or shaking (Schedel et al., 2016). It was impossible for the Kinect to "lock onto" the skeleton of people with tremors; the team needed to lock the training data onto a team member with a similar body type. As with Green-Mateu's experience, once the system had created a map, it was possible to switch the control over to the individual with Parkinson's Disease. Once locked on, the system was able to track the movement and quantify the tremors.

Flesh/Light/Movement

In this instalformance (a system that both exists as an installation and has a scored/choreographed performance) *Flesh/Light/Movement* (2006), Schedel programmed a computer to track the shadow cast by a dancer. In the piece, a dancer stands between a light and a translucent screen; behind the screen is a web camera that tracks the shadow of the performer. The software is programmed to divide the image into 18 boxes: a set of 12 boxes across the top served as simple triggers, and when more than 50 percent of the area was covered in shadow, a bell sounded. The rest of the screen was divided into six larger boxes with more complex mapping to create richer interaction. It was used to develop a system whereby a single dancer was able to reach up and ring the bell. However, creating an installation version required more room between the light and the screen so that shorter individuals, children, or people in wheelchairs could still ring the bells. Ideally, the audience will have a chance to interact with the system before seeing a virtuosic performance, so they gain an understanding of the rules governing the interaction. The first time a bell is rung in the performance, the dancer kicks her leg above her head to trigger the sound—often creating an audible gasp in the audience who had only thought to use their hands to trigger the bells.

In the next handography exercise, *Shadows of Light* (see Figures 14.1 and 14.6), we look at shadows as a metaphor for mapping bodies and challenge the notion of a one-size-fits-all approach when quantifying and mapping the body.

Locus

Until now, all the pieces we have discussed used wireless tracking, either through the Magic Leap, Kinect, or custom hardware. Composer/movement/music technology researcher Jung In Jung used the GameTrak controller, a tethered spatial position controller created for a golfing video game (Freed et al., 1), during her PhD research to create various works. Jung used multiples of this restrictive motion tracking in several pieces as a test to bridge communication of abstract musical concepts between software design and contemporary dancer collaborators. *Locus*, Jung's first work with Gametrak, utilized the controllers:

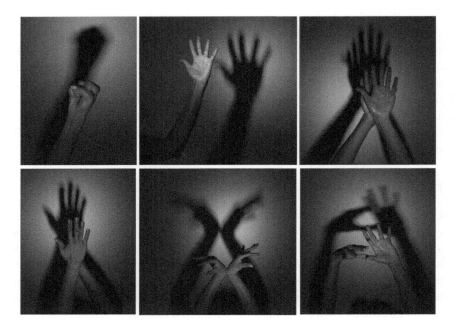

FIGURE 14.6 *Shadows of Light*
Source: Susie Green, 2020.

not only as an interface, but also as a common medium in which to think and work on the compositional process together. Both abstract sound and choreographic ideas were bridged through a concrete object—co-opting the affordances of the restrictive motion.

Jung 2020, 345

In her research, she cites Forsythe's techniques; his influence can be seen in her use of restriction as a means to create a structure within which improvised movements can be explored. Her intention was to "introduce the collaborative model from the field of contemporary dance to the field of computer music, and to adopt it into [her] compositional processes for sound" (ibid.). *Locus* is an example of an interdisciplinary piece that works within restrictions to evince adroitness, blurring the distinction between dance and music, choreography and music composition, interactive environment, and instrument design—and in Jung's case, between performers and creators.

Instead of simply choreographing the dance, Jung prompted the dancers to improvise with the tech and space while she observed them: "My dancers quickly adapted my composition process as they were trained with similar choreographic techniques" (Jung 2018, 358). She and the dancers then chose a combination of movements from the rehearsals which they found interesting physically, visually,

FIGURE 14.7 *((re) frame/bound)*
Source: Susie Green, 2020.

and sonically. Through this observational process and cycle of actions, the human beings become the technology and work through an algorithmic process much like machine learning. Jung decided to change the set-up of the Gametraks from performance to performance. The changing of the set-up ensured that the dancers had a fresh spatial landscape to discover and navigate, which produced new choices in improvisation, and subsequently new choreography from piece to piece. In the following handography exercise, *((re) frame/bound)* (see Figures 14.1 and 14.7), we introduce a new technology—the rubber band. You will explore a new spatial landscape through restriction, limitation, and adaptation of your hands' kinesphere.

III: Once Removed

Just as practitioners repurpose systems like the Kinect for use in medical contexts, artists have repurposed medical sensors, often called biosensors, for art (Naccarato and MacCallum 2017, 1). Collaborators Naccarato and MacCallum used a combination of computers and a variety of biosensors before focusing on the use of hospital grade electro-cardiogram (ECG) sensors in their artistic practice that sits at the intersection of dance, music, improvisation, and meditation with technology. In their performance *III: Once Removed*, they use heartbeats to explore processes of attempted measurement and representation of constant circulation that is never capturable and are ever-overlapping. Fascinated by the human construct of time, in their performances the duo explore Eagleman's proposition that "time is not a single entity. Instead, it is likely that a diverse group of neural mechanisms mediates temporal judgments" (Eagleman, 135). Their first pieces, exploring fluid timing and heartbeats, had players synchronize their performances to click tracks from the peaks of ECG sensors worn by the duo (Naccarato, 33). Later, they amplified the noisy electric signal produced by the biosensors directly into sound and sent this to musicians who were given a set of highly structured rules to play with. In the video documentation, Naccarato and MacCallum could be seen center stage, on their knees across from one another with locked eyes; throughout the performance, their hands touched one another's faces. Their breathing and interconnected heartbeats fluctuated, adding to the changes in time. In this way, their bodies became a part of the technology as the musicians improvised according to the predeveloped rules. In our interview with the duo, they explained that the musicians had to listen to the variable ECG rhythms while watching for the collaborators' subtle movements, and this multi-modal awareness resulted in a much better-synchronized performance.

Naccarato and MacCallum have developed four principles for representing the body with sensors, summarized as follows:

1) It is impossible for the human body to be measured in its entirety, no matter how many biosensors are used ... there exists no stable, complete body to be measured in the first place.
2) Bodies are continually becoming ... complex systems of relationality will always exceed representation.
3) Biosensor data is never only a result of biology, but rather carries traces of the system design from which it was derived.
4) Analysis of biosensor data requires interpretation and imagination on the part of the designers, users, and observers (Naccarato and MacCallum 2016, 59).

The design of interfaces which quantify bodily movement, is not neutral in any step of the process—from choosing or building a sensor, through interpreting the data, to displaying the data through media. Bodily experience is relative and unique; any quantification system is an external mathematical average. So too is the subjective sense of time. The following handography, *Entanglement* (see Figures 14.1, 14.8 and 14.9), expands the kinesphere to include the neck and voice, explores temporality, isochrony, rational listening, alignment, and possibility/impossibility, and illustrates various ways the body, systems, and time can be used in performance.

Audimance

Thus far, we have covered accessibility on several axes, but have not discussed how visually impaired people can experience performances involving the body. Access to

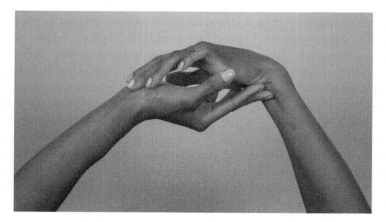

FIGURE 14.8 *Entangled Pulse*
Source: Susie Green, 2020.

FIGURE 14.9 *Entangled Voice*
Source: Susie Green, 2020.

dance, theatre, and film for non-visual audiences has traditionally been in the form of audio description. Most people are familiar with closed captioning, where words appear on screen transcribing the dialog and describing the music and soundscape for television viewers who are deaf. Another accessibility feature is designed for people with visual impairments; Descriptive Video Service (DVS) is a secondary audio channel carrying enriched verbal descriptions of what is going on visually in a scene (Cronin and King, 504). In theater, DVS is often called an audio description, or AD, and it is usually designed with *neutral* verbal narrations of visual information (Snyder, 935). An AD transcription from a 2019 Kinetic Light dance offered a new and *expressive* description:

> Head, neck, rocking, undulating.
> Frenzied movements quicken and hasten.
> Quicken.
> Releases hand in band.
> Quickens and hastens, frenzied.
> Rocking *left* and right and *left* and right and *left* and right and *left* and HUP!
> High and low.
> Reaching with the space.

Pounding with arms and feet on floor.
Frenzied.
Collapse.
HuuuuuuuuuHaaaaaaaaaaaa
Breath.
Fingers twitch.

Dinneen

Kinetic Light, an ensemble of three artists—Sheppard, Lawson, and Maag—created a compelling artistic experience for their blind and low-vision fans; they stress the importance of thinking about accessibility from the beginning of any artistic process. Even this reading of their performance with the emphasis on *left*, and the drawn-out *HuuuuuuuuuHaaaaaaaaaaaa*, pushes the boundaries of audio description, which is usually more literal in tone. During the *I Wanna Be With You Everywhere* festival at Performance Space NY, the audio description included live microphone feeds from the stage to allow the audience to hear real-time movement. AD interpreters were encouraged to perform with the dancers. For audience member James Dinneen, "at its most vivid, [the narrator's] voice became the dancing body, rolling, collapsing, and fighting for air" (Dinneen).

Inspired by the success of expressive AD, Kinetic Light created a new app, Audimance, for audio portrayal of choreographic experiences. The app offers audiences choices of "different styles of description, soundscapes, poetry, prose … [creating an] aural artistic experience" (Kinetic Light). During performances, designers included varying soundtracks represented by pastel dots on the screen with which audiences interacted. Through Audimance, Kinetic Light transformed AD into an engrossing artistic experience, gave agency to the audience in how they wanted to hear the dance, and rendered dance in sound for the purposes of equity.

Manifesto

Earlier in this chapter, we discussed inclusion for differently abled artists in the process of creating experiences and devices tailored for their personalized embodied expression. Centering *access to technology as an equity*, we challenge disparities that have been leveraged to block technology and education regarding the workings and processes behind the making of technology, such as economic, gender, race, age, physical, and mental abilities, and the intersectionality of any or all of these. The right to enchantment, expression, and erudition is available to all beings, and should be honored.

We recognize our privilege of having access to these systems, and we manifest a call to place humanity back into human–computer/human–human interaction as an intimate and personalized relationship. We call on curiosity and the access to the knowledge of systems along with the reimagining of them as an act of resistance to the patriarchal/hierarchical proclivities of owning, selling, and limiting knowledge, tech, space, place, expressivity, methods, and practices. Our Cynosuric Bodies are surrounded by a constellation of collaborators sharing time, opportunities, and knowledge which serve to center individual needs for a healthy and whole collective.

Acknowledgements

Special thanks to all the individuals we interviewed for this chapter for their time and work. We extend extra gratitude to handography performer/model Erin Leigh and photographer Lina Martinez-Espada. Finally, many thanks to the editors of this book for their thoughtfulness and inclusion.

Bibliography

Alessandrini, P., and F. Abtan. "*Mondgewächse*: A Collaborative Methodology for Inclusive Audiovisual Mappings in Instrument Design." Paper delivered at *International Conference on New Musical Interfaces*, Birmingham, UK, 2020.

Baudoin, P., and H. Gilpin. "Proliferation and Perfect Disorder: William Forsythe and the Architecture of Disappearance." 2004. www.hawickert.de/ARTIC1.html (accessed 15 May 2013).

Birringer, Johannes. "Interactive Dance, the Body and the Internet." *Journal of Visual Art Practice* 3, no. 3 (2004): 165–178.

Cronin, Barry J., and Sharon Robertson King. "The Development of the Descriptive Video Services." *Journal of Visual Impairment & Blindness* 84, no. 10 (1990): 503–506

Dinneen, James. "This Is What Accessibility Sounds Like" *The Brooklyn Rail*, September 2019. https://brooklynrail.org/2019/09/dance/This-Is-What-Accessibility-Sounds-Like.

Eagleman, David M. "Human Time Perception and Its Illusions." Current Opinion in Neurobiology 18, no. 2 (2008): 131–136.

Finch, Mark, Susan LeMessurier Quinn, and Ellen Waterman. "Improvisation, Adaptability, and Collaboration: Using AUMI in Community Music Therapy." Voices: A World Forum for Music Therapy 16, no. 3 (2016).

Freed, Adrian, Devin McCutchen, Andy Schmeder, Anne-Marie Skriver, Dan Overholt Hansen, Winslow Burleson, Camilla Nørgaard, and Alex Mesker. "Musical Applications and Design Techniques for the Gametrak Tethered Spatial Position Controller." In Proceedings of the 6th Sound and Music Computing Conference, edited by Fabien Gouyon, Alvaro Barbosa, and Xavier Serra. Porto, Portugal: Institute for Systems and Computer Engineering, Technology and Science, 2009, pp. 23–25.

Garland Thomson, Rosemarie. *Extraordinary Bodies: Figuring Physical Disability in American Culture and Literature*. New York: Columbia University Press, 2017.

Green-Mateu, Susan. The Tesseract: Using the Body's Movement to Shape My Compositional Practice. Masters by Research thesis, University of Huddersfield, 2018.

Johnson, Steven. *Interface Culture: How New Technology Transforms the Way We Create and Communicate*. New York: Basic Books, 1999.

Jung, Jung In. "Bridging Abstract Sound and Dance Ideas with Technology: Interactive Dance Composition as Practice-based Research." Paper delivered at *International Conference on Live Interfaces*, Porto, Portugal, June 2018.

Jung, Jung In. "Sound–[Object]–Dance: A Holistic Approach to Interdisciplinary Composition." In *Sound and Image: Aesthetics and Practices*, edited by Andrew Knight-Hill. Abingdon, UK: Taylor & Francis, 2020.

Kinetic Light. https://kineticlight.org/audimance (accessed 21 May 2021).

Kirsh, David. "How Marking in Dance Constitutes Thinking with the Body." *Versus: quaderni di studi semiotici* 112 (2011): 183–214.

Laban, Rudolf. *The Language of Movement: A Guidebook to Choreutics*. Boston, MA: Plays, Incorporated, 1974.

McKerrow, Steve. "Wheelchair Dancer, Peabody Create Music from Motion." *The Baltimore Sun*, 1 April 1993.

Merleau-Ponty, Maurice, and Colin Smith. *Phenomenology of Perception*. London: Routledge, 1962.

Morrison, Elise. "Cyborg Theatre: Corporeal/technological Intersections in Multimedia Performance." *Contemporary Theatre Review* 22, no. 3 (2012): 428–430.

Mulder, Axel. *Human Movement Tracking Technology*. Hand Centered Studies of Human Movement Project, Technical Report 94-1. 1994.

Naccarato, Teoma, and John MacCallum. "From Representation to Relationality: Bodies, Biosensors and Mediated Environments." *Journal of Dance & Somatic Practices* 8, no. 1 (2016): 57–72.

Naccarato, Teoma, and John MacCallum. "Critical Appropriations of Biosensors in Artistic Practice." In *MOCO '17: Proceedings of the 4th International Conference on Movement Computing*, edited by Marco Gillies and Kiona Niehaus. New York: Association for Computing Machinery, 2017, pp. 1–7.

Naccarato, Teoma. Re/contextualization: On the Critical Appropriation of Technologies as Artistic Practice. PhD dissertation, Coventry University, 2019.

Parker-Starbuck, J. *Cyborg Theatre: Corporeal/Technological Intersections in Multimedia Performance*. London: Palgrave Macmillan, 2011.

Phelan, Peggy. "Reconsidering Identity Politics, Essentialism, and Dismodernism: An Afterword." In *Bodies in Commotion: Disability and Performance*, edited by Carrie Sandahl and Philip Auslander. Ann Arbor, MI: University of Michigan Press, 2005, pp. 319–26.

Puckette, M., and K.L. Hagan, "Hand Gesture to Timbre Converter." In *Proceedings of the International Computer Music Association*. San Francisco, CA: International Computer Music Association, 2020. http://msp.ucsd.edu/Publications/icmc2020-reprint.pdf.

Schedel, Margaret, Daniel Weymouth, Tzvia Pinkhasov, Jay Loomis, Ilene Berger Morris, Erin Vasudevan, and Lisa Muratori. "Interactive Sonification of Gait: Realtime Biofeedback for People with Parkinson's Disease." In *Proceedings of the ISon 2016 Interactive Sonification Workshop*, edited by Jiajun Yang, Thomas Hermann, and Roberto Bresin. Bielefeld, Germany: CITEC, Bielefeld University, 2016.

Scherbina, Anna, C. Mikael Mattsson, Daryl Waggott, Heidi Salisbury, Jeffrey W. Christle, Trevor Hastie, Matthew T. Wheeler, and Euan A. Ashley. "Accuracy in Wrist-worn, Sensor-based Measurements of Heart Rate and Energy Expenditure in a Diverse Cohort." *Journal of Personalized Medicine* 7, no. 2 (2017): 3.

Siegel, W., "Dancing the Music: Interactive Dance and Music." In *Oxford Handbook on Interactive Dance*, edited by Roger T. Dean. Oxford, UK: Oxford University Press, 2009, pp. 191–213.

Siegel, Wayne, and Jens Jacobsen. "The Challenges of Interactive Dance: An Overview and Case Study." *Computer Music Journal* 22, no. 4 (1998): 29–43.

Snyder, Joel. "Audio Description: The Visual Made Verbal." *International Congress Series* 1,282 (2005): 935–939.

Winters, Amy. "Building a Soft Machine: New Modes of Expressive Surfaces." In *Design, User Experience, and Usability: Technological Contexts*, edited by Aaron Marcus. New York: Springer International, 2016, pp. 401–413.

Zhang, Zhengyou. "Microsoft Kinect Sensor and Its Effect." *IEEE Multimedia* 19, no. 2 (2012): 4–10.

15
THE VIOLINING BODY IN *ANTHÈMES II* BY PIERRE BOULEZ

Irine Røsnes

Introduction

The term *violining* derives from Christopher Small's *musicking* (Small 1998), and invites us to consider music as a process and practice which is built on interaction and relationships alongside cultural, historical, and material objects (such as instruments and scores) (Green 2013, 20), and which contributes to a dynamic and embodied understanding of music. Violining therefore signifies an enacted process that goes beyond the mechanics of playing the instrument and is considered in the widest sense of violin-specific musicking, which incorporates a complex myriad of contingencies and interrelations at play. To draw on what seems to be a meaningful and comprehensive presentation of violining in mixed music, this chapter aims to illuminate a circular interrelation of idiosyncratic affordances of the practice which come to fore through interrelation with the environment and the extended notion of the instrument. The term "violining" relates primarily to practice, to something that I *do* – and is therefore used as a verb throughout the chapter. With that in mind, the primary concern of this section is to explore the technologisation and mediatisation of the violining body through – and coupled with – the creative use of electronic music technology. As will be argued further in the chapter, the technologisation of the violining body ought not to be regarded with a sense of neutrality as it fundamentally changes the nature of sound production and perception. To illustrate my argument, a performative analysis of *Anthèmes II* (1994) by Pierre Boulez will be presented. The piece is widely recognised as a key work for violin and live electronics. A canon of the chamber mixed music genre, it stands apart from the centuries-long tradition of acoustic virtuoso playing coupled with electronic sound mediation. The reflections presented here through the example of *Anthèmes II* address idiosyncratic elements and specific challenges of the violin mixed music genre which distinguish the setting from other chamber music genres.

DOI: 10.4324/9781003008217-20

With that in mind, this chapter aims to give a better understanding of how despite technologisation of the extended performative body (Rodgers 2010), specifically the electrified violining body, through amplification of the instrument and migration of the sound source from the resonance of the violin to the speakers – the body of the violinist remains at the centre of the performance and sound production. Yet, through the embodied account of violin mixed music performance practice which draws on the current interdisciplinary discussion of embodiment theory[1] as a dynamic, decentralised, non-linear interactive system of cognitive, bodily, and environmental processes (Smith and Thelen 1994), (Clark and Chalmers 1998), (Gallagher 2005), this chapter argues that the violining body expands beyond the skull, skin, and limbs and incorporates the instrument, the sonic space, and the sound of the electronics as an extended notion of the performative body while creating a non-hierarchical interrelationship of the electrified violining body with its surrounding environment. The characteristics of the practice are formulated from the point of view of a phenomenological[2] observation of the violining body performing with electronics which specifically focuses on its idiosyncrasy in relation to the acoustic violin sound production.

The chapter aims to consider and answer the following questions: What are the implications of the electronics on the embodied agency of the violinist? How is the historical notion of violin playing re-imagined and transformed in mixed practices? What is the violin-technical means through which the violinist relates to the electronics? These questions are approached through positioning my own practice at the centre of the investigation, and will be illustrated by specific examples of the phenomenology of performance of *Anthèmes II*. The structure of the chapter is as follows. The section "Electrified-Violining-Body" explores the notion of how the music-making body expands the corporeality of the physical body to the violining body, and ultimately grows into a dynamic interactive system of electrified-violining-body. The next section, "The Body Mixed in Practice", connects the gestalt of electrified-violining-body to a specific instance of performing *Anthèmes II* by Pierre Boulez. Specifically, issues of sound projection and dynamic differentiation, accents/onsets, and haptic feedback will be discussed closely. The observations presented in this chapter are part of a larger piece of practice research into the repertoire for violin and electronics that I have conducted at the University of Huddersfield between 2017 and 2021.

The Electrified-Violining-Body

Following Varela, Thompson and Rosch (1991),the music-making body can be viewed as a gestalt which is irreducible to a single element, functionality, or directionality of actions. That position opens a fruitful avenue for viewing my violining body in a continuous dialogue with the sonic environment, which informs my approach to listening and sound production, and which is embedded in the environment (Gallagher 2019). My electrified-violining-performance-body as the locus for all activity on and behind the stage is the starting point for this investigation.

As a performer, I work in, though, from, and on my body while performing; the body is always at the centre of performance and extended into the instrument, equipment, and the sonic environment, constituting the electrified-violining-body.

My engagement with a multitude of contexts that present themselves across musical traditions and historical eras, performance rituals and aesthetics, skills, agencies, and affordances (Gibson 1979) means I rarely experience my body as a singular, isolated agent while performing or musicking otherwise (Laws 2019, 109). I engage not only with the sound production in relation to the sonic material present in the room, but also the wealth of knowledge received from all instances of musicking ((Small 1998), whether conscious or sub-conscious. Therefore, the violining body is not just a physical entity with the movement of fingers, arms, ability to recognise pitch, play together, think phrases, etc. Rather, it is a well-tuned system that emerged out of a multitude of experiences (Laws 2019). Through thousands of practice hours, ensemble rehearsals, and decades of living with the instrument, my body is shaped by the practice and my sense of self as performer is intertwined with the instrument (Torrence 2019). The notion of a singular dynamic entity contributes to the wider critique of the Cartesian view of the mind-body-environment divide (van der Schyff 2015).

But what happens when music technology enters the sphere of Acoustic music-making? Do boundaries of the violining body merge into the realm of electrified musicking? How do amplification, sound diffusion, controllers, and the lack of visual reference affect violining and in what ways can electronic music technology be experienced as a continuation and extension of the violining body? As Berweck (2013) suggests, electronic music technology is often outside the skill set of acoustic instrumentalists, something which means that mixed settings can be experienced as destabilising to the violining embodiment.

The various roles that the body engages with during mixed music performance are experienced as an unseparatable whole, an ecosystem of actions and perceptions manifested as bodily actions (listening, use of limbs, swaying and movement of the body, making communicative gestures, etc.), as bodily extensions (the violin and the bow amplification, loudspeakers, and control contraptions like effects pedals), as well as functionality of spatial positions (the choreography of the body and the equipment in the space as a well-tuned system). It is important to note that the challenges of the practice are piece-specific and must be addressed in relation to each composition.

Despite the emerging presence of "the performer" in mixed music discourses of recent decades (Berweck 2013; Kimura and Risset 2006; Pestova 2008), there is a further need to understand the specificity of violin practice in the context of mixed music performance. Following Gibson's understanding of affordances as possibilities for action shaped by interconnectedness between the violinist, the instrument, and the environment, it is sensible to assume that through developing an intimate notion and connection with the instrument, the musical thinking and the body image of the performer are influenced and shaped by the idiosyncrasies of the instrument (Laws 2019). The loop of actions and perceptions that occur as a result of such interrelationship points in the direction of the necessity of studying the particularities of the setting in relation to the instrument. The generalised notion of "performer" (Dogantan-Dack 2015) therefore omits central violinistic questions of sound production, intonation, tradition of playing, even identity, and leaves the subtleties and idiosyncrasies of instrument-specific knowledge and skills without detailed consideration.

The violin shapes the body of the violinist in a multitude of ways. As most violinists working with mixed music repertoire are educated in the traditional conservatoire educational system,[3] the violin becomes an integral part of the physical and mental development of a child from an early age, and in some cases the formal training starts as early as the age of 2 or 3 (Suzuki Association of America n.d.). Years of training imply that the violinist develops physically, mentally, and culturally hand-in-hand with the instrument, with stages of one's physical growth mirroring the change and the growth of the instrument. Starting off with a small violin as a young child, by the teenage years one reaches the point of playing a full-size violin – an important and often memorable stage in the development of young violinists. As such, the physical growth of a child is interconnected with the "growth" of the violin –they grow together. That process is different, for instance, from the development of young pianists, percussionists, or wind and electronic instrumentalists, and presents a specific type of embodiment that can be characterised as mutual synchronicity between the subject and the object, which thus matures into the violining body. Such development over time intertwines and shapes the body image of a violinist as a 'complex set of intentional states – perceptions, mental representations, beliefs, and attitudes – in which the intentional object of such states is one's own body" (Gallagher and Cole 1995, 371).

Moreover, the violin shapes the physical body of the performer over time. My left shoulder may carry more tension than the right one; my left ear, may wear out quicker than the right one; calluses and permanent "violin rash" on the left side of my neck, the different shapes of my right and left hands (as if they belong to two different people), the way I stand, the strength of my arms – my entire body is shaped by my instrument, and the violin is imprinted and embodied in my music-making body (Torrence 2019). The violin is a part of my body image, and I am quick to recognise the subtleties of the sound-producing gestures in playing of other violinists, just as teachers who have lost their top form can advise students on the finest details of sound production without playing. The notion of body image leads us to the understanding that the music-making body of the violinist is *mediated* by its life-long entanglement with the violin.

The Body Mixed in Practice

The physical position of the violin in relation to the apparatus is crucial in regard to feedback and sound quality. As discussed by Tremblay and Mclaughlin (2009), being outside of the speaker circle prevents the violinist from hearing her own sound, assessing the volume and the overall balance, unless using monitors (which in its own right is problematic, as monitors present an indicative, reduced sonic picture). The uncertainty created by the inability to hear a full sounding complexity destabilises the embodied notion of sound production and the sense of control. Specifically, the violining embodiment is affected by the following points:

1. the necessity for amplification (for real-time processing and balance of the acoustic and the digital)
2. sound diffusion (eight channels in *Anthèmes II*) – the mediation of the acoustic sound through amplification and speakers
3. synchronisation between the violin and electronics (here, the Antescofo score follower system)
4. dialictic of the acoustic and electronic sound sources
5. the responsibility of producing and sourcing the electronic sound through the violin.

Affordances of electronic augmentation present a number of challenges in relation to sound production. As problematised by McLaughlin (2012), the multidirectional sound wave of an acoustic source must be amplified and sent through a speaker system to blend with the axis-directional electronic sound. However, McLaughlin points out that the solution of amplification is challenging and creates an "acousmatic dislocation" (Emmerson 2007) which affects but the embodiment and the technique of sound projection. Directing the sound toward the far end of concert hall through the means of violin technique but must be achieved through the correct positioning of microphones and noise-free, clear sound production. Much of the responsibility is outsourced to the correct use of technology, its correct positioning and quality.

Another example of extended or distributed sound production is the inability of the violinist to control the volume or balance of the sounding result and the necessity for an external assessment, which is often done by a sound engineer. These examples show that a large part of the projection and miscibility of sound sources is distributed and enacted outside the violining-body, thus forming an extended embodied sonic apparatus. That stands in opposition to an acoustic duet playing, where both players are equally responsible for their own sound production and of the duo as a whole.

The violining embodied gestalt expands through exposure to new ways of musicking with electronics, and adopts an inherent notion of causality, reactivity, and exploration of the extended practice. The indicative topology of roles that the violinist might occupy within a single composition may be outlined as follows: the violin can act as a controller, sound source, and follower. It is important to note that in all instances, mixed music ought to be perceived as a chamber music genre, and not as a solo with an electronic accompaniment, as the violinist is at all times in a co-dependent relationship with the media and the environment even if the electronic part is a fixed media, albeit through different means. The way to identify and differentiate the roles of the violin in a single mixed piece is by practising with electronics. As Mieko Kanno suggests,[4] the electronics part ought to be internalised by the violinist during the phase of preparation. Berweck emphasises the importance of understanding the properties of the software and its functionality, investing in one's own equipment, and practising with electronics in a similar way as one would in an acoustic ensemble. Both approaches enable the violinist to embody the work with electronics through practice, thus expanding the violining body into an electrified violining body. Importance of the individual preparation of pieces with real-time processing cannot be underestimated. While playing in time and in tune remain the very of the preparation, amplification exposes imprecision and poor execution. By incorporating electronics into the violining body framework and expanding it to the electrified-violining-body, we enable a sense of a dynamic interaction and embodiment within the extended sonic system.

To illustrate these ideas in practice, I will discuss my experience of performing *Anthèmes II* (1994) for violin and live electronics by Pierre Boulez, which took place at Phipps Hall, the University of Huddersfield on 20 January 2019. The performance was delivered in collaboration with Pablo Galaz (sound design) and Laurens van der Wee (sound engineer). The setup of the piece consisted of an eight channel system (2+6) surrounding the audience, a mixing desk, a digital reverb unit, an interface, a DPA4061 microphone for the violin, and a MacBook Pro running Max MSP software. The score following is handled by the Antescofo module, which uses an encoded score to track the violin part. The preparation for the performance happened over a period of nine months, and the electronics materials were generously lended by Cyril Béros of IRCAM.

Projection and Dynamic Differentiation

> The difference between the soft and the loud is narrow. It feels narrow. I can put the bow on the string, and effortlessly, there is a dramatic amount of sound coming out without me even trying to shape it. The shape is different, though. It needs more space and silence around it. Like a large truck, it needs some space and time to manoeuvre.
>
> *from the performance dairy (January 2019)*

After the very first run-through of the piece in the venue, it became clear that the amplification changed the way I perceived and embodied dynamics: the compression of the amplified sound lessened the extremes of soft and loud, flattening the expressive capacity. The first part of *Anthèmes II*, "Très lent" (1–16, Figure 15.1), is one of the softest parts in the piece, fluctuating between *pp* and *mp* throughout the entire section. The rich harmonisation and the compression of the sound by the electronics challenges fragility and flexibility of the sound – the texture of the sound feels thicker and richer than I envision a *pp* to sound. I experience my sound as lush and full, primarily because the violin triggers a whole set of electronics that harmonise with it like an electronic a capella, enhancing a sense of interconnectedness with the sonic fabric of the electronics. As the level of the

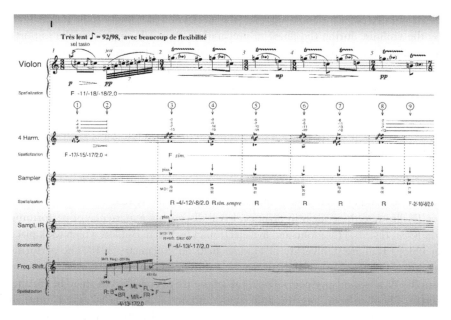

FIGURE 15.1 Pierre Boulez, *Anthèmes II*, "Très lent"

violin amplification is set to be equal to the electronics, all in all it gives a sense of a general elevation of the dynamics and leads me to realise that dynamic contrasts here must be achieved through different means than volume. After rehearsing the section, I realised that my ears had begun to identify the dynamic threshold of the electronics and my violining body started to respond to the software, embodying the sequential, pragmatic "thinking" of it. The threshold of the dynamics was not immediately dependant on my technique, but was a prerequisite of the apparatus, enhancing an extended notion of instrumentality.

After experimenting with various microphone positions, bow placements, and pressure, it became clear that a useful approach to solving the issue of dynamic insensitivity was to redirect attention from dynamic variation to timbral differentiation and tonal contrast. The character indications and bow positions of "Très lent" are "avec beaucoup de flexibilité" and "sul tasto", which suggest a delicacy and fragility of timbre. My translation of these directions to violin playing suggests an extreme, airy *flautando* playing with little bow pressure, transparent in colour, shimmery vibrato – to match the electronics. As Mieko Kanno points out: "timbre creates illusion by manipulating the cognitive faculty that is formed through our physical and emotional experience" (Kanno 2001) - the timbral colouration alters the perception of the dynamics and creates an illusion of fragility and softness.

Figure 15.2, the transitional material of "III Lent" (1–4), is another example of colour-as-dynamic. The approach suggests the use of *sul ponticello* in a high register,

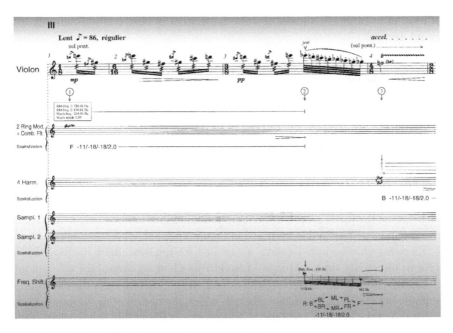

FIGURE 15.2 Pierre Boulez, *Anthèmes II*, "III Lent"

followed by a rapid one-note crescendo until the following section. This fragment is interesting for several reasons.

A meaningful way to transition from *mp* to *pp* in *sol ponticello* here was through timbral colouration, and specifically by creating a shimmery colour, alternating the gradation of *sol ponticello* and the rapidness of the tremolo – and not by means of a volume decrease. The transition note of bar 4 is especially interesting because the dynamic increase here proved to be most effectively achieved by creating a timbral illusion of a dynamic increase though a larger amount and speed of the bow rather than using a "glued-to-the-bridge" bow position, which can be problematic on its own right as there is a danger of the amplification picking up the higher partials that are more apparent to the ear through bowing next to the bridge, which will ultimately make the sound thinner.

Here we explored how the approach to creating soft dynamics, dynamic differentiation, and increase in volume relies on adopting a more pragmatic listening attitude and embodying the thresholds of the digital parameters into the violin playing. Because of the sound compression and the rich electronic augmentation, the difference between loud and soft is narrower than in acoustic playing, and is most effective when approached as a timbral colouring, rather than relying on volume. These observations inform our understanding that the amplification changes the perception of the sound and its embodiment in relation to the instrument. At the same time, it presents the violinist with a whole new set of expressive modalities in relation to timbral colouration and exaggeration of bow positions, timing, and sound density.

Accents – Onsets

> By stretching the time before the onset, slightly delaying or going ahead – letting the sound ring and decay in the environment – I am sculpting the piece.
>
> *from the performance dairy (January 2019)*

Another issue that was identified during the preparation for the performance was the role of accents in the piece, as opposed to accents in a Romantic style. Throughout the piece, accents often indicate a rapid shift to new sonic material and are used as its trigger, as demonstrated in Figure 15.3.

Knowing that accents provoke an immediate response from the electronics informs my way of approaching it – I am learning how to control the effect of my violining actions in relation to the electronics. My ability to predict the electronics' response is a means of interaction through which the notion of my violining body goes beyond the boundaries of the body-instrument physicality. In the given scenario, the accent proves to be not so much about energy and intensity as it might be in, for example, the Romantic repertoire, but rather about timing. This becomes clear from observing the shape of the attack as a consequence of the length and intensity of the previous note (bar 4 in Figure 15.2): the decay of the material preceding the accent is a tool for shaping the next onset, which triggers a new section

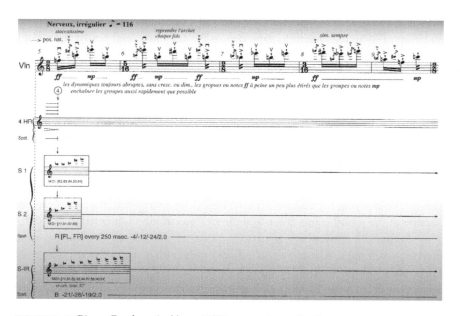

FIGURE 15.3 Pierre Boulez, *Anthèmes II*, "Nerveux, irregulier"

of the piece. The accent becomes a way of phrase signposting, and the timing with which it is approached serves as a tool for interaction. This example demonstrates that accents have different meaning in mixed music than in acoustic repertoire, and do not necessarily signify an emphasis or a climax, but a cue for new material and a point of interaction between the violin and electronics.

Haptic Gap

> The amplified sound feels faster. As if there is no friction, no resistance, no physical weight to it – only responsiveness. It puts me off a little bit, I do not feel in control.
>
> *from the performance dairy (January 2019)*

Rehearsal of section VI – which is essentially a tight dialogue and mirroring of gestural material between the violin and electronics, in particular demisemiquavers – presented as a conversation between the electrified-violining-body and the electronic response which is haptically imbalanced: the embodied velocity and resistance of the sound produced on the violin is different to the resonance of the electronics, and the disembodied response of the electronics produces weaker haptic feedback and feels lighter and faster. According to Papetti and Saitis, haptic feedback:

> supports performance control (e.g., timing, intonation) as well as expressivity (e.g., timbre, emotion). In particular, skilled performers are known to establish an intimate, rich haptic exchange with their instruments, resulting in truly embodied interaction that is hard to find in other human–machine contexts.
>
> *Papetti and Saitis (2018, 2)*

Given that the haptic feedbacks of acoustic and electronic instruments are different, it presents a performative challenge: how to create an illusion of narrowing the haptic gap – the difference in the embodied resistance of sound production and perception?

The electronic sound travels through space on an axis as opposed to the multidirectionality of normal acoustic sound, and doesn't resonate through the body, the floor, and the instrument (Papetti and Saitis 2018, 2) in the same way as an acoustic violin does. As Figure 15.4 demonstrates, the parts are closely intertwined, and represent a continuous line divided between the instruments. To create that illusion, I decided to experiment with quicker bow speed, a lighter left hand and a *flautando* colour of the sound – and most importantly, the timing between phrases. It became evident that weaker haptic feedback may be compensated for by avoiding interfering with the decay of the electronic sound. Allowing the decay to fade out, making space between phrases by embodying the electronics' decay threshold, enabled me to strategically navigate and create an illusion of narrowing the haptic gap.

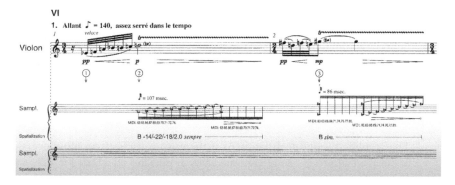

FIGURE 15.4 Pierre Boulez, *Anthèmes II*, "VI Allant"

Conclusion

Through an extended embodiment approach, the music-making body of the violinist performing with electronics can be viewed as a dynamic action-perception system, which is enacted through a dialectic of embodied interconnectedness constituting the electrified-violining body. Its role in the context of mixed music is different from other genres of chamber music, primarily because of the physical properties of acoustic and electronic sound. This chapter has illustrated how various elements of the violin sound production are distributed between the violinist, amplification, and sound diffusion equipment. The control of the sounding result is no longer a singular responsibility of the violinist: the quality and correct position of microphones is as important as the ability of the violinist to produce the desirable sound, while the issues of volume and balance are often outsourced to the sound engineer, leading to the notion of distributed sound production. Thus, the performing agency is distributed through the environment external to the body, creating an expanded notion of the violining embodiment.

The embodied violining gestalt is modified and expanded by the electronics in the following ways. The sound compression narrows the embodied understanding of the dynamics. That can be compensated for by adopting an embodied notion of the dynamic threshold of the electronics and approaching dynamic contrasts as timbral coloration. The meaning of accents/onsets in violin mixed music is different from the accents in the Romantic repertoire. They often trigger new sonic material, and when approached with that notion, may be used as a tool for interaction between the violin and electronics. The phenomenon of a different haptic feedback generated by the violin and electronics may be compensated by embodying the notion of electronic sound decay and allowing space between phrases.

As we have explored throughout this chapter, circular implications of the electronics on the violin sound production and vice versa, are at the core of the practice, and cannot be ignored by adopting a soloistic approach to performance of mixed music repertoire, and ought to be practised as a type of chamber music.

Furthermore, the sonic environment with which the violining body interacts transforms the technical means of violin sound production. The electronic mediation of the violining body idiosyncratically changes the way sound projection, dynamic differentiation, haptic gap and accents may be approached in relation to acoustic practice, and are therefore specific to the setting.

The adaptation of the violining-body to the electronics happens over time. It requires the violinist to develop new ways of preparation that enable an intimate understanding of the electronic processes and the ability to gain better control of sound production. As rapid changes and evolution in electronic music technology quickly find their way into new mixed music compositions, it is crucial for the violinist to keep the notion of "work-in-progress" in relation to understanding the mixed music apparatus. Destabilising, yet yielding new and rich potential for expression, the incorporation of electronics into the violining gestalt creates a dynamic ecological notion of the electrified-violining-body.

Notes

1 The concept of embodiment is a larger theoretical classification that originated in the study of phenomenology; see Heidegger (1978, first published in 1927), Husserl (2012, first published in 1913), Maurice Merleau-Ponty (2014, first published in 1945), and von Weizsäcker (1940). This work is primarily reliant on frameworks presented by Clark and Chalmers (1998), Gallagher (2005), Colombetti and Roberts (2015), Ryan and Schiavio (2019), Lakoff and Johnson (2002), and Parviainen (2002).
2 Here understood as a direct access to human experience (Varela, Rosch and Thompson 1991).
3 A series of interviews with violinists performing mixed music repertoire was conducted to inform this work. The artists interviewed included: Irvine Arditti, Mieko Kanno, Barbara Lunenburg, Dejana Seculic, Darrah Morgan, Josh Modney, Aisha Orazbayeva, and Linda Jankowska – all classically trained violinists.
4 Interview with Irine Røsnes, 16 December 2019.

Bibliography

Anon. 2021. "10 Tips on Maximising Tone Quality & Projection." The Strad, 4 November. www.thestrad.com/10-tips-on-maximising-tone-quality-and-projection/22.article.
Berweck, Sebastian. 2013. *It Worked Yesterday*. Huddersfield, UK: University of Huddersfield Press.
Borgdorff, Henk. 2012. *The Conflict of Faculties: Perspectives on Artistic Research in Academia*. Leiden, the Netherlands: Leiden University Press.
Born, Georgina. 1995. *Rationalizing Culture: IRCAM, Boulez, and the Institutionalization of the Musical Avant-garde*. Berkeley, CA: University of California Press.
Boulez, Pierre, and Andrew Gerzso. 1994. *Anthèmes II for Violin and Live Electronics*. Paris, France: IRCAM.
Clark, Andy, and David Chalmers. 1998. "The Extended Mind." *Analysis* 58(1): 8–19.
Colombetti, Giovanna, and Tom Roberts. 2015. "Extending the Extended Mind: The Case for Extended Affectivity." *Philosophical Studies* 172: 1243–1263.
Cook, Nicolas. 2013. *Beyond the Score: Music as Performance*. New York: Oxford University Press.

Cox, Arnie. 2006. "Hearing, Feeling, Grasping Gestures." In *Music and Gesture*, edited by Anthony Gritten and Elaine King, 46–60. Aldershot, UK: Ashgate.

Dogantan-Dack, Mine. 2015. "The Role of the Musical Instrument in Performance as Research: The Piano as a Research Tool." In *Artistic Research in Music: theory, Criticism, Practice*, edited by Mine Donagtan-Dack et al., 169–189. Farnham, UK: Ashgate.

Emmerson, Simon. 2007. *Living Electronic Music*. Aldershot, UK: Ashgate.

Friston, Karl. 2010. "The Free-energy Principle: A Unified Brain Theory?" *Nature Reviews Neuroscience* 11: 127–138.

Gallagher, Shaun. 2005. "Philosophy". In *How the Body Shapes the Mind*, 196–200. Oxford, UK: Oxford University Press.

Gallagher, Shaun. 2018. "Extended Mind." *Southern Journal of Philosophy* 56(4): 421–447.

Gallagher, Shaun. 2019. "Educating the Right Stuff: Lessons in Enactivist Learning." *Educational Theory* 68(6): 525–641.

Gallagher, Shaun, and Jonathan Cole. 1995. "Body Image and Body Schema in a Deafferented Subject." *Journal of Mind and Behavior* 16(4): 369–390.

Gibson, James. 1979. *The Ecological Approach to Visual Perception*. Boston, MA: Houghton Mifflin.

Green, Owen. 2013. User Serviceable Parts: Practice, Technology, Sociality and Method in Live Electronic Musicking. Unpublished doctoral thesis, City University, London.

Heidegger, Martin. 1978. *Being and Time*. Hoboken, NJ: Wiley-Blackwell.

Husserl, Edmund. 2012. *Ideas: General Introduction to Pure Phenomenology*. Abingdon, UK: Routledge.

Kanno, Mieko. 2001. *Timbre as Discourse*. York, UK: University of York Press.

Kimura, Mari, and Jean-Claude Risset. 2006. *Auditory Illusion and Violin: Demonstration of a Work by Jean-Claude Risset Written for Mari Kimura*. Paris, France: NIME.

Lakoff, George, and Mark Johnson. 2002. *Metaphors We Live By*. Chicago, IL: Chicago University Press.

Laws, Catherine et al. 2019. *Voices, Bodies, Practices: Performing Musical Subjectivities*. Ghent, Belgium: Leuven University Press.

Leman, Marc. 2010. "Music, Gesture, and the Formation of Embodied Meaning." In *Musical Gestures: Sound, Movement, and Meaning*, edited by Mark Leman and Rolf Inge Godøy, 126–153. New York: Routledge.

McLaughlin, Scott. 2012. "If a Tree Falls in an Empty Forest: Problematization of Liveness in Mixed-music Performance." *International Journal of Performance Arts & Digital Media* 5(1): 17–27.

Merleau-Ponty, Maurice. 2014. *Phenomenology of Perception*. London: Routledge.

Mozart, Leopold. 1756. *Versuch einer gründlichen Violinschule*. Augsburg, Germany: Johann Jacob Lotter.

Papetti, Stefano, and Charalampos Saitis. 2018. *Haptic Musical Instruments; Haptic Psychophysics; Interface Design and Evaluation; User Experience; Musical Performance*. Champaign, IL: Springer Nature.

Parsons, L.M. 1990. "Body image." In *The Blackwell Dictionary of Cognitive Psychology*, edited by M.W. Eysenck, 46–47. Oxford, UK: Wiley-Blackwell.

Parviainen, Jaana. 2002. "Bodily Knowledge: Epistemological Reflections on Dance." *Dance Research Journal* 34(1): 11–26.

Pestova, Xenia. 2008. *Models of Interaction in Works for Piano and Live Electronics*. Montreal, Canada: McGill University Press.

Rodgers, Tara. 2010. *Pink Noises: Women on Electronic Music and Sound*. Durham, NC: Duke University Press.

Røsnes, Irine. 2021. *Theatre of Transformations*. Huddersfield, UK: University of Huddersfield Press.
Ryan, Kevin, and Andrea Schiavio. 2019. "Extended Musicking, Extended Mind, Extended Agency: Notes on the Third Wave." *New Ideas in Psychology* 5: 8–17.
Small, Christopher. 1998. *Musicking: The Meanings of Performing and Listening*. Middletown, CT: Wesleyan University Press.
Smalley, Denis. 1997. "Spectromorphology: Explaining Sound-shapes." *Organised Sound* 2(2): 107–126.
Smith, Linda B., and Esther Thelen. 1994. *A Dynamic Systems Approach to the Development of Cognition and Action*. Cambridge, MA: MIT Press.
Suzuki Association of America. n.d. "About the Suzuki Method." https://suzukiassociation.org/about/suzuki-method/.
Torrence, Jennifer. 2019. "The Foregrounded Body: A Mutation from Executing Musician to Co-creating Performer." The Research Catalogue. www.researchcatalogue.net/view/533313/533314.
Tremblay, Pierre Alexandre, and Scott McLaughlin. 2009. "Thinking Inside the Box: A New Integrated Approach to Composition and Performance." In *Proceedings of the 2009 International Computer Music Conference*, 379–386. Montreal, Canada: International Computer Music Association.
van der Schyff, Dylan. 2015. "Music as a Manifestation of Life: Exploring Enactivism and the 'Eastern Perspective' for Music Education." *Frontiers of Psychology* 6(345): 1–15. doi: 10.3389/fpsyg.2015.00345.
Varela, Francisco J., Eleanor Rosch, and Evan Thompson. 1991. *The Embodied Mind: Cognitive Science and Human Experience*. Boston, MA: MIT Press.
von Weizsäcker, Victor. 1940. *Der Gestaltkreis: Theorie der Einheit von Wahrnehmen und Bewegen*. Leipzig, Germany: Thieme.

16

"TRY TO WALK WITH THE SOUND OF MY FOOTSTEPS SO THAT WE CAN STAY TOGETHER"

Sonic presence and virtual embodiment in Janet Cardiff and Georges Bures Miller's audio and video walks

Sophie Knezic

Janet Cardiff and George Bures Miller have created a distinctive body of performative sound art of which a key output is the ongoing series of interactive audio and video walks, known as the Walks, that inaugurate a nuanced and layered experience of perception, memory, embodiment and time. The Walks are produced from sonic compositions featuring ambient sound, fragmented narration, excerpted historical accounts and personal musings spoken by the guiding persona of 'Janet' that afford a unique, multi-dimensional listener experience. The techniques of binaural sound recording heard through stereo headphones, Janet's acousmatic voice and the format of the solo walker positioned as a participant-listener are central to the Walks' overall effect. Through carefully constructed technological, sensorial and narrative elements – and crucially, their virtual dimension – the Walks generate an experience of sensory perception that I am terming 'sonic presence and virtual embodiment'. Philosophical perspectives on the virtual from Pierre Lévy, Roberto Diodato, Brian Massumi and Henri Bergson are recruited into the argument to demonstrate the ways in which Cardiff and Bures Miller's Walks mobilise a metaphysics of virtuality. This hinges on the interchange of virtual and actual phenomena, becoming a process whereby the experience of sensory perception, embodiment and temporality are recalibrated and intensified.

To date, Cardiff and Bures Miller have produced 28 audio and video Walks in varied international locations, from major cities like London, Sydney and Venice to smaller townships and forest terrain. The format of the Walks is consistent: the participant-listener is given a pair of stereo headphones and a connected device at a designated starting point, and then follows the instructions of the audio recording,

DOI: 10.4324/9781003008217-21

which invariably impel the listener to walk a circuitous path through a series of locales, simultaneously navigating the prescribed route intermixed with a sonic composition emanating from the headphones alongside ambient sounds in the real-time environment. The compositions feature a range of human and non-human sounds, sonic objects specific to the area or sourced elsewhere – such as footsteps, humming, vehicular traffic, church bells, splashing water, whinnying horses, birdsong and thunder – interwoven with the central feature of Janet's voice. The rich tapestry of sonic textures is spliced with fragmented texts such as existential reflections, brief historical accounts, reflections of transient figures and dream narratives all spoken by the persona of Janet's voice. It is this voice that acts with centrifugal force to suture the other sonic elements into an experiential whole that nonetheless remains porous. Through their dovetailing of virtual and real-life elements enabled by the interactive experience, the Walks oscillate between pre-recorded objectivity and contingent potentiality, in so doing recomposing the relationship between virtuality, embodiment and perception.

Cardiff has referred to the initial trigger for the development of the Walks as an inadvertent audio recording made while wandering in a graveyard in Banff, Alberta in 1991. Although the site recording was intentional, Cardiff had neglected to switch off the voice recorder when placing it into her bag, resulting in a continuous recording of her physical motions on the return journey. Listening later to this unintentional surplus recording awakened Cardiff's realisation of its artistic possibilities:

> When I played back the tape to find where I had left off I heard the sound of my body while walking, my voice describing what was in front of me and also my breathing. I began to walk with my *virtual body* [italics mine]. It was one of those 'aha' experiences. I knew I had to use the format because it was so peculiar. I produced the first walk, Forest Walk, about two weeks later.
>
> *Cardiff, in Schaub (2005 pg 79)*

Cardiff's retrospective identification of the consequentiality of this event as a point of origin is not uncoincidentally framed in terms that articulate the Walks' primary, interconnected elements of virtuality, embodiment, perambulation, sound and the acousmatic voice. As tracings of an acoustic environment through former physical attendance, the Walks are indices of a sonic presence that is re-activated by a subsequent listener-participant, expanding the bounds of virtual experience and sensory perception as relays across subjectivities and temporal registers.

The Walks (initially credited to Cardiff, but developing into a collaborative practice with Georges Bures Miller) can be situated within the historical lineages of 20th-century artists' walks.[1] Cardiff's point of distinction within these varied walking practices is the cultivated deployment of her own voice as a malleable persona known as 'Janet', which functions as the sound composition's key structural element. As Cardiff has acknowledged, this persona is mutable, fluctuating in mood and character.[2]

Yet curators, historians and participants have identified one vocal persona as particularly seductive and intimate. Schaub (2005 pg 20) has referred to this as 'the artist's voice', describing it as:

> a seemingly ageless, pleasantly deep, feminine voice that ranges from matter-of-fact to sexy to solicitous. It is a voice that is neither too harsh nor too soft and that you find pleasant to listen to and are happy to follow.[3]

In my experience of the Walks, this voice derives its seductive power from Cardiff's precise modulation of timbre, pacing and amplitude (a soft speaking that veers towards whispering) that anchors it in an affective register. It is a voice that solicits proximity and imbues the narration with intimacy even when the spoken words are not divulging personal material, but conveying straightforward information such as directional instructions.

It is the oft-repeated imperative to 'stay together' spoken by this solicitous Janet persona that intensifies the sense of proximate intimacy, positioning the voice as a kind of incorporeal confidante. 'Go around the corner to the front of the main stairs. Walk up the stairs. I'll walk slowly so we can stay together,' Janet bids in the audio walk *Chiaroscuro* (Cardiff and Miller 1997). 'Listen to me, follow my footsteps,' she instructs in *The Empty Room* (1997) (Schaub 2005 pg 236). 'Try to walk with the sound of my footsteps so that we can stay together,' she coaxes in the *Villa Medici Walk* (Cardiff and Miller 1998a); a refrain repeated in *Wanås Walk* (Cardiff and Miller 1998b). In contrast to the convention of the museum or tourist audio guide where vocal instructions are neutral and remote, in Cardiff and Bures Miller's Walks, an effect of confidentiality is produced through the tenor of Janet's voice and the instructions themselves, often predicated on the necessity to 'stay together', situating Janet's sonic presence as unerringly close.

Another element which intensifies the sense of Janet's proximity is the listener-participant's use of stereo headphones to hear her voice. Stereo headphones offer a unique sense of spatial intimacy as they herald a sonic field that appears simultaneously external and internal. 'In-head' acoustic imaging is the term invoked by Stankievech to refer to the way that headphones are able to resituate the sonic field to the interior of one's head, effecting a shift in the paradigm not only of listening, but of consciousness: 'The imaginative powers of the mind's ability to imagine space coincide with a literal location of an interior space "in the head"' (2007 pg 56). Headphones permit whole new imaginary sonic worlds to be transposed into this mental spatial realm, and if four technical criteria are fulfilled, then sound is experienced as an interior acoustical field.[4] While the apparatus of headphones facilitates this audio-perceptual conceit, the sense of sonic intimacy is augmented by the timbre of Janet's voice. The sensation of being cocooned in headphones is coupled with Janet's confiding expressions and coaxing tones to make it seem as if Janet is speaking to the individual listener in a highly personalised form of address.

On a technical level, this interior acoustical field is achieved not just through the use of headphones, but the specific technique of binaural sound recording. By placing an omni-directional microphone in the position of each ear on a dummy head then moving that head through a physical environment while recording, the resulting playback offers an effect of sound as if heard by a person traversing that very environment. As well as imitating the perspective of naturally binaural human hearing, the key feature of binaural recording is of sound with its spatial unfolding preserved, producing a powerfully realistic sonic presence. The ambient sounds in the Walks appear to be occurring in real space because they are physically localised in the very spots that the listener-participant traverses (through a door, under an alcove, against a brick wall): the sound waves reach our ears spatialised as if we ourselves are hearing them in situ. As Hanssen notes, the listener thus experiences sound as real yet constructed, in a kind of perceptual ambiguity that makes the recording technique a sonic equivalent of *trompe l'oeil* (2010 pg 42). The recorded sounds have no discernible physical source, yet have potent sonic presence, collapsing the notion of evidentiary sound.

A concomitant effect is a sharpened sense of embodied perception. As the varied sonic textures and sound fragments appear – birdsong, footsteps, traffic and the sonorous timbre of Cardiff's own voice – the surrounding world in all its sensorial richness appears curiously magnified. As Schaub (2005 pg 132) remarks:

> Suddenly, familiar sounds from ordinary experiences, such as geese passing overhead, sirens in the streets, or other nearby voices have the potential of achieving heretofore unfathomable intensity. Her spoken references give the participant a curious sense of synaesthetic immediacy. You can smell what she is describing and you can taste the salt from the sea in the air.

Hanssen argues that this intensification of sensory awareness is a direct result of the binaural recording technique, which 'makes the auditory experience more physical, as something felt and remembered *with* the body, instead of as something detached' (2010 pg 43). Fisher goes further, claiming that the recorded sounds appear as if internally located within the listening subject, almost part of one's interoceptive bodily processes (Fisher 1999, quoted in Hanssen 2010 pg 42).

Yet this heightened sense of corporeal consciousness is also produced through the very element of perambulation. As Witmore notes, the necessity to maintain a walking pace with the artist, coupled with Janet's intimate confessions, enhances the participant's bodily senses (2005 pg 61). This corresponds to Massumi's assertion that an intrinsic connection exists between movement and sensation (2002). The participatory element of shared locomotion is reinforced by Janet's frequent injunctions to closely follow her footsteps. Alongside the binaural recording technique and the cocooning experience of wearing headphones, this mode of companionate walking becomes the catalyst for environmentally attuned sensory and bodily awareness.

Cardiff is explicit about her objective to stimulate sensorial awareness through sonic textures. 'How do we discern "reality," if not from our senses?' she asks. 'The sound of footsteps behind us excites an innate urge to see what made the sound. So, by manipulating basic aural indicators, then the participants begin to question their understanding of the physical world' (Schaub 2005 pg 134). Cardiff elevates this dimension of intensified embodiment through the character Janet's acute sense of her own sensorial awareness. In *Wanås Walk* (1998), Janet narrates: 'Dead leaves under my feet. Nettles against my bare legs. My shoes are wet through to my toes. The wind is on my face … the leaves are moving in the breeze' (Schaub 2005 pg 236). In *MoMA Walk* (1999), the character coquettishly observes, 'What do I collect? Pieces of conversations, the sunlight on my kitchen table, the feel of his fingers touching my hair, the smell of my dog's fur' (Cardiff and Miller 1999). In *Her Long Black Hair* (2004), Janet invites the listener-participant to engage in sensual acts:

> I want you to do another experiment. Put your finger in your mouth, now put the wet saliva on your cheek. It feels cold, bothersome, like a separate part of your face. See how long you can stand it there.
>
> *Schaub (2005 pg 102)*

Yet the intensification of sensorial experience is a result not merely of the components outlined above, but a paradoxical effect of the deliberate reciprocity between real and virtual sonic elements. The Walks' heightened sensoriality is achieved through the interplay between a virtual sonic presence (principally the softly spoken words of the persona Janet) and the listener-participant's physical situatedness in a surrounding environment. Together, these combine as imbricated elements to produce the modality of sonic presence and virtual embodiment. Bures Miller has acknowledged the way in which the Walks sensitise listener-participants to their immediate environment through the technology of headphones and a media player; a point furthered by Stankievech and Hanssen.[5] However, it is not just audio technology that produces this effect, but a philosophically specific notion of the virtual. Although the term 'virtual' is often used in reference to the immateriality of computer networks and digital media as well as virtual reality, this is a limited field of its meaning. The etymology of the term in fact derives from the Medieval Latin *virtualis*, from *virtus*, meaning power or strength. In philosophical terms, the virtual indicates the capacity for potential form or existence, opposed to the actual or materially real. Hence, the virtual can be defined as potential existence.

Lévy speaks of the virtual as a 'knot of tendencies or forces' that accompany a situation or event (1998 pg 24). The term 'knot' suggests an entanglement of diverse strands, not all of which may be actualised in an event. A particular environmental or external circumstance might activate an element of the virtual, but as the virtual entails the metaphysical existence of a cluster of possibilities – in relation to the world's fundamental contingency – the transition into manifest form cannot be gauged in advance. In other words, an irreducible aspect of undetermined existence remains nestled within the realm of the virtual. For Lévy, an important characteristic of virtualisation is the way it '[undoes] the here and now' and 'open[s] the way to new spaces, other velocities' (1998 pg 93). This understanding of virtualisation foregrounds its radical heterogeneity. The virtual is not simply the development of nascent forms or the manifestation of latent qualities. Rather, as the virtual materialises, it mobilises alterity and difference. The process of virtualisation entails a transformation of identity: as the virtual shifts into actual form, it dovetails with the material world in a deterritorialising and hybridising manner.

Diodato similarly views the virtual as formed of heterogeneous tendencies in multi-dimensional movements towards actualisation. Although he is keen to retain the virtual's link to the digital, understanding it as a form of interactivity with the digital image, Diodato emphasises its transformative dimension. The virtual's quintessential attribute is its mode of interactivity. Virtuality may take the form of an immersive environment, as Grau would argue, but its essential condition is a special kind of interactivity that only virtuality can provide.[6] This is an interactivity that precipitates unforeseen dimensions of the real, allowing the body to be 'phenomenalized through interaction' (Diodato 2012 pg 6). More specifically, it is an interactivity comprised of a relation between the virtual body and the non-virtual body.

The particular format of Cardiff and Bures Miller' Walks – a solo walker fitted with headphones listening to a sonic composition, tracing a path coaxed by Janet's vocal promptings – is one premised on a kind of interactivity that is best described as virtual, whereby the participant's body is 'phenomenalized through interaction'. While the Walks' compositions are pre-recorded and scripted in advance, as they are listened to by the participant their sonic layers subtend the sensory elements of the physical environment in all its immediate, ephemeral and complex contingency. Degrees of familiarity or unfamiliarity with the locale, historical awareness of place, seasonal atmosphere, and the unique material and social circumstances, ages, genders and ethnicities of diverse bodies in motion constitute layers of situated

FIGURE 16.1 *The City of Forking Paths*

perception that mean that the kind of interactivity the Walks instigate cannot be strictly confined to the scripts' parameters. As they interweave non-synchronous layers of the actual and the potential, the Walks' mosaic of voice and sonic textures precipitates states of virtualisation: 'becoming-events' inaugurated through the listener-participant's locomotive, sensorial and cognitive interactivity.

In *The City of Forking Paths* (2014), a work commissioned for the *19th Sydney Biennale*, this interactivity triggered a dimension of vigilant alertness, as the Walk is nocturnal. Designed to commence at dusk in the foyer of Customs House, it wends its way through Circular Quay up through the back streets of The Rocks, down narrow laneways and semi-private terraces. The soundtrack is interspersed with ambient sounds, interpolated with historical narrative fragments, while Janet's coaxing voice ushers the listener-participant onwards. While standing next to the railing over the water's edge at Circular Quay, she tells us that when the Second Fleet sailed in, the corpses of those who did not last the journey were tossed into the water at this very spot, 'naked corpses resting on the rocks' (Cardiff and Miller 2014).[7] More than once, we hear Janet accosted by male strangers attempting to engage her in conversation, some with threatening intent.

The menacing tone of the Walk is reinforced by the fact it takes place at night. As a solitary female walker wandering through the vacant and dimly backstreets of the Rocks while listening to *The City of Forking Paths*, I shared in Janet's anxiety and wariness. 'I wish I could walk without fear in this darkness,' she confesses (Cardiff and Miller 2014). The spoken narrative's conjuring of fear phenomenalised my own primal instincts, producing a knot of intersecting forces, a reciprocity between interior and exterior states. The Walk adumbrated a handful of baleful characters whose immaterial presence was belied by their vocal proximity, jeering voices advancing and encircling, virtualising a psychological state of potential threat. Janet's wary tones activated latent cultural misgivings of women's vulnerability to nocturnal violent assault, precipitating a visceral state of unease. Although akin to other Walks in its noirish elements, *The City of Forking Paths*' crystalline sonic textures – rain falling or the tapping of iron railings – triggered a heightened sensory awareness whereby such sounds could be read as signals of danger, the suggestion of threat oscillating between virtual and actual realms.

More than any real-time interpersonal interaction, this particular modality of sonic presence and virtual embodiment complexifies one's sense of embodiment, splitting it from the realm of immediate presence to form another register of perceptual experience. When we listen to the Walks' heterogeneous elements – of atmospheric sounds, relayed historical events, narrative fragments and Janet's private musings – these intersect with the listener-participant's own aggregate of sensations, emotions, knowledge and memory. The Walks give rise to a hybridised state of being, an oscillation back and forth between dimensions of the immaterial and the real, the actual and the potential that exemplifies another crucial condition of the virtual: its doubled nature. The virtual situates the subject in a zone that is neither fully installed in the physical present nor circumscribed in immaterial space. The virtual inaugurates a dimension of hybridisation that escapes the conventional dichotomies of interiority and exteriority attributed to bodies considered real, encouraging the subject to toggle between different dimensions whose overlappings never fully cohere.

This doubled environment is a specific effect of the Walks, like *The City of Forking Paths*, that feature video of the surrounding locale (on a device such as an iPhone) alongside the audio composition heard through the headphones. While walking, the listener-participant is compelled to continually adjust the height and orientation of the iPhone to as closely as possible 'match' the screen-image, as a digital-virtual analogue of the real. Yet this is a doubled environment whose dual layers never resolve. Instead, the listener-participant is caught in a disjunctive overlap between the digital image and the real-world locale, the screen image both accurately and imperfectly mirroring the locale in which the Walk is set. The video Walks' critical dimension is this layered off-register experience as an aporetic space between the actual and the virtual.

We never see Cardiff herself onscreen, and this is significant, as it augments the authority of her voice and the illusion of aural fidelity that suggests we are situated in intimate proximity to her subject position. The lack of Janet's visual image simultaneous with her sonic presence defines her as an *acousmêtre*, or acousmatic voice. As extensively theorised by Chion, the *acousmêtre* is a sound heard without a visible source, the term having been coined by the experimental composer Schaeffer. Unlike Schaeffer, who restricted his study of the acousmatic voice to the sound technologies of radio, phonography and telephony, Chion believed the appearance of the *acousmêtre* in cinema inaugurated a mode of 'visualised listening'. The acousmatic voice was not simply disembodied sound, but a particular nexus of vision to sound. In this regime, certain things may be given visual form, but not the voice that speaks, the effect of which is to intensify the authority of that voice.

The *acousmêtre* is a sonic phenomenon that exemplifies virtuality. When Chion writes 'Neither inside nor outside: such is the *acousmêtre*'s fate in the cinema' (1999 pg 23), he identifies a fundamental characteristic of the virtual – its fluctuation between interiority and exteriority, presence and absence. Chion memorably refers to the *acousmêtre* as having 'one foot in the image' (1999 pg 24), but this can be reconfigured to contend that the *acousmêtre* has *one foot in the virtual*. Chion's discussion of the acousmatic voice focuses on its force, its panopticism, omniscience and omnipotence. Conversely, I suggest, the very liminality of the acousmatic voice, its perpetually unresolved relation of the absence to presence, links it to the processes of virtualisation. When a voice is separated from a tangible body that remains unseen, this unsettling matrix of *there and not there* forms the kernel of *virtualis* in its sense of potential existence.

A fundamental shortcoming of most theorisations of the virtual is their ocular bias. Diodato, for example, argues that the virtual body is an interactive *image-body*, and that the operation of virtualisation is discerned sensibly but only through 'an eminently corporeal gaze' (2012 pg 7). The concept of the image is in fact so central to his understanding of the virtual that Diodato claims that 'we can consider "image" as the *proper name* of the virtual body', betraying a deep-rooted ocularcentrism. Conversely, Cardiff and Bures Miller's audio and video Walks reveal how potent a virtual-*sound*-body can be. The visual absence of Janet in tandem with the crystal clear proximity of her voice draws on the *acousmêtre* to produce a unique modality of sonic presence and virtual embodiment that structures the operation of the Walks.

This is a virtual movement anchored in the corporeal. The Walks' sonic objects – particularly Janet's voice – without their visual counterparts incite a process of virtual embodiment by the listener-participant that involves a kind of fusing or hybridising with the Walks' panoply of sonic elements. These are formed through a combination of pre-recorded sounds of the composition alongside the actual sounds experienced by the listener-participant in the contingency of real time, as an imbrication of virtual and actual elements. The interlaced combination of sonic presence with, we might say, *missing parts*, opens up a space of virtuality that is neither absent nor fully present, composed of sonic stimuli which penetrate us yet are neither completely internal nor external, but exist in a space, borrowing from Chion, 'that has no name' (1999 pg 24). As the Walks' sonic textures are spatialised through binaural recording and amplified through 'in-head' acoustic imaging, transforming their virtual or non-tangible existence into *sonic presence*, so too is our experience of embodiment *virtualised* in the process as our bodies and sensorial perception are assimilated into the virtual field.

The virtual field functions to both intensify and perforate the real, correspondent to Diodato's designation of the virtual as 'a kind of unmarking, or a "not" of presence' (2012 pg 95). The virtual cuts a hole in the real, effecting a transformation in our subjectivity and corporeality: we are delocalised and relocalised, re-created and dispersed. In this regime of virtualised embodiment, evidentiary sound dissolves. We hear an approaching brass sextet whose physical proximity is utterly convincing, or an absent cellist whose strings are heard with full resonance in front of the very spot where we now stand, yet these binaurally recorded sounds intermingle with our immediately present sensorial field, producing a complex amalgam of virtual and actual sonic phenomena. We are caught between dimensions. No longer contained within the circumscription of immediate physical presence, the phenomenally real is interpolated with the virtual presence of the other – the other who is both there and not there, or more precisely, who was once there and is no longer there.

Another element that subtends the consciousness of the listener-participant is the experience of temporality. This is not simply owing to the fact that the Walks take place through time, but through the interpolation of different temporal dimensions: the present tense of the listener-participants as they perambulate, overlaid with Janet's 'present' as she maps out the path spoken in the present tense; Janet's address to the listener's future present tense, experienced as an awareness of Janet's experiential past; the past ambient and musical sounds captured by the binaural recording technique; and the pastness of historical events linked to architectural or geographic sites narrated by Janet, witnessed by the listener-participants in their own presents. This configuration of temporal planes is rent with fissures,

Cardiff and Bures Miller's walks

constructed through a conscious moving in and out of multiple folds of the virtual and the actual, compelling one to toggle between these intersecting strata.

This sense of being caught between timescales is accentuated through the act of perambulation, whereby the experience of the body unfolds in motion. A moving body, according to Massumi, does not fixedly coincide with itself so much as with its capacity for transition. A body in motion precipitates 'an immediate, unfolding relation to its own nonpresent potential to vary' (Massumi 2002 pg 4). 'Nonpresent' implies the body's ability to slip in and out of temporal registers, to be drawn into the past as well as to be open to the indeterminacy of potential, future existence. When Massumi asserts 'The body, sensor of change, is a transducer of the virtual' (2002 pg 135), he underscores a foundational virtuality to corporeal life. This points to the experience of embodiment as conditioned by both presence and non-presence, formed through an interaction of virtual and actual dimensions.

The matrix of temporal layers in the *Alter Bahnhof Video Walk* (2012), produced by Cardiff and Bures Miller for *Documenta (13)*, prompts an especially ruminative interchange between past and present. Set in Kassel's former central railway station, the Walk traces a route through the station's various spaces, from the central depot to private rooms up hidden stairways, down corridors and onto track-side platforms. The Walk acquires an unexpected solemnity when, coaxed by Janet's voice, the listener-participant is led to the farthest platform and informed that during World War 2, on this very platform, the entire Jewish population of Kassel (numbering approximately 500 in 1942) were unwillingly herded onto trains bound for the concentration camps. In my experience of the *Alter Bahnhof Walk*, this episode of Holocaust atrocity lost a conventional sense of historical distance through the particular convergence of orally relayed account in tandem with the

FIGURE 16.2 *Alter Bahnhof Video Walk*

tactile physicality of the station platform itself. Walking down the platform, feeling its gravelly texture underfoot while stirred by the surrounding currents of air and quietude, prompted to dwell on the parallel yet horrifically different way a community was coerced along this very path 60 years prior, simultaneously opened and sutured the temporal chasm between lived present and historical memory. Unlike a standard audio guide offering a comprehensive history of place, this abrupt and fleeting step into history was an unexpected plunge from which we were drawn back seconds later into another temporal register: a fluctuating between past and present, gravitas and lightness.

This movement back and forth across temporal intervals implodes any linear notion of time and crystallises the relation of memory and perception. In his metaphysics of time, Bergson argues that despite their assumed independence, memory and perception are deeply intwined. In abstract terms, they may be conceived as separate, but lived experience melds them. 'There is no perception which is not full of memories,' Bergson asserts. Concomitantly, with the immediate data of our senses, 'we mingle a thousand details of our past experience' (Bergson 2007 pg 24). Virtuality is central to memory, because memory in its pure state exists in the realm of the virtual and can only be brought into conscious awareness when it finds a point of affinity with the body's present actions, perceptions or sensations. As memory-images are summoned from the virtual realm, they emerge and amalgamate with present perception through the process of actualisation.

The virtual memory or sensation is continually open to being actualised in the present, and conversely, the present experiences or sensations of the body will dissolve into the virtual realm. This means that processes of virtualisation and embodiment are inherently linked as relays between past and present, the immaterial and the actual. Intriguingly, Bergson uses the metaphor of a borrowed body to explain the reciprocity between perception and memory, virtuality and embodiment: 'Our perceptions are undoubtedly interlaced with memories, and inversely, a memory … only becomes actual by *borrowing the body* [italics mine] of some perception into which it slips' (2007 pg 72). This suggests that not only do perception and memory interpenetrate, but a body must be 'borrowed' for a memory to be actualised.

This notion of bodily recruitment represents a striking correspondence with Cardiff and Bures Miller's Walks, activated through interaction with the individual listener-participant's body. Bergson's conception of a memory that slips into present perception through the means of embodiment correlates to the structure of the Walks, whereby Janet's memories (and her conjuring of historical events) slip into the consciousness of the listener-participant corporeally, through the act of perambulation which follows in the footsteps of Janet's own former bodily motions. Cardiff's realisation in 1991 that she could retrace her forest walk with her *virtual body* – before even embarking on the ongoing project of the Walks – forecast the very process by which memory and perception occur, as transits between virtuality and embodiment, activated through the phenomena of sound.

FIGURE 16.3 *Night Walk for Edinburgh*

In the most recent Walk, *Night Walk for Edinburgh* (2019), Janet muses:

> There are moments when you go out of sync with yourself. When you feel that you don't know the person inside's body that you're walking with. But you have to keep coming back, retracing your steps ... then you can find yourself again.
>
> *Cardiff and Miller (2019)*

This narrative fragment echoes Massumi's postulate of a moving body's lack of self-coinciding, and acknowledges how the subtle alignments of embodiment and subjectivity can fall out of sync. Perhaps this is why in so many of the Walks, Janet enjoins the listener-participant to follow the sound of her footsteps so that 'we can stay together': to get close enough to borrow our body to launch her thoughts, memories and desires, as we in turn reciprocally borrow her virtual body to animate manifold experiential encounters. With vivid sonic textures and narrative detail, the Walks not only induce sharpened states of sensory awareness, but demonstrate how intricately interconnected virtual and actual phenomena are in the processes of embodiment and perception.

Through the listener-participant's physical present overlapping with a narrated, recorded past, Cardiff and Bures Miller's Walks prompt a doubled experiential register. The sharp sense of Janet's proximity via her acousmatic voice and the unerring clarity of ambient sounds achieved through the binaural recording technique produce a powerful sonic presence. Yet this is a presence underscored by a virtual realm that activates and intensifies sensory perception, inaugurating a specific modality of sonic presence and virtual embodiment. Ultimately, this is a modality in reciprocal exchange with its obverse, of *sonic virtuality and actual embodiment*. The Walks exemplify Diodato's concept of the virtual as a phenomenalising through interactivity that undoes the fixity of the 'here and now'. The Walks also correspond to Bergson's theory of perception as alloyed with memory and, correlatively, memory as stirred by immediate sense perception. As Bergson observes, the virtual can only be actualised by 'borrowing a body' – the body of perception into which it slips. In other words, the virtual is a movement premised on embodiment, just as embodiment, as Massumi reminds us, is premised on the virtual. The Walks catalyse a heightened sensory awareness, opening out to a multiplicity of experiential moments in a temporal frame more expansive than the present. As relays between the virtual and the actual, past and present, interiority and exteriority, memory and perception, the Walks remain open to continual re-inflection by each listener-participant, never reaching a point of closure, alive to the contingencies of each moment and its potential existence.

Notes

1 These include walks conceived as an artistic practice, such as French collective International Situationist Internationale's *dérive* as a psycho-geographic exploration; British land artists Richard Long and Hamish Fulton's walks through rural terrain in the 1960s, American artist Max Neuhaus's *Listen* walks, Belgian artist Francis Alys's urban endurance walks and Australian artist Sarah CrowEST's urban peregrinations. Secondly, through the feature of a headphone-connected audio device, Cardiff's walks subtend the paradigm of the technological sonic walk such as Christina Kubisch's *Electrical Walks* as well as more conventional museum audio guides and the art practices that satirise this, such as Andrea Fraser's *Museum Highlights*.
2 'I use different types of "Janet" voices to evoke different atmospheres. A flat, intense voice will suggest a more removed, filmic reading, while a conversational tone creates a sense of reality. A quiet thinking voice exists on a different spatial level, creating the ability to penetrate the listener's brain as if it were voicing their own thoughts' (Cardiff, quoted in Schaub 2005 pg 143).
3 Other responses include an anonymous entry in the San Francisco Museum of Modern Art comment book: 'I love your voice. I would follow you anywhere' (quoted in Schaub 2005 pg 22). When the San Francisco Museum of Modern Art curators were asked what was special about Janet Cardiff's voice, Madeleine Grynsztejn said: 'What do I think about her voice? It's absolutely integral, it's equivalent to Jackson Pollock's brushstroke, it's absolutely unique in that sense, and you recognize it as hers and hers alone. It's got this sort of Lauren Bacall resonance to it that's simply unforgettable and that gets under your skin …. It completely seduces you and absorbs you and compels you to go with her: I mean she hardly needs to say follow me, you would follow that voice almost anywhere' (quoted in Schaub 2005 pg 176).
4 The four technical criteria are: identical sound is simultaneously exposed to both ears at once; there is no temporal delay in the sound event; phasing of loudspeakers doesn't occur; sound enters directly entering the ear canal, with no filtering (Stankievech 2007).

5 George Bures Miller states: 'We're trying to connect right away to the remembered experiences that your body knows ....The walks ... make you hyper-aware of your environment around you. I thought it would take away from that because you put a headphone on and walk around with a Discman, but all of a sudden, your senses are alert. They say media kills your senses, but it is not true because it can actually enliven them' (quoted in Schaub 2005 pg 24).
6 The most straightforward definition of the virtual is by Oliver Grau, who defines the virtual primarily in terms of immersion: a virtual world has a tendency to enclose the observer and take them away from external visual impressions, providing them instead with an image-space that moves towards a state of totality – or immersion. The virtual inaugurates what he calls the 'vanishing interface' – a fusion of the user with the medium to the degree that the user loses awareness of the apparatus of the medium as he or she is transported to a fictional realm (Grau 2003).
7 Noted when I participated in the Walk on 24 October 2015.

Bibliography

Bergson, Henri (trans. N.M. Paul and W.S. Palmer). 2007. *Matter and Memory*. New York: Cosimo Classics.
Cardiff, Janet and Miller, George Bures. 1997. *Chiaroscuro*. Audio walk and telescope. 12 minutes. Janet Cardiff & George Bures Miller – Walks. https://cardiffmiller.com/walks/chiaroscuro/.
Cardiff, Janet and Miller, George Bures. 1998a. *Villa Medici Walk*. Audio walk. 16 minutes, 22 seconds. Janet Cardiff & George Bures Miller – Walks. https://cardiffmiller.com/walks/villa-medici-walk/.
Cardiff, Janet and Miller, George Bures. 1998b. *Wanås Walk*. Audio walk. 14 minutes. Janet Cardiff & George Bures Miller – Walks. https://cardiffmiller.com/walks/wanas-walk/.
Cardiff, Janet and Miller, George Bures. 1999. *MoMA Walk*. Audio walk. 12 minutes, 50 seconds. Janet Cardiff & George Bures Miller – Walks. https://cardiffmiller.com/walks/moma-walk/.
Cardiff, Janet and Miller, George Bures. 2012. *Alter Bahnhof Video Walk*. Video walk. 26 minutes. Janet Cardiff & George Bures Miller – Walks. https://cardiffmiller.com/walks/alter-bahnhof-video-walk/.
Cardiff, Janet and Miller, George Bures. 2014. *The City of Forking Paths*. Video walk. 64 minutes. Janet Cardiff & George Bures Miller – Walks. https://cardiffmiller.com/walks/the-city-of-forking-paths/.
Cardiff, Janet and Miller, George Bures. 2019. *Night Walk for Edinburgh*. Video walk. 55 minutes. Janet Cardiff & George Bures Miller – Walks. https://cardiffmiller.com/walks/night-walk-for-edinburgh/.
Chion, Michel. 1999. *The Voice in Cinema*. New York: Columbia University Press.
Diodato, Roberto (trans. Justin L. Harmon). 2012. *Aesthetics of the Virtual*. New York: State University of New York Press.
Grau, Oliver. 2003. *Virtual Art: From Illusion to Immersion*. Cambridge, MA: MIT Press.
Hanssen, Tina Rigby. 2010. The Whispering Voice: Materiality, Aural Qualities and the Reconstruction of Memories in the Works of Janet Cardiff and George Bures Miller. *Music, Sound, and the Moving Image* Vol. 4 No. 1: 39–54.
Lévy, Pierre (trans. Robert Bononno). 1998. *Becoming Virtual: Reality in the Digital Age*. New York: Plenum Trade.
Massumi, Brian. 2002. *Parables for the Virtual: Movement, Affect, Sensation*. Durham, NC: Duke University Press.

Schaub, Mirjam. 2005. *Janet Cardiff: The Walk Book*. Vienna, Austria: Thyssen-Bornemisza Art Contemporary in collaboration with the Public Art Fund.

Stankievech, Charles. 2007. From Stethoscopes to Headphones: An Acoustic Spatialization of Subjectivity. *Leonardo Music Journal* Vol. 17: 55–59.

Witmore, Christopher L. 2005. Four Archaeological Engagements with Place Mediating Bodily Experience through Peripatetic Video. *Visual Anthropology Review* Vol. 20 No. 2: 57–72.

17
BREATHING (AS LISTENING)
An emotional bridge for telepresence

Ximena Alarcón-Díaz

In search of an interface

I am a migrant woman and a listening sound artist working with networking technologies. I have lived for more than 20 years outside Colombia, my native country, in Catalunya, the United Kingdom, and Norway. For me, migration is not a theme nor a label, but an embodied condition emerging from the experience of moving between geographies and cultures. Female migrancy seems to be a way of transitioning between status and identities, "on an uncertain journey towards new roles and understandings" (Brooks and Simpson, 2013). Since 2011, I have been listening to the *in-between sonic space* of the human migratory experience. Inspired by Pauline Oliveros' Deep Listening® practice (Oliveros, 2005), I have developed a practice of improvisatory telematic[1] sonic performances, with other migrants, to access this in-betweenness, which is foremost an embodied experience. Using synchronous surround sounds, spoken word, voice, memories, and dreams, I have developed a number of works which weave fragments of individual and collective migrations (Alarcón, 2017).

In this context, I have been looking for *interfaces* that help me to listen together to the pieces from stories belonging to distant times and locations, to relations *in-between* native and host lands, to understand these as a whole, thus expanding my *sense of place* where I reside, my *sense of presence* in the distance, and my sense of *agency* to move with free will across such in-betweenness. Gallagher (2005) explains our embodied sense of agency as purposive actions, "which are best described in terms of intentions, rather than neurons, muscles, reachings, etc." (Gallagher, 2005, p.240). In human–computer interaction (HCI), a *sense of agency* can be understood as "the experience of controlling both one's body and the external environment" (Limerick, Coyle and Moore, 2014), and it constitutes an important measure for interface design: an embodied interface can increase the sense of human agency.

Thus, one of my challenges is to explore interfaces that respond to our voluntary and involuntary actions, unveiling intentions through sensing, feeling, memory, and metaphor, listening for place and presence in our human migrations while exercising free will.

Within my latest project INTIMAL: Interfaces for Relational Listening, I have explicitly placed embodiment at the centre of the improvisatory experience. I have questioned the role of the body as an interface that keeps the memory of place, interrelating body, memory, migration, and telematics. I have proposed *relational listening* as one approach to the design and experience of technologically mediated embodied interfaces. These can help migrants, the general public, researchers, and artists to explore at once the *sense of place* and *sense of presence*, key human preoccupations in the context of geographical migration (Alarcón, 2019).

INTIMAL

INTIMAL is an "embodied" physical-virtual system for relational listening in the context of human migration, to be used in telematic sonic performance. The INTIMAL system combines interactive audio and transmission software as well as sensor-based technology to create interrelations between body movement, oral archives, voice, and spoken language within an improvised performance situation. The system was developed in a Marie Skłodowska Curie-funded postdoctoral research project at the RITMO Centre in the University of Oslo, and was informed by the listening experiences of nine Colombian and Latin American migrant women whose field test performance, on May 7, 2019, connected them across the sites of Oslo, Barcelona, and London. They listened to their own migrations and to an oral archive of testimonies of Colombian women which have been collected by the organisation Diaspora Women and annotated in the INTIMAL research (Alarcón et al, 2019b). The improvised performance was the last step of a research process combining the practice of Deep Listening® with methods of Embodied Music Cognition and human–computer interaction.

Deep Listening practice helped women to access their migratory experiences sensorially by listening, sounding, and improvising freely, expanding their awareness of sound across time and space. Embodied Music Cognition helped me to record, see and analyse their body movements, and HCI methods supported the implementation of technologically mediated interfaces, such as sensors and tracking devices, that transmit the collected data in order to create meaningful sonic interactions across distant locations, including the use of oral archives.

Thus, INTIMAL is *physical* – that is, it is experienced in the physical body and by connecting with the surroundings. It can be experienced using wearable technologies such as mobile phones and breathing sensors. Through Deep Listening, INTIMAL embraces unconscious dreams and *virtuality* as metaphors of migration. INTIMAL is *virtual*, as in detachment, uncontrollable, dream-like, volatile, and facilitated, and amplified with the mediation of streaming data, audio, and connection technologies. Using technologies of transmission, my approach is in tune with Suzanne Kozel's understanding of the virtual as based on "a reconfiguration of physical dimensionality and an experience of sensory saturation occurring between people and computer technologies" (Kozel, 2007:79); the virtual, Kozel suggests, is a space "of radical potential, with scope for existential, artistic, and political transformation" (ibid., 82). In what follows, I will describe the process that led to the conceptual, artistic, and technical implementation of the INTIMAL system.

Listening deeply to Colombian women's migration

Deep Listening practice and philosophy, developed by the composer Pauline Oliveros (2005), invites us to expand our perception of the continuum of sound as it travels in time and space. This perception expands as we engage in a 24-hour-a-day listening practice, including listening in dreams (IONE, 2005) and listening deeply to our bodies, involving vibrations which are activated by body movement (Gold, 2008). I invited nine Colombian migrant women living in London, Barcelona, and Oslo to explore their sonic memories of their migrations, and also to listen to their unconscious dreams (IONE, 2012), through Deep Listening. Using Google Hangouts as a telematic platform, they amplified and shared such memories through sonic improvisation with free body movement and voice (Figure 17.1). At a later point, they attended an intensive Deep Listening session where they explored individual and collective inner geographies with different sonic meditations such as *TAPPING into your inner PLANT* by Sharon Stewart, improvising with voice

FIGURE 17.1 *Listening in Dreams*, via Google Hangouts
Source: Drawing by Silvia Esperanza Villalba Martínez.

FIGURE 17.2 *Listening to the Land*, Gran, Norway
Source: Photo by Sharon Stewart.

and body movement. They also examined their relationships with the land, using *Environmental Dialogue* by Pauline Oliveros (2005), and listened deeply to their bodies practicing *Early Morning Walks* and *Embodying the Five Directions* (Gold, 2008) (Figure 17.2).

Bringing a collective memory of migration, and specifically migration from Colombia, they explored improvisation scores I composed, such as *Chiddiomatikflui* and *Histomemoriology*.[2] With *Chiddiomatikflui*, I invited them to move their body according to the repetitive voicing of words in different languages that were close to their heart; my intention was to explore what Julie Choi (2007) calls "multivocalities", where the learning of a language is inseparable from the constant search for a voice. With *Histomemoriology*, I invited them to respond with spoken word and voice to words that they shared with the group from their dreams. I played on words to create the name *Histomemoriology*, coming from *histo* (from body tissue, or web, interconnectivity), and also from "history"; I added the word "memoriology", implying a science dedicated to exercising collective memory. This is different from, although related to, the definition of memoriology in social science, which entails a form of collecting history derived from oral accounts, and the value of speech, which defies the written form (Weyner, 2020). My intention with the score was to use sonic improvisation as an exercise of collective remembering, which can acquire acoustic and textual forms (Wertsch, 2002).

The intensive Deep Listening session equipped the nine women with a repertoire that would allow them to build trust and a space to navigate individually, and with others, through a *migratory journey*. I proposed this journey as structured in a listening and sounding score including *four spheres of migratory memory*: body stories,

FIGURE 17.3 Score for *A Migratory Journey* by Ximena Alarcón

social body, native place, and new lands, including soil, nature, and other living beings (Figure 17.3).

The *migratory journey* acted as an orientation and spatial metaphor (Lakoff and Johnson, 2003), which some of the women followed spatially, while others incorporated the spheres of migratory memory alongside and with their body movements. They improvised with their memories, finding directions by walking, rotating, and pausing.[3] The spheres were derived from my listening to and annotation of the testimonies of the Diaspora Women's oral archive (Figure 17.4). Within the oral archive, the spheres constituted an ontology of migratory memory, which provided me with a number of excerpts from the testimonies to be played back to the women in an exercise of collective memory.

Understanding body movement in a migratory journey

I used methods of Embodied Music Cognition to record women's *migratory journeys* in a Motion Capture lab. These methods involved using a number of different technologies to record movement of the body, as well as biodata, "to reveal motion features that contrast with the original audio, or to reveal motion features that are not easily visible to the naked eye" (Jensenius and Godøy, 2013). I used infrared

FIGURE 17.4 The four spheres of migratory memory, an Ontology by Ximena Alarcón

markers on face and body, electromyograms, and breathing sensors, and recorded two *experiments*: the first, improvising on their *migratory journeys*, and second, their listening to the oral archives via earbuds. Both experiments offered different elements to envision the INTIMAL system, the interfaces, and possible interactions. In the Motion Capture lab, *capture* technologies brought limitations as well as expansions as they "framed" the embodied experience (Figure 17.5), revealing traditions of seeing the "body as an object" (Reeve, 2011). These technologies have a history of medical and surveillance uses, therefore control is embedded in their in-built narrative, becoming problematic for envisioning forms of interaction that respond to the migratory condition and art development. To divert that path of seeing the body "as the locus of the experience ... assuming a separation between body and mind" (Hunter, 2013), I needed a holistic approach to envision these technologies as performance-tools. *Migratory Journeys*[4] recorded in the lab (Figure 17.6) contrasted with the *raw* Deep Listening experience the women had in a more natural setting when they first improvised sharing their stories in the intensive Deep Listening session. In the lab, some women reported feeling strange and constrained to move, or in contrast, some of them reported feeling freer and in control. In her soma design manifesto, and for the design of embodied technologically mediated interfaces, Kristina Höök (2018) argues for a design engagement that "starts from the human condition, in which mind-body-emotion-sociality are seen as a unity, inseparably communicating and influencing one another" (ibid., 197). In

Breathing (as listening) 249

FIGURE 17.5 The experiments' suits and markers, screenshot from a video capture of Qualisys software

FIGURE 17.6 *Experiment 1 Migratory Journeys*, video screenshot
Source: https://vimeo.com/304188356.

my methodology, while Deep Listening and improvisatory practice were bringing forth sensations, feelings, and conscious and unconscious expressions of the migratory experience, methods of Embodied Music Cognition helped me to "see" body movement from a systematic perspective with the biodata collected. Also, these helped me to anticipate what might or might not work for the implementation of interactive technologies in the INTIMAL system.

Design and implementation of the INTIMAL "embodied" physical-virtual system for relational listening

In women's *migratory journeys*, amongst many body movements, walking, running, and rotation allowed a mobility that can be tracked in relation to directionality and the steps' dynamics (Alarcón et al, 2019c), and created space between them. Thus, I integrated into the system the practical and emotional activity of searching for location and place, for a *sense of place*, in the context of human migration.

Breathing emerged as a set of key data points that highlighted moments of togetherness between three people listening and improvising. Breathing additionally underscored a rhythmical movement that accounts for someone's *presence* without forcing performativity (Figure 17.7). This finding led me to imagine the artistic and technical implementation of RESPIRO in order to feel *presence* across distant locations.

Thus, in the INTIMAL system I proposed to develop interaction by focusing on the movements of walking to *sense place*, as if looking for directions,[5] and breathing to *feel* others' *presence* across distant locations via telematics.

The system involved the prototyping and artistic-technical implementation of three software modules, MEMENTO, RESPIRO, and TRANSMISSION (Figure 17.8),[6] and these were tested in *INTIMAL: A Long-Distance Improvisation*, a performance which took place on May 7, 2019 between the cities of Oslo, Barcelona, and London (Figure 17.9).

The MEMENTO software was designed to semantically and thematically interrelate fragments of the oral archive.[7] To listen to these fragments, MEMENTO used a mobile phone as a sensor to track listeners' body movement in space, specifically walking and rotation (Figure 17.10). Each step triggered a new fragment from the archive, using proximity of semantic relations between the stories, as the listener advanced and rotated. These movements acted as a metaphor for locating directions in space and searching for one's place.

In this logic, a sense of agency is embedded in the intention given by the steps – for instance quality and tempo – one takes, and the listening attention to breathing. The triggering of voices from the oral archive with the testimonies of Diaspora Women's conflict and migration was activated by the walking, and the responses weaved expressions from collective improvisation between the physical, the virtual, the emotions, and the memory of people's own migratory *journeys*. These resembled a *histomemoriology* (discussed earlier) which interrelated oral stories and helped the listener to have an individual and collective reflection of deep conflicts of individual and collective memory. These memories might be kept as *embodiments*, understood as body movement, as in sensation and emotion, as incorporation of non-verbal and verbal expression.

Breathing (as listening) **251**

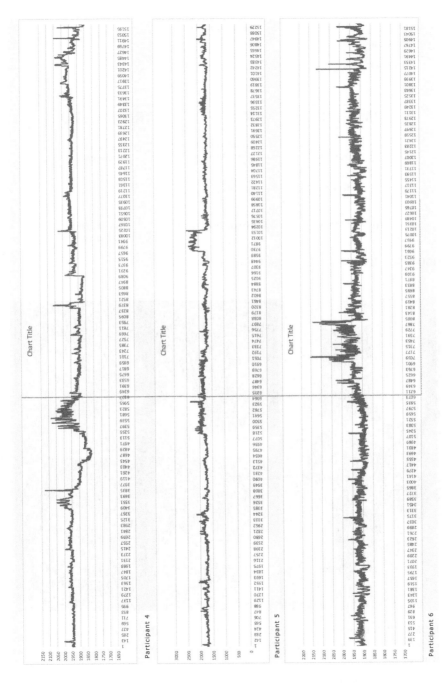

FIGURE 17.7 Breathing data from improvisers while performing *Migratory Journeys*, screenshot from plot

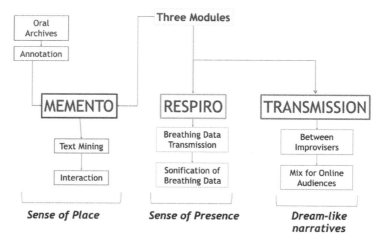

FIGURE 17.8 INTIMAL System for Relational Listening

FIGURE 17.9 Improvisers using INTIMAL in locations in the three cities: Iklektic (London), Melahuset (Oslo), and Phonos Foundation, University Pompeu Fabra (Barcelona)

Source: Screenshot composition by Ximena Alarcón.

Breathing (as listening) 253

Mobile Phone in MEMENTO

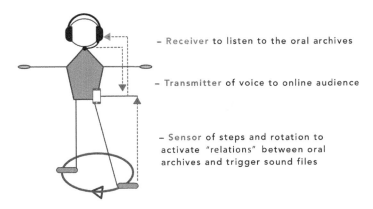

FIGURE 17.10 Use of the mobile phone as a sensor in MEMENTO

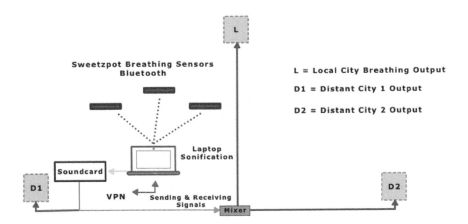

FIGURE 17.11 Signal flow of RESPIRO: collecting, transmitting, sonifying, and amplifying breathing data

Source: Screenshot from *INTIMAL Documentary 2021*: https://vimeo.com/512586450.

RESPIRO was implemented as a transmission and sonification[8] solution for the breathing data of improvisers, transmitted through FLOW™ breathing sensors.[9] This breathing data allowed the improvisers to listen to their individual and collective breathing, and to feel a sense of co-presence within a co-located space in each of the three cities, and a sense of telepresence across distant locations.

With RESPIRO, improvisers could hear a mix of their sonified breathing through one loudspeaker in their local city while simultaneously hearing the sonified breathing of the other six improvisers located in the other two cities (Figure 17.11) through the other two loudspeakers (Figure 17.12). These abstract

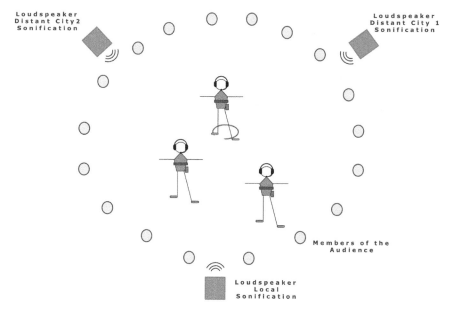

FIGURE 17.12 Listening setting: loudspeakers used to listen to the sonification of breathing data via RESPIRO

sounds had characteristics resembling the inner breathing sound (Oslo), the sound of wind (Barcelona), and the sound of human mobility in a dynamic city (London).

TRANSMISSION was the set of technologies that was used to mix the sounds from RESPIRO with the vocal responses of the improvisers in the three venues using the Discord app, and to transmit it for the online audiences. The audiences could hear a fragmented sound signal alongside scattered yet interconnected memories (Figure 17.13).[10]

The combination of these three software modules invited the improvisers to explore and listen to their *sense of place* and *sense of presence* in a relational way, opening paths for new understandings of their migration experiences (Alarcón et al., 2019a). With INTIMAL, the body became an interface for the materialised sonic experience through headphones (to listen to the oral archives) and loudspeakers (to listen to the sonification of breathing data from the local city and from the distant cities). The vibrations of a shared experience were felt through the physicality of the sonic medium, with an emphasis on sonification of breathing data, in between co-located and distant communications.

Breathing in the INTIMAL performance: an emotional bridge for telepresence

During the 30 minutes of performance pre-determined by a time score (Figure 17.14), narrative traces emerged with the complexity of connections and disconnections.

Breathing (as listening) **255**

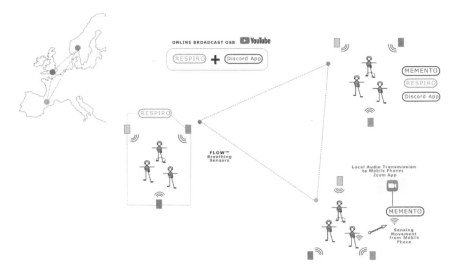

FIGURE 17.13 Signal flow in TRANSMISSION

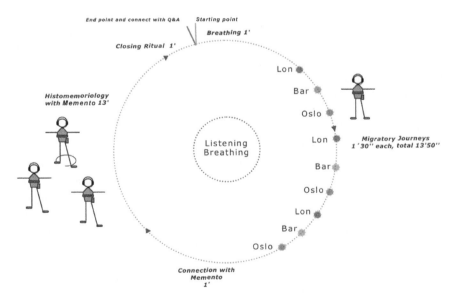

FIGURE 17.14 Time score of *INTIMAL: A Long-Distance Improvisation*

Relationality emerged as a complex embodied narrative (Grishakova and Poulaki, 2019) of a "migratory journey", engaging the embodied mind, complex scripts of communication, and reuse of narratives in social and technological environments, with the most varied approaches to body movement and voice, ranging from stillness and silence to dance movement, singing, and screaming (Alarcon & Jensenius, 2019).

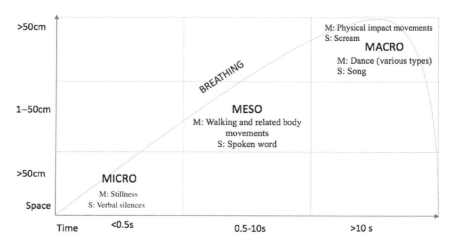

FIGURE 17.15 Analysis of INTIMAL and breathing as an emotional bridge using Jensenius' Taxonomy of Body Motion

Source: Alarcon and Jensenius (2019).

While MEMENTO served the functionality of navigation of an oral archive, it raised questions regarding control over the body (for instance, taking decisive steps to enable the software to work), the interaction with RESPIRO promoted a more fluid relationship with others who were co-located across distant locations. The sonification of breathing, and breathing itself, emerged as an emotional bridge *in between* improvisers, their distant locations, the oral archive, their body movements, words, voicings, and memories.

For instance, laughter in the INTIMAL improvisation was prominent amid histories of loss and death. At the end of the performance, the improvisers commented on why they laughed, and one improviser (LR) responded: "because laughter is contagious". As part of my methodology, in my post-performance interviews, I asked her, "Where did you hear laughter?", and she said, "I heard it from the others in the other cities, I heard it!" Technically, the acoustic laughter was not transmitted for the improvisers; the only transmission they received was the sonification of each other's breathing, which became active according to their soundings. In a recent conversation with the artist and scholar Kristine Diekman,[11] she suggested that this experience might be embraced by Julia Kristeva's concept of "semiotic *chora*",[12] including "crying, screaming, grunting, cicadas, whistling, chants, protests, bodies together in sound rhythm", as a contribution to "connect us to each other and the natural world of non-human animals and plants". Thus, I wonder how our most profound emotions could be transmitted in between distant locations without words, but by only breathing as *chora*. Next, I will be exploring moments of the INTIMAL performance that expand the understanding of sonified breathing in the distance as *chora*, which is naturally embedded in the improvisers' narratives.

Breathing as chora

Breathing, with its voluntary-involuntary vital character, is in the realm of our intention, in the sense of agency or free will, and at the same time unconsciously reveals our bodily functions and emotions. Dynamics of affect can be explained in the sense that we are breathing the same air, which is also distinct in between distant locations. Breathing, as Magdalena Górska (2018) proposes, is a relational force that "not only materializes, recognizes, and manifests social power relations but also forces social and environmental transformation" (ibid., p.253).

Kristeva (1984) explains *chora* as "a modality of signifiance [*sic*] in which the linguistic sign is not yet articulated as the absence of an object and as a distinction between real and symbolic." (p.26). To me, *chora* is inspiring for flexibly informing a synchronous option of sonic telematic connection and transmission, far from fixed signatures of meaning, gestures, and controlled data. If the *chora* "precedes and underlines figuration and thus specularization, and it is analogous only to vocal or kinetic rhythm" (Kristeva, 1984, p.26), it cannot be seen, but can be heard and transmitted. Furthermore, going deeper into embodiment, Kristeva suggests *chora* as a space, as the poet and scholar Kika Dorsey (2008) writes:

> this space before meaning, where the self has not yet learned to recognize his or herself, is associated with the maternal body. It is through the rhythm of the heart beating, the breath, that musicality in language creates new forms through its brush with emptiness. It is a primordial experience analogous to that of the newly born infant that has not developed its ego.

Breathing thus potentially bridges the relationality of discursive impositions and standing as deeply embodied, rhythmical, intimate, and primal.

In the performance's first minute, there is a breathing connection between the nine improvisers in the three cities. In the online transmission,[13] we can hear sonified breathing [in square brackets] and voices that come and go with different references to breathing, shown *in italics* (with English translations):

> [a little explosion] *chaa!*
> *Somos colombianos* (We are Colombians)
> *Respira para no morirnos. Respira para salvarnos* (Breathe so we don't die. Breathe so we save ourselves)

One can hear exhalations of air, coughing. The background sonifies a melody, it is more than abstraction. Breathing awareness involves emotions, communication, and relationality with all the other beings and their rhythms, weaving in the impact of our transformative listening.

In the INTIMAL system, breathing is not detached from walking and speech. I am interested in how interrelations between breathing, walking, and speech can provide an embodied experience of remembering and transforming our sense of place and presence through people's memory. The emotional dynamics in the improvisation are rooted in the collective memory of the women improvisers. This is informed by their experiences of loss and death, but also by the vitality of Colombia, which continues its life as one of the most biodiverse and exuberant natural places on the planet, a lung for the planet:.

> [at minute 7 there is a sound like an explosion]
> *Respira* (Breathe)
> *¿Cómo es que uno se prepara para la guerra?* (How is it that you get ready for war?)
> *la guerra es ridícula* (war is ridiculous)
> [at 9 minutes and 25 seconds there are sounds of sonified breathing]
> *Volver a nacer* (Being born again)
> *Que no se muera* (So it doesn't die)

Care for each other emerged in the realm of stories of divisions and contradictions. For an improviser in Oslo, the sounds of sonified breathing were remembered by one of the improvisers (LN) as a "blanket of colours" between the three cities. In London, improvisers came together to create a shape with their bodies that evoked a human lung; in their body voice improvisation, one of them expelled a piece of paper carrying words about identity and migration that she had been ripping up and chewing in her mouth. Meanwhile, the telematic connection sounded almost like Morse code:

> [chiflido (whistle) sounds ...]
> *¡Aquí!* (Here!)
> [sonification of breathing gets more lively in between the three cities]
> *Aquí toca cantar en Quechua* (Here we must sing in Quechua)
> *Mejor volemos, volemos para soñar o soñemos para volar* (Better we fly, let's fly to dream,
>   or let's dream to fly)
> *Porque las memorias duelen también si no se recuerdan* (Because memories also hurt if you don't remember them)
> *Hay que respirar* (We need to breathe)
> [minute 15]
> *Más rápido* (Faster)

The part of the score called *Histomemoriology* starts. The women interact with MEMENTO, which triggers the oral archives:

> *Hay unas mujeres hablando sobre Colombia y los alemanes que lo llevaron* (There are some women talking about Colombia and the Germans who took it)
> *Yo me acuerdo* (I remember)
> *Árboles y plantas* (Trees and plants)

Las plantas (Plants)
Usted aquí no tiene nada que hacer (Here you have nothing to do)
Yo no sabía qué hacer (I didn't know what to do)
Los mataron a todos (They killed everyone)
Te lo dije (I told you)
A todos (Everyone)
¿Qué hacemos, grito? (What do we do, scream?)
A todos, a todos, todos los mataron (They killed everyone, everyone)
Si quieres gritar yo te resueno (If you want to scream, I resonate with you)
Podemos reirnos (We can laugh)
[at 17 minutes and 48 seconds there is laughter coming from Oslo, and in London there is a response with more laughter, and after that there is a scream and the breathing sensors become highly active]
La planta medicinal (The medicinal plant)
Vamos a tener plantas (We will have plants)
Vamos a sanarnos (We will heal)

In the INTIMAL performance, by interrelating breathing and different walking speeds together with emerging improvisatory speech, this sonic emotional bridge potentially influenced the improvisers' distinct levels of individual and collective agency across the distant locations. In London, they engaged in a childhood ride, singing and dancing:

El puente está quebrado (The bridge is broken)
¿Con qué lo curaremos? (How are we going to repair it?)
Con cáscaras de huevo, burritos al potrero (With eggshells, donkeys to the prairie)
Que pase el tren, que ha de pasar (Let the train pass)
¡Lleva! (Caught!)
[at minute 30 there is a Closing Ritual, and another story of childhood is heard while the colour green contrasts with war]
No me maltrates (Don't treat me badly)
Verde que te quiero verde (Green, how I want you, green – from García Lorca's *Romance Sonámbulo* poem)

In these examples, if listening to breathing in relation to body movement brings such an awareness of collective memory, perhaps Kristeva's *chora* space might be understood in this work as an alternative materiality underlying togetherness across the distance, tapping into pre-verbal stages, touching deep memory of childhood states to achieve growth and transformation. *Chora* as underlying concept supports the *in-between sonic space* in the context of migration and displacement, nourishing sonification of breathing as an emotional bridge for telepresence.

Chora supports emerging narratives of rebirth and reinvention of ourselves in the context of migration, far from our native land, in the loss of family connections, and potentially in other contexts of geographical, social, and cultural dislocation.

Furthermore, it supports the listening to oral archives containing stories that might be painful to hear, including voices with emotions and rhythms that might not have sufficient air. Listening to the sonification of improvisers' serene or agitated breathing creates a compelling relationship with the listening to the voices of the oral archive. It creates space to listen to difficult stories, as their presence is not removed and it is highlighted as another as yet not signified *chora*.

Back to the interface, in 2020

Two years after the INTIMAL telematic performance experience, I reflected on accessible technology that conveys breathing as an emotional bridge for telepresence. This time, my questions and search for *sense of place* and *sense of presence* expanded from the migratory context to the one of the pandemic. I wanted to make this experience accessible and the interface hybrid: serving both walking and breathing without the need for breathing sensors.

As a resident in The Studio, and with the support of internships at Bath Spa University and The Studio Recovery Fund,[14] I created the INTIMAL App©, bringing together relations between different actions – breathing, emotions, walking, and speaking – in a set of rhythmic and kinetic relations that are technologically mediated. Derived from the experience with the INTIMAL system, the app invites people to navigate migratory journeys using South, East, North and West as coordinates, to trigger voices recorded from INTIMAL research participants in a set of relations: (1) walking steps and directions, (2) breathing sonified as *chora*, and (3) speech, the significance on top of which we walk and breathe, also the random utterances that emerge from mindful walking and breathing. Portability as well as listening amplification technologies, such as headphones, make a difference not only in the perception of the sound (being physically surrounded by it), but linked to intimacy and distance.

In my ideation for this newly created INTIMAL App©, which is subject to continuous technological and artistic exploration, I have drafted here a pseudo code to state its essence:

> If I walk, I breathe
> If I breathe
> You breathe
> If we listen to our breathing together, we experience joy
> And entrainment
>
> If I run
> You listen
> My steps are interdependent with my breathing
>
> If I speak I cannot hear my breathing
> If I hear my breathing

I might speak
With more pauses

If I hear speech
I might mimic their breathing, or their no breathing
If I walk I hear my breathing
If I walk and I hear my breathing
I sense place

If I listen to a speech of conflict
I might change my speed
If I walk and hear my breathing
The listening of the conflict might ease
As it might the conflict in the mysterious sonosphere[15]
across time.

I speak in between pauses of breathing
I make pauses between my speaking
of words

I might hear others (humans and non-humans)
I open space

I sense place

I breathe and listen at once
To my presence and to your presence
That supports our emotions
That surpass meaning

I cross a sonic bridge
In my imagination which is
Your synchronous reality

We are live
We have experienced telepresence.

Acknowledgements

The INTIMAL project received funding during 2017–2019 from the European Union's Horizon 2020 research and innovation program under the Marie Sklodowska-Curie grant agreement No. 752884, and was partially supported by the Research Council of Norway through its Centres of Excellence scheme, project number 262762. Since September 2019, I have been working independently to continue this research, and have become a resident at The Studio, Bath Spa University's Enterprise and Innovation Hub, which allows me to access co-working space and business advice. I have received start-up funding through The Studio Recovery Fund to develop and test the INTIMAL App©.

Notes

1 I use the term "telematic" to refer to a performance transmitting sound or sonic data bidirectionally and synchronously through the Internet and across distant locations.
2 To listen to and see excerpts of this process, watch the online INTIMAL documentary: https://vimeo.com/512586450 (accessed September 13, 2021).
3 The displacement of the body as well as the stories of mobility emerged in their walking and pauses, and in finding directions influenced by Heloise Gold's scores and IONE's invitation to explore one's agency in the dream world, in which we notice how active and passive one can be in the dreams.
4 See the video *INTIMAL Experiment 1 Migratory Journeys*: https://vimeo.com/304188356 (accessed September 13, 2021).
5 Although the walking and triggering of files was local, the same action was taking place in the distant locations. The transmission of the triggered fragments of the oral archive was via the Zoom app, using the mobile phone of each improviser and their earbuds for private (from audience's listening) and shared listening (between them).
6 The implementation of the INTIMAL system was a collective effort involving the research assistants Paul Boddie and Lucia Nikolaia López Bojórquez, the PhD student Çagri Erdem, the Postdoctoral Researcher Victor Evaristo González Sánchez, the Master's students in Music Technology and Communication at the University of Oslo and NTNU Eigil Aandahl, Elias Sukken Andersen, Eirik Dahl, and Mari Lesteberg, and with the supervisory advice of Alexander Refsum Jensenius (Alarcon et al., 2019a).
7 MEMENTO software is designed to be used by anyone in a performance which includes oral archives that have previously transcribed and annotated.
8 Sonification is a process that translates data to sound, and has been defined as "the use of non-speech audio to convey information or perceptualize data" (Kramer, 1992).
9 FLOW™, developed by Sweetzpots.
10 To listen to the full telematic performance, see: https://youtu.be/m30yRwG1Tp8 (accessed September 13, 2021).
11 This conversation took place at the *Simbiosis* event, which took place on June 18, 2020, designed to showcase different artists' works and the role of art in the context of COVID-19. It was staged by Fronda, an artistic organisation based in Pachuca, Mexico.
12 Suggested by Kristine Diekman to me during the talk "Listening during Times of COVID" presented at *Simbiosis 2020*.
13 https://youtu.be/m30yRwG1Tp8 (accessed August 20, 2020).
14 Two Bath Spa University internships allowed me to work with Ricardo Graça, a graduate student, on a working prototype of the INTIMAL App© for mobile phones. In 2021, I was awarded a grant by The Studio Recovery Fund to develop further and test the INTIMAL App© with ten women in Bath. For the test, I worked in collaboration with the Service Designer Dr. Liliana Rodríguez, and I further implemented the App with the programmer Kieran Harte. See a demo of the INTIMAL App© at : https://vimeo.com/554809254 (accessed August 25, 2021).

15 Pauline Oliveros' concept, described as "the sonorous or sonic envelope of the Earth that is comprised of two irrevocably interwoven layers, the biospheric layer and the technosphenic layer" (Oliveros, 2010).

References

Alarcón, Ximena. 2017. "On Dis-location: Listening and Re-composing with Others." *Reflections on Process in Sound* 5: 24–37.
Alarcón, Ximena. 2019. "Conceptual Design for INTIMAL: A Physical/virtual Embodied System for Relational Listening." *Journal of Somaesthetics* 4(2): 6–24.
Alarcón, Ximena and Alexander R. Jensenius. 2020. "'Ellos no están entendiendo nada' ['They are not understanding anything']: Embodied Remembering as Complex Narrative in a Telematic Sonic Improvisation." In *Proceedings of RE:SOUND 2019*. London: BCS Learning and Development. http://dx.doi.org/10.14236/ewic/RESOUND19.32.
Alarcón-Diaz, Ximena, Paul Boddie, Cagri Erdem, Eigil Aandahl, Elias Sukken Andersen, Eirik Dahl, Mari Lesteberg, and Alexander Refsum Jensenius. 2019a. "Sensing Place and Presence in an INTIMAL Long-Distance Improvisation." *Journal of Network Music and Arts* 1(1). https://commons.library.stonybrook.edu/jonma/vol1/iss1/3.
Alarcón-Diaz, Ximena, López Bojórquez, Lucia Nikolaia, Olivier Lartillot, and Helga Flamtermesky. 2019b. "From Collecting an Archive to Artistic Practice in the INTIMAL Project: Lessons Learned from Listening to a Colombian Migrant Women's Oral History Archive." *Acervo. Revista do Arquivo Nacional* 32(3): 48–63.
Alarcón-Díaz, Ximena, Gonzalez Sanchez, Victor Evaristo, and Çagri Erdem. 2019c. "INTIMAL: Walking to Feel Place, Breathing to Feel Presence." In *Proceedings of the International Conference on New Interfaces for Musical Expression 2019*. Rio Grande do Sul, Brazil: Federal University of Rio Grande do Sul.
Brooks, Ann and Ruth Simpson. 2013. *Emotions in Transmigration: Transformation, Movement, and Identity*. Basingstoke, UK: Palgrave Macmillan.
Choi, Julie. 2017. *Creating a Multivocal Self: Autoethnography as Method*. Farnham, UK: Routledge.
Dorsey, Kika. 2008. "Embodied Language: Julia Kristeva's Theory of Poetic Language and Tantric Buddhism According to Reggie Ray." *Not Enough Night* (Fall): 1–8.
Gallagher, Sean. 2013. *How the Body Shapes the Mind*. Oxford, UK: Oxford University Press.
Gold, Heloise. 2008. *Deeply Listening Body*. Kingston, NY: Deep Listening Publications.
Górska, Magdalena. 2018. "Feminist Politics of Breathing", in Lenart Skof and Petri Berndtson, eds, *Atmospheres of Breathing*, 247–259. Albany, NY: State University of New York Press.
Grishakova, M. and M. Poulaki. 2019. *Narrative Complexity: Cognition, Embodiment, Evolution*. Lincoln, NE: University of Nebraska Press.
Höök, Kristina. 2018. *Designing with the Body: Somaesthetic Interaction Design*. Cambridge, MA: MIT Press.
Hunter, Kate. 2013. "The Cognitive Body: Using Embodied Cognition as a Tool for Performance-making", in Sandra Reeve, ed., *Body and Performance*, 163–175. Axminster, UK: Triarchy Press.
IONE. 2005. *Listening in Dreams*. Lincoln, NE: iUniverse.
IONE. 2012. "Deep Listening in Dreams: Opening to Another Dimension of Being", in Monique Buzzarte and Tom Bickley, eds, *Anthology of Essays in Deep Listening*, 299–313. Kingston, NY: Deep Listening Publications.
Jensenius, A. R. and R. I. Godøy. 2013. "Sonifying the Shape of Human Body Motion Using Motiongrams." *Empirical Musicology Review* 8(2): 73–83.

Kozel, Susan. 2007. *Closer: Performance, Technology, Phenomenology*. Cambridge, MA: MIT Press.

Kramer, Gregory. 1992. "Auditory Display: Sonification, Audification, and Auditory Interfaces." Paper delivered at *First International Conference on Auditory Display*, Santa Fe, NM, 1 October.

Kristeva, Julia. 1984. *Revolution in Poetic Language*. New York: Columbia University Press.

Lakoff, George and Johnson, Mark. 2003. *Metaphors We Live By*. Chicago, IL: University of Chicago Press.

Limerick, Hanna, David Coyle, and James W. Moore. 2014. "The Experience of Agency in Human-computer Interactions: A Review." *Frontiers in Human Neuroscience* 8(643): 1–10.

Oliveros, Pauline. 2005. *Deep Listening: A Composer's Sound Practice*. Lincoln, NE: iUniverse Books.

Oliveros, Pauline. 2010. *Sounding the Margins. Collected Writings 1992–2009*. Kingston, NY: Deep Listening Publications.

Reeve, Sandra. 2011. *Nine Ways of Seeing a Body*. Axminster, UK: Triarchy Press.

Wertsch, James. 2002. *Voices of Collective Remembering*. Cambridge, UK: Cambridge University Press.

Weynet, James. n.d. "History, Narrative, Ethnohistory 12: History, Oral History, and Memoriation in Native Title." Australian National University Press. http://press-files.anu.edu.au/downloads/press/p64921/mobile/ch12s02.html. Accessed November 15, 2020.

18
FOLEY PERFORMANCE AND SONIC IMPLICIT INTERACTIONS

How Foley artists might hold the secret for the design of sonic implicit interactions

Sandra Pauletto

Introduction

In the credit list of any major film or TV series, Foley artists are found under the sound department, among sound editors, dialogue editors and sound mixers. A Foley artist is someone who performs and records sound effects in synchronization to the picture after the film has been shot and edited, i.e. in post-production. While an analysis of how the art of Foley has come to be and how Foley artists contribute to filmmaking can be found in a number of publications (e.g. Ament 2014; Wright 2014; Hagood 2014; LoBrutto 1994), both academic and not academic, this chapter aims to shed light on the role of the body, its physicality and performative aspects, and on Foley art as a source of design knowledge for the creation of future technology.

Jack Donovan Foley (1891–1967) is often recognized as the Hollywood pioneer who first developed the techniques and practice of creating sound live in synchronization with the picture. The practice of Foley, as it came to be known in honour of its pioneer, has not changed much from its beginnings. The artist works in a recording studio, where the picture is projected on screen, surrounded by a large amount of sounding objects (selected for their sound qualities, not visual or tactile characteristics, which means that they are often indistinguishable from what one could call "junk") and surfaces that will allow them to create many different sounds. Descriptions of the practice often emphasize the quantity of objects collected (almost characterizing Foley artists as "hoarders"), their mundane, low-tech and cheap nature (often found in second-hand or junk stores) and the surprisingly (for people not familiar with sound) deceptive nature of sound: the sound of horses galloping can be re-created with coconuts, breaking bones with celery sticks, and a broken skull with a smashed watermelon.

DOI: 10.4324/9781003008217-23

These are highly fascinating aspects of the practice, but I would argue, not the most important ones. In fact, on the basis of these descriptions, one would not be wrong in thinking that collecting a large enough number of different sounding objects, and learning (from books, from interviews, from talking to Foley artists) the "recipes" for making a number of different sounds could be sufficient for someone to become a Foley artist. After all, many might describe it as a low-tech practice, since the artist does not need to deal with computers or electronics (a sound engineer usually does this) and anybody can do the movements they perform such as walking, or cracking a celery stick. But many Foley artists seem to disagree. Gary Hecker says, "a lot of people try it, and they fail at it" (Hecker 2010), and similarly, Kitty Malone remarks: "a lot of people through the years have tried, and, don't ask me why, some people have a feel for it and some don't" (Molina 2016). And even some acclaimed Foley artists admit that they have not always been good at some aspects of it: "I was terrible. I couldn't get in sync, period!" says James Nelson (in ibid.).

In this chapter, I argue that what really sets a Foley artist apart from other people is how they make use of their body, and their ability to perform and act through sound, expressing both explicit and subtle behaviours and intentions. Furthermore, I advance that understanding this unique expertise, how it manifests itself in sound, is key to developing new everyday sonic interactions for digital objects, or other applications such as games or virtual reality, that can be rich in meaning as well as subtle. In implicit human–computer interaction, systems are developed to respond to user actions that are not primarily aimed at interacting with a computerized system. The goal is to pre-empt needs and suggest options in an unobtrusive way. An example of implicit human–computer interaction is when a person passes near an automated door with or without the intention of entering, and the door opens, providing the option to enter. Between humans, information is often communicated implicitly through everyday sound. Research (e.g. Tajadura-Jiménez et al. 2015; Houel et al. 2020) has shown that we can understand a lot about a person's emotional state by the way they walk, run, or knock on a door, for example. The question then is: how can we design, or synthesize, similarly expressive and subtle sounds for new silent digital objects? In other words, how can we create "sonic implicit interactions"? Foley artists are able to "act" these implicit interactions through their body and objects to produce meaningful sounds. By understanding in more depth what they do, we might find the key for designing similarly expressive new sonic interactions. Joe Sabella and Kitty Malone allude to the key skills of Foley practice in as follows:

> I like using all my senses, my hearing, my touch, sight, hand eye coordination. To be a good foley artist you have to have all those facilities, and they need to work very well together. Doing stuff in real time in sync to picture is difficult, very difficult.
>
> *in Sabella (2015)*

And moreover: "We go back to imagination, tempo, coordination, and then love. You don't know which comes first, maybe love comes first" (in Molina 2016).

A note about acting

The sounds Foley artists create are predominantly those meant to have been produced by the characters on screen: footsteps, the sound of clothes when moving and the sound of interactions with objects. Characters can be represented on screen not only by human actors, but also by puppets or animated drawings. Foley artists create the sounds for all of these characters as they act. It is perhaps, then, interesting to reflect, even if very briefly, on what acting is:

> In its simplest form ... acting is nothing more than the transposition of everyday behaviour into a theatrical realm. Just as the language of poetry is not different in kind from the language in a newspaper, so the materials and techniques used by players on the stage [or screen] are no different in kind from those we use in ordinary social intercourse.
>
> *Naremore (1988 pg 21)*

The actor's body, poses, gestures, voice, costume all contribute to depicting the character. Of course, there are different types of acting. A group of people going shopping in a scene's background can be considered to be acting even if they are simply repeating an everyday activity that does not need much skill. At the other end of the spectrum, we might find virtuoso actors such as Charlie Chaplin, who can range between highly naturalistic and highly stylized (e.g. miming) modes of acting. The examples mentioned above rely solely on the actors' bodies, they do not need voices to be understood as examples of acting. We would probably not hear the actors in the background of a scene talking, and many of Chaplin's movies are silent, which demonstrates that despite the obvious importance of voice in cinema (exemplified by the centrality of the script), acting exists also in the absence of the voice.

Technological developments throughout the history of cinema have amplified the role of the body and gestures in acting. As Bette Davies remarked: "the screen is a fantastic medium for the reality of little things" (quoted in McBride 1983 pg 106) Close-up shots facilitate more subtle gestures, and an actor "can register, with a whisper, a glance, a contraction of a muscle, in a manner that would be lost on stage" (Cronyn 1949 pg 46). If the full figure is not often shown, then editing increases its power to create meaning and, one could say, to create "acting", movements, actions and reactions that might never exist in a continuous manner. In a situation in which acting can be created by editing together visual fragments, sound acquires the ability to render "intimate, low key behaviour in ways that would have dazzled Stanislavski" (Naremore 1988 pg 39), whose acting techniques often assume that "emotional life may sometimes be more easily aroused and fixed for performance through work on the physical life of the role, rather than through inner work" (Carnicke 2000 pg 16). Tight framings, camera movements away from the subject and similar techniques suggest a world beyond the screen, which is rendered often with off-screen sounds, and support the possibility of directing the audience's focus.

Furthermore, a naturalistic and more intimate type of acting emerges in which actors, while appearing to be doing nothing, use the manipulation of objects as a way to express character. As Naremore writes: "only the most vulgar empiricism regards the objects around us as inanimate. Once those objects have entered into social relations and narrative actions, they are imbued with the same 'spirit' as the humans who touch them" (Naremore 1988 pg 87), and actors turn objects into "signifiers of feeling. Sometimes the player dexterity is foregrounded, but more often it is hardly noticeable, lending emotional resonance to the simplest behaviour" (ibid.).

Foley sounds, then, the result of movements or object manipulations, also become "actors" as they represent the character in the aural domain, sometimes together with the picture, sometimes by themselves in off-screen scenes. Clothes, for example, shape not only bodies, but also behaviours, poses and gestures, both visually and sonically. The following examples highlight the performative, physical and creative efforts that the sound of clothes can demand of Foley artists. Alison Dee More describes the task of creating the sound of the cape in *The Dark Knight* (Nolan 2008): "the cape was a gruelling task because, just getting the "flumph" and how heavy that cape was, sustaining it for a long time, for me that was hard" (Molina 2016). Shelley Roden describes making the sound of a metal jacket in *Doctor Strange* (Derrickson 2016):

> we had to come up with a jacket, but is made of metal and comes off the wall in parts. John [Roesch] and I actually performed that together because we could do different notes like we were an orchestra. He handled the low heavy metal part of it, and I was the little accents.
>
> *Roesch and Roden (2018)*

So if these sounds are actors, fully participating in the creation of a character in a film, are Foley artists acting? When we concede that body movement, gestures and interactions with objects are central to acting and to the creation of character, then it becomes clear that the expression of acting on screen is only partially delivered through the images: a large proportion, or in the case of an off-screen character, the whole of it, is conveyed by Foley artists. The ability to create and express a character through sound interactions, or acting through sound, is the truly unique ability of Foley artists, and the skill that makes them, as we will see in the next sections, extremely valuable for the design of the sounds of current and future technology such as smart objects or automated systems.

The body, acting and Foley artistry

Through the analysis of interviews with established Foley artists, I will attempt to bring to the surface comments and reflections relating to the body, performance and acting in Foley. Although Foley artists are credited under the sound department, one might be surprised to discover that many do not have a sound engineering or even a music-related background. Sue Harding mentions that many Foley artists are "ex-performers, or have some kind of performance bones in their body, because it really helps with the movement, there are many ex-dancers, that kind of thing" (Harding 2019). Greg Barbanell, for example, trained as an actor (Crockett 2015), Kitty Malone was a dancer, and did all the footstep dancing of Liza Minelli in *Cabaret* as well as the footsteps of Mr T in *The A-Team*, and Marco Costanzo was a magician (Molina 2016). For Shelley Roden, Foley "is a combination of being a professional athlete, and a musician, and an actor all in one" (in ibid.). The job is described as very physically demanding by many – "This is one of the truly physical art" (Sabella 2015), "It is a very physical job" (Crockett 2015) – to the point that at times, "people have gotten some serious injuries," remarks Alicia Stevenson (Hecker, Lunsford and Stevenson 2016). Sarah Monat and Robin Harlan emphasize that "you need to be quite physically fit", and their advice to newcomers is to "make sure that they hone their skills in performance, dance, music. Those things are important to apply to what we do" (Monat and Harlan 2012).

The physical aspects of the job do not only relate to the movements needed for the creation of the sound, but also those needed to "hide" the real physical characteristics of the Foley artist that might not match the character, as well as the incredible mental focus required by the job. Stevenson remarks how Foley artists have "to control our breathing so you are not hearing my female breathing while I am doing a heavy man running for blocks" (Hecker, Lunsford and Stevenson 2016). Greg Barbanell explains:

> you are focused, and you are waiting for that move, and all your muscles are getting ready to fire ....At the end of a shift, I am mentally fatigued, from the amount of focus that's required ....You got to be alert, your reflexes have to be good, and it's tiring.
>
> *in Molina (2016)*

Foley artists do seem to see themselves principally as performers. Alicia Stevenson notes, "In order to get the right feel of a character, you need to really know how they are feeling" (Hecker, Lunsford and Stevenson 2016), and again:

> I think it is acting. Are they sad? Are they energetic? Are they drunk? Are they stumbling? Are they cautious? Are they sexy? Trying to be quiet. Trying to intimidate. When I am walking a character, I immerse myself into that

character, and it helps me to anticipate what they are gonna do. So, I think it helps my performance.

ibid.

Alyson Moore feels "we are storytellers with sound" (Moore, Moriana and Lang 2017). Sue Harding, while describing how a simple sound, for example putting a glass on the table, can be performed with many different emotions and meanings, describes the overall feeling to be portrayed in a movement as something that initially can be communicated from director to actor: "the director has told the actor *do that in a certain way* so we need to make sure that those moments are caught with the right sound as well" (Harding 2019), and then transmitted from the actor to the object the Foley artist sees on screen in postproduction: "whatever the emotion the actor is feeling at that time, [it] travels through the body to the glass" (ibid.).

For Foley artists, just like for actors, "before performance comes interpretation" (Albertson 1947 pg 65), and therefore an analysis of the character and the scene. Actors will analyse characters, their motivations, their personalities and their actions primarily through the script, while Foley artists do this typically through an analysis of movements, expressions and the appearance of the characters and objects on screen (in addition, they might receive some directions or notes from the director or the picture editor) (Pauletto 2019). Elisha Birnbaum states that:

> to be a good Foley man, you have to transform yourself to the character on the screen, when you become one of the character on the screen, whether it is going to be a man or a woman, or a child, or a dog, you are the dog, you are the man, and not everybody can do it!

in Molina (2016)

Marco Costanzo regards himself as a performer, and Foley as performance art:

> You need to act out the character you see on screen. If someone is coming in drunk, I will slop my body and start doing this, and drag my feet and trip on a little bit of the carpet … I look at the character and I say *Ok this guy is 150 pounds, he is a mad man, he has got sneakers on, he is like on crack so we are going to do something that emulates that,* so every person that I look at: I become that person.

ibid.

Similarly, Shelley Roden recalls working on *The Blind Side* (Hancock 2009): "I walked Big Mike and I had to become a 270–300 pound man who was feeling alone and no one cared about him. So, I really felt heavy, and I gave myself a sense of heaviness" (in Molina 2016).

Breathing, and sometimes the voice, are important aspects of Foley, too. Gary Hecker, for example, uses his voice and breaths to "carve" and manipulate other sounds with the help of his Foley mixer (Hecker, Lunsford and Stevenson 2016). For Peter Burgis, Foley "is really about self-expression and about building up a library within your head and a dexterity with objects" (Burgis 2018), while Joe Sabella equates Foley to "a good jazz song. When you get sucked in, you feel the flow, and all the tempos, and all the textures, and how every note just fits in. To me that's the art of Foley" (Sabella 2015). Foley artists very often work in pairs because it allows them to create simultaneous sounds, but also because, like actors in a dialogue scene, they can play off each other. David Lee Fein and Ken Dufva worked together for about 20 years, and remark on how they understood each other, and had, to a large extent, matching temperaments and sensibilities, but also enriched each other with new, different, ideas (Molina 2016).

It is rare to have the opportunity to see a Foley artist at work – after all, the cinematic spectacle does all it can to hide the apparatus that produces it. But in two recent documentaries, *Actors of Sound* (ibid.) and *The Secret World of Foley* (Jewel 2014), we have the chance to see, either through a split screen or the inclusion in the framing of the screen, what the Foley artist is looking at and how the artist acts out a character on film. First, we notice how focused on the picture the artists seem to be. They seldom look at what they are manipulating, having placed all the sounding objects at hand to be grabbed and dropped as necessary. When Foley artists work in pairs, they seem to become dancers, at one with each other's movements. Alyson Moore loves "paper work": "there is a lot of detail to paper, there is a lot of texture to paper" (in Molina 2016). We can see her acting the sound of multiple paper airplanes in the animated short *Paperman* (Kahrs 2012). The sounding object seems nothing: just a couple of sheets of paper. But their consistency and texture have been chosen carefully. She is sitting on a table with the paper in her hand. Her movements are fast and precise. The paper interacts with the table, the air and hands when she folds it and slides her finger down the edge. Fingers tap frantically on the paper when the airplanes are meant to stab the paperman, or they are moved rhythmically up and down to indicate flying. It is a complex and fascinating performance to watch. Earlier in *Actors of Sound*, we see Shelley Roden doing the footsteps of rugby players during a match. Again, her eyes are fixed on the screen projecting the film. Her posture is quite similar to that of a rugby player, or someone who is running, with the upper body projected forward and the feet stomping hard and fast on the ground. In contrast to that, we see Catherine Harper doing dance footsteps. She is dancing elegantly and smoothly, the feet sometimes tap and at others slide. All of her body is dancing, especially her arms and hands (even if they are not making a sound). In *The Secret World of Foley*, Peter Burgis and Sue Harding work together to create the sound of a silent short movie in which fishermen prepare to go out on a boat to catch crabs and lobsters. We see how Burgis performs with fine detail the movement of the rope against the wooden boat, where sometimes the rope is caught against the wood, and sometimes it is sliding. At the same time, Sue Harding performs the lobster pot attached to the rope. It slides against the wood, it bumps against it, and finally splashes in the water and then settles. Everything flows extremely naturally, as if Burgis and Harding were connected, just like the rope and the lobster pot. It is clear, just by even watching a few of these examples, that Kitty Malone is right: "some people have a feel for it".

From low tech to high tech: Foley artists as designers of sonic implicit interactions

Thus far, I have argued that Foley artists are primarily actors – in other words, they *transpose everyday behaviour into a theatrical realm* – and that this transposition happens in the sound domain. In sound computing terms, the Foley method of creating sounds could be equated to digitally creating sounds by procedural audio (Farnell 2010). In procedural audio, a sound, for example the sound of fire, is decomposed into its basic physical components, e.g. crackle, hiss, roar. These components are then digitally modelled using a variety of synthesis techniques, which can range from additive synthesis to frequency modulation, or from granular synthesis to physical modelling. Then the composite model's parameters are modified in time through a function that represents, or "mimics", a fire-like behaviour. In Foley, a fire would be made by identifying appropriate objects that can make the sound of the main components heard in fire, e.g. cellophane, potato chip bags, etc., then the Foley artist would "act" the fire, i.e. create the sonic behaviour of fire through object manipulation (e.g. scrunching up and releasing the objects).

Foley artists, like procedural audio, are "potential sound" (Farnell 2011). They have the objects to make many sounds, and the knowledge of how to transmit a behaviour onto these objects to make them sound like the target sound in a specific context and with a particular intention. Behaviour, in the context of procedural audio, can be described as the way something can sound given its physical characteristics. It is highly dependent on context, which "places particular emphasis on certain features" (ibid.). A ball moved by the wind on a surface will roll, not slide, for example, but in a confined space, in a specific context, it might change behaviour and bounce from wall to wall. Similarly, a typical Foley sound like knocking on a door might be short and regular if there is no urgency, but if the person knocking is escaping an assassin (specific context), then the knocks will be irregular, fast and timbrically changing if the person uses both palm and fist (Houel et al. 2020). In my research, I have found that a professional Foley artist is able to produce hundreds of expressive variations of the same sound, in this case a sequence of knocks, in only one hour. These were then acoustically analysed and used to digitally synthesize similarly expressive sounds (Barahona-Rios and Pauletto 2020b). This is a very practical example of how it is possible to extract expressive features from the highly skilled performance of a Foley artist and use it to inform the sound design or digital synthesis of expressive everyday sounds.

Currently, there exist only a limited number of sound and behaviour models, some working perceptually better than others, but ideally, if all the possible sounds, behaviours and contexts could be modelled, creating sounds in this way during, for example, a game or a virtual reality experience would resemble having a very cheap (in terms of computer storage) Foley artist inside the computer generating unique sounds as and when required on the basis of the human–computer interaction. Studying which objects Foley artists use to create particular sounds, how they are able to express different emotions through manipulating these objects, and implementing that knowledge as digital models can contribute to advancing procedural audio for games (Barahona-Rios and Pauletto 2019; Barahona-Rios and Pauletto 2020b) or other applications. But while many entertainment applications might strive to create primarily foreground sounds, I believe that Foley artists have a much more crucial role to play for the development of subtle sounds that might help us interact with today's computer systems in new and seamless ways.

The vast majority of sounds created by Foley artists are sounds that we, the audience, are not meant to pay attention to, or even be aware of. In everyday life, communication between humans largely relies on implicit contextual information coming from gestures, body language and voice. And every footstep, every body movement and every interaction produce sound. These sounds do reach our ears, but we do not always consciously hear them. Our brain "judges" their importance (Did the footsteps signal danger? Did the movement of the clothes demonstrate intimacy?) and determines what sound should fully capture our attention.

During films, our brain employs a similar mechanism (Anderson 1996) and utilizes primarily what Chion (2019) calls *causal listening* (where our primary concern is to identify the cause of the sound) and Gaver (1993), in a slightly different definition, refers to as *everyday listening*. The result is that the audience is usually unaware of how Foley sounds affect their perception. They still *feel* the presence and behaviour of a character on screen rendered through the Foley sounds, but generally do not attribute this perception to sound because, instead of perceiving Foley for what it really is, an acoustic event produced completely independently from the picture, they perceive it as an aspect, a *trace* of an object or gesture on screen. As Leman writes, "We hear the sounds, but we perceive their causes" (Leman 2010 pg 51), even when causes are fictional. This is exactly what Foley artists want us to perceive. When I asked Foley artist Gareth Rhys-Jones, during an observation of his practice in the studio, how he knows when a sound is "correct", he replied: "when you [the audience] don't notice it" (Pauletto 2019 pg 78). It seems that Foley artists know the secret of how to produce the "unhearable", or perhaps we could say "implicit", sounds.

With the development of smart objects, ubiquitous computing and autonomous systems, explicit human–computer interactions (where a user needs to explicitly interrogate a computer in order to get a desired output) are not a feasible option, as it would make many of our day-to-day interactions very awkward and demanding. Implicit human–computer interaction has been defined as "an action performed by the user that is not primarily aimed to interact with a computerised system, but which such a system understands as input" (Schmidt 2000 pg 192). Additionally, the interaction is implicit if "the exchange occurs outside the attentional foreground of the user" (Ju and Leifer 2008 pg 74). In implicit interactions, the assumption is that the computer has a certain understanding (by virtue of the way it has been programmed, the sophistication of which can vary from a simple rule system up to machine learning, for example) of our behaviour in a given situation and context. To do this, the system needs to be able to perceive our behaviour, environment and circumstances, interpret what it senses (what the system hears, sees or feels), then apply this information to produce an output. For implicit interactions to work well, the perception of context and the interpretation of that information, including potentially the user behaviour, needs to be sophisticated. The previous implicit interaction, for example, is not fully accomplished, because doors can open unnecessarily. More sophisticated perception and interpretation stages (where the system is able to know when a person wants to pass through the door) could significantly improve the result (examples of how this and other interactions could be improved can be found in Schmidt 2000 and Ju and Leifer 2008).

Hearing is perhaps the sense we use most in our day-to-day implicit interactions. That is because it is omnidirectional, it reaches beyond physical barriers (we hear sounds through walls), and has a relatively long range. However, while there is a wealth of research on how to design sounds that are meant to be attended to (alarms, sonification of data, for example in medical contexts, etc.), research on how sound should be designed to elicit interactions implicitly, subtly and unobtrusively, but nonetheless effectively, is lacking. This type of sound design, which relies on our everyday and causal listening skills to perceive, interpret and elicit behaviours, must consider at all times how intentions and behaviours express themselves through the body and gestures of the characters or objects they are implicitly referring to. In this context, I suggest that the focus of the design process should shift from being mainly concerned with the acoustic characteristics of the sound, or from solely modelling the sound source, to how these sounds are articulated by intentions and behaviours through the *body* of the implied source. In my research, I utilize methods from sound and music computing, ethnography and design thinking to elicit knowledge from sound design practice to inform sound computing. Through interviews and design sessions with sound professionals and performers (Pauletto et al. 2009; Pauletto 2012; Pauletto 2019; Pauletto et al. 2021; Selfridge and Pauletto 2021), I attempt to identify what is unique about this knowledge. Through the development of professionally produced Foley sound datasets that articulate a number of emotional intentions (for example, the dataset on knocking sounds we recorded with Swedish Foley artist Ulf Olausson and made available to others – see Barahona-Rios and Pauletto 2020a), researchers are able to analyse how emotional intentions shape everyday sounds, furthering knowledge on how to detect behaviours from everyday sounds, and how to digitally model and synthesize performance sounds. In our research on the synthesis of expressive knocking sounds, we took, for example, a machine learning approach (Barahona-Rios and Pauletto 2020b). Finally, the investigation and modelling of historical sounding objects in performance – for example, our analysis and modelling of a wind machine in performance (Keenan and Pauletto 2017) – allow us to further explore the complex space where sound source characteristics and performance gestures meet to create sound.

In the context of implicit interactions where sound is the primary conveyor of information, which I refer to as "sonic implicit interactions", sound can the signal sensed by the computer or the signal produced by the computer to initiate an interaction. Let us imagine two scenarios, first as a human–human interaction and then as a human-computer interaction, that exemplify these possibilities. We are at home and we hear the slow, sad footsteps of our partner around the house. We think that they have had a bad day at work, therefore we switch the kettle on to make a cup of tea for them. In the corresponding human–computer context, this could become: the mobile phone perceives our partner's footsteps and compares it to a database of emotionally labelled footsteps performed by Foley artists. The mobile phone interprets the footsteps as sad, and it sends a message to the smart kettle to switch on when the person comes into the kitchen. In this example, Foley artists, who could be considered footsteps virtuosos given their ability to perform footsteps with many different emotions, can contribute to this sonic implicit interaction by providing large datasets of emotional footsteps that can be analysed to develop robust and nuanced knowledge of the acoustic correlates of emotions in footstep signals, so that appropriate interpretation models can be created for implicit interactions that use footsteps as input signals. In my research, I have conducted these studies (creating an expressive dataset, producing acoustic analysis of it, and using that knowledge to synthesize expressive sounds) for knocking sounds, but in principle the process can be applied for a number of other everyday sounds. The great advantage of involving Foley artists in this process is their unique ability to provide many examples of everyday sounds performed with a vast range of expressions.

In the following example, the sound is the system's output. We are at home, and we hear our flatmate sighing. We think that they are not feeling well, and decide to make a nice dinner to cheer them up. In the human–computer context, this could become: the smart plant pot system senses that the plants are not doing well, they are low in water and nutrients. When the owner is at home, and passes near the plants, the plant pots make a sound to hint to the owner that they might want to attend to the plants quite soon. What should the plant pots "sighing" sound like? Should it sound like sighing, or something else? In order for this system to provoke a caring behaviour towards the plant, how intrusive and varied should the sound be? What makes a sound suggestive of an action? When is a sound felt, but not explicitly heard? A design process that involves the expertise of Foley artists (not only audio programmers and potential users) could yield a much wider solution space for such a project. In my current research project, "Sound for Energy – Sonic interaction design to support energy efficiency behavior in the household", I use this approach in the sound design ideation process of new sonic interactions for the household.

Foley artists are the sound professionals who have expert knowledge on how to express behaviours through sound for characters, even for those characters that do not have a sound in the real world. Additionally, they know how to create sounds that can be ignored as well as attended to without fatigue. This is often an embodied and tacit knowledge that is difficult to define and extract. I have outlined how I attempt to address this complex issue in my research through the use of a variety of methodologies. This approach is extended in recently funded projects which will model sounding objects (Pauletto et al. 2021),[1] and their performance, used in radio production, and apply this and related findings, using a design thinking framework (Design Council UK 2021), to the development of new sonic interactions to be embedded in smart objects for energy efficiency.

Overall, research related to the design of sonic interactions, and in particular implicit sonic interactions, reveals a complex picture in which we can no longer underestimate, or exclude from the design process, the experts in the field: the Foley artists, their acting knowledge and their ability to express through their bodies, often implicitly, intentions, suggestions and behaviours through sound.

Conclusion

Foley artists are actors able to *transpose everyday behaviour into a theatrical realm* through sound. They express a character's behaviour through the sound produced by their body and interactions with objects. They have such acute sensibility that they are able to create sounds that are implicit to a behaviour, but are "unhearable" – in other words, sounds that one can feel and even understand, but not explicitly be aware of. In the past, there have been attempts to digitally create a Foley artist, usually by providing a large database of sounds and automated ways of selecting and synching these sounds. But these approaches have not, so far, proved successful. This is because Foley is not simply a large database of sounds or sounding objects, it is "sound by acting". And acting is, at least to date, difficult to model with any great level of sophistication. Instead, I suggest that Foley artists have today more avenues to utilize their skills. Their knowledge and skills should be called upon by current sound design research and development. One particularly relevant area is that which I named "sonic implicit interactions", in which Foley artists can both inform how a system can interpret perceived sounds produced by everyday behaviour and contribute to designing "unhearable", unobtrusive, but meaningful sound for future technology. I wonder, for example, what sound Alyson Dee Moore would create for a smart plant pot? Perhaps her exquisite and subtle paper work could provide the answer.

Note

1 See the following projects: "Sonic interaction design to support energy efficiency behavior in the household" funded by the Swedish Energy Agency (2021–2023) at www.soundforenergy.net, "The Radio Sound Studio: developing novel digital sound design tools through the modelling of historical sound effects", funded by NAVET, KTH (2021) at www.kth.se/navet/research/projects/the-radio-sound-studio-1.1046432 and SonicFunc at www.kth.se/hct/mid/research/smc/projects/sonicfunc-sound-design-methods-for-the-digital-society-1.951664.

Bibliography

Albertson, Lillian. 1947. *Motion Picture Acting*. Funk & Wagnalls.
Ament, Vanessa Theme. 2014. *The Foley Grail: The Art of Performing Sound for Film, Games, and Animation*. CRC Press.
Anderson, Joseph, 1996. *The Reality of Illusion: An Ecological Approach to Cognitive Film Theory*. SIU Press.
Barahona-Rios, Adrián, and Pauletto, Sandra. 2019. "Perceptual Evaluation of Modal Synthesis for Impact-based Sounds." Paper delivered at *SMC Sound and Music Computing Conference 2019*, Málaga, Spain, May 28–31.
Barahona-Rios, Adrián, and Pauletto, Sandra. 2020a. "Knocking Sound Effects with Emotional Intentions." Dataset. Accessed October 30, 2021. https://doi.org/10.5281/zenodo.3668503.
Barahona-Rios, Adrián and Pauletto, Sandra. 2020b. "Synthesising Knocking Sound Effects Using Conditional WaveGAN." Paper delivered at *SMC Sound and Music Computing Conference 2020*, Turin, Italy, June 24–26.
Burgis, Peter. 2018. "Inside the Pinewood Foley Studio." YouTube. Accessed October 30, 2021. www.youtube.com/watch?v=tQl_-MghIjo.
Carnicke, Sharon M. 2000. "Stanislavsky's System." In *Twentieth Century Actor Training*, edited by Alison Hodge. Routledge, pp. 11–36.
Chion, Michel. 2019. *Audio-vision: Sound on Screen*. Columbia University Press. https://doi.org/10.7312/chio18588.
Crockett, Zachary. 2015. "The Man Who Makes Hollywood's Smallest Sounds." Priceonomics. Accessed October 30, 2021. https://priceonomics.com/the-man-who-makes-hollywoods-smallest-sounds/.
Cronyn, Hume. 1949. "Notes on Film Acting." *Theatre Arts* 35: 45–48.
Derrickson, Scott (director). 2016. *Doctor Strange*. Film. Marvel Studios.
Design Council UK. "What Is the Framework for Innovation? Design Council's Evolved Double Diamond." Design Council. Accessed October 30, 2021. www.designcouncil.org.uk/news-opinion/what-framework-innovation-design-councils-evolved-double-diamond.
Farnell, Andy. 2010. *Designing Sound*. MIT Press.
Farnell, Andy. 2011. "Behaviour, Structure and Causality in Procedural Audio." In *Game Sound Technology and Player Interaction: Concepts and Developments*, edited by Mark Grimshaw. IGI Global, pp. 313–339.
Gaver, William W. 1993. "What in the World Do We Hear? An Ecological Approach to Auditory Event Perception." *Ecological Psychology* 5.1: 1–29.
Hagood, Mack. 2014. "Unpacking a Punch: Transduction and the Sound of Combat Foley in Fight Club." *Cinema Journal* 53.4: 98–120.
Hancock, John Lee (director). 2009. *The Blind Side*. Film. Warner Bros.
Harding, Sue. 2019. "On the Black Art of Foley – an Interview with Sue Harding." YouTube. Accessed October 30, 2021. www.youtube.com/watch?v=j7J9d8j-qsU.
Hecker, Gary. 2010. "Gary Hecker – Veteran Foley Artist." Vimeo. Accessed October 30, 2021. https://vimeo.com/11436985.
Hecker, Gary, Lunsford, Dawn, and Stevenson, Alicia. 2016. "Foley Artists: How Movie Sound Effects Are Made." YouTube. Accessed October 30, 2021. www.youtube.com/watch?v=U_tqB4IZvMk.
Houel, Malcolm, Arun, Abhilash, Berg, Alfred, Iop, Alessandro, Barahona-Rios, Adrian, and Pauletto, Sandra. 2020. "Perception of Emotions in Knocking Sounds: An Evaluation Study." Paper delivered at *SMC Sound and Music Computing Conference 2020*, Turin, Italy, June 24–26.

Jewel, Daniel (director). 2014. *The Secret World of Foley*. Film. Shorts International.
Ju, Wendy and Leifer, Larry. 2008. "The Design of Implicit Interactions: Making Interactive Systems Less Obnoxious." *Design Issues* 24.3: 72–84.
Kahrs, John (director). 2012. *Paperman*. Film. Walt Disney Animation Studios.
Keenan, Fiona and Pauletto, Sandra. 2017. "'Listening Back': Exploring the Sonic Interactions at the Heart of Historical Sound Effects Performance." *The New Soundtrack* 7.1: 15–30.
Leman, Marc. 2010. "An Embodied Approach to Music Semantics." *Musicae Scientiae* 14.1 suppl.: 43–67.
LoBrutto, Vincent. 1994. *Sound-on-film: Interviews with Creators of Film Sound*. Greenwood Publishing.
McBride, Joseph. 1983. *Filmmakers on Filmmaking: The American Film Institute Seminars on Motion Pictures and Television*, Volume Two. Tarcher Press.
Molina, Lalo (director). 2016. *Actors of Sound*. Film. Freestyle Digital Media.
Monat, Sarah and Harlan, Robin. 2012. "Foley Artists." YouTube. www.youtube.com/watch?v=MHAIgJsMoXw.
Moore, Alyson, Moriana, Chris, and Lang, Mary Jo. 2017. "The Magic of Making Sound." YouTube. Accessed October 30, 2021. www.youtube.com/watch?v=UO3N_PRIgX0.
Naremore, James. 1988. *Acting in the Cinema*. University of California Press.
Nolan, Christopher (director). 2008. *The Dark Knight*. Film. Warner Bros.
Pauletto, Sandra, Selfridge, Rod, Holzapfel, Andre and Frisk, Henrik 2021. "From Foley Professional Practice to Sonic Interaction Design: Initial Research Conducted within the Radio Sound Studio Project." Paper delivered at *Nordic Sound and Music Computing Conference*, Copenhagen, Denmark, November 11–12.
Pauletto, Sandra, Hug, Daniel, Luckhurst, Mary, and Barrass, Stephen. 2009. "Integrating Theatrical Strategies into Sonic Interaction Design." Paper delivered at *Audio Mostly 2009 – a Conference on Interaction with Sound*, Glasgow, UK, September 2–3.
Pauletto, Sandra. 2012. "The Sound Design of Cinematic Voices." *The New Soundtrack* 2.2: 127–142.
Pauletto, Sandra. 2019. "Invisible Seams: The Role of Foley and Voice Postproduction Recordings in the Design of Cinematic Performances." In *Foundations in Sound Design for Linear Media: A Multidisciplinary Approach*, edited by Michael Filimowicz. Routledge.
Roesch, John and Roden, Shelley. 2018. "The Foley Team of Skywalker Sound." YouTube. Accessed October 30, 2021. www.youtube.com/watch?v=G2qpEabgeMU.
Sabella, Joe. 2015. "Crew Call: 'Back To The Future' Foley Artist Joe Sabella on Creating Sounds." YouTube. Accessed October 30, 2021. www.youtube.com/watch?v=B0E0yXp4tEo.
Schmidt, Albrecht. 2000. "Implicit Human Computer Interaction through Context." *Personal Technologies* 4.2: 191–199.
Selfridge, Rod and Pauletto, Sandra 2021. "Investigating the Sound Design Process." Paper delivered at *Nordic Sound and Music Computing Conference*, Copenhagen, Denmark, November 11–12.
Tajadura-Jiménez, Ana, Maria Basia, Ophelia Deroy, Merle Fairhurst, Nicolai Marquardt, and Nadia Bianchi-Berthouze. 2015. "As Light as Your Footsteps: Altering Walking Sounds to Change Perceived Body Weight, Emotional State and Gait." In *Proceedings of the 33rd Annual ACM Conference on Human Factors in Computing Systems*. New York: Association for Computing Machinery, pp. 2943–2952.
Wright, Benjamin. 2014. "Footsteps with Character: The Art and Craft of Foley." *Screen* 55.2: 204–220.

INDEX

Note: Page numbers in **bold** indicate tables; those in *italics* indicate figures.

Abilities First School, *Play the Drum* 59–60
Ableton software 204
Abramovich, Marina 1
Abtan, Frieda, *Mondgewächse* 203
Abya Yala 138, 140, 141, 149nn11, 14
acousmatic dislocation 218
acousmatic listening 57, 60, 159
acousmatic voice 228, 229, 235, 239
acting 267–272, 276
Actors of Sound (2016) 271
Acustemology 149n2
Adams, Mags 169
Adaptive Use Musical Instrument (AUMI) 197
Adoo, Clarence 203
affective bodies 12, 52, 54, 61
affective reports from listening 155, 157–162, 164n4
affordances 24, 26, 206, 214–218
AfroNordestinas 68, 69, 71
Ahimsa 147
Ahmed, Sarah 55, 61
Akama, Ryoko 18–20, *19*, 21
Alarcón-Díaz, Ximena 243–264; *Chiddiomatikflui* 246; *Histomemoriology* 246, 258–259; *INTIMAL: A Long-Distance Improvisation* 250–260, *252*, *255*; INTIMAL App© 260, 262n14; INTIMAL: Interfaces for Relational Listening 244–261; *Migratory Journeys* 246–250, *247*, *249*, *251*

Albertson, Lillian 270
Alessandrini, Patricia, *Mondgewächse* 203
Alice, Maria 66
Alys, Francis 240n1
Amacher, Maryanne 190
Amaral, Heloisa 87
amefricanity/*amefricanidadei 140*
American Sign Language (ASL) 199–201
amplification: Alarcón-Díaz's INTIMAL 244–245, 260; low frequency sound 183–184, 186–189, 191; violining body 215–216, 218–220, *221*–224
Anderson, Ruth 86
anechoic chamber 47n15
Antescofo score follower system 218, 219
Anthonissen, Christine 124
Anzaldúa, Gloria 140
Arendt, Hannah 114, 127n2
artethnography 95–106, 108n6
artists' walks 229, 240n1
As Calungas 76n6
Ashley, Mary 90n5
Ashley, Robert 90n5
assemblage 12–14, 16–18, 21–22, 155–156
assonances of silences [collection] 35
A-Team, The 269
Athelstan Sound 85
audio description (AD) 209–210
audio walks, Cardiff and Bures Miller's 228–242

aurality 139, 149n2
Azevedo, Reinaldo 165n9

Bakhita, Sharylaine 67
Baltar, Brígida, *Collecting* series – *mist, sea air and dew* 42
Barad, Karen 80, 87, 88
Barbanell, Greg 269
Bárbara, A (The Barbarian) 106
Barker, Paul Alan 4
Barthes, Roland 124
bass cannons 188, 192
bass clarinet 183
bass drum 188
bass flute 186, 187
bass guitar 191–192
Batalha das Heroínas, A (The Battle of the Heroines) 94, *98*, 99, 100–102, *101*
Batuca 173–174, *174*, *175*
Baudoin, P. 198
Beagle Boys 165n9
BEAST speaker system 63n6
Bechara, Nanda 70
Behrman, David 90n5
Belê, Sandra 66
Benjamin, Walter 45
Bennett, Jane 12–14, 17, 18
Bergson, Henri 228, 238, 240
Béros, Cyril 219
Berweck, Sebastian 216, 219
Between the suspended word and porous listening [investigations under sound propositions] project 35, 46n2
Beyoncé 70
Bhowmik, Samir 133
Bia Boa (Nice Bia) 106
Bieckman, Kristine 256
binaural recording, Cardiff and Bures Miller's Walks 230–231, 236, 239
Bines, Rosana Kohl 45
biodata 247, 249
biographemes 124
Bione, Clara 66
biosensors 207–208
Birnbaum, Elisha 270
Birringer, Johannes 201
Bixarte 76n7
Black Women Parade 139
Blacking, John 28
Blackman, Lisa 80
blind people 208–210
Blind Side, The (2009) 270
Blueberry techno 128, *129*, *132*
Bolsonaro, Jair 158, 160

Bonafé, Valéria 149n2, 153–165
Born, Georgina 2
borrowed body 238–240
Boudry, Pauline 79, 81
Boulez, Pierre, *Anthèmes II* 214–215, 218, 219–224; score *220*, *221*, *222*, *224*
Bowman, Jason, *In Case There's a Reason: The Theatre of Mistakes* 82
Braidotti, R. 192
Brazil: COVID-19 pandemic 158; feminist methodologies in the sonic arts 3, 166–178; festivity cycles 109n9; *The Lunar Howls of Wolves* 138–148; *mar paradoxo* 36–46, 46n7; *Microfonias* project 158–161; music technology 171–172; Tejucupapo women 92–110; women's music in Paraíba 65–77
break dancers 67
breathing: Foley artists 269, 270–271; as listening 250, *251*, 253–260, *254*
Brooks, Ann 243
Brown, Trisha 82
Bures Miller, Georges: *Alter Bahnhof Video Walk* 237–238, *237*; *Chiaroscuro* 230; *The City of Forking Paths 233*, 234, 235; *The Empty Room* 230; *Her Long Black Hair* 232; *MoMA Walk* 232; *Night Walk for Edinburgh 239*, 239; *Villa Medici Walk* 230; *Walks* 228–242; *Wanås Walk* 230, 232
Burgis, Peter 271
Burtle, John 89n1
Butler, Judith 167
Bynum, Caroline 32

Cabaret (1972) 269
Cabnal, Lorena 140, 143
Caesar, Rodolfo 149n2
Caetano, Jessica 76n7
Cage, John 47n15; *Notations* 82, 84
Camarão, Maria 100, *101*
Campesato, Lílian 153–165
Cara da Mãe (Their Mother's Face) 106
Cardew, Cornelius 83
Cardiff, Janet: *Alter Bahnhof Video Walk* 237–238, *237*; *Chiaroscuro* 230; *The City of Forking Paths 233*, 234, 235; *The Empty Room* 230; *Her Long Black Hair* 232; *MoMA Walk* 232; *Night Walk for Edinburgh 239*, 239; *Villa Medici Walk* 230; *Walks* 228–242; *Wanås Walk* 230, 232
Carnicke, Sharon M. 267–268
Carroll, Lewis, *Alice's Adventures in Wonderland* 47n14

cartographing and sharing listenings 153–164
Carvalho, Carlos 101
Casseano, Patrícia 67
Catarine, Raab 66
Catholic Church 108–109n8
causal listening 273, 274
cavalo marinho 109n10
Central Única das Favelas (CUFA, Central Union of the Favelas) 69
Chaplin, Charlie 267
Chemero, Anthony 25
Chion, Michel 235, 236, 273
Choi, Julie 246
chora 256–260
Chrisou, Jani 83
Christian meditation tradition 117
Cimini, Amy 53, 63n3
ciranda 97–99, *98*, 107, 109n10
Clark, Lygia 46n5
classical music, low frequency sound in 181
closed captioning 209
coastal silences 36–46
coco de roda 97–99, *99*, 107, 109n10
Cole, Jonathan 217
Collins, Rebecca 3, 175
Colombetti, Giovanna 27, 30
Colombian women's migration 243–260
color constancy, effect of memory on 20
Comadre Fulozhinha 109
computational theory of mind 29
conative bodies 13
Conka, Karol 69
conversation method, *Microfonias* project 154–155, 157, 164n3
Corner, Phil 90n5
corpographies 122, 124, 125
Costanzo, Marco 269, 270
COVID-19 pandemic 7–8; Alarcón-Díaz's INTIMAL 260; "Listening to yourself and the world" project 149n7; *Microfonias* project 155–158, 160–161, 164n7; *Simbiosis* 262n11; Sound Poetics of Territory-Spirit-Bodies for Well-Living 139, 140
Coyle, David 243
Crasnow, Sharon 177
Crockett, Zachary 269
Cronyn, Hume 267
CrowEST, Sarah 240n1
curator, embodied 78–80, 87–89
Curtiss, Charlene 201–202
cynosuric bodies 196–213

da Silva, Luzia Maria 94, 95, 97, 99, 100
Daher, Katia *103*, *104*
Dark Knight, The (2008) 268
Davis, Bette 267
Dawsey, John 102
De Jaegher, Hanne 27
deaf people 209
Decibel: *WHITE LINES* 187–188; *your sickness is felt in my body* 186
deep listening 243; Alarcón-Díaz's INTIMAL 244–249, *245*, *246*; situated 51–64; soundwalking 168, 171, 173, 175
Deep Listening album 58
deep situated listening 51–64
Del Santos 66, 76n6
Deleuze, Gilles: affect 51, 53, 54; assemblage 12, 13; deep situated listening 60, 61; difference 41; non-sense paradox 47n14; plane of immanence 51, 53–54; situated knowledge 56
Descriptive Video Service (DVS) 209
Di Franco, Karen 83
Di Paolo, Ezequiel 27
Diaspora Women 244, 247, 250
DIMI Ballet 201
DIMI-O 201
Dinneen, James 210
Diodato, Roberto 228, 233, 235–236, 240
disability: Audimance 210; audio description 209–210; Descriptive Video Service 209; human–computer interaction 201–3; *Instrument of Balance and Grace* 201–202; *Stretched Boundaries* 58–60
Discord app 254
dispatches, *Microfonias* project 155–164
disruptive listening 44–45
Divine, Kyle 2
Doctor Strange (2016) 268
Documenta 14 exhibition 83
Domenich, Mirella 67
Donato, Val 66
Dorsey, Kika 257
double bass 181, 183
Doucet, Brian 171
dreams: agency in 262n3; listening in 245, *245*
dub plates 187, 192, 193n4
Duby, Marc 4
Dufva, Ken 271
Duignan, Enda 171
Durand, Gilbert 105
dynamic systems theory 26
Dźuverovič, Lina 83

Eagleman, David M. 207
ECOAR Group 167
ecological psychology 24, 25
Egloff, Deborah, *Prometheus* 59
El Haouli, Janete 154
electroacoustic music (EAM): deep situated listening 51–53, 57–62; New York City (2011) concert 52, 53, 57–60; as plane of immanence 53–55; Tillburg, Holland (2018) concert 52–53, 61–62
Electroacoustic Music Studies (EMS) network 53, 57–58
electro-cardiogram (ECG) sensors *III: Once Removed* 207–208
electronic music: low frequency sound 181, 183, 185–190, 192; violining body 214–225; *see also* electroacoustic music
emancipatory methods 169
Embodied Music Cognition 23, 28, 244, 247, 249
enactive-ecological musical approaches 23–34
Encuentro Sagrado con si misma/Sacred Encounter with oneself project 149n7
energy expenditure sensors 204
English, Lawrence 185
ethics of care 24, 27, 28
ethnomusicology 149n2
Eurynome 140–142, 146, 147
Evangelical Church 97, 109n8
Evaristo, Simone *103*, *105*
everyday listening 273, 274
Ewá 144, 146
exclusive listening 58
exhibitions, embodied curator 78–89
Experimental Intermedia Foundation 86, 90n5
Ezcurra, Mara Polgovsky 2

f(r)iction artists 102, 105
feedback: haptic 223–224, 225; sensuality of low frequency sound 191–192; violining body 218, 223–224, 225
Fein, David Lee 271
Feld, Steven 149n2
female: pressure 137
Feminaria Musical: Research Group and Sound Experiments 138–139
Feminismos del Abya Yala (UACM) 149n7
feminist artivism 139, 140, 149n6
feminist politics of listening 154
Fernandes, Priscila 76n6
fiction-score, *Microfonias* project 155, 156–157
Finch, Mark 197

Flores, Luana 66, *67*, 76n5
FLOW™ breathing sensors 253
Fluxus 79
Fodor, Jerry 25
Fogo de Monturo (Surprise Element) 106
Foley, Jack Donovan 265
Foley artists 265–278
forces at play 11–22
Forsythe, William 197–198, 202, 206
France, electroacoustic music 57
Frasch, Heather 11–22; Digital Boxes *14*; objects in studio *12*; *Post-Paradise Series* (Birmingham, UK, 2019) *14*, *16*
Fraser, Andrea, *Museum Highlights* 240n1
Freedom, Song and Dance 114
Freire, Ida Mara 113–127
Freire, Maria Angélica 96, 100, 101
f(r)iction artists 102, 105
Fronda 262n11
Fulton, Hamish 240n1

Gaeta, Angela 66, 76n6
Galaz, Pablo 219
Gallagher, Shaun 217, 243
Gametrak 205, 207
Gargallo, Francesca 140
Garland Thomson, Rosemarie 202
Gautier, Ana Maria Ochoa 149n2
Gaver, William W. 273
Gibson, Beatrice 83
Gibson, James J. 24, 25–26, 216
Gilpin, H. 198
Giovando, Chiara 83
Girls and Science project 175
Godden, Vanessa 185–186, *186*
Godøy, R. I. 247
Gold, Heloise 262n3
Gonzalez, Lélia 140
Górska, Magdalena 257
Graça, Ricardo 262n14
Grau, Oliver 233, 241n6
Green, Lucy 65–66, 71, 75, 176
Green, Susie 196–213
Green-Mateu, Susan, *Inter-Act* 204–205
Greie-Ripatti, Antye 128–137
Grosz, Elizabeth 142–143
grounded theory 168
Groupe de Recherches Musicales 57
Grynsztejn, Madeleine 240n3
Guattari, Félix 12, 13
Guerreiras (Warriors) 102–104, *103*, *104*, 105, *105*
Guerrilla Girls 2
Guirraiz, DJ *69*

Hagan, Kerry, *Who Was That Timbre I Saw You With?* 199
hand as body 197–199
handography exercises 196, 197–198; *Entanglement* 208, *208*, *209*; *Multi-Dimensional Isolation* 199, *200*; *Perception* 197, *198*; QR code *197*; *((re) frame/bound)* 207, 207; *Shadows of Light* 205, *206*
Hanssen, Tina Rigby 231, 232
haptic feedback 223–224, 225
Haraway, Donna 51, 53, 55–57, 60, 61
Harding, Sandra 169
Harding, Sue 269, 270, 271
Harlan, Robin 269
Harper, Catherine 271
Hartman, Hanna 18
Hayes, Lauren 23–34, 147
Hayles, N. Katherine 29
headphones: Alarcón-Díaz's INTIMAL 254, 260; Cardiff and Bures Miller's Walks 230–233, 235
HeadSpace 203
hearing heads paradigm 51–52, 55, 60, 62
hearing impairment 209
Hecker, Gary 266, 270–271
Henrick, Mark 185
Henriques, Julian 182
Her Noise: Feminisms and the Sonic programme 79
Higgs whatever, *Who Was That Timbre I Saw You With?* 199
hip hop and rap 66–75
histomemoriology 246, 250
Homens e Caranguejos (Men and Crabs) 105, 107
Höök, Kristina 248
hooks, bell 140
Hope, Cat 181–195; *Shadow* 190; *Tone Being* 190, *191*
human–computer interaction (HCI): agency, sense of 243; Alarcón-Díaz's INTIMAL 244, 247–260, *249*; cynosuric bodies 201–206, 210; enactive-ecological musical approaches 23, 29, 32; Foley artists 266, 273–276; implicit 266, 273–276; O Keeffe 3
Hunter, Kate 248

I Wanna Be With You Everywhere festival 210
If I were Me 176
implicit interactions 266, 272–276
inclusive listening 58
Indigenous Women Parade 139

individuation 16–17
infrared motion-detection devices *see* motion-detection devices
infrasound 181, 188, 192n1
Ingleton, Lee 79
Instrument of Balance and Grace 201–202
International Association of Black Dance (IABD) 118
International Situationist Internationale 240n1
intersectionality: sound poetics of territory-spirit-bodies for well-living 140; soundwalking 169, 177n2
IONE 262n3
Iyer, Vijay 32

Jacobsen, Jens 203
JamBoxx 59
Jawad, Karolina 2
Jensenius, A. R. 247; Taxonomy of Body Motion *256*
Joan of Arc 94
Johnson, Steven 198
Jornadas Sonoras (Sounding Journeys) project 66
Ju, Wendy 274
Juliana, Maria 66
Jung, Jung In, *Locus* 205–207

Kahn, Douglas 47n15
Kanno, Mieko 219, 220
Katz, David 20
Kim, Christine Sun 1; *Binary Reality with a Delay* 59
Kim-Cohen, Seth 46n6
Kinect 198–199, 201, 205, 207; Green-Mateu's *Inter-Act* 204; Parkinson's Disease 205
kinesphere 197–199, *200*, 202, 207–208
Kinetic Light: Audimance 210; audio description 209–210
Kirsh, David 198
Knezic, Sophie 228–242
Knowles, Alison: *Notations* (with John Cage) 82, 84; Sounds Out Of Silent Spaces 86; *Womens Work* (with Annea Lockwood) 78–87
Kotz, Liz 82, 85
Kozel, Suzanne 245
Kramer, Gregory 262n8
Kristeva, Julia 256, 257, 259
Kristiansson, Thérèse 169
Krogh Groth, Sanne 51–64
Kubisch, Christina, *Electrical Walks* 240n1

Kubota, Shigeko 90n5
Kundalini 144, 146
Kurenniemi, Erkki 201

Laban, Rudolph 197–198
Lady Gaga 70
Lambert, Leandra 149n2
Lane, Cathy 79
Langy, Preta 69, *69*, 70–71, **72**, **73**
Larsson, Peter 203
Laurie Anderson/Trisha Brown/Gordon Matta-Clark exhibition 82
Le Guin, Ursula, *The Dispossessed* 130
Leach, Mary Jane 86–87
Leão, Alessandra 102–103, 109n13
LeapMotion 198–199, 201; Higgs whatever's *Who Was That Timbre I Saw You With?* 199
learning difficulties, people with 24, 30–31; day centre *31*
Learning from Athens exhibition 83
Lefebvre, Henri 170
Leifer, Larry 273
Leite, Giordana 69, *69*
Leman, Marc 24–25, 28–29, 273
Leung, Ghislaine 83; *Colour Hides the Canvas, Moulding Hides the Frame* 84
Lévy, Pierre 228, 232
Lima, Glaucia 66
Lima, Kalyne 66–75; Campo Minado" lyrics **72**, **73**; photographs *68*, 69
Lima, Priscila 69, *69*
Limerick, Hanna 243
Lingis, Alphonso 182
Lispector, Clarice 43, 45; "As águas do mundo" ("The Waters of the World") 43–44; "Se eu fosse eu" (If I were me) 167, 177
listening networks 164n4
"Listening to yourself and the world" project 149n7
Lloyd, Barbara 90n5
Loaiza, Juan M. 28, 31–32
Lockwood, Annea: *Piano Transplants* 80, *81*, *84*, 84, 85; Sounds Out Of Silent Spaces 86; *Womens Work* (with Alison Knowles 78–87
Long, Richard 240n1
Lopes, Nei 150n17; "Senhora Liberdade" 127n3
Lorenz, Renate 79, 81
low frequency sound, sensuality of 181–195
Lucier, Alvin 90n5, 190
Lucier, Mary 86, 90n5

Lugones, Maria 73–74
Lunar Howls of Wolves, The 140–148
Lyra, Luciana 92–110; *A Bárbara* (The Barbarian) 106; *Bia Boa* (Nice Bia) 106; *Cara da Mãe* (Their Mother's Face) 106; *Fogo de Monturo* (Surprise Element) 106; *Guerreiras* (Warriors) 102–104, *103*, *104*, 105, *105*; *Homens e Caranguejos* (Men and Crabs) 105, *107*; *Obscena* (Obscene) 105–106; *Pour Louise ou a desejada virtude da resistência* 106; *Quarança* 106; *Salema – sussurros dos afogados* (Salema Porgy) 105, *107*; *Therèse* 106; *Yriadobá* 106

MacCallum, John 204; *III: Once Removed* 207–208
machine learning 207, 274
Maderuelo, Javier 47n16
Madonna 70
Madu, Viviane *103*, *104*
Magic Leap 205
Malacar, Deborah 76n5
Malone, Kitty 266, 269, 272
Mann, Elena 89n1
Manning, Erin 16–17, 153
mapping (cynosuric bodies) 201
mar paradoxo 36–46; documentation of process *37*; printed material *36*, *38*; seabed typologies *41*
maracatu-rural 109n10
Marashinsky, Amy Sophia, "The Goddess Oracle" 139, 140
Massumi, Brian: perception 20, 21, 22; virtuality 228, 231, 237, 239, 240
Matyja, J. R. 25
Max MSP software 219
Mayakovsky, Vladimir 118
Mazé, Ramia 169
Mbembe, Achille, "The Universal Right to Breathe" 131
McCoy, Peter 136
McIntyre, Sally Ann 187
McLaughlin, Scott 218
McRobbie, Angela 78
meditation 117
Meira, Biba 173, *174*
Mello Neiva, Tânia 65–77
Melodia, Luiz, "Dores de Amores" 116–117
MEMENTO software 250, *252*, *253*, 254, 256, 258, 262n7
memoriology 246
menstruation 139, 142–144
Merleau-Ponty, Maurice 197

Microfonias: Invention and Sharing of Listening project 153–164
microphones: Cardiff and Bures Miller's Walks 231; violining body 217–218, 219, 220, 221, 224
migration 243; Alarcón-Díaz's INTIMAL 244–260; memory 247, *248*
Miller, Leaf 59
Minelli, Liza 269
Mogrovejo, Norma 149n7
Monat, Sarah 269
Mondgewächse 203
Moore, Alyson Dee 268, 270, 271, 276
Moore, James W. 243
Moreira, Inaê 149n9; "#Breathing in" 138
Morgan, Frances 84, 86
motherhood 160
motion-detection devices 198–199, 201; Alarcón-Díaz's INTIMAL 247–250, *249*; Green-Mateu's *Inter-Act* 204
Motta, Zezé 114, 116, 127n1
Moura, Soraia Maria de 143
multivocalities 246
Mumma, Gordon 90n5
musical patriarchy 66, 71, 74, 75
musicking: enactive-ecological musical approaches 26, 28, 30, 32; violin-specific 214–227
mythodology in art 105–106

Naccarato, Teoma 204; *III: Once Removed* 207–208
Naremore, James 267, 268
Nelson, James 266
Nepomuk, Katarina 76n5
Nery, Miguel 68
Nettleton, Sarah 32
Neuhaus, Max, *Listen* walks 240n1
Neumann, Andrea 17
New Interfaces for Musical Expression (NIME) 29
Nogueira, Isabel 1–8, 149n2, 166–178
Norberg, Kathryn 169

O Keeffe, Linda 1–8, 166–178
Obscena (Obscene) 105–106
octobass 183, 193n3
O'Dwyer, Aine 84
Oiticica, Hélio 46n5
Olausson, Ulf 274
Oliver, Mike 169
Oliveros, Pauline 39, 262n15; deep listening 51, 53, 55, 58, 60–61, 168, 243, 245;

electroacoustic music concert 53, 57–59, 60; embodied curator 88; *Environmental Dialogue* 246; *Her Noise: Feminisms and the Sonic* programme 79; *Slow Runner* project 81; *Sonic Meditation* 85; *To Valerie Solanas and Marilyn Monroe in Recognition of Their Desperation* 79, 82, 85; Women's Ensemble 86, 89n5
Ono, Yoko 1
Optical Organ 201
ORGASMIC STREAMING ORGANIC GARDENING ELECTROCULTURE exhibition 83–84, *84*
or-life (impulse 1 and impulse 2) 156, 160–162, *162*

Pagnes, Andrea 1
Pape, Lygia 46n5
Paperman (2012) 271
Papetti, Stefano 223
Parker-Starbuck, J. 202–203
Parkinson's Disease 205
participatory sense-making 27, 32
Partido dos Trabalhadores 165n9
Pauletto, Sandra 265–278
perceptual collapse 185
permeable listening 39, 42
Perse, St John 119
Phelan, Peggy 202
Philip, Marlene NourbeSe 113–114, 117–120, 124–125; *Looking for Livingstone: An Odyssey of Silence* 120, *121*; *Zong!* 120, *121*
piano 183
Pinto, Makota Valdina 140
Play the Drum (Abilities First School) 59–60
porous listening 39–41, 42, 44
Potter, Roy Claire 83
Pour Louise ou a desejada virtude da resistência 106
Praying to the Goddess (Rezo para a Deusa) 139, 146–147
Primary Information 85
procedural audio 272–273
Processes of writing/Listening of processes [articulations between voice, word, and silence in sound publications] project 46n1
Prodger, Charlotte 83
Puckette, Miller, *Who Was That Timbre I Saw You With?* 199

Quarança 106
queer theory 31

Rajko, Jessica 24, 33
rap and hip hop 66–75
raw listening 44, 39, 41, 42, 47n18
Raw Reality/Raw Reality Street Culture Social Project 68
Reeve, Sandra 248
relational listening 244–261
relationality 20, 208, 255, 257
religion: Catholic Church 108–109n8; Christian meditation tradition 117; Evangelical Church 97, 109n8; low frequency sound use in services 181
representational theories of mind (RTMs) 25
Research Group in Body and Art Studies 176
Research in a Box: Educating Women in Sound 3
"Resonating the Female Body in Space" workshop 171–173
RESPIRO software 250, *252*, *253*, 253–254, *254*, 256
Revell, Irene 78–91
Reybrouck, Mark 25
Rhys-Jones, Gareth 273
Rocha, Camila 69, *69*, 70–71, **72, 73**
Rocha, Chris *103*
Rocha, Janaina 67
Rockmore, Clara 1
Roden, Shelley 268, 269, 270, 271
Rodrigues, Teresa Cristina 66
Roesch, John 268
Rolnick, Neil, *Mono Prelude* 59
Rolnik, Suely 177
Rosa, Laila 138–152; *Bleeding and giving birth to* Shakti 144–145; *Lunar Shakti, Siren's chant 145; Uterus in flower, I snaked* 145
Rosch, Eleanor 25
Rosenfeld, Marina 187–189, 191, 192; *The Accompanists* 187; *Cannons* 188, *189*, 189; *Sheer Frost Orchestra* 187; *Teenage Lontano* 187; *theseatheforesthegarde* 188; *WHITE LINES* 187–188, 190
Røsnes, Irine 214–227
Ross, Fiona 124
Rousseff, Dilma 165n9
Ryngaert, Jean-Pierre 103

Sabella, Joe 266, 269, 271
Saitis, Charalampos 223
Salema – sussurros dos afogados (Salema Porgy) 105, *107*
Samson, Kristine 63n2

Santos, Del 66, 76n6
Schaeffer, Pierre 57, 58, 235
Schafer, R. Murray 46n10
Schalk, Meike 169
Schaub, Mirjam 230, 231
Schechner, Richard 100
Schedel, Margaret 196–213; *Flesh/Light/Movement* 205
Schiavio, A. 25
Schmidt, Albrecht 274
Schmidt, Ulrik 51
Schneemann, Carolee, *Parts of a Body House* 83, *84*
Schneider, Rebecca 1
Schwartz-Shea, Peregrine 169
Secret World of Foley, The (2014) 271–272
self-listening 164nn3–4
self-taught performers 3, 4, 8n3
sensuality of low frequency sound 181–195
Shakti 141, 144, *145*, 146, 147
Shani, Tai 83
Shannon, David Ben 32
ShareMusic & Performing Arts' In: fluence Ensemble 203
sharing listenings and cartographing 153–164
Shiomi, Mieko 83; *Spatial Poem* 80
Siegel, Wayne 201, 203
sign language 199–201
silences: in the body 113–127; coastal (*mar paradoxo*) 36–46; as sound propositions 35
Simpson, Ruth 243
sine tones 189–190, 192
Sinta A Liga Crew (Feel the League Crew) 66–70, 74–75; "Campo Minado" (Minefield) 70–71, 71, **72–73**, 74; photograph *69*; videoclip image 71
sky-only, a vertigo 156, 157–160, *159*, 162
slow listening 44
Slow Runner project 81
Small, Christopher 28, 214
Smalley, Denis 63n6
Smith, Colin 197
social cognition 24, 27
Soddell, Thembi 184–189, 191, 192; "Erasure" 185–186, *186*; *Held Down, Expanding* 184; *Love Songs* 185–186, *186*; *your sickness is felt in my body* 186–187, 190
somatic perception 182
somatic turn 23, 32
sonic arts, feminist methodologies in the 166–178
Sonic Arts Union 86, 89–90n5

sonic body 182–184, 192
#sonicwilderness 128–137; *Blueberry techno* 128, *129*, *132*
sonification 262n8, 274; Alarcón-Díaz's INTIMAL 253–254, *254*, 256–260
sonology 138–1399, 141, 149nn2, 6
sonority 149n2
sound engineers 266; violining body 218, 219, 224
sound mapping 171, 173, 175
sound propositions 35, 38
#soundasgrowing 128, 131, 137
Soundings: An Exhibition in Five Parts 89n1
Sounds Out Of Silent Spaces 86, 90n5
soundscapes: feminist methodologies in the sonic arts 166–168, 170–171; interactive networks 11; *mar paradoxo* 37, 42, 44, 45; meaning 46n10; #sonicwildnerness 128
soundwalks 44; Cardiff and Bures Miller's Walks 228–242; feminist methodologies in the sonic arts 168–171, *170*, 173, 175
South Africa: dance as a witness 123–124; dance elements 113; toyi-toyi 115–116, 125
Spinoza, Baruch de 12–13, 53, 55, 60, 61
Stabenow, Carsten *130*
Stanislavski, Konstantin 267–268
Stankievich, Charles 230, 232
Stepanoff, Alexandra 1
Stevenson, Alicia 269–270
Stewart, Sharon, *TAPPING into your inner PLANT* 245
Stolf, Anna 46
Stolf, Raquel 35–48; *FORA [DO AR]* (OUT [OF AIR]) 39, *40*; *mar paradoxo* 36–46
Stretched Boundaries 58–60
Ström, Caspar 136
structural coupling 29, 33n2
sub-contrabass flute 183, 193n3
subtones 189–192
subwoofers 183, 186, 188, 190, 191
Summers, Elaine 86
SuperCollider software 3
Synapse software 204
Szlavnics, Chiyoko 190

tam-tam 190
Tanaka, Jarue 66
Teixeira, Adriana Gabriela Santos 138–152; *Dancing with the Goddess Vila* 141–142, 146
Tejucupapo, Brazil 92–110; *A Batalha das Heroínas* 94, *98*, 99, 100–102, *101*;

festivities 97–100, *98*, *99*; *Guerreiras* (Warriors) 102–104, *103*, *104*, 105, *105*; mangrove forest 93, *93*, 95–97, *96*, 103, 108; oyster gatherers *94*, *96*, 96
telematics 243–245, 250, 257–258, 260, 262n1
telepresence 254–260
temporality, Cardiff and Bures Miller's Walks 236–238
territory-body-spirit 138–152
Terto, Julyana 68
Thérèse 106
These Are Scores 79, 85–87, *86*
thing-power 12, 21
Thompson, Evan 25
Thompson, Marie 2, 63n3
Tomaz, Clara, *Deviations and Straight Line* 59
Torrance, Steve 27, 30
Torrence, Jennifer 216
toyi-toyi 115–116, 125
transgender people 171, 172, 176
TRANSMISSION software 250, *252*, 254, *255*
Tremblay, Pierre Alexandre 218
Truman, Sarah E. 32
tuba 181
Turkle, Sherry 18
Turner, B. 23
turntablism 187–188

uncanny 18, 21, 161
United Kingdom: electroacoustic music 57, 63n6; feminist methodologies in the sonic arts 166; *The Lunar Howls of Wolves* 138; music technology 171
Urban, Petr 27–28

van der Wee, Laurens 219
van Schalkwyk, Marthinus 116
Varela, Francisco J. 25, 215
Veganism 140, 147
Velardi, Marilia 167, 176
Vergueiro, Viviane 140
very low frequency (VLF) sound, sensuality of 181–195
vibrational therapies 182
video walks, Cardiff and Bures Miller's 228–242
Vila 140–142, 146
violining 214–227
virtuality: Alarcón-Díaz's INTIMAL 244; Cardiff and Bures Miller's Walks 232–240; definition 241n6
visual impairment 208–210
Voegelin, Salomé 87–88

WACK! exhibition 79, 82
Wacquant, Loïc 100, 109n11
Walton, Kendall 182
Weavers of Existence 113, 114, 116, 121, 123
Web of Affections exhibition 113
well-living 138–152
Westerkamp, Hildegard 44, 177n1
Whalen, David 59
Wii controllers 3
Winter, Julie 86, 90n5
Witmore, Christopher L. 231
witness, dance as a 122–127
Women in Sound Women on Sound (WISWOS) 8n1; *Educating Women in Sound* symposium 2–3
Women's Ensemble 86, 89n5

Womens Work 78–85, *81*; *These Are Scores* 79, 85–87, *86*
Wood, Catherine, *Yvonne Rainer: Dance Works* 82
workshop as curatorial format 79–80, 84–89
Wright, Geoffrey 201

Xambo, Anna 2

Yee, Lydia 82
Yoga 140, 143, 147
Young, La Monte 190
Yriadobá 106

Zhang, Zhengyou 199